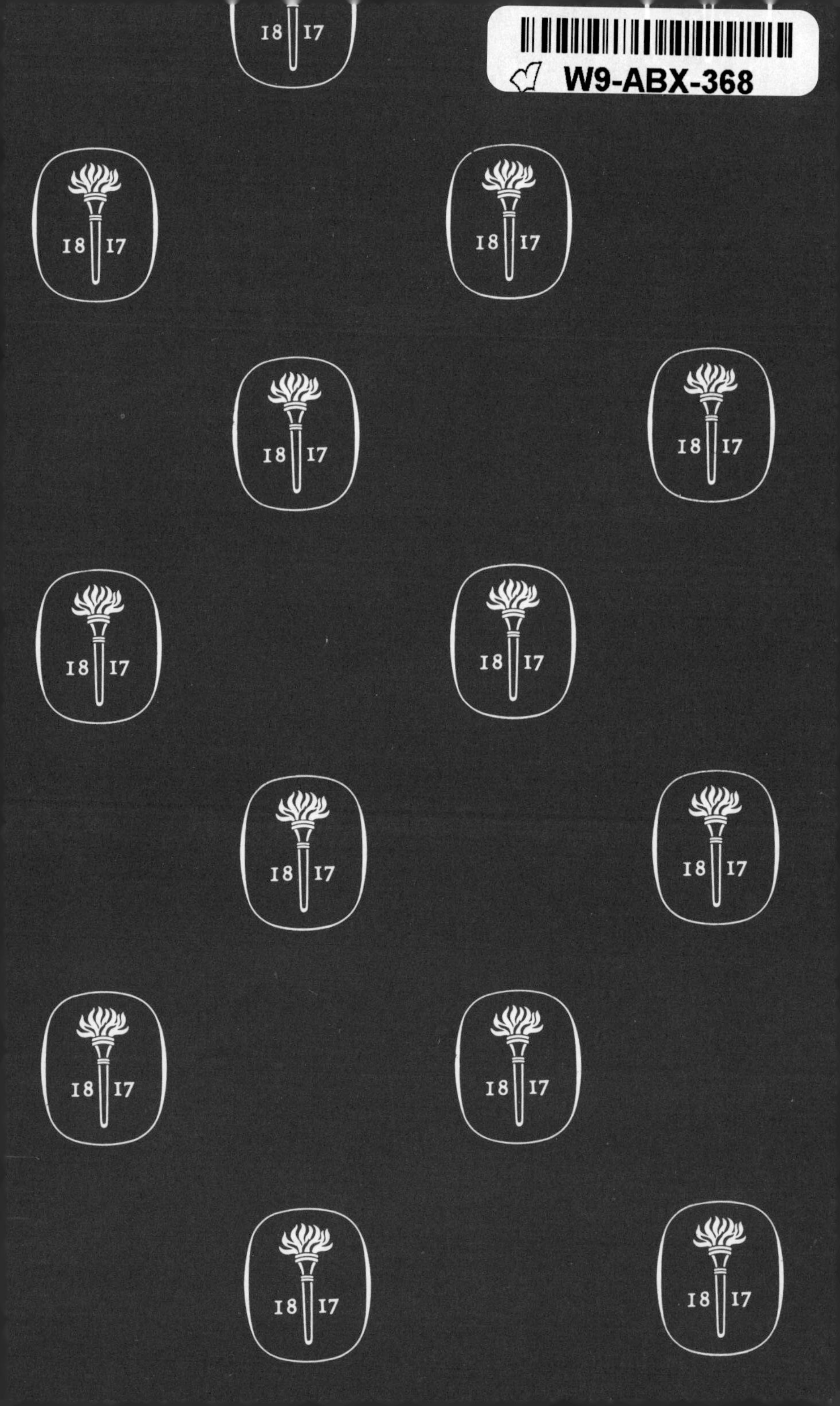
18 17
W9-ABX-368

ADMINISTRATION OF PHYSICAL EDUCATION

To Wally Hood:
One of the finest young men in the Profession. Best wishes.
Ed. Masonbrink

Harper's Series in

School and Public Health Education,

Physical Education, and Recreation

under the editorship of

Delbert Oberteuffer

Administration of Physical Education

Glenn W. Howard

Edward Masonbrink

Harper & Row, Publishers

New York and Evanston

ADMINISTRATION OF PHYSICAL EDUCATION

A-N

Library of Congress Catalog Card Number: 63-7145

CONTENTS

PREFACE

THIS text emphasizes the functions of administration in planning, organizing, conducting, and evaluating a program of physical education at the school and college levels. It is designed for the professional student of physical education. It relates administrative "know-how" to the principles of education that have emerged from experience in all areas of education.

Rather than presenting a formal narrative description of the physical education program, the book is written from the point of view of the administrator who faces the task of planning, organizing, developing, and conducting a program. What are his problems? What questions will he face in the beginning, and later? What kind of program will he plan? How will he proceed to organize that program and put it into operation? How will he work within his institution? As the program is outlined through answers to these and other questions, many pertinent administrative functions are woven into the discussion, and administrative interrelationships are suggested. Not every question that the administrator may have will be answered, and not all possible solutions to the questions raised are included; however, desirable practices are described, and suggestions for acceptable alternatives have been added. The administrator must make his own decisions, using the best information available to him.

The emphasis throughout is on program. Primarily, the text deals with the instructional or "activity" part of a total program of health and physical education. Special chapters are also devoted to the related areas of intramural and interscholastic sports programs, safety programs, and health education programs, although the text does not claim to give a full discussion of these areas.

The first chapters of the text set forth a point of view concerning the function of administration, both in schools and in colleges. The intention is to create in the student an attitude toward his work which will lead him to a professional consideration and performance of whatever task he undertakes. The text repeatedly affirms that administration exists solely to enable the total school organization to achieve the purposes of education in a democracy by the most efficient means.

Subsequent chapters stress the importance of setting goals, establishing directions for the program; suggestions are made of ways to involve the staff or faculty in such planning. The activities to be selected for teaching are discussed in relation to their contribution to these goals, and are thus considered as the means or the instruments by which educational outcomes in personal growth are achieved.

Following the presentation of the program of physical education are chapters on special topics, such as facilities, office management, and administrative responsibilities in areas other than instruction. The administrator's concerns regarding the instructional staff receive detailed treatment. Teaching is a resource as well as a means by which other resources are brought into proper use, and the effectiveness of an instructional staff determines the degree to which the educative opportunities of a program are realized. One of the administrator's most important duties, therefore, is to meet fully his obligations to his staff.

This, then, is the pattern of the text. One theme runs throughout: physical education is a form of education, not something apart. The physical education administrator is first a professional educator. His position as an administrator means that he approaches his task with the broad view of the educator whose principal obligation is to make the best educational opportunities available to all children, youth, and adults participating in his program.

Reference to college practices is made from time to time because a greater range of administrative responsibilities is found at this educational level. One should not infer, however, that the text is intended to prepare persons only for administrative work in colleges and universities. School practices are described also, and where wide differences exist the discussion is extensive.

The authors express their appreciation to the many persons to whose works reference has been made in this text, and particularly to the following who have kindly given permission to quote from their publications: Appleton-Century-Crofts, Inc., for materials from *Methods of Research* by Carter V. Good and Douglas E. Scates; The Ronald Press Company for materials from *Administration of Physical Education—for Schools and Colleges,* by William Leonard Hughes and Esther French; John Wiley & Sons, Inc., for materials from *Measurement and Evaluation in Psychology and Education,* by Robert L. Thorndike and Elizabeth Hagen; and the Rice University for the record forms which are reproduced in the Appendix.

G. W. H.
E. M.

August, 1962

ADMINISTRATION OF PHYSICAL EDUCATION

Chapter 1

ORIENTATION FOR THE EDUCATIONAL ADMINISTRATOR

ADMINISTRATION encompasses the procedures, the direction, and coordination required for doing a job. Administration involves planning and taking the steps by which an organization, an institutional group, or public reaches its goals. In brief, administration is and should be concerned with the performance of purposeful work.

Administration, therefore, is not defined by a single concept but is described in part by the nature of the undertaking and the goals which provide direction for the work being done. Almost any aspect of the job may become an act of administration. In a simple organization, with a small number of persons involved, administering and actually doing the work may go together for a large part of the task. The one-teacher department requires that the administration as well as the work be performed by the same person.

In more complex organizations, involving the participation of a relatively large number of people, the administrative tasks alone require the full-time services of several people. The superintendent of schools for a large city devotes his entire time to administration and has a sizable staff to assist him.

In order to understand and to use effectively the information contained in this text, one must accept the idea that administration is concerned with accomplishing defined ends and that its duties are described specifically by the nature and purposes of the functions being administered. The nature of administration is derived from the nature of the work performed.

THE FUNCTION OF ADMINISTRATION

Although common usage may define administration as management, in educational practice administration also includes leadership in the process of defining goals and of setting standards by which practice is to be judged. An educational administrator is expected to manage effectively that unit of the system or institution for which he is responsible, as well as to raise questions concerning the purposes being sought with a view to furthering the pertinence and value of the outcomes gained by the students.

One who approaches the study of administration may anticipate learning a body of rules which he will follow in carrying out any job in the field of education. Such anticipation will be unrewarded. On the other hand, the student may be delighted to discover that administration is an area in which one who has vision for growth in a field may be given the opportunity to make such growth possible. Admittedly, he may be one step removed from the teaching and research which really produce the growth, but, without his vision and his ability to make it possible for others to work in their chosen ways, effective teaching and research would be hampered.

What is the relationship of this concept of administration to the field of physical education? Because it is an integral part of the educational program of the school and college, physical education must be administered in a way that is consonant with the total educational administration. Whatever principles are set forth the administration of the school and college must apply equally to all departments of those institutions.

The program of physical education has several subdivisions and may sometimes be complex. Where the program includes instructional courses, intramural athletics, intercollegiate athletics, and supervised recreation, as well as shared responsibilities in the health service field, the administrative demands are numerous and exacting.

The breadth of the program of physical education, and the fact that certain phases attract the attention of many persons in the community, place the responsibility for both effective management and educational leadership upon the program administrator. Furthermore, physical education programs vary from one school or college to another. The broad philosophy guiding the programs may be the same, but emphases shift, community needs change, school or college organizational structures differ; hence the specific characteristics of a given school or college will suggest to the administrator the steps to take in order to get his job done.

Here a brief word should be said about the phrase "getting the job done." What are the implications? Does it mean doing any job regardless of its value? Does it mean that the administrator must maintain a situation as he finds it, regardless of its relationship to accepted educational goals? Is he allowed any choice in the ends which give direction to his work? Does it mean simply the performance of routine (management) tasks?

If one is to look upon administration as comprising more than management functions, the answer can be only that getting the job done not only requires the skillful application of management principles and techniques, but demands the participation of the administrator in the selection of the job and the procedures which will be used to do it. In order to get the job done, he must be sensitive to changes in student needs, to alterations in school or college administrative practice, to new interests in the community, to pertinent findings discussed in research literature, to staff suggestions, and to almost any factor which may influence the direction and conduct of the physical education program. The administrator must be able to adapt administrative practices to facilitate the accomplishment of chosen goals.

The coach who has brought essentially the same team through three or four years of play, realizing in its final year the achievement of goals which were remote in the first year, wistfully remarks that he would like to have the team another year now that the boys (or girls) have learned to play. The administrator may feel the same way after he has been working for a while. He, however, unlike the coach, may keep the same policies and practices long after they have passed their useful life. If he does, he gradually loses sight of the job to be done and remains primarily the manager of routine procedures which slowly hamper the effective accomplishment of the job.

To return to the question concerning the relationship of the concepts of educational administration to the field of physical education, one can say that the principles and practices, the functions and purposes, which are acceptable in general administrative concepts are equally a part of the concept of administration in physical education.

CHARACTERISTICS OF ADMINISTRATION

The major portion of this text will deal with the various phases of the physical education program. The nature of many jobs will be described, the goals will be discussed, experience from which knowledge has come will be related, and responsibilities of persons associated with the program will be set forth. The intention is to describe the job as it may be encountered and to discuss the ways of doing it within the scope of an educational profession.

Before beginning this study, one may wish to know more about the characteristics of modern educational administration. A clear knowledge of his administrative responsibilities and functions will protect one against becoming too deeply engrossed in the techniques which were once developed for performing a certain task at a certain time. Four questions, when answered, may provide a better understanding of administration and of an administrator's function. They are:

1. Does educational administration require trained administrators?
2. Does administration require leadership?
3. Does administration require democratic practices?
4. Does administration require research on the job?

When the answers to these questions have been studied, the reader will perceive that administration is more than management, that it is a highly demanding professional obligation, rich in opportunity to render satisfying service to his own field. The remainder of the chapter is concerned with these answers.

DOES EDUCATIONAL ADMINISTRATION REQUIRE TRAINED ADMINISTRATORS?

The answer to this question must be strongly affirmative. Administration is a complex process which includes planning, organizing, and operating the school or college, the department of instruction, and the larger community programs. Thorough professional preparation is required if the administrator is to carry on the functions of his position.

Although one could conceivably administer a program in terms of general management without a complete knowledge of the subject matter in his field, it is unlikely that he could ably administer an educational program. The first requirement in training, therefore, is a substantial and adequate preparation in general education and in the specialized field. Examples of the unfavorable effect of the person without advanced training upon the physical education program are all too common in universities where men with no specialized preparation in either education or physical education have been promoted to the chairmanship of the department. When writing about the need for trained administrators, one assumes that the minimum qualification is educational competency in the specialized field.

MANAGEMENT RELATIONSHIPS. The importance of preparing persons for administrative work is indicated by the nature of the responsibilities which the administrator must carry. These relate to management, staff, students, statesmanship, research, and planning. In addition he should possess certain personal qualities, although these are more difficult to define and are not acquired as easily as knowledge about specific functions.

The day-to-day operation of a department involves the management of personnel, facilities, equipment, finances, records, and reports. Effective management practices mean the full utilization of the departmental resources in conducting an excellent physical education program. Poor management practices divert energies and resources into wasteful and unproductive expenditures. The administrator, therefore, must learn and use the best procedures for carrying out his responsibilities.

The administrator is expected to recruit new teachers, supervise and guide his teaching staff, provide for in-service training, involve his staff in departmental planning and policy formulation, encourage them to improve their own work through study and research, and generally give stimulating professional leadership. There are several ways of fulfilling these functions, and it is the responsibility of the administrator to choose the way which will raise the professional performance of his staff. Furthermore, if he is to do his work well, he must know policies, regulations, and practices for his own institution and for institutional administration in general.

PROGRAM ADMINISTRATION. The subject of this text is the program of physical education. The administrator is principally responsible for the program and for the curriculum of physical education which it contains. He must know the procedures of curriculum planning, implementation, and evaluation. He must be able to estimate his facilities, equipment, and supply needs, and to fulfill them. Administrative competency is crucial. If it is lacking, the program falters. If it is present, the program flourishes and grows.

The administrator works constantly with many people. He will have professional relationships within his own field; he will have significant relationships with colleagues in other fields within his own institution. There will be many occasions for him to represent his work to the community. These functions fall into what Kefauver has called social statesmanship, because they are conducted in terms of long-range planning and related policies. This kind of statesmanship reflects the understanding, attitudes, and skills of the administrator.

He should be able to plan and conduct research into various aspects of his own work in order to secure valuable information in planning and making decisions. He need not be a research specialist himself, but he should know how to describe his problems so that appropriate research procedures can be applied to their solution.

The word *planning* will appear many times in the text. No administration can be effective, except by accident, when there is no plan or when it is imperfectly executed. The administrator must have skill in the procedures of planning itself. Curriculum development, for example, is based upon a plan. The acquisition of new facilities is possible only if a plan has been prepared beforehand.

Because staff members and others in the institution will participate, the guidance of this operation requires a knowledge of suitable techniques.

THE NEED FOR TRAINED ADMINISTRATORS. One will conclude, therefore, that educational administration requires trained administrators. The duties and responsibilities of the position can be performed adequately only by persons who have prepared for the work. The administrator, too, continues his studies in service to keep his preparation in step with the development of the job.

Attention is given today not only to the kind of preparation which the potential administrator should have, but to the personal qualities which will be important factors in his performance. Grace[1] lists ten attributes of personality which candidates for educational positions should possess. These include such items as the ability to think rationally, the ability to avoid tactless or harmful remarks about others, emotional stability, regard for the laws of physical and mental health, recognition of the attainment of others, and ability to cooperate with others.

A list of personality traits is never complete. There is the possibility, too, that a particular list reflects the preferences of its author. The purpose of presenting one is to indicate that administrative effectiveness also depends upon the personal qualities of the administrator. If by objective criteria one judges that a program of physical education is being carried out effectively, he will assume that the administrator possesses at least some of the desirable personal attributes.

Training for school administration has been going on for more than thirty years. The earlier training was concerned with management matters: budgets, building, legislation, and handling of staff. Later, administrators were encouraged to apply fact-finding methods to assembling information about their schools. Decision-making and policy formulation were to be aided by having an abundance of information. The importance of preparing capable educational administrators is given added support by the development of special programs and centers for their training and by the increase of pro-

[1] Alonzo G. Grace, "The Professional Preparation of School Personnel," Forty-Fifth Yearbook, Part II, National Society for the Study of Education, University of Chicago Press, 1946, p. 178.

fessional literature about educational administration. Administration in physical education has also received attention.

Programs of research designed to improve the administration of public schools have been established. One of these programs aims to find ways to develop the role of administrative leadership in American education and to explore means by which school administrators can work together to improve their respective jobs. In New York State a move was started by the State Association for Health, Physical Education, and Recreation to develop a basis for the certification of directors of health, physical education, and recreation in city public school systems. In June, 1953, the Board of Regents of the State of New York established certification requirements for these positions. In anticipation of the Regents' action, the Association, through its section on administration and supervision, started a project to establish "standards, methods and procedures by which a director would be able to do better the job in which he is employed and certificated." After two years of intensive work, the Association published a brochure entitled *Administration*[2] which "indicates the responsibilities of directors as determined by best present opinion and suggests principles and policies which schools may use in establishing these responsibilities." The emphasis is upon preparing individuals for the special features of public school administration of programs of health, physical education, and recreation. The need, as well as the desirability, for trained administrators is amply demonstrated. The person who has no particular training for administration and who never seeks more than the minimum of information which the job forces upon him, and the departmental head who follows traditional practices without questioning their effectiveness for the current situation, are not meeting the obligations of their positions in physical education. Increasing complexity of school and college organization, broadening educational programs, greater community concern for the effectiveness of education, and generally increasing costs are some of the reasons for demanding better prepared administrators.

In physical education, as in any subject area, an ever-increasing

[2] Joint Study, Directors Association, Administration, New York State Association for Health, Physical Education, and Recreation, New York State Education Department, 1955, p. 21.

importance is attached to the obligation to conduct a thoroughly professional, educationally rich, and economically productive program of instruction. The administrator must be prepared to lead in educational matters as well as to manage the departmental program if he is to fulfill this obligation.

DOES ADMINISTRATION REQUIRE LEADERSHIP?

An affirmative answer to the question seems so certain that the reader may wonder why it is raised at all. However, practice in education, and in physical education, provides too many examples of administration without leadership. Furthermore, the opening statement about administration as "the procedures, the direction, and coordination required for doing a job" does not necessarily include leadership as one of the characteristics. If one holds the view that administration is only management, he will see little need for leadership since the job is to keep a function operating according to standard procedures.

The evidence today points to leadership as an obligation of administration, not just an optional phase. Administration can do its job effectively only when it exercises appropriate leadership. This fact applies to the administrative functions of the physical education teacher who is responsible for the subject in the elementary school as well as to the multitude of duties which a state supervisor may perform in his work. Wahlquist emphasizes the position of leadership which the administrator holds. He states, "They key person in American democracy is neither the business man nor the politician. It is the public school administrator who, in the long run, shapes the communities, the states, and the nation. . . . Their [administrators'] leadership may not be so obvious, but it is they, and the teachers under their supervision, who are quietly, and inconspicuously shaping the ideals, attitudes, and beliefs of future generations."[3]

Although educators at times seem to be trying to anticipate the changing ideas of lay populations concerning what the schools should be doing, the professional educator of stature is really setting

[3] John T. Wahlquist, *et al., The Administration of Public Education,* The Ronald Press Co., 1952, p. 4.

the pattern of learning so that education presents in the best way the fundamental knowledges and values of a democratic society. The importance of this function of leadership is described by the Overstreets. "Educators, in short, are those deliberately trained leaders to whom society entrusts the task of harmonizing individual rights with social rights, progress with stability. Only when well equipped with educators can democracy tap the riches and run the risks inherent in allowing myriad types of leadership to bid for a following."[4] To be an educator is to be a leader at some level in the educational organization.

LEADERSHIP AND INSTRUCTION. Educational administration has complex responsibilities, with the effort centered on the instructional work of the school or college. Leadership is an essential quality of administration if its instructional obligations are to be fully met. Foshay, in writing about the need for improving instruction, states, "What all these efforts [to improve instruction] have in common is a recognition that the school leader is still the key to the quality of the school program. The quality of instruction, in the long run, cannot rise above the insights about instruction held by the school principal or superintendent."[5] To this final phrase may be added "the city or departmental administrator of physical education."

The administrator must exercise leadership by providing for study of new methods of work, for establishment of new goals, for necessary evaluation of a program or of a job. He must understand all the purposes of his job so that he can direct the above steps toward an improved education for children and youth. He must assume the responsibility for his own continuing professional development and for improving his own methods of work; by example, stimulation, and encouragement he must provide that leadership which encourages others to strive for their own self-development.

The administrator is not the sole possessor of all the desirable qualities and professional knowledge among his staff, nor is he the

[4] Harry A. Overstreet and Bonaro W. Overstreet, *Leaders for Adult Education*, American Association for Adult Education, 1941, pp. 2–3.

[5] Arthur W. Foshay, "The Key Is Still Leadership," *Educational Research Bulletin*, March 14, 1956, pp. 74–76.

only one capable of being a leader or even of performing as one. All teaching jobs involve leadership. If an educational staff is considered as a unit, however, the administrator occupies the central position. His actions, his ideas, and his goals are bound to influence others. In order to do his job to the full measure required by the field of education, he must be a leader.

Education today is more important than ever, if that is possible, in American life. Certainly the need for both more liberal and more specialized education is urgent. What the schools and colleges do and how they do it are matters of vital concern to everyone. The administrator is in the responsible position. It is he who must guide the operation of the educational institutions; it is he who must utilize fully the professional personnel resources, the physical facilities, and the community capacities to serve modern and effective education. Educational administration, therefore, requires devoted leadership of professional quality. The schools maintain a position of responsible service in preparing children, youth, and adults for full and mature participation in a democracy; they depend upon strong, forthright leadership in their administrators, as well as in their teachers.

The administrator of an instructional department of physical education must also be a leader if his program is to meet the obligations of a subject in the schools of a democracy. The need for this quality in professionally conducted, scientifically based programs is as great today as at any time in the history of physical education.

DOES ADMINISTRATION REQUIRE DEMOCRATIC PRACTICES?

In the schools and colleges of a democracy, administrative practice must fully reflect democracy and testify to a deep conviction that it is a superior way of life. The administration of the educational unit, whatever it may be, should strengthen the beliefs of students, teachers, and citizens in democracy at work.

In the *Forty-Fifth Yearbook,* published by the National Society for the Study of Education, Kefauver states, "The concept of democracy in educational administration is now generally accepted. . . . The movement is encouraged by the greater attention being paid to education for democratic citizenship and the belief that the practice of democracy is a more effective teacher than mere talk about it."[6] Spalding, writing on organizing the personnel of a democratic school system, stresses the fact that modes of behavior in a democracy must be learned, and that the fundamental social aim of the schools of the United States is to facilitate the learning of these behaviors by the young people who attend. He states, "If schools are to develop persons who will behave democratically, they should be staffed with teachers who are learning to behave in these ways."[7] Administrative personnel as well must learn and practice democratic ways of working.

Wahlquist writes, "It is the conviction . . . that educational problems should be solved democratically within the framework of laws and machinery under which the schools operate in our republican scheme of government."[8] The concept of democratic school administration has been actively promoted through the study and published yearbooks of the National Conferences of Professors of Educational Administration. The report for the 1948 Conference emphasized that the inner convictions of the democratic leader were more important than organizational arrangements of particular methods. The report lists what the conference has set forth as the inner convictions. They present ideas characterizing democracy and will be included in the discussion to follow.

THE NEED FOR PERSONAL CONVICTIONS. It should be said here, and perhaps repeated, that democratic administration is possible only when the administrator holds clear personal convictions. An attempt to be democratic according to a formula has weak spots and actually may fail under pressure because there is only information about democracy but no deep understanding supported by strong belief. A discussion of democratic practices as essential to administration without considering the nature of a democracy may lead nowhere. While democracy is spoken of in terms of inner convic-

[6] Grayson N. Kefauver, "Reorientation of Educational Administration," *Forty-Fifth Yearbook,* Part II, National Society for the Study of Education, University of Chicago Press, 1946, p. 5.

[7] Willard B. Spalding, "Organizing the Personnel of a Democratic School System," *Forty-Fifth Yearbook,* Part II, National Society for the Study of Education, University of Chicago Press, 1946, p. 58.

[8] Wahlquist, *et al., op. cit.,* p. 29.

tions, and as a great social faith, there must be a more specific characterization if it is to be distinguished from fascism, authoritarianism, or any other social ideology.

The student will be aware of the mainsprings of democratic living. The Educational Policies Commission has set forth the following broad generalizations to include the basic essentials of democracy.

1. The General Welfare. One who lives in accordance with democracy is interested not only in his own welfare but in the welfare of others—the general welfare.
2. Civil Liberty. One who lives in a democratic way respects himself. And to self-respect he adds respect for the moral rights and feelings of others, for the sanctity of each individual personality.
3. The Consent of the Governed. Democratic processes also involve the assent of the people in matters of social control and the participation of all concerned in arriving at important decisions.
4. The Appeal to Reason. Peaceful and orderly methods of settling controversial questions are applied by a democracy to matters of national and international policy as well as to private disputes.
5. The Pursuit of Happiness. Democracy sets high value upon the attainment of human happiness as a basis for judging the effectiveness of social life.[9]

In a later publication of the Educational Policies Commission,[10] democracy is spoken of as a "great social faith," embodying within it beliefs concerning the great worth of the individual, the fact that men can and should rule themselves, and that the human mind can be trusted and should be set free.

The few references given touch upon important aspects of the democratic concept. Government by the consent of the governed, concern for the welfare of all, faith in the ability of the individual to share in choosing his government, and placing a high value on the worth of each individual are the aspects of democratic belief frequently dealt with in the literature of educational administration. They can be the guides for developing democratic administrative practices in a school, a college, a department of instruction, or a classroom.

[9] Educational Policies Commission, *The Purposes of Education in American Democracy*, National Education Association, 1938, pp. 7–8.

[10] Educational Policies Commission, *The Education of Free Men in American Democracy*, National Education Association, 1941.

How does democracy work in the administration of a school or college, or of a department of physical education? In the first place, the school is an agency of the democracy with selected, specialized functions assigned to it. General policy governing the organization and structural pattern of the school, as well as its major objectives, is established by the state. Administration of this policy becomes the function of the local district or community, which in turn may create additional policies to aid in fulfilling the task of education. Administrative personnel and teachers are obligated to carry them out. Policies at the state level arise out of legislation approved by the people. The state in turn must conform in its actions to policies embodied in the basic tenets of the federal government and in federal legislation related to education.

In the second place, the methods of conducting education, the specific selection of curriculum for each age group, the determination of achievement levels, and the coordination and integration of the many activities within the school which work to achieve the goals of education are left to the school administration and teaching personnel for decision and implementation. Furthermore, the policies governing personnel selection, promotions, assignment of responsibilities, sometimes salaries, and other items related to interpersonnel activities are primarily the responsibilites of the administrator and his staff. Opportunities for developing and practicing democratic concepts in the administration of these phases of the program are numerous.

PARTICIPATION IN ADMINISTRATIVE PROCESSES. The administrator who, in his work, practices the democratic concept referred to earlier will need the full cooperation of all those working with him in the program, and in some instances he will look to student participation for guidance, too. Those who discuss democratic administration emphasize sharing in both planning and problem-solving. Such participation must be in accord with concepts of trust, respect, common goals, freedom of expression, responsibility for decisions, and others pertinent to the action taking place. Attention is directed, however, to the need for broad participation in contrast to centralized decision-making and directing. Discovering the best ways to secure full group cooperation in problem-solving is important to the administrator. When he gets his staff to take part readily in arriving at solutions to their educational problems he has entered one of the significant phases of democratic administration.

Hughes and French support the idea of participation as the mark of democratic administration in physical education. "While central authority and responsibility are essential to good administration the wise administrator attempts to follow the principle of democratic representation in administration. In general, this means that every individual affected by an administrative principle or policy has some voice in framing and adopting the policy."[11]

A realistic interpretation of the final statement in the preceding quotation would be that those administrative principles and policies which are developed at the departmental level should take into account the expressed judgments and recommendations of the departmental staff. It is possible for any individual within a state to express his wishes on legislative matters to his representatives and to the responsible officers of the state government. To this extent he is participating at the state level. As one proceeds down the steps from state government to city government, the opportunity for personal participation grows. In practice, teachers in both schools and colleges can take part in policy formulation through their organized staff and faculties. The extent to which this is possible depends upon the practice of the school or college administration. At the departmental level, participation is readily possible and should be the established practice. A lengthier discussion of teacher participation in departmental administration is given in Chapter 11.

Teachers can express their opinions and recommendations through various organizations. Professional organizations related to subject matter fields frequently offer resolutions in order to transmit to administrative and legislative bodies the consensus of their members on a stated matter. Active teacher organizations are set up specifically to deal with matters of policy and practice affecting the work and status of teachers. The National Education Association, with its many member organizations, is the best example of this type of organization. In the year 1959–1960 the Association spent more money on lobbying for federal legislation than any other person or group reporting. Legislation establishes policy; hence the

[11] William L. Hughes and Esther French, *The Administration of Physical Education for Schools and Colleges,* A. S. Barnes and Co., 1954, p. 6.

NEA members, through their national office, were expressing their wishes on legislation. The American Association of University Professors represents university teachers. Administrators are not eligible for membership. Through committee reports and studies which are made and published in its journal, the Association expresses its opinions on general university policies and occasionally on specific institutional policies and actions.

There are local teachers' organizations, occasionally formed as unions, which concern themselves with policies and practices governing working conditions, qualifications, salaries, and other related matters. In New York State, a teachers' organization filed suit seeking a decision on the constitutionality of the law which barred strikes by governmental employees.[12] Action of this type is another means of expressing opinion and participating in the formulation of policy.

Kefauver has stated in some detail the impact of democratic practice upon administration. His words are worth reviewing here:

> A detailed consideration of administrative organization and procedure would show that the question of democratic procedure touches upon many aspects of the life of the school. It affects the role of the administrator and the methods by which he carries on his work. It gives to the staff and to the individual teacher a larger role. It gives to the students a more active part in the life of the school. It calls for a modification of the procedure in the classroom. It provides for a greater degree of cooperation of persons with a spirit of equality, with each contributing according to his special experience. It is concerned with the equality of opportunity for all students and with the flexibility required to make adaptation to the special needs of the individual. It provides for leadership by the administrator and by the teacher and by students. It increases the extent to which agreement is sought and reached among all interested parties in dealing with educational problems. It provides for the study of different alternatives when dealing with controversial questions so that students can acquire the basis for making their own decisions.[13]

Again it must be said that the administrator should understand clearly the meaning of democracy as a social philosophy, and be-

[12] "Theobald Hails Strike-Law Test," *The New York Times,* September 28, 1960, p. 41.

[13] Kefauver, *op. cit.,* pp. 5–6.

lieve firmly in its superiority for education if he is to employ its concepts and methods in the variety of educational situations listed in the previous quotation. Failure to meet this criterion can result in the introduction of superficial and wasteful practices under the democratic label. Thus, basing policy decisions on popular opinion polls, trying to give a crowd "what it wants," asking students, who have had no previous opportunity to study the purposes and means for achieving them, what they wish to do in a physical education class, trying to establish knowledge by the process of voting—these and similar kinds of popular participation are used all too frequently as examples of democratic practice in administration, in the classroom, and in the gymnasium.

A charge frequently directed against democratic practice is that no one takes responsibility for anything. The answer is that, on the contrary, each participant shares in the responsibility for whatever is under consideration. The degree of responsibility depends upon several factors; one may be the age of the participant, another may be the previously determined areas of duties of the participant, another may be his ability or training for meeting their requirements.

AREAS OF RESPONSIBILITY. In an organization, such as the school, certain areas of responsibility are defined by law and are assigned by law or official regulation. It is impossible for persons working in these areas to ignore, or to pass to others, their assigned duties. For example, a board of education employs the teachers. The superintendent may prepare recommendations for appointment but the board does the actual appointing.

Other fields, or areas of responsibility, have grown through customary practice to belong to stated positions. These responsibilities can be reassigned by law or group agreement, but until a change is made, they are understood to belong to certain positions. For example, the supervision of physical education facilities is generally assumed to belong to the head of the department. A superintendent or a college president may decide that another person should have charge of the facilities and make such an assignment. Except for this kind of direct action, however, the position of chairman (or administrator) of the physical education department carries with it responsibility for supervising the department's facilities.

In a third area there are unassigned responsibilities which grow out of the developing and changing nature of the educational task. Within this area the administrator may make assignments by direction or he may, by utilizing the advice of his staff, arrive at assignments on which there is general agreement and which are made to best meet the need which has arisen. Within this latter area lies a great deal of the opportunity for working toward a better curriculum, improved class arrangements for pupils, more effective methods of evaluation, improved teaching standards as well as teacher status, and better community relations. It is worth emphasizing that from this area, in which the school or departmental staff may participate to the fullest extent, will come new developments and new recommendations which ultimately may be incorporated into the general operating policies for the entire school or college.

It is true that people who do not have a clear idea of their own responsibilities as well as those of others may neglect theirs in favor of the others'. If the concepts of democratic practice are understood and if the duties of a position are clearly described, there seems to be little reason for democratic administration to falter or for responsibilities to be shunned. Administration is not a legislative function, but it has the obligations of carrying out the enactments of legislation and giving leadership in the formulation of desirable legislative proposals. In both cases it can and must operate according to the concepts of democratic administration.

Does Administration Require Research on the Job?

If administration is concerned with getting a job done, then its nature is determined by the nature of the job. How does one learn the nature of the job? Obviously, by studying it with adequate and objective methods and by investigating its many aspects to discover the problems, the needs, the outline, and details of the job. Administration is in demand only to the extent that it can accomplish the assigned task. Research is a requirement if administration is to perform its duties satisfactorily. Without such study, important decisions are made with insufficient data at hand, planning is wishful rather than purposeful, and problems are classified according to surface clues and not in terms of their full and specific nature. Administration, whether it is that of a large university, or of a small department within the institution, must study objectively and constantly its accomplishments in terms of stated purposes, the effectiveness of its methods, and from time to time the acceptability and pertinence of the goals toward which its work is directed. The importance of research in administration will be brought out more fully in later sections.

SUMMARY

The topics considered thus far have been presented more from the standpoint of the total school or college administration than from that of the subject or department of physical education. Administration of physical education, however, cannot be different in kind and quality from that of education in general. Only professionally interested and qualified people can bring to administration the knowledge and devotion needed to do the job. These people must stand for the best in physical education philosophy and practice and must be forthright in influencing educational growth. Schools in a democracy must have consistency in administrative practice and will expect the administrator to exemplify democratic practices. Finally, education is a profession of high calling. One must be scholarly in his administration if he justifies his position in the profession.

Chapter 2

THE TOTAL PROGRAM OF HEALTH AND PHYSICAL EDUCATION

THIS text will be concerned with that part of the health and physical education program usually termed *instructional* or simply called *physical education.* It is one part of a multi-faceted unit in the educational organization of a school or college. Attention should be directed to the relationship between these units and the physical education program. In the following material the interrelationships will be indicated. Full descriptions and detailed consideration of purposes, organization, and conduct of these other units of the total program will be found in texts devoted especially to each one.

EDUCATIONAL EXPERIENCES IN THE TOTAL PROGRAM

Each aspect of the total program makes a significant contribution to the education of children and youth. Each aspect has some unique quality in its materials and methods. To list the educational experiences which any student might encounter in the total program of health and physical education would be an almost impossible task. Furthermore, the impact of these experiences upon each individual student cannot be determined with a high degree of accuracy. If the school is seeking to influence the development of its pupils in emotional, intellectual, social, cultural, and healthful ways, it can be confident that the total program of physical education contributes to each of the areas.

The specific part which physical education plays is described in detail in Chapter 3. In a very real sense those closely related aspects of the total program, namely intramural athletics, interscholastic and intercollegiate athletics, and recreation, make similar contributions. Each emphasizes one kind of experience more than others. Their resources are similar to or identical with those of physical education; their immediate goals, however, may vary from the principal ones which guide the instructional program of physical education.

This program forms the base of the total physical education program. Without it only a limited number of individuals would be able to enjoy active recreation, intramural athletics, and interscholastic and intercollegiate athletics. Where there is a rich program of physical education instruction, more students take part in the intramural programs, more want and are able to continue active recreation, and those who are attracted to the intense activity of competitive athletics can join squads from which teams are organized for play.

By approaching the value from another direction, one can say that intramural athletics, competitive sports, and active recreation are the means for developing the knowledge and skills which have been acquired through the instructional program. These activities provide for improvement in skills, for continued practice, for greater personal and social development. One can retrace his steps, then, and say that the possibility of securing the best values from these related activities occurs when the instructional program is educational, completely organized, and professionally conducted.

Physical education as an educational unit and as an instructional program contributes to and utilizes the health education program of the institution. Several aspects of health education are more closely related to physical education than to any other subject in the school and college curriculum. The interrelationships of physical education with these other units will be discussed briefly in order that the emphasis of this text upon physical education will not cause one to ignore the fact that the administrator may be, and often is, in charge of a program embodying all the units making up the total program of health and physical education.

HEALTH EDUCATION

In our American society, health is always held high in importance for the individual and society, regardless of the changes in other values. The World Health Organization defines health as a state of complete physical, mental, and social well-being and not merely the absence of disease or infirmity. Williams states that health is the "best functioning of the whole person,"[1] or "the quality of life that renders the individual fit to live most and serve best."[2] As an institution concerned with the education of the whole child, it is incumbent upon the school to carry on those health programs suited to its particular purposes and resources.

A list of health problems confronting society would include the prevalence of accidents, continued high incidence of certain communicable diseases, pollution of water resources, need for adequate health services for all people, high death rates from degenerative diseases, and persistence of attitudes which lead the individual to select ineffective means for meeting his health problems. The school alone cannot solve many of these problems. On the other hand, education about the nature of the problems, and especially education concerning the citizens' responsibilities to make better health possible, are within its province. To meet these obligations for health education the school conducts three major programs: health service, health instruction, and healthful school living.

HEALTH SERVICE. Health services in the schools and colleges have long been closely related to physical education. In the early years of school and college physical education the administration of this program occasionally fell to the person who also was responsible for the health service. Conferences which have been held periodically on health in colleges stress the interrelationships between the two.

For a long time health services paid greater attention to the medical aspects of their services than to the total health education pro-

[1] Jesse Feiring Williams, *Healthful Living*, 4th ed., The Macmillan Co., 1947, p. 2.

[2] Jesse Feiring Williams, *Personal Hygiene Applied*, W. B. Saunders Company, 1941, p. 2.

gram. Physical education has emphasized increasingly its educational contributions and has incorporated special activities, such as intramural and intercollegiate athletics, into its total program with the result that the emphasis upon strictly healthful outcomes has diminished. Nevertheless, there remains today an exceedingly close relationship between health services and physical education. Each depends upon the other in several ways.

The physical examination of the student reveals facts which his educational program must take into account. These facts are essential to the physical education teacher if he is to utilize his teaching resources in the best interests of the individual student. Those students whose physical activities are restricted usually require supervision, exercised through the periodic examination which the health service arranges and often carries out. In those instances where the restriction is temporary, the health service personnel working with the physical education teacher can plan a program leading to an early return of the individual to normal status.

Students are admitted to intramural and intercollegiate athletic programs on the basis of their physical status as determined by the health examination. When individuals are injured in any of these activities it is the responsibility of the health service to render emergency care, to advise with regard to further services, and to determine when the individual is ready to return to activity.

The health service assists the teachers of personal health courses by helping them to identify the significant school and community problems and providing a program which coordinates the activities required to maintain generally good health.

The physical education teachers assist the health services to fulfill their functions by identifying and referring individuals who show need for examination and counseling, by creating favorable attitudes among the students toward the effective use of health services as well as toward their responsibility for maintaining good health, and by carrying out the recommendations of the health service in the matter of injured students and those who are restricted in their activities. The teacher of physical education is in a favored position to perform these valuable services.

The school health coordinator may be one of the teachers of physical education. In institutions which maintain health councils, the chairman of the council may be the physical education teacher. The close relationship between physical education and health services (as well as other aspects of health education) is treated in detail in texts on health education. For purposes of this text it is sufficient to show that this important relationship exists.

HEALTH INSTRUCTION. Health instruction today is part of the professional assignment of teachers of health and physical education. This is based historically upon the fact that these persons were best qualified to teach the subject because of their own preparation. Growth in health knowledge has encouraged a trend to prepare teachers of health. The movement has been extremely slow and is likely to remain so because of the realistic problems faced by a superintendent in staffing his schools and because of the continuing close relationship between the preparation of the physical education teacher and that proposed for the teacher of health.

The teacher of physical education who also meets students in the classroom to discuss the subject of health finds himself in a good position to do an effective teaching job. The playfield and gymnasium are laboratories in which the students reveal their needs for healthful living. Conversely, these laboratories offer the teacher the means for putting into practice healthful attitudes which lead the student to use information gained both in the laboratory and in the classroom. The physical education teacher must be alert to opportunities for increasing the student's competence in healthful living. He must not narrow his concern to the skill of the physical activity.

HEALTHFUL SCHOOL LIVING. Healthful school living is the third large area contributing to the health program of every school system. It furthers health services and health instruction and is interrelated with both. Healthful school living denotes the influence of all factors in the school environment upon the individual's health. In other words, it is the result of the individual's interaction with his total school environment, with particular attention being given to the healthful outcomes.

The physical education department, with its own specialized facilities has a major responsibility in this aspect of the health education program. Facilities should be constructed for safety. They should be maintained in a clean condition. Instruction should include recognition of hazards and ways to minimize them. However the program of physical education involves the students, the circumstances surrounding them should represent the most acceptable of healthful conditions and practices.

Every aspect of the school—its building, equipment, appointments, curriculum, staff, services, administrative policies, and methods of instruction—affects healthful school living. The physical education administrator attends to all these factors within his own area of jurisdiction so that the student may live in school under optimum health conditions.

THE PHYSICAL EDUCATION PROGRAM

The physical education program is often called the service or basic instruction program. It is usually that part of the total which is mandated by law and is required of all students. Beginning in the primary grades, it continues into college, and is designed to serve the needs of the whole student population. It is part of the individual's schedule and is treated like any other subject in the curriculum.

The basic instructional program makes a unique contribution to the total educational program. It occupies a place in the school and college curriculum which is equal to that of the other subjects. The administrator and the teacher of physical education are also expected to be concerned with the general education of children and youth and with the major aspects of the field of education.

Matters regarding the professional responsibility of the physical educator will be discussed in detail throughout the text. Interrelationships and responsibilities shared by physical education personnel are presented briefly in this chapter in order to bring into focus the total program of health and physical education, as well as to indicate that the text does not ignore the broader relationships.

The basic instructional program in physical education underlies the programs of intramural athletics, interscholastic and intercollegiate athletics, and active recreation. Children, youth, and adults who attend educational institutions acquire the knowledge and learn the skills and rules which are essential to further active participation.

The programs referred to in the following material are normally part of the responsibility of the physical education administrator in the public schools, colleges, and universities. Administrative organization in institutions of higher education may have a separate department of intercollegiate athletics for men or a separate division of intramural athletics for men. In colleges and universities the women's program encompasses all these aspects with that of intercollegiate athletics found in a relatively small number of institutions.

INTRAMURAL ATHLETICS. Intramural athletics were developed to meet the interests of students in highly organized competitive sports at a level lower than intercollegiate competition. They include the organization and conduct of leagues, tournaments, meets, and special events. The program, which began in colleges, has spread to all educational levels. Although instruction is given occasionally to intramural participants, it is limited, for the professional personnel available is not large. Intramural athletics do provide the means for an individual who has learned a game in his basic instructional class to continue improving his skills and knowledge in play.

Institutions which offer intramural athletics as one phase of the total physical education program have a unified administration. Where the intramural athletic program is administered as a separate division, or under an office other than that of physical education, close cooperation between the two departments is necessary. Again, let it be said that the instructional program is basic; intramural athletics follow. It should be pointed out, however, that intramural athletics at the college level will assume greater importance as the entering students become better educated in games and sports by the high schools.

It is possible to coordinate the instruction in physical education with the intramural athletic program. For example, if the intramural program opens in the fall with speedball or soccer, those particular sports can be taught in physical education classes. Student officials can be prepared for their duties. If the entry lists are large, some students may be trained to supervise the events.

Intramural athletics provide an answer to the criticism of having too many spectators and not enough participants. They are athletic or sports programs for all. The quest for carry-over and leisure time sports is solved by intramurals. Intramural sports offer a basis for keen competition but do not require the time to master the skills of the varsity athlete. The desire to compete on an equal basis is gratified in the intramural program. Since the total range of athletic activities can become a part of the intramural program, all students should be encouraged to take part and all schools should offer adequate opportunities.

INTERSCHOLASTIC AND INTERCOLLEGIATE ATHLETICS. Interscholastic and intercollegiate athletics are programs of interinstitutional competitive sports events in which selected teams representing their institutions meet each other, almost always on a scheduled basis. The program of competitive sports is conducted largely for male students. In recent years there has been a renewal of interest in interinstitutional competitive sports for girls and women but on a very limited basis. More informal sports programs have been typical of girls' and women's athletics.

Competitive sports have been part of popular cultures through the recorded history of mankind. Their part in the lives of people in the United States demonstrates without question that this type of sports activity is an integral part of American culture. The fact of significance to the educator is its place in the educational curriculum.

The history of intercollegiate athletics in the United States reveals that athletics were generated and developed as student activities outside the domain of the school or the college. When physical education programs were introduced in the colleges and later in the schools, these were not athletic or sports programs but rather graded exercises fashioned after the gymnastic programs of Germany and Sweden. Although the German gymnastic movement incorporated games and sports into its total program, the colleges and schools adopted only part of the program. The insistence of a few that physical education should include those activities which were of natural interest to children and youth, and also intrinsic to the American people, stimulated physical educators to consider them as part of the resources to be utilized.

Along with this change of view, there was a growing acceptance by colleges of the responsibility for intercollegiate athletics. Administratively and professionally it became the practice to place intercollegiate athletics within the department of physical education. Often this would become the department of physical education and athletics.

Public school athletics have developed more within the boundaries of regular school organization, although part of the financial support for the interscholastic athletic program has to be derived from other than tax levy funds.

Today the conduct of interscholastic and intercollegiate athletic programs presents the professional educator with cause for concern in many situations and for satisfaction with the educational integration of programs in others. For purposes of this text it can be said that programs of interscholastic and intercollegiate athletics, organized and conducted for educational purposes, are a part of the total program of health and physical education and, as such, are closely related to and dependent upon the instructional program of physical education.

The Educational Policies Commission has defined its position on school athletics when it states that, "We believe in athletics as an important part of the school physical education program. We believe that the experience of playing athletic games should be part of the education of all children and youth who attend school in the United States."[3]

If this belief is to influence practice, instructional programs of physical education will have to be expanded and intensified in order for all boys and girls who are physically able to develop their skills, strengths, and knowledge for successful experiences in competitive sports. Even more significant will be the change in the competitive sports programs themselves from concern with a small number of selected and intensively trained players to a broader interest in competitive sports programs for a larger number of youth.

Although the competitive sports programs in high schools and colleges are often at the top of the pyramid of activities, as a part of the total health and physical education program these highly skilled and organized events are educationally useful only as long as they have the quality of progression. When the events become professionalized in the sense that they are repetitive, or that they are modified to make them more entertaining, they do not even belong in the pyramid. In a sense a pyramid is not a good educational analogy, because it has a terminal point at the top. No event of

[3] Educational Policies Commission, *School Athletics—Problems and Policies,* National Education Association, 1954, p. 3.

value can be kept in the curriculum when it reaches the point of termination of learning.

Later discussion in this text will reinforce this point of view, because the educational aspects of physical education will be emphasized repeatedly. As one of the resources of the program of physical education, interscholastic and intercollegiate athletics have a firm and important place. The relationship between the basic instructional program and the interinstitutional program is that between an elementary and an advanced course.

RECREATION. One can repeat what many have said, namely, that worthwhile recreation is an essential aspect of living in an industrialized society. Furthermore, the movement of people into cities and suburban areas creates problems for individuals who seek recreation. Schools and colleges are recognizing their obligations and constructing facilities which can be used for recreational as well as educational purposes. In the basic instructional program of physical education, children learn skills, games, and dances which they perform out of school. They also learn to play with others. Older children and youth also acquire knowledge which enables them to participate in active recreation. College students and adults carry on in their leisure time those activities which they have learned in their physical education instructional program. The recreational needs of individuals at each age, therefore, influence the content and conduct of the physical education program.

Not all recreation is active. Active recreation, however, is needed for its physically stimulating value, which is one of concomitant outcomes. Developing ability in an active recreation and bringing about an interest in continuing participation are important purposes of physical education.

SUMMARY

The total program of health and physical education has several major phases, each with its own particular purposes and resources, and each related to the other. The central program—the instructional program of physical education—will concern the remainder of this text.

Chapter 3

ADMINISTRATIVE RESPONSIBILITY FOR GOALS

IF THE nature of the job determines the administrative tasks, then a knowledge of the goals which physical education strives to achieve is of primary importance. Furthermore, because physical education is only one part of the total educational program of the school or college, there will be administrative relationships and lines of responsibility between the person in charge of the physical education program, those responsible for other subject areas, and those responsible for the program and operation of the entire school system, college, or university.

THE GOALS OF PHYSICAL EDUCATION

The goals of physical education are not static. They must be restudied periodically in the light of both educational purposes and newer knowledge concerning the contributions of the field to larger educational goals. Again, in this subject area as in all education, opinions differ as to what the goals should be. The following discussion of purposes of physical education will indicate how difficult it has been for this field to agree upon its goals. Foshay, in a recent discussion of educational goals, has defined two levels of consideration. The first deals with the ultimate goals being sought. This is the level for study in this chapter. The second deals with the operational goals, those steps to be followed in moving toward the ultimate. The operational goals will be considered in the section on the physical education program.

What are the professional goals of physical education today? How are they selected? How much agreement is there on the ultimate purposes of physical education?

The history of physical education reveals that there have always been goals guiding the conduct of any physical education program. In the United States, leaders advocating its establishment as part of the school program stated the purposes to be achieved by such instruction and practice. A chronological series of the definitions of physical education is not intended here. It is important to note that the purposes of the profession in its work today may include earlier purposes, but today's goals are set in the pattern of an educational endeavor rather than that of a specialized discipline.

In 1929, the College Physical Education Association created a Committee on Curriculum Research. The task of this committee was to study the curriculum of physical education with respect to purposes, content, administration, and evaluation. The stimulus for organizing the committee was a belief that there was a need for a more uniform program of physical education throughout the schools of America. The question at hand concerned the practicability of creating a program which could be used by schools with varying facilities, in widely spread geographic regions, and under the supervision of personnel with differing viewpoints. Although this committee was a college group, its concern was with the physical education program from the elementary school through the secondary school. The major proportion of the study was directed to the public school programs. The college program was considered an extension of the secondary school curriculum, with minor modifications in the emphasis upon types of activities and the level of achievement expected of the student.

At the beginning of its work, the committee formulated five objectives to govern its activities. These became the objectives of the program outlined by the committee, although they were used originally as criteria for evaluating the contributions to the curriculum of a number of physical activities. Because these statements represent the concurrence of a group of men studying the curriculum of physical education, they are given here first. The student will find that later statements by the committee are broader in some ways than these; nevertheless, the following objectives have served as guides for many years.

According to the Committee on Curriculum Research, physical activities should contribute to:

1. Physical and organic growth and development of the child and the improvement of body function and body stability.
2. Social traits and qualities that go to make up the good citizen and the development of sound moral ideals through intensive participation under proper leadership.
3. Psychological development of the child, including satisfactions and emotional stability resulting from stimulating physical and social experiences.
4. Development of safety skills that increase the individual's capacity for protection in emergencies, both in handling himself and in assisting others.
5. Development of recreational skills that have a distinct function as hobbies for leisure time hours, both during school and in afterschool life.[1]

Individual writers have presented their own lists of objectives. Voltmer and Esslinger analyzed stated objectives from a number of sources and grouped them according to previously selected criteria into two categories: those most worthy of general pursuit, and those less worthy of general pursuit.[2] The specific aims listed within each category deal with physical and psychomotor outcomes, social and cultural values, personality development, and recreational and safety skills. In their objective approach to setting up aims of physical education, the writers cannot avoid disagreement with other authorities on the relative importance of the various aims. The problem arising from such a list is that needs are not alike in all situations. Any detailed statement of objectives in which there is a ranking of importance faces the same problem.

[1] Adapted from William Ralph LaPorte, *The Physical Education Curriculum*, rev. ed., Parker and Co., 1951, p. 8.

[2] Edward F. Voltmer and Arthur A. Esslinger, *The Organization and Administration of Physical Education*, 3rd ed., Appleton-Century-Crofts, Inc., 1958.

Other statements of aims and objectives, of which there are many, follow closely those groupings designated by the LaPorte Committee. Each individual's list is tempered by his own interpretation of the purposes of physical education. The similarity of the statements is more noteworthy than the differences between them.

A summary statement of the objectives which guide the organization and conduct of a physical education program should be preceded by consideration of the nature of the objective itself. Nash speaks of *remote* objectives, the larger guiding ones, as the standards of health, recreation, and citizenship. Physical education is expected to make a substantial contribution to these objectives. More immediately, he treats the development of the child as an objective of physical education and describes it on four levels: (1) organic, (2) neuromuscular, (3) interpretative, and (4) emotional. Again the wording may vary, but the intent resembles that of other statements of objectives.[3]

DEFINITION OF GOALS, AIMS, OBJECTIVES, AND PURPOSES

At the beginning of the chapter, reference was made to Foshay's division of objectives into immediate and ultimate, and it was stated that this discussion would focus on the ultimate objectives. At this point a brief observation about the several interpretations given to the words *goals, aims, objectives* and *purposes* will help the student to understand the professional literature on this subject whenever and wherever he encounters it.

Today the word *objective* is used generally to describe all that is sought, whether it be the ultimate or the immediate. *Purpose* also is commonly used as a synonym for *objective*. Williams makes a clear distinction between the aim of physical education and its objectives. He states that "an aim is not really conceived unless the means are visualized and organized for the end in view." For Williams, the aim is the ultimate end which guides all work under the heading of physical education. "Objectives, on the other hand, are precise, definite, and limited statements of steps in procedure of realization of the aim. Between aim and objectives there arises the

[3] J. B. Nash, Francis J. Moench, and Jeannette B. Saurborn, *Physical Education: Organization and Administration,* A. S. Barnes and Co., 1951, pp. 62–63.

need for statement of purposes which are not general enough to be an aim and not precise enough to be objectives."[4] Objectives are the attainable steps along the way, and may be as numerous as one wishes, according to the limitation of the step to be taken. Occasionally the word *goal* describes the larger end, and at times even this term is modified by *major* and *minor*.

Whether one uses aims, goals, ends, purposes, or objectives, it is well to remember that there are degrees of directing power and that an aim, an ultimate objective, or a major goal is essential to give the fundamental direction and value to the endeavor. Physical education must have this kind of aim. Without it, there can be no physical education program.

Williams has proposed the following as the aim of physical education. "Physical education should aim to provide skilled leadership and adequate facilities which will afford an opportunity for the individual or group to act in situations which are physically wholesome, mentally stimulating and satisfying, and socially sound."[5] There is a quality about an ultimate objective or aim, as Williams has chosen to call it, which distinguishes it from lesser objectives. His statement provides a concise point of view which is not surpassed. According to this, the teacher may very well achieve the major share of the ultimate goal in a given situation at a certain time. If the situation is repeated, this accomplishment will permit the teacher and students to progress further toward the ultimate goal rather than repeating something already attained. The aim is a constant, guiding influence which keeps a professional field moving ahead, doing its job, and serving society as it should. The student, the teacher, and the administrator must think in terms of the ultimate as they plan for the immediate.

Ultimate objectives, and the more immediate ones leading to them, fall within the following groups of values. These are the areas in which professional physical educators establish their objectives. They are part of the framework of goals for all education:

1. Those dealing with the area of organic development, fitness, and physiologic well-being.

[4] Jesse Feiring Williams, *The Principles of Physical Education,* 4th ed., W. B. Saunders Company, 1944, p. 248.

[5] Jesse Feiring Williams, *The Principles of Physical Education,* 6th ed., W. B. Saunders Company, 1954, p. 222.

2. Those dealing with the area of personality development, psychological growth, and verbal learning.
3. Those dealing with the area of social development and citizenship in terms of human relations.
4. Those dealing with the development of attitudes, skills, and activities for use in leisure time.
5. Those dealing with development of neuromuscular skills for specific reasons in addition to those of recreational use.

How does one develop objectives according to the principles set forth above, and how does he achieve them? Several answers may be given to these questions.

One of the major goals of education as given by the Educational Policies Commission is the self-realization of the individual. Objectives in this category relate to the development of personal skills, capacities, and qualities which make it possible for the individual to take a full part in his society and to secure satisfaction from living because of his ability to seek them. What objectives of self-realization can be sought through physical education, and how can they be achieved?

Personal capacities which the individual develops through his active participation in physical education are physical strength, physiologic endurance and adaptability, and neuromuscular skills. In addition, there are possible gains in emotional stability and means of expression, social maturity, and knowledge growing out of intellectual activity. Stated objectives to describe the specific outcomes sought for each of the above capacities can be prepared by the physical education teacher for his school and age groups. Such objectives would include standards of performance in a physical activity demanding strength and organic endurance. There would be standards sought in bodily control and in skill performances. An understanding of emotional expression would be developed, as well as emotional control, both of which improve one's ability to participate in an activity and to meet the situations which arouse emotion. An appreciation and expression of the finer emotions of affection, understanding, joy, and others would be sought. Social qualities appropriate to the age group would be described and worked for as the means of participating successfully within a group and of gaining an understanding of one's responsibility in a society.

The student can achieve his objectives only by engaging in purposeful activities which take place under planned instruction. In physical education, the resources are bodily activities, and there is a wide variety in the degree to which these offer learning opportunities. When a teacher uses any one activity, the immediate goal is bound up with the nature of the activity. For example, if the activity is a folk dance for children, the immediate goal becomes the learning of the dance and practice to make performance of the dance possible. The skill of the dance is immediate and must be acquired before the dance itself becomes the means for achieving other objectives. In the process of learning the skills, the child develops physically and physiologically according to the time spent in practice, the vigor of the dance, and the vigor with which he participates. Furthermore, he learns more about learning. He acquires additional knowledge in the form of new vocabulary and new meanings related to the origin and meaning of the dance itself. Emotions of joy, as well as others, are outcomes of the dancing. These are possible expressions of the dance. Obviously, factors stimulating the expression of fear, dislike, and even hatred can also be introduced into the situation. Control of unsuitable emotions may be learned, and the teacher may try to redirect those which hamper educational growth. Social maturity is enhanced through the student's participation in the group and through achieving both skill and responsibility for his part in the dance.

When a skill has been acquired so that the individual can continue his participation without instructional supervision, he develops the ability to take part voluntarily in recreational activities. Further socialization is possible and continuation into similar activities is given impetus. He reaches a new level of awareness of activities; his curiosity and interest are aroused, leading him into further participation and learning.

Emphasis must be given to the fact that the starting point and the principal means are the activities. All the objectives which have been mentioned are achieved because they are important to engaging in the activity. Without an activity, whether it be folk dancing, basketball, or track, there would be little meaning to the objectives and very limited achievement. For this reason it is necessary to develop more specific statements of objectives within the situation where the teaching and learning occur. It is also necessary to recognize that objectives such as physical stamina, when taken out of the context of living purposes and meanings of the individual, are extremely difficult to achieve and really are seldom attained to any acceptable degree. If the same objectives are placed within the scope of meaningful activity, levels of achievement can be set as high as one desires.

Objectives in the areas of human relationships, economic efficiency, and civic responsibility can be defined and achieved through the same procedures. The teacher of physical education is fully aware of the fact that although his subject may contribute to attaining these objectives, it is not the sole means for their accomplishment. Objectives in physical development, stamina, and motor learning, however, cannot be fully achieved, except through the resources of physical education.

SIMILARITY OF GOALS OF EDUCATION AND PHYSICAL EDUCATION

Leaders in physical education today make little if any distinction between the goals of education and those of physical education. They do emphasize the unique contributions which physical education can make to the ultimate goals of education. There is a growing tendency not to establish special objectives or goals for physical education with respect to the ultimate ends to be sought, but rather to emphasize the function of education in a democracy and relate the purposes of physical education to this function.

Kozman, in *Group Process in Physical Education,* describes objectives broadly and orients them toward the outcomes sought primarily through the group process. She states:

> We share with all other teachers a common concern for the developing person; we share with these same others the same goals, each using different materials and a wide variety of experiences and methods to attain them. In addition, physical education has unique contributions to make in the education of students. Jointly with others we are concerned with education for leisure, for health, and for democratic citizenship. Our unique contribution lies in the area of educating for the understanding and use of the body as the instrument for daily living, for expressing ourselves, for communicating with others.
>
> How the individual feels about his body, what insights he gains through

its expressive use, how clearly he realizes the value of its responsiveness, how consciously he appreciates the esthetic nature of movement when it is a union of thinking–feeling-doing–all are basic to what he is and what he does as a person and as a member of a group.[6]

In the matter of objectives, Oberteuffer[7] makes no distinction between education and physical education. His argument consistently states that physical education, as part of the school curriculum, must seek, through its unique resources, the same ends that the total school has chosen for itself. These values must be a part of the planned learning opportunities in the program.

Helen Manley combines the specialized outcomes of physical education with the general goals of education in describing the essentials of physical education for women.

Physical education is but one area of the total curriculum in education. It is the one primarily concerned with activity and which teaches democratic living through the physical. The body is the vehicle; the large motor area, the tools. The activities should promote organic vigor and neuromuscular skills, but always accompanied by social experiences provocative of democratic living. The human organism is unified, the physical cannot be taught alone, and so the method of teaching and the environment of instruction will affect the learning. Strength, skill, fitness, endurance are part of this great profession, but those who believe so sincerely in physical education believe above all else in the American democracy–physical education is merely one powerful vehicle for developing human relations. Dr. Jesse F. Williams, one of our outstanding physical educators, has said that without this higher purpose we find ourselves "devoted to strength with no cause to serve, skills with no functions to perform, and endurance with nothing worth lasting for."[8]

Physical education today has goals which are consistent with and contribute to the achievement of the purposes of the total school curriculum. Physical education, sometimes considered as a separate program or curriculum, shares with other school subjects the re-

[6] Hilda Clute Kozman, ed., *Group Process in Physical Education,* Harper & Brothers, 1951, p. 11.

[7] Delbert Oberteuffer, *Physical Education,* rev. ed., Harper & Brothers, 1956.

[8] Helen Manley, "Essentials of Physical Education for Girls and Women," *Report of the International Congress on the Essentials of Physical Education for Youth,* American Association for Health, Physical Education and Recreation, 1955, p. 136.

sponsibility for educating youth in the many qualities which will insure their own fullest development and participation in society. The teacher and administrator need to understand this fact thoroughly, to share the convictions of those who have pointed the way, and to work to fulfill the claim that physical education is an integral part of the school program.

There is not space here to discuss the many studies and arguments which have backed this point of view and led to its formulation. The student who has not already acquainted himself with the literature on this matter will wish to read from the original sources. The road leading from the middle of the nineteenth century, when physical education was considered strictly an exercise program designed to overcome weaknesses and handicaps of children, to the present day, when physical education offers not only physiological values but rich learning in other vital aspects of the person's life, has been filled with detours, obstacles, rough spots, conflicts, and even opposition to its construction. Even today it is not smooth, but the force directing it is increasing in size, power, and fundamental knowledge. The opportunity for improving physical education as a part of the school and college program is greater than ever, and the need for improvement presents a great challenge.

In order to indicate the universality of the educational viewpoint concerning the outcomes of physical education, several statements from papers submitted at the International Congress on the Essentials of Physical Education for Youth in 1954 are given below. Mr. A. Bilbrough of England stressed the education of the whole child and the importance of social learning.

In the world of education we have become increasingly familiar with the demand to cater for the physical, mental, and spiritual needs of the child and to realize that the mind, body and spirit make up the "whole" child, and that the "whole" child needs our attention. Briefly, then we understand the aim of education to be the preparation of the child physically, mentally, and morally for the business of life. This, of course, is no new theory but because in "physical education" all these things are receiving attention, physical education is rightly given its present important and prominent place in modern education.

Though the necessity to cater for the needs of the individual and to provide opportunities for individual expression are generally recognized as essential, an equally important essential is the need for individuals to be able to live happily together, to be tolerant and appreciative of each other and to respect the other person's point of view. How do we hope to achieve success in educating children to these ideals? We consider that it helps if they are able to dance or swim together or to join together in games of hockey, badminton, golf or tennis. In the excitement of a game or the keen rivalry of competitive sport, there are frequent opportunities for emotions to be out of control and for feelings to be expressed in unpleasant and undesirable ways—but good physical education will train children to control their feelings and express themselves in more gentlemanly fashion; thus the development of good sportsmanship is only another way of describing invaluable social training.[9]

Sadanand D. Chopde of India emphasized the meaningful experiences which physical education may provide for youth of university age.

In trying to meet the needs of the youth, the appropriate point of focus should be the individual as we find him in his complex environment. The wholeness and freedom of the individual is constantly at stake in our modern life; it is especially so in the highly developed societies. . . . It is our function as educators to restore to each individual in some ways, his faith in the worth and dignity in his individual personality, and in that of other individuals in the society. Life is a struggle; involving constant and continuous responsibilities of making decisions affecting one's own life and that of others. Being an individual, whole and free, means the right to make decisions, and further to live by their consequences. This will have meaning for the youth, and as such there is scope for his growth and development in this direction. It will besides increase his understanding and appreciation of his dependence on others. From our experiences, we are led to believe that physical education programs conducted with intelligent leadership can provide those meaningful experiences which the complex life of the modern society is depriving him of.[10]

Pointing to the obligation of the individual to prepare himself to serve others, Joyce M. Tyrrell of Canada wrote the following: "To sum up, I believe that it is essential that our college physical edu-

[9] A. Bilbrough, *The Report of the International Congress on the Essentials of Physical Education for Youth,* American Association for Health, Physical Education and Recreation, 1955, pp. 104–105.

[10] Sadanand D. Chopde, "Essentials of Physical Education for University-Age Youth," *The Report of the International Congress on the Essentials of Physical Education for Youth,* American Association for Health, Physical Education and Recreation, 1955, p. 118.

cation in Canada be broad, of high standards, and positive. It must provide release from tension. It must contribute to the wholeness of education, and it must be so presented that those who receive it will, after graduation, serve their fellows, with vitality and with dedication."[11]

None of these speakers emphasized strength, endurance, or muscular skills as the essentials of physical education for youth in their countries. Were these time-honored qualities ignored? Not at all. They are only means by which the youth realizes more fully his educational potential, by which he can meet more surely his obligations as a citizen in his country. Physical education in the United States cannot shun its responsibility to strive for the fullest development and education of the individual in a country and in a world where the understanding of human relationships is a means to better living for all.

OBJECTIVES FOR COLLEGE PHYSICAL EDUCATION

With only a few exceptions, the literature referred to in this discussion of objectives concerns the physical education curriculum for schools below the college level. In choosing the broad goals of the program, therefore, one must assume that the ultimate objectives for physical education in colleges are the same as those stated for the lower schools. The education of youth in colleges should follow the goals of education as society sees them.

LaPorte, in *The Physical Education Curriculum,* makes the following statements about the college program. Objectives are not defined, but the suggested curriculum implies that the college is concerned with preparation for leisure time.

> At the college level a strong emphasis was placed on making the activities elective as to type in place of a specified, required program.
>
> In general, there was definite opinion favorable to giving emphasis, where facilities were available, to such carry over activities as badminton, bowling, boating, camping, golf, hiking, riding, skiing, skating, snowshoeing, social recreation activities and tennis with a wide list of choices

[11] Joyce M. Tyrrell, "The Essentials of Physical Education for University Women in Canada," *The Report of the International Congress on the Essentials of Physical Education for Youth,* American Association for Health, Physical Education and Recreation, 1955, p. 136.

particularly in the specialized equipment activities so that a given school could select those for which it is equipped without having to teach all activities.[12]

Hughes and French set forth objectives similar in scope and intent to those given previously for the elementary and secondary school physical education curricula. They refer to the aim of modern education to develop the whole individual rather than to train the mind alone (if this is possible). According to Hughes and French, the program which a staff will be expected to organize and administer should seek the following goals:

The Biological Objective. Participation in physical education and athletics should assist in the normal growth and development of the skeletal and organic systems, in the development and maintenance of proper functioning of these systems, and in the development of sufficient strength and endurance to perform the ordinary, and occasional extraordinary tasks of life without undue strain.

The Skill Objective. Participation in physical education and athletic activities should assist in the development of recreational and utilitarian skills involving rapid and adaptive choice and action, and in the development of the coordination of the special senses with body movement, including the ability to judge accurately speed, distance, force, weight and timing of movement.

The Social Objectives. Physical education and athletics should offer children and youth the opportunity to develop desirable citizenship traits through harmonious and cooperative participation in group activities, including those involving intercultural relationships. They should lead to attainment of sportsmanship, leadership, self-discipline, sociability, and social cooperation.

Attitudes, Appreciation, and Understanding as Objectives. Participation in physical education and athletics should help the participants develop wholesome interests in physical activities; such positive mental traits as joy, enthusiasm, self-confidence, persistence, and courage; understanding of their own aptitudes and limitations; appreciation of the beauty of body movement; and knowledge of rules, techniques, tactics, health procedures, and wise and constructive use of leisure time.

Administrative Objectives. Administration should be designed to set the stage for the educational process.[13]

[12] LaPorte, *op. cit.*, p. 25.

[13] William L. Hughes and Esther French, *The Administration of Physical Education for Schools and Colleges*, A. S. Barnes and Co., 1954, pp. 3–4.

Since these objectives are compatible with those accepted for the field of physical education, it might be assumed that they also guide the programs of physical education in colleges and universities. This assumption, however, does not hold up under examination.

A study of the purposes of physical education for college men made by Wise and reported to the meeting of the College Physical Education Association in 1952 indicated that the chairmen of college and university departments of physical education for men held a wide variety of objectives, and, where there was any semblance of agreement, the resulting objectives did not cover the range of those accepted for the lower schools. Several of the implications from the Wise study follow.

> The fact that there was not complete unanimity of opinion concerning the importance of any objectives of the college physical education program may appear to lend some validity to the claim that the physical education program lacks direction.
>
> . . . the objectives of physical education which were of primary importance to the college men's programs were a development of motor skill, habits of participation for the present and the future, interest in physical activity, and providing fun of participation.
>
> The objectives of college physical education rated of high importance were generally not related to the intellectual and cultural development of students. Only a few specific objectives of the program dealing with intellectual pursuits were considered important. Intellectual-Cultural objectives considered in the most important section included the extension of knowledge of techniques and rules of the activities, personal and group health knowledge, and the development of appreciation as a spectator.
>
> Those objectives which were rated as most important to the program were also those which the directors indicated may most practically be measured. Physical education objectives seemed to be generally related to the objectives of general education at the college level.[14]

A wide range of objectives for the college program may be expected, although it is not necessarily considered desirable. College curriculums are not identical nor even alike in many instances, because the state does not demand such uniformity. Colleges differ in the nature of their origins; hence they may hold different views

[14] A. R. Wise, "The Purposes of Physical Education for College Men," *Proceedings,* The College Physical Education Association, 1953, pp. 132–135.

concerning the purpose of physical education. For example, a college may believe that education is for the mind alone. This institution may have no program of physical education for its general student body, but may conduct an elaborate program of intercollegiate athletics for a small number of its students. Furthermore, administrators and teachers in colleges are not necessarily prepared professionally in the field of education; in physical education such lack of preparation may be reflected in the objectives selected and in the methods used to reach them.

Even if none of the above conditions existed, and if all personnel were professionally trained, there would still be diversity in objectives among the colleges because of the differences in their major purposes and in the nature of their student bodies. On the other hand, the guiding purposes of all physical education programs should be consistent with the major purposes of higher education. Therefore, the objectives chosen by a college for its particular physical education program should contribute in the fullest measure to the goals of higher education. In view of this criterion, the objectives listed by Wise as most common in programs for college men are inadequate. The goals listed by Hughes and French are more appropriate, although their application at the college level requires careful planning and definition. The larger view expressed by Kozman and by Oberteuffer[15] provides a lasting goal.

The college teacher or administrator will establish his or her program so as to utilize the resources of physical education to aid the students in achieving the stated goals of the institution, thus fulfilling the major purpose of higher education. He can then see clearly the objectives, the basis for evaluation, and the methods required to achieve the objectives.

SUMMARY OF MAJOR PURPOSES

In summarizing this discussion of physical education goals, one wishes to emphasize both the identification of the field with all of education and the uniqueness of its resources for producing outcomes which other fields of learning can reach only to a limited degree. Because it is a part of the total educational program, "physi-

[15] Kozman, *op. cit.*, p. 11. Oberteuffer, *op. cit.*, p. 288.

cal education aims for the same general goal that gives purpose to all the other learning experiences of the school—the well-rounded development of all children and youth as responsible citizens in our democratic society."[16] The outcomes considered important by the profession are also in a sense the major objective areas. They are listed as:

1. The development and maintenance of maximum physical efficiency.
2. The development of useful skills, especially those which make movement of the body in a large variety of activities easy and satisfying. Fundamental skills, safety skills, and the more complex expressive and game skills are considered useful.
3. The development of socially acceptable conduct. Physical education is not the sole means of teaching this kind of conduct, but when its activities are learned and practiced under good leadership, physical education can be a major influence in the development of desirable conduct.
4. The development of an appreciation and enjoyment of wholesome recreation.[17]

If one has read the previous material carefully, he will conclude that the listing of specific goals means only that these matters are important and must be taken into account in setting up learning situations. He will also realize that an educational experience should contain all these elements if the teacher hopes to develop the whole individual, rather than a brain or a set of muscles. The teacher decides upon the emphasis and directs the learning toward the major aim, while at the same time the more specific values are sought directly.

RESTRICTIVE ATTITUDES

It is necessary to comment upon two attitudes concerning the implementation of programs leading to the achievement of acceptable and desirable objectives. Both decry the view that the professional educator should accept and strive for higher goals. The first attitude presumes that limitations of facilities, narrowness of

[16] W. K. Streit and Simon A. McNeely, "A Platform of Physical Education," *Journal of the American Association for Health, Physical Education and Recreation,* March, 1950, p. 136.

[17] *Ibid.,* pp. 136–137.

outlook of the school or college administration, low prestige once accorded to physical education in the institution, and primary emphasis on interschool or intercollegiate athletics restrict as well as decide the goals toward which one may strive.

Limitations always exist, no matter how favorable the physical and intellectual atmosphere of an institution may be. The question is, do the limitations determine forever the kind of program which is to be conducted in the school or college? The authors think not. Furthermore, it is a matter of common experience that those who have no worthwhile goal have no worthwhile programs. There is nothing quite so tragic as an educational program aimed at procuring meager outcomes. One must work within the existing limitations, but he need not live by them indefinitely nor should he set his goals entirely within them.

The second attitude is that one should give the people what they want. If they seek a recreational program, let them have it. If they wish only a program of highly organized competitive sports on an interinstitutional basis, let them have it. If they encourage the continuance of activities whose outcomes run counter to the generally accepted purposes of education, go along with them.

Literature in education often contains statements supporting the thesis that the schools should serve the public. A hasty and shallow interpretation of this statement would suggest that the direction and conduct of education must follow the rather amorphous wishes of a public—which actually may be several publics, each with a special interest—with only vague notions about the function of education in American democracy. In dealing with laymen, whether members of a board of education, members of a board of trustees, a parents' group, or a local business or service organization, the professional educator, teacher, or administrator, by virtue of his training, must provide the specialized knowledge upon which lay groups base their actions.

In discussing the relationship of a school superintendent with a board of education, Sears states that "the superintendent's position in the government mechanism, by its own nature, clearly makes him responsible not merely as a consultant, but as a leader." Whether matters are brought before the board by the superintendent or by someone else, his function in the overall process of governing the schools is "positive and aggressive."[18] Foshay has raised a question about the source of our goals. He outlines the problem as follows:

> The great problem for any school person is to reconcile what is expedient with what is significant. It is expedient, and perhaps prudent, to set the operational goals of a school on the basis of some averaged-out opinion among the patrons of the school. In some few very tense communities, this may be all that is possible. But a great school was never developed on the basis of an average of public opinions. Moreover, if we are frank about it, we must admit that we, who interpret the average, tend to make it mean what we ourselves value most about a school. Now, the question is, What should be the source of our goals? Is it wrong for the values of the public educator as a person to enter into his curriculum decisions? Even if he consults with others in his community concerning the goals of education, should he bear the responsibility for finally developing such goals? Every one of us here knows that there is a fine line between the prudent and the possible. Some of us play it so safe that we never express a personal opinion of any consequence; we take no personal responsibility for our beliefs; we resort to group process to the exclusion of thinking in the armchair—and all in the name of democracy and considerateness.[19]

The fact is that school programs which do not take advantage of the knowledge and guidance of professionally competent educators will flounder, run the risk of seeking limited objectives, and sometimes even accept unworthy objectives. This danger applies equally to any part of the total school program. The physical education curriculum should be determined by the professional physical education personnel.

Does this mean that the interests and needs of the local community must be ignored? Indeed not! The professional educator, mindful of the major task of the school or college, will learn the requirements of his own students and also those of the community. He will be alert to needs and interests which extend beyond the local community. Equipped with this knowledge and with a full understanding of the guiding purposes of the school, he will be able to utilize completely the physical education resources both

[18] Jesse B. Sears, *The Nature of the Administrative Process,* McGraw-Hill Book Co., Inc., 1950, p. 421.

[19] Arthur W. Foshay, "Educational Goals," *Educational Research Bulletin,* February 13, 1957, pp. 35–36.

to achieve the objectives which relate to physical education and to attain the goals of the total program.

Oberteuffer states clearly and forcefully the relationship between the objectives of a subject, or curriculum, and the society in which the school operates. He writes: "Furthermore, the curriculum in physical education must be sensitive to community problems, national movements, social customs, and to any and all of the influences which shape American schools. It should present no values or objectives at variance with the stated purposes of education in a democracy.[20]

The teacher and the administrator of physical education can do no less than to make every effort to live according to this philosophy.

[20] Oberteuffer, *op. cit.*, p. 289.

Chapter 4

LINES OF ADMINISTRATIVE RESPONSIBILITY

An individual who begins working in any organization soon learns that he is not working alone but is under the authority of someone else. Successful administration results when the administrator recognizes these facts and when he determines the areas where he has authority and those where he does not. Administration is concerned with getting the job done according to accepted goals; the administrator must learn the lines of responsibility and work in accordance with them.

The statements in the above paragraph are clear and definite. If every job involved an organization in which the people follow a pattern, the administrator would need only the skill to learn his duties, responsibilities, and limits and the ability to work within his findings. Because organizations, including schools and colleges, are administered by people who are neither robots nor identical to one another in their administrative practices, there are digressions from the defined pattern of administrative responsibility. Some who occupy positions of responsibility neglect their obligations, some try to usurp the responsibilities of others, some have never learned their own responsibilities, some are unfamiliar with the larger organization within which they work and confine themselves to their own small sphere.

The administrator accomplishes his goals by working with others in positions of responsibility, sometimes above him, sometimes on his level, and sometimes subordinate to him; hence, being able to work within established lines of authority is important. The ability to deal effectively, however, with those matters which come within undefined or poorly defined areas of responsibility will require insight, tact, and skill as well as the ability to adhere to the general organizational pattern.

It is not intended to support the idea that an administrator who finds desirable actions blocked by the organized lines of responsibility must always accept defeat. Organizations usually provide for appeals from the decision of an immediate superior. Furthermore, organizational patterns in a democratic society are subject to change. Whether or not the administrator chooses to appeal or to work for a changed organization will depend upon his values and the particular circumstances.

The major purpose of the following presentation is to describe institutional organizational patterns as they relate to the lines of administrative responsibility and to place in perspective the role of the administrator of health and physical education as he works through his own educational program to achieve the purposes of the school system or higher institution to which he belongs. Because colleges usually permit their departmental heads greater freedom of administrative action than do school systems, the following materials treat in detail the lines of administrative responsibility in a college or university. The same pattern exists in a school system and will be summarized at the end of the discussion.

EDUCATION—A STATE FUNCTION

In the United States the state is the authority for all organized education. "For nearly three hundred years America has regarded the state as the responsible agent for the development and maintenance of a system of public education, available to all children of all the people, irrespective of race, creed, political affiliation, or economic status. Legally and historically, then, education is a state function."[1]

[1] Alonzo G. Grace, "The State and the Educational System," *Forty-Fifth Yearbook,* Part II, National Society for the Study of Education, University of Chicago Press, 1946, p. 7.

State control extends to institutions of higher education, both public and private, wherever they intend to award any kind of certificate, degree, or diploma for succesful completion of a course of study. The state serves as an organizer and supporter of higher education on the one hand, and as an agent of the people in holding institutions to educational standards on the other.

The departmental administrator in a college may not be aware of the role played by the state unless his work concerns the preparation of teachers. He should know that colleges and universities are chartered by the state to carry on certain types of programs. The degree, or degrees, which an institution may grant are authorized by the state, and usually the curriculum of the institution, its faculty, and facilities are studied carefully before authority to grant degrees is given.

The administrator and the teacher have the obligation of knowing the basis for the institution's charter, the purposes for its existence, and the state's requirements for the institution in terms of curriculum, faculty, and facilities. There is reason to believe that institutions themselves neglect their part in helping their employees to fulfill this obligation. The teacher is employed to work in a subject matter area; rarely is he asked to concern himself with the larger purposes of the institution. Since the departmental chairman will have to act for the institution, he must be familiar with the purposes of his college or university.

AIMS OF COLLEGES AND UNIVERSITIES

Stated aims of colleges and universities are similar in general, but the emphasis which is given to selected aspects of aims does vary. Even if the statements seemed alike from one institution to another, it would still be important for the departmental administrator to be familiar with the statement of aim as his own institution publishes it in order to know the local implications and emphases which influence its instructional program.

Statements of aims presented here are taken from the official bulletins of colleges and universities. They will serve to direct attention to those matters which the institution considers important. Physical education is a required subject in each of the institutions cited below.

A large private university describes its purpose as follows:

> The University motto, *Eruditio et Religio,* reflects a fundamental faith in the union of knowledge and religion, the advancement of learning, the defense of scholarship, the love of freedom and truth, a spirit of tolerance, and a rendering of the greatest service to the individual, the state, the nation, and the church. Through changing generations of students the objective has been to encourage each individual to achieve to the extent of his capacities an understanding and appreciation of the world in which he lives, his relationship to it, his opportunities, and his responsibilities.
>
> . . . [The] University is concerned with developing the whole man. In its classrooms, libraries, and laboratories it is concerned with his mental and moral development, in its gymnasiums and on its playing fields, with his physical growth, and in its Chapel and religious program, with his spiritual well being.[2]

A small liberal arts college presents a challenging statement of general purpose and follows this with its own aims, which point to the larger guiding purpose of college education.

> The function of a college is to produce young men who will be the future leaders in the great callings of life. To this end [it] aims to give its students every opportunity to train the mind, to build up the body, to kindle the imagination, to discipline the emotions, to strengthen the will, to cultivate conscience. It introduces the young man to classroom, library and laboratory, to playing field and gymnasium, to great teachers and promising young men of his own age, to all the wide world about him, and to the great records of the past—and bids him make the most of them and of himself.
>
> It does this in the confident expectation that his training here will fit him in his own life to fulfill his capabilities and to recognize and discharge his obligations to his fellow man and the society in which he lives.[3]

In the above statement no assignment of special function is made for physical education. The implication is that physical education must take its place with other disciplines in the college in realizing the stated purposes. In such an institution, a departmental chairman receives direct guidance in setting his own departmental goals and in choosing the means by which he will attain them. Should he

[2] *Bulletin of Duke University, Undergraduate Instruction,* Duke University Press, March, 1956, p. 8.

[3] *Wesleyan University Bulletin,* Wesleyan University Press, Inc., October, 1956, p. 6.

be unfamiliar with the college's statement, he could make serious errors in the kind of program which he planned and attempted to conduct.

A large state university sets forth its aims and objectives for the entire institution in terms of a general purpose and in the light of proposed accomplishments.

Aims and Objectives: To provide an education to fit the times for the young men and women who enroll here; to disseminate and advance knowledge in the fields of learning in which programs of instruction and research are maintained; to bring the services of the institution to the people of the state wherever and whenever there is evidence of need which the resources of the university can best satisfy.

What the Institution Hopes to Accomplish: The University hopes to provide an education which will enable its graduates to contribute to the economic well-being of the state and nation to the limit of their creative and productive skills; to contribute to social stability by their understanding of the world around them; to contribute to the moral fabric of society by a sense of personal integrity; belief in deity, and devotion to American principles of government; to contribute to the political welfare of the state and nation by a reasoned and thinking approach to public affairs; in brief, to be truly educated men and women, effective citizens, well qualified to assume leadership in their communities, in the state, and in the nation.[4]

A large municipal liberal college of arts and science aims

1. to prepare young men and women of proved ability for rich and purposeful living and participating citizenship;
2. to help them identify their interests and formulate their vocational plans;
3. to give them an adequate background of knowledge and skills to pursue successfully professional studies in professional schools;
4. to prepare select groups to teach in elementary and secondary schools, to hold junior positions in social service, and to serve effectively in such callings as newspaper and magazine writing, laboratory technicians, research assistant and the like; and
5. to provide an opportunity for adults to continue their education toward cultural, professional, or vocational goals, and to develop skills in recreational and leisure-time activities.[5]

[4] *Michigan State University Catalog,* 1956–1957, Michigan State University, April, 1956, pp. 17, 67.

[5] *General Catalog,* Queens College, 1956–1957, p. 17.

One broadens his awareness of man's aspiration for his own development and for a better social environment as he reads the purposes of these colleges and universities. In spite of the expressed hope that the individual will achieve "to the extent of his capacities," the significant emphasis is given to man's integrity, and his service to society. The view is always forward and upward. English is studied not only to develop skill in writing, speaking, and reading but also to open to the student the richness of communication so that his thoughts may find the fullest expression and the ideas, ideals, thoughts, emotions, and experiences of others, written and spoken, may increase his understanding and knowledge.

Physics and mathematics enable man to plot his way into space. Philosophy helps man to identify himself within a vast universe. Physical education adds to man's understanding of his capabilities and provides situations for learning effective social interaction. Physical education today helps man to prepare for travel in space.

Institutional charters are granted in order that the high educational purposes of the institution can be achieved; the administration and faculty of the institution are the means of such achievement. The instructional departments become the organizational units by which this work is planned and conducted. When colleges and universities set for themselves the high aims and purposes described in the previous statements, no department may ignore them and settle for lower, less significant purposes. The departmental program must align itself with the goals of the institution. The departmental administrator has the major responsibility for guiding the formulation of the program and for directing the energies of his staff toward the goals set by the college.

THE GOVERNING BOARD

A college or university chartered by the state is represented by a body or corporation, a board of trustees, of regents, of overseers, which is the actual governing unit for the institution. In organizing a new college, some responsible body must first be established. The authority given to this body permits it to secure the site, facilities, and faculty which become the college or university as people know it.

The following is a description of the organization and authority of a board of control for a large state university.

Michigan State University is under the control of a constitutional board known as the State Board of Agriculture. The members are elected from the State at large for a period of six years, two being elected each odd year.

The President of the University is appointed by the Board and is by constitutional provision the presiding officer of that body.

The Board likewise appoints a Secretary and a Treasurer, who hold office at its will.[6]

The board, like the board of education for the public schools, is a governing, policy-making body. Final authority for all matters pertaining to the conduct of the institution resides in it. Much of its work is of a routine nature and is carried on without either the faculty or the general public being concerned with it. When matters of conflict or controversy arise which concern the institution, the authority and responsibility of the board become clear. Although the board has final authority on all matters pertaining to the institution, it is responsible to the state for the proper conduct of the institution, for maintaining acceptable educational standards, and for fulfilling the provisions of its charter.

THE INSTITUTIONAL HEAD

A body, such as a board of trustees, has difficulty in carrying out policy in the day-to-day life of an institution. Furthermore, since members of these boards are usually not salaried, they are not expected to administer the policies which they create. The responsibility for making policies effective in an institution rests with its head, usually the president. According to Harmon, "The chief executive is responsible for four major phases of the university's life: internal institutional administration, program development, promotion, and educational interpretation."[7]

Up to this point the organization and administration of the college seem remote to the teacher or departmental administrator. Often the faculty member has not met the members of the govern-

[6] *Michigan State University Catalog, op. cit.,* p. 17.

[7] Henry G. Harmon, "Effective Organization of the President's Office for University Service," *Proceedings,* Institute for Administrative Officers of Higher Institutions, XIX, 1947, p. 28.

ing board of the institution. He may not even know their names unless he reads regularly and carefully the first pages of the institution's bulletin. His closest relationship is likely to be with the college president, or in large universities with the dean of his college, for the president is not as immediately involved with departmental matters as he may be in the smaller colleges.

Regardless of the size of the institution, its president or head is responsible for carrying out the provisions of the institution's charter under the policies set forth by the governing board. The faculty member and the departmental administrator will do well to remember this fact in order to avoid misunderstanding with respect to spheres of jurisdiction. If there are exceptions to this placing of responsibility, the policies of the governing board must be explicit in defining them.

College and University Organization

Colleges and universities are similar in general organization. A university, however, contains several colleges or schools, each of which may be organized as a separate college. Generally, the internal organization of a college will be described in this text because the college is made up of basic units, departments, or other similar instructional units. What is true of the separate college is likely to apply to the college within the university.

College organization is arranged to manage three major areas: instruction, administration, and service. The following is not intended to include every function belonging in each category, but to indicate the important jobs which come under each heading.

The instructional functions include planning courses, preparation of the curricula leading to the various degrees, selection of evaluative procedures, maintenance of college educational standards, conduct of instruction, keeping records of student accomplishment, operation of the library, counseling and testing students, research, and guidance of new teachers on the faculty.

Setting up a category of administration separate from instruction or service means not that these latter areas do not concern the college administration, but that there are functions which are primarily the job of college administrative personnel. These functions include preparation of budgets, approval of recommendations for employment of new personnel, maintenance of personnel records, purchase and distribution of supplies and equipment, maintenance of all physical facilities, determining need for new capital items (and often securing funds to pay for them), planning new capital facilities, dealing with discipline of both students and employees, maintaining suitable public relations with off-campus groups, interpreting legal responsibilities of the institution, and recommending policy changes and new policy to the board governing the institution.

In the area of services, colleges provide for supervision of student health, for sanitary conditions on campus, for feeding students and faculty, for the general safety of all persons using the college grounds, buildings or special facilities, for housing students and occasionally faculty, and for vehicular parking.

The reader will recognize immediately that the categories are not discrete. Instructional concerns involve budgets, health, capital improvements, and so on. Administration must be mindful of all instructional and service matters. Services are aimed at facilitating the educational function of the institution to the greatest extent possible.

The college president is responsible for managing and directing the entire institution. He is assisted by provisions of policy which delegate duties to individuals and departments within the institution. The major unit, which acts almost entirely as a complete educational organization, is the department, usually defined by the limits of a subject matter area. The department's primary responsibility is the conduct of an educational (instructional) program. Other departmental duties are related to teaching. The preparation of departmental budgets, the employment of personnel, and the supervision and management of facilities are responsibilities defined and carried on according to the educational program of the department. One can readily observe that departments will vary widely in the variety and extent of these related responsibilities. All departments must select personnel and supervise their work. On the other hand, very few departments are directly responsible for the physical facilities which they use. In many departments the budgetary needs are primarily for personnel and to a limited extent for instructional supplies.

The department of health and physical education will have a greater number of responsibilities beyond personnel and supplies than will almost any other subject matter unit. Specialized facilities, programs conducted outside the classroom, and service to students and staff of the entire institution are examples of such responsibilities. Consideration will be given to these various functions from time to time in this text.

THE DEPARTMENTAL CHAIRMAN

Chairmen of the departments are important members of the college administrative organization. Although the president of the college is the authority, his immediate control and direction will usually, and should, be exercised through the departmental chairmen.

A person entering upon a departmental chairmanship should study the policies which define his job and his relationships with other administrative officers of the college. He will need to know the limits of his own authority. There may be unusual assignments of responsibility based on a previous situation in the department or the college. If he did not study the purposes and some of the historical background of the college before becoming chairman, he should do so now. The ability to utilize his position to fulfill a progressive, effective educational program is the primary responsibility of the departmental administrator. This responsibility is delegated by the state to the governing board of the institution, to the president, to the departments.

THE FACULTY

In colleges and universities the faculty occupies an important position in the formulation of policy relating to the curriculum. The faculty as a body usually establishes the course requirements for degrees, certificates, and diplomas, acts upon the proposals for additions and modifications in the course offerings, creates committees to study the standard of instruction, and in general deals with matters related to these functions. Faculties usually are charged with responsibility for the extra class program of student activities.

The role of the faculty is a powerful one, especially in view of the fact that its authority is derived from the governing board of the institution, and its actions are final when they are approved by the board. In the organization of a college or university, no other body does the work of the faculty in the area of curriculum. The board may act upon faculty curriculum proposals, but it would be almost impossible for it to inaugurate them.

An instructional department of the college must submit its curricular matters to the faculty for approval. Similarly, the department through its faculty representatives acts upon curricular matters presented by other departments.

Lest the reader think that two opposing statements have been made when, in one paragraph, the departmental administrator is charged with the responsibility for a forward looking, effective educational program, and, in the next paragraph, the faculty is said to formulate policy relative to curriculum, let him note the difference between the two functions.

The faculty, representing the entire college, gives meaning to the stated goals of the institution and guides the instructional program so that the institution's nature and purposes may be fully realized. It may actually determine whether there shall be departments, or interdepartmental or area studies units, and which instructional departments shall be represented in the institution. In this latter area the faculty is somewhat limited by the broad requirements of the institution's charter from the state and by the authority and power of the college administration.

Once the educational policies and curriculum have been established, the department conducts its own program almost as an autonomous unit. From time to time, however, the faculty may examine the status of any program in the institution. The following description of an actual incident portrays the relationships between the department, the faculty, the governing board of the institution, and the state. Although the president of the institution was involved at almost every step, the authority for acting upon curricular matters belonged to the faculty, the board, and the state.

In a liberal arts college the department of health and physical education, which conducted required courses in the liberal arts program for all students, also offered several elective courses in its instructional program. With the growth of the college the department decided to develop a plan to prepare teachers of physical education. The department of education was in favor of this.

One serious obstacle faced the department of health and physical education. The state requirements for the certification of teachers in physical education plus the college requirements for courses in liberal arts subjects exceeded the number of credit hours required for graduation. One of the general policies of the college was that students should have about one fourth of their course work in areas of free choice, not necessarily in the subject matter field of their concentration (or major) study. In order to allow for some free electives in the proposed concentration in physical education, the department developed a plan whereby the student could earn his bachelor's degree in the college within the prescribed 128 credits, with about seven or eight hours of free electives included. In order to meet the requirements for state certification, however, he would have to earn seven credits in undergraduate courses taken beyond the 128 credits required for graduation. Although his undergraduate education was tuition free, he would have to pay for courses taken after graduation.

The proposal passed the faculty, although a few questions were raised about the limited elective credits available to the student. When it reached the governing board it was rejected, because the state, which was heavily subsidizing the education of teachers, held that the student should be able to secure all his required undergraduate preparation within the 128 credits and without the necessity of paying for extra courses. The state would not pay for the credits beyond those required for graduation. The board returned the matter to the faculty without acting upon it. The department of health and physical education now revised its proposal to include the required courses for teacher certification within the 128 credits, but in doing this it had to eliminate all free elective credits. When the revised proposal was brought before the faculty again, it was strongly opposed, not because of the nature of the concentration, but because of the elimination of all elective opportunities for the student. It was a basic policy in the college that all students should have the privilege of choosing subjects from the total range of elective offerings, and this policy would be set aside in the proposed concentration for the preparation of teachers in physical education. Only the fact that the department itself through its earlier proposal had supported the need for elective study and that its revision was dictated by the state education policy caused the faculty to approve the revised proposal.

In this situation all major administrative units were brought into the picture. The authority of each is indicated. Obviously, in matters of administration, the departments, faculties, colleges, boards, and state departments are represented by their heads. In this situation these persons were functioning with, not apart from, other members of their respective bodies.

An incident recounted in the *Journal of Health and Physical Education*[8] demonstrates two points. The first, as in the incident just described, is that the faculty is responsible for curricular policy in the institution. The second is that a department of health and physical education must conduct its program as professionally and effectively as possible and should contribute to the achievement of the institution's major goals. The degree to which the department meets its obligation will depend largely upon the leadership and skill of the departmental administrator.

The work of the departmental administrator is described in detail in Chapters 5, 6, and 7. His responsibilities and duties in planning, organizing, directing, coordinating, and controlling the program are considered. Other relationships with administrative personnel within an institution or system are discussed.

SCHOOL ORGANIZATION

The schools of a locality are established under the authority and by action of the state. Jurisdiction over the schools lies with the state. A body created by the state, such as a state board of education, may be officially designated as the agency to promote, develop, and supervise the educational system within the state. The purposes for

[8] S. C. Staley, "The Illinois Story," *Journal of Health, Physical Education and Recreation,* October, 1957, p. 15.

which the schools are to be established are set forth by the state.

Local boards of education are organized under state law and have powers and authorities similar to those of a college or university board of trustees. In many areas the board of education has the additional power to levy and collect taxes to support the schools. The board is the policy-making body and has authority over financial matters as granted by state laws.

The body known as the local school board evolved from committees of laymen who were chosen to handle the business and related administrative matters of the schools. The professional leadership resided in the principal, when the school was large enough to have one. Growing size and complexity of school districts required better administrative organization and resulted in the employment of an administrative officer, the school superintendent. Boards did not readily transfer all administrative management to the superintendent, however, and today the boards or individual members may exercise more direct control than is desired. By and large, the board is the policy-making and appraising group which exercises its powers through a superintendent of schools. If the board is to fulfill its role, it must study the purposes of education as well as the functions of its own schools; it must appraise the effectiveness of its schools and be in a position to recognize the need for improvements.

The executive officer of the school system is the superintendent of schools, who carries out the policies established by the board of education. If the system contains several schools, there will be a principal in charge of each one. The principal is the immediate administrative superior of the departmental head.

At this level the similarity between college organization and that of the schools ceases. In a large secondary school it would be possible to have departmental staff organization and also total school faculty organization. Because the secondary school curriculum is not subject to regular and frequent change, the curriculum functions of the staff are minimal. On the other hand, there is as much opportunity for changing the methods by which the goals of instruction are achieved as in the college.

In a large secondary school, a departmental chairman is responsible for the administrative guidance and supervision of his program and staff. His working relationship with the principal is close.

Policies governing the majority of school functions are established from above, that is, from the board or superintendent level. There is no supportable reason why faculty consideration cannot be given to policy proposals. A departmental chairman and his staff can suggest policy, whether there is a regular practice of inviting such action or not.

Elementary schools are less likely to have any kind of departmental organization. In the first place, since the curriculum itself is not departmentalized, staff members are not associated with a particular department, except for the small number of special teachers who serve all classes in the school. At the elementary level, the schools should function as a unit where faculty action is sought. Supervisors, especially those for special areas, may be thought of as representing the subject area rather than the specialized staffs. At this level, therefore, administrative consideration of physical education will be determined by the principal within the school and by the special teachers and supervisory personnel outside the school. Supervisors, because they are in staff rather than line positions, can make recommendations about policy directly to the superintendent, or to an assistant superintendent in the case of a very large city. In the special subjects, there may be an administrator at the city or district level for the entire system. In this event the supervisors in his area are responsible to him.

There may be additions to the organization within a district without affecting the structure just described. If the system is large, there may be curricular supervisors who work with the teachers in several schools. There may be a city or district head for a field such as art or physical education. While these persons are on the central staff, under the direct jurisdiction of the superintendent, the teachers with whom they are associated work under their respective principals. The schools maintain their own organizational unity.

One can compare the positions of college president and school superintendent, or dean of a college within a university and the school principal, and discover that within their own organizations they perform similar administrative functions. Departmental heads within the schools, however, seem to have lower administrative standing than their counterparts in colleges and universities. There is less variety in school curricula, creating less demand for administrative action in this area. On the other hand, if the principal were to allow the department head greater responsibility and expect more of him, or her, in matters of instruction, supervision, new planning, and budgetary control, perhaps his own work could be carried forward more effectively.

What has been written concerning the attitudes, outlooks, and functions of the administrative officers in colleges can be applied to those serving in equivalent positions in the schools.

Chapter 5

PLANNING AND ADMINISTRATIVE RELATIONSHIPS

PHYSICAL education shares in the common effort of the school and college to achieve the major goals of education. The program is the particular means through which the physical education teacher works toward these goals. A program of physical education is planned to suit the individuals for whom it is intended; that is, the specific objectives for an age group will be formulated upon such basic factors as the age and maturity of the students, their degree of development in motor, intellectual, emotional, and social abilities, their principal interests, and their particular needs. For example, a major objective of education is the development of the individual so that he is able to utilize his capacities for his own fullest self-realization. In the ability of movement, the objectives sought for and by the six-year-old are the relatively gross bodily skills which, when mastered, give him greater freedom in using his body and expressing himself through movement. The objectives of the high school youth in the matter of movement may be the complex coordinations required for pole vaulting, basketball, or dancing. The guiding objective is the same for both groups, but the specific objectives suit the particular group. The following discussion of program assumes this kind of adaptation at each appropriate step.

While one may write and talk about physical education, he cannot discuss a specific program unless he has all the necessary information concerning the situation in which the program is to operate. The teacher and the administrator, therefore, must build their program within the concept of physical education as a means for educating young people; they must plan the pattern and cut the cloth according to the form of the organization or institution within which they work. To apply the discussion of the program of physical education to any situation without change or modification would create an anomaly in the attempt to educate people. An administrative position is like a personality, often resembling others, but also possessing its own unique qualities which are shaped by all the aspects of the institution. If these qualities are ignored, the total personality cannot be fully understood. If they are taken into account, one will find the personality congenial and productive.

This presentation of the program of physical education will have more meaning for the prospective administrator if it is developed as an analysis of his duties and responsibilities. An analysis requires a starting point. In this case it is the assumption that the person is being employed to develop and administer a program of physical education. How does he go about doing this? The assumption permits consideration of almost all aspects of the institution, the community, the staff, and the task of organizing the program itself. For those already engaged in administering a program of physical education, there may be points in the discussion which previously have not received adequate attention and which now should be studied for whatever help they can give.

This section will raise questions concerning the program of physical education in the total educational span. The discussion which follows each question will treat some aspects generally, that is, in terms of all educational levels, and others according to a particular educational level. These latter items will present parallel discussions, one for colleges and universities, and one for schools, i.e., for grades from elementary through high school.

The major questions which the administrator may ask himself at the start of his new job are:

1. What does he need to know first about the assignment, the institution and the community; where and how will he secure the above information?

2. Assuming that the program starts with instructional classes, what policies and procedures will he establish?
3. How will he handle usual administrative matters related to the students?
4. If he is in charge of a staff of teachers, what kind of supervision will he employ? How can the staff be used as a team in planning and evaluating phases of the program?

Assume now that he is placed in the school, or college, and is to develop a program of physical education for the students. What does he need to know first? There are two large areas of essential knowledge. One has to do with matters of general administration, the other with matters directly related to the program of physical education and to departmental operation. Perhaps one would say that the first area is collegewide or systemwide in scope and is under the direction of others, whereas the second area is departmentally encompassed and is primarily the responsibility of the physical education administrator. Matters of collegewide and systemwide scope about which the physical education administrator will need information are discussed in the materials which follow. The method in this section will be to present first the question (or item), next a statement of its importance to administration, and last, a brief description of common practices where they exist. These three points will be followed by a listing of suggested steps which the administrator may take to secure information which he needs.

GENERAL ADMINISTRATION

To Whom Is the Administrator Directly Responsible?

IMPORTANCE TO ADMINISTRATION. Establishing lines of authority and responsibility are essential at the beginning of a job in order for the administrator of physical education to define his jurisdiction and to know the channels which he must follow to gain approval for proposals of actions which are required or which he wishes to take. This line of authority defines the administrator's responsibility. In matters of disagreement with other departmental heads, or even with his own staff, it is well for him to know who besides himself has the power to make and enforce decisions and to resolve conflicts.

To ignore the authority of others, or to attempt to avoid using the regular channels for accomplishing one's purpose is to court immediate frustration and ultimate opposition to whatever one is attempting. The point is not that administrators are jealous of their particular powers, although some are, but that an organization works best when its various units are used for their intended purposes.

In seeking to identify the person to whom he is responsible, the administrator is likely to find that there are several persons, each responsible to the head of the institution or the system, each also responsible for some aspect of the total job, such as budget, personnel, or curriculum, and each a person to whom the administrator of physical education must himself be subordinate. The important point is to recognize these administrative channels and to learn quickly how to work with and within them.

GENERAL PRACTICE: COLLEGE. In an earlier chapter it was pointed out that colleges are organized and operated under a governing board, such as a board of trustees, and that the administrative head of the college is a person usually designated as president. Working under the president in a small college, and next in line administratively, will be a dean of the college. In a larger college there may be a vice-president. In a large university there may be several vice-presidents, as well as a dean for each of the constituent colleges. In each institution there will be a dean of students; in a coeducational institution there are a dean of men and a dean of women.

While each of these positions has defined duties, the scope of the duties is often unique to the institution. For example, in a small college a dean may be responsible for the full operation of the college, except for approving the budget. He or she may also fulfill the duties as dean of students. In a large university all financial matters may be under the jurisdiction of a vice-president, but the preparation of budget requests may be a duty of each of the deans of the constituent colleges. In a large university, a dean of students may be responsible for the welfare of all students and especially for the conduct and activities of students outside the classroom. On the other hand, the constituent colleges may have associate deans whose concern is the curricular guidance of students in their respective colleges. To some extent, their work unavoidably will overlap or coincide with that of the university's dean of students.

In colleges and universities, unlike most lower schools, the teaching staff, or faculty, has jurisdiction over instructional matters. Approval of courses, of curricula, and of requirements for a degree and the granting of degrees are matters generally delegated to the faculty, which usually is also charged with the supervision of student activities, i.e. so-called extra-class activities.

GENERAL PRACTICE: SCHOOL. The superintendent of schools is the administrative head of a school system. If there is only one school in the district, he is head of the school.

The school principal usually administers the instructional program in his school and is responsible for student welfare and discipline. He is responsible for class schedules, for the work of the teachers, and for the effective use of facilities and supplies. In a school system, the building principal generally is the one to whom the teachers and departmental administrators are responsible. He may, if he chooses, utilize his teaching staff in an advisory capacity, as a college dean or president customarily does.

SUGGESTED STEPS FOR ANSWERING THE QUESTION. The person who enters a new position will have made the acquaintance of the one in authority who employed him. In a small college this person may be the head of the institution. In situations in which a departmental administrator is employed by a dean or other administrative officer, he may learn the lines of responsibility during his interviews.

Usually the superintendent of schools interviews and employs or recommends new teachers to the board. In a large system, however, the principal may conduct the interview with applicants and make recommendations for appointment to the superintendent. Occasionally board of education members may do the interviewing, but this practice is less common as well as difficult to follow and to justify in a school system of any size. In New York City a Board of Examiners receives applications, prepares tests, conducts interviews with applicants, and certifies those who are eligible for appointment to teach. From the office of an associate superintendent the building principals receive the names of candidates who are available for assignment to their staffs. In this situation a departmental chairman is selected from among those teachers who have taken and passed a series of tests for the position of chairman.

A newly appointed chairman must become familiar with the administrative organization of the school. The school or college may provide the newcomer with a staff manual or handbook describing institutional policies, giving information on administrative practices and on school or college regulations. Minutes of college faculty meetings will contain a record of actions which constitute policy and also will indicate the limits of faculty jurisdiction. Conferences with the president or superintendent and with other officers of administration will help to define duties, authority, and limitations of the administrator's position. In some instances, the board of trustees provides copies of its regulations and of its minutes for faculty or teacher use. These sources describe the authority as well as the duties of the administrator.

The following statement sets forth the duties of a departmental chairman in a liberal arts college:

> The chairman shall be the executive officer of his department and shall carry out the department's policies as well as those of the faculty and the Board which are related to it. He shall be responsible for (a) the administrative work of the department such as departmental correspondence and records; (b) the assignment of courses to, and the arrangement of programs of individual teachers; and (c) the general supervision of the department. He shall have authority to initiate policy and action concerning departmental affairs subject to the powers delegated by these by-laws to the staff of the department in regard to educational policy, and to the appropriate departmental committees in the matter of promotions and appointments. He shall represent the department before the faculty council, the faculty and the Board. He shall preside at meetings of his department. He shall prepare the tentative departmental budget which shall be subject to approval by the department's committee on appointments or departmental committee on personnel and budget, after which he shall transmit it to the president together with his own recommendations. He shall also be charged with the responsibility for assuring careful observation and guidance of those members of the instructional staff of the department who are on temporary appointment. The chairman of the department, when recommending such temporary appointees for permanent appointment shall make full report to the president and the committee on faculty personnel and budget regarding the appointees' teacher qualifications and classroom

work, the relationships of said appointees with their students and colleagues, and their professional and creative work.[1]

There can be no doubt about the powers of the chairman as outlined in the above description. In a like manner, the functions of the faculty are described.

> . . . The faculty shall be responsible, subject to the Board, for the formulation of policy relating to the curriculum, the granting of degrees, the student activities and student discipline. The faculty . . . shall also be responsible for and shall establish rules governing the use of the college name by organizations and clubs. It shall make its own bylaws and conduct the educational affairs customarily cared for by a college faculty. The president shall preside at its meetings, or in his absence, the dean of faculty or a dean designated by the president.[2]

WHAT ARE THE MAJOR GUIDING AIMS OF THE INSTITUTION?

IMPORTANCE TO ADMINISTRATION. Aims give direction and meaning to the work of the educational institution and system. They may be detailed, attempting to define carefully and specifically the task which the institution faces, or they may be far-reaching and general in scope.

Whatever are set forth as the goals of the institution or the school system are also the goals of each instructional unit within the school system and each instructional department in the college. Not only is it important, therefore, that there be stated aims, but it is equally important that each department or instructional unit know them, understand them, and above all organize and conduct its own instructional program in accord with them.

GENERAL PRACTICE: COLLEGE. A sufficiently comprehensive discussion of aims of colleges and universities was presented in an earlier chapter. One may say that it is general practice for colleges to state their aims.

GENERAL PRACTICE: SCHOOL. The purposes of public education are published in a number of books and reports. Reference has been made to the statement of the Educational Policies Commission in its publication, *Purposes of Education in American Democracy*. The

[1] *By-laws of the Board of Higher Education of the City of New York*, September, 1956, pp. 29–30.

[2] *Ibid.*, p. 23.

purposes of education are under almost constant study and discussion. Great social crises cause people to review critically the work of their schools. The results of such reviews have not caused drastic changes in the major purposes of the schools in the United States, but they do stimulate improvements in methods and practices.

The purposes of education in a particular locality are those set forth by the state government in its legislation setting up the schools and in subsequent acts governing and regulating the conduct of education in the state. An administrator of physical education should be familiar with the legislation pertaining to the schools, especially with those pronouncements concerning the purposes which the schools are to serve.

SUGGESTED STEPS FOR ANSWERING THE QUESTION. It is a common practice to list the aims of the institution in its official bulletin. The administrator may also inquire of the president or may study the records of the institution for statements of aims, if they are not carried in the official bulletin. Because colleges do occasionally revise their statements of purpose, the administrator may find an historical account of the institution's development, as well as minutes of faculty meetings in which purposes have been discussed and new statements made.

A city system of education may encourage the investigation of its purposes, especially of the degree to which its schools and curricula are meeting local needs. Published reports of these investigations provide added sources of information about the purposes of the school system in which the administrator may be working.

WITH WHICH ADMINISTRATIVE OFFICERS WILL THE NEW ADMINISTRATOR WORK?

IMPORTANCE TO ADMINISTRATION. The organization of an educational institution is complex. Growth in the size of institutions at all levels has forced stricter organization to improve their management. Functions of an institutional organization are delegated to individuals whose job is to see that they are performed. Because an institution is in reality an organization of instructional units, all management functions are concerned with these units in some way. The departmental administrator will work with those officers whose duties relate to the departmental program. His obligations to some of them are clearly designated. Generally, these are the officers responsible for instruction, curriculum, finances, personnel (employment, supervision, discipline), admissions, student welfare (including discipline and health), student activities, records, counseling, testing and guidance, and plant and grounds. In large institutions there may be officers in charge of research and development, public relations, alumni services, ceremonial occasions, and other divisions or services unique to a particular institution.

A school system includes a similar list of functions, for which one or more persons are responsible, depending upon the size of the system. In a large system a staff under the jurisdiction of the superintendent may be assigned responsibilities for the administrative supervision of these functions. Curriculum may be supervised by an associate superintendent who heads a curriculum research organization, an evaluating unit, as well as subject matter supervisors. Finances, which include the purchase and issue of supplies and equipment, the accounting function for the system, and studies of projected costs, may be under the direction of a business manager, or financial officer serving the entire system.

GENERAL PRACTICE. Persons responsible for several of these functions were named in the previous chapter. The following outline will review that discussion and include the titles of other officers with whom the chairman will work.

Instruction, curriculum. Those responsible for this area are:

1. Dean of faculty
2. Chairman of a college curriculum committee
3. Faculty council, or faculty as a body
4. Other departmental heads
5. On rare occasions, a member representing the governing board of the institution
6. President of the institution
7. Board of education
8. Superintendent
9. Principal

College. Curricular matters usually originate with the department, pass through the hands of a college committee, and are recommended to the faculty for final college action. It should be noted that departments may be asked to work on curricular matters by the president, the dean, or the faculty, who in turn may be guiding the development or revision of the college curriculum.

School. The public education curriculum is determined in part by the state, sometimes broadly, at other times in terms of specific subjects. Because the state requirements do not absorb all the school time, the local administration can develop a curriculum which serves local needs, too. Institutions of higher education generally have greater latitude than schools in the choice of curricula and course content.

The chairman of a high school physical education department may find that the state has specified the minimum time to be devoted to his subject in the weekly school schedule. This may consume all the time that he is allowed by his administrator. On the other hand, he may learn that more time is available if he can develop an acceptable plan for utilizing it.

Finances: budgets, purchase, consumable supplies. The financial operations of the institution are administered by the following officers:

1. President; superintendent of schools
2. Dean of administration
3. Vice-president for financial administration
4. Business manager; treasurer of the board of education
5. Purchasing officer
6. Dean of faculty, or dean of the college (for instructional personnel budget)
7. Principal of the school

College. The finances of a college are usually most carefully administered. Funds for the operation of the institution, for capital expenditures, and for new developments are allocated by the governing body on the basis of available money. Because the sources for funds are limited, and because the amount of money at hand varies from year to year, financial planning is one of the vital jobs of administration. Educational policy and its implementation depend upon the way in which money is used. The president of the institution, therefore, is the primary financial officer with respect to the use of available money and planning for the future financial needs of the institution.

Administration of the funds according to a specified plan may be the function of a dean of administration or of a business manager. Keeping the financial records is the duty of the business manager. If there is a dean of administration, the business manager will be subordinate to him.

In a large university, a vice-president in charge of finances serves in a capacity similar to that of a dean of administration in a college. If there is a purchasing officer, other than the business manager, his responsibility will be to secure materials, supplies, and equipment required by the various departments, offices, divisions, and shops of the institution in accordance with requests submitted to him. He also may serve as a consultant to any member of the staff, advising him on sources of supply, previous experience with purchased items, prices, reliable suppliers, and other information which will assist the staff member in securing the item most suited to his need. It should be emphasized that the purchasing officer can honor only those requests for which funds are available to cover the cost of the purchases.

A purchasing officer will buy instructional supplies and equipment as he receives approved requisitions from the departments. Certain supplies which are used in common by the entire institution will be purchased directly by him according to the anticipated need and stocked in a central store. Individuals and departments can secure these items by submitting an order to the central storekeeper.

In a later discussion of budgets, attention will be given to the various parts of a budget. At this point, for purposes of clarity, one should know that institutional operating budgets are divided into two major parts, namely, personal services and other services. Relationships of the administrative officers to these two divisions of the budget may be somewhat complex and will warrant careful definition in each institution.

The business manager and the purchasing officer may have limited jurisdiction over the expenditure of money in the nonpersonal service division of the budget. As a rule they do not have jurisdiction over personnel to be employed with budget funds except to advise the responsible officer as to the amount of money available. The dean of administration may be responsible for all personnel or he may be concerned only with noninstructional personnel. In the latter case, a dean of faculty will administer the instructional personnel budget. Both deans are supervised by the president, who must approve the employment of the instructional staff.

Perhaps further clarification of the relationship of the departmental administrator to these financial officers of the college should await the discussion of the budget. Of one fact he can usually be sure: the president is the final authority *within* the institution for the expenditure of allocated or appropriated funds.

School. The budget of a school district or school system is adopted by the board of education. Approval of the budget may be the same as adoption by the board, or it may require favorable action by the voters of a district or by the city government. When a budget has been approved, the superintendent has the authority to disburse operating funds. Capital expenditures are generally authorized directly by the board. Usual procedures of requisition and purchase are followed. If the departmental administrator has received an allocation of funds to cover the purchase of budget items, he should submit the necessary requisitions from which bids and purchase orders may be prepared.

In a large school system, consumable office and maintenance supplies are purchased for the entire system and are kept in a central store. Each school may requisition its supplies from the central store. Because distribution of these supplies is usually made according to schedule, the departmental administrator should send his requests to the school office in time to have them included on the school's order. It is likely that items which are used regularly will also be stocked by the school.

Instructional personnel. The following officers are responsible for supervising the teaching staff:

1. Dean of faculty in a college
2. Dean of the college in a university
3. Dean of administration
4. President
5. Superintendent of schools
6. Principal

College. The selection and employment of his teachers is one of the administrator's most difficult and important jobs. Occasionally, a dean or president may recruit and select college teachers, but more commonly this duty belongs to the departmental chairman.

As a matter of accepted policy, colleges and universities seek to employ the best persons available for their instructional staffs. The criteria according to which candidates are judged are not identical in all institutions, however, in terms of characteristics and qualities. Whatever the criteria, the dean of faculty or the president will wish to know that each prospective employee meets them. The meaning given to *criteria* is broad and indicates a rather general description of an acceptable staff member. The dean or president is the only person authorized to assign a salary to a person being considered for employment.

When a department needs a new teacher, the administrator proceeds as follows:

1. Decides upon the kind of person needed and the qualifications he or she should have, the salary to be paid, and the instructional rank to be assigned.
2. Confers with the dean or president to secure authorization to fill the job and to learn the salary possibilities.
3. Seeks a candidate who meets the requirements and will accept the job at the instructional rank and salary specified, if the job is offered.
4. Presents the recommendation to the dean or president for approval.
5. If approval is given, notifies the candidate and asks for his or her acceptance.

In colleges and universities approval of a recommendation by the dean or president is usually tantamount to formal employment. The departmental administrator should know that an applicant officially becomes an employee only after he has been approved by the governing board of the institution and has been notified by a duly authorized administrative officer. Failure to follow the basic five steps listed above leads to misunderstandings between prospective staff members and the college administration. For instance, an embarrassing situation can be created if one quotes a salary to a candidate before securing administrative authorization and afterward learns that a lower salary is all the administration will allow.

Other matters dealing with the recruiting and selection of teachers will be presented in the chapter on staff relationships. This section pertains to the college administrative officers with whom the departmental administrator will work when he seeks to employ a new teacher.

Procedures which have been described for employing new staff members usually apply to the annual reappointment of departmental staff members and to the preparation of recommendations for promotion. In colleges which grant tenure to teachers who have met the requirements, the same general procedures apply.

In the case of an employee who is not to be recommended for reappointment, the departmental administrator will be expected to explain the reasons for the decision and, of course, will follow the stated college procedures for notifying the employee of the action.

School. The role of the school superintendent and principal in the employment of teachers has been described. A departmental administrator may have no part in recruiting and employing new teachers. In a school system, however, teachers may take part in the recruitment and selection of new personnel if the principals and the superintendent invite and encourage their participation. Departmental administrators should seek to become involved by stating their own personnel needs, by aiding in the search for the best candidates, by reviewing credentials and interviewing candidates, and by making their recommendations to the appropriate administrative officer.

If the school is to become a center for studying the functions of education and instructing pupils and students, teachers and departmental administrators will have to demonstrate greater concern in the selection of new teachers and the criteria used for reappointment of teachers already in service.

Noninstructional personnel. Those employees who are not members of the teaching staff come under the jurisdiction of the following:

1. Dean of administration
2. Personnel officer
3. President
4. Superintendent of plant and grounds
5. Business manager
6. Principal

College. There are many classifications for occupation of noninstructional personnel. In general, these include secretarial and clerical employees, laboratory assistants, custodial, maintenance, and engineering personnel, business machine operators, cafeteria and dining room employees, and others. The practices concerning responsibility for administering this body of employees are less uniform than those dealing with the instructional staff.

The department of physical education is likely to employ persons in several of these classifications. In some instances, too, responsibility is determined by the source of authority for the expenditure of money. The six administrative officers listed above usually administer matters pertaining to employment, dismissal, promotion, assignment, discipline, and salary for members of the noninstructional staff. In his own institution, the departmental administrator will learn the lines of responsibility to follow in these matters.

School. Departmental administrators in public schools are unlikely to be directly responsible for noninstructional personnel, except in a large department which has a clerical assistant. If the department is large and nonteaching jobs are numerous, the administrator can make a request to his principal for clerical assistance.

Student records, reports, admissions. The record-keeping functions, an important phase in every institution, are administered by the following officers:

1. Registrar
2. Director of admissions
3. Dean of students
4. Principal
5. Counselor
6. Nurse

College. Official student records are maintained by the college registrar and his staff. Each teacher is required to provide the registrar with grades and any other reports, such as attendance, which may be required by the college as part of its record.

In a large institution the task of admitting students to the college or university is assigned to the admissions officer or the director of admissions. He usually works with a board or a committee who assist in setting policy and handling special cases when the need arises. In a small institution the registrar or a member of his staff may also serve as the admissions officer.

The dean of students, whose office is responsible for many aspects of student life, maintains student academic records and will also have information which is not commonly entered on the record. Scores on special tests, notes on counseling interviews, record of participation in student activities, and reports of other experiences and achievements will be part of these records.

The departmental administrator is responsible to these officers of administration for managing his own department so that the data is kept correctly and ready to be recorded when it is due. Grades to be reported at the end of a term should be transmitted promptly to the registrar's office. Routine reports to the dean of students should be made on time and special reports rendered promptly when they are requested. In turn, the registrar and the dean of students will supply the departmental administrator information about individual students. Many times during the year the chairman will need the previous record of a student or will wish to learn whether or not the difficult student in his department is a problem student in other departments. The chairman can secure this kind of information from the offices of the registrar and of the dean of students.

Schools. In schools the matter of admissions is based upon the residence of the child's family in the school district. Special cases which fall outside the residence qualification are handled by the office of the superintendent.

Student and pupil records are kept in the principal's office. Because the state requires standard reports, especially about pupil attendance, all teachers must keep records and report them. Attendance and marking reports, notes on student conduct, results of measures of ability, records of special events, and grade standing of the student are all part of the record maintained in the principal's office. In addition special records may be kept by the school physician, or nurse, and by the guidance personnel.

The administrator's problem is to make record keeping and report preparation as simple and economical as possible in the teacher's interest and to make really effective use of the recorded data which are kept in the administrative and service offices of the school. The purpose of records, of course, is to use them, not merely to keep them.

Student activities, welfare, and discipline: college. The following officers are concerned with the various aspects of college student life:

1. Dean of students
2. College physician
3. Dean of faculty
4. President
5. Faculty of the institution
6. Superintendent of plant and grounds

Student Activities. Generally, student activities come under the jurisdiction of the faculty, which delegates immediate responsibility for supervising the activities to a faculty committee or a faculty-student committee. Because the president is charged with preserving the good name of the institution, protecting its property, and generally maintaining its moral and academic character, he may act independently when he judges that circumstances demand it.

The dean of students supervises the realm of student activities, working under the supervision of a faculty committee but also as an officer of the college administration in his own right. His office is the center for working control and guidance of student activities. The one exception to this organization is the departmentally sponsored and managed student activity. Although intercollegiate athletics are a collegewide activity, the control and management of this program falls to some type of departmental organization. This may have its own supervising committee, sometimes known as an athletic board, with policy-making powers and administrative functions, especially with respect to the budget for athletics. (The administration of intercollegiate athletics is a subject treated fully in several texts.)

The pattern for the administration of student activities commonly places all activities, including intercollegiate athletics, under the jurisdiction of the faculty. Boards or committees are created by the faculty and given authority to provide immediate supervision over the activities according to policies approved by the faculty.

The dean of students is the faculty administrative officer for most collegewide student activities. Departmental activities are sponsored and managed by the departments within the faculty policies governing such activities.

Thus far no reference has been made to the college or university student government organization, which also may share in the development and administration of student activities. Student government is organized under faculty approved policies and may become the actual immediate administrator of policies concerning student organizations. However, it is not the final authority in their administration.

Historically, the control of intercollegiate athletics was lodged in the hands of student or student-alumni organizations. That kind of control has been replaced generally by faculty control in colleges and universities. In some institutions, student organizations still retain considerable power over the operation of the intercollegiate athletic program, but only because the faculty and college administration permit it.

A department of physical education may invest its resources heavily in student activities. Intramural athletics, recreational activities, off-campus outdoor programs, dance recitals and festivals, gymnastic exhibitions, and intercollegiate athletics are some of the nonclass activities conducted by or under the direction of the department. Such a variety of student activities touches all the patterns of college or university administration, compelling the departmental chairman to learn the administrative policies and work with the responsible administrative officers and committees.

Student welfare. The term *student welfare* refers to health services, housing, food service, campus safety and sanitation, vehicular parking, loan funds, counseling and guidance (also a part of the instructional services), and recreation. The officers who may be involved and their respective areas are the following:

1. Dean of students: Health, housing, loan funds, counseling and guidance, parking, recreation
2. College physician: Health, housing, campus safety and sanitation, food service, counseling and guidance
3. Superintendent of plant and grounds: Housing, parking, campus safety and sanitation, food service

4. Residence halls manager: Housing, food service, recreation, campus safety and sanitation
5. Manager of the dining halls: Food service, campus sanitation, recreation
6. Dean of faculty: Counseling and guidance, student loan funds, housing, health

In a small institution each of these officers coordinates his duties in this area with any of the others, making whatever working arrangements are most satisfactory. Larger institutions may have a council or committee whose membership consists of those officers of administration who head the several services listed. Such a body may also have student members.

The departmental chairman works directly with these officers on matters of mutual concern. He may belong to the college or university committee and take part in planning and coordinating the several services. Although this text emphasizes physical education, a department frequently lists both health and physical education in its title, thus establishing its chairman as one of the college officers responsible for student health. A department of physical education alone has primary objectives and values in health which align it with other departments or services in this field.

Student Activities: School. The many extra class activities are assigned to departments or to individual teachers by the school principal. Because the administration and responsibility for curricular and co-curricular activities belong to the principal, he delegates the several tasks to those who are best fitted to carry them out.

A program such as interscholastic athletics normally is part of the total program of the physical education department. A principal may, however, make specific coaching assignments without consulting the chairman.

A student organization, usually in the form of student government, is typical of secondary schools. Such an organization will have at least one faculty advisor. The organization may sponsor all-school events, initiate service projects, collect dues to support its activities, and exercise some disciplinary functions over other student organizations.

Student welfare. The items previously listed under this heading are also the administrative responsibility of the school principal. Specific duties may be designated to individuals on the school staff, and it is with these persons that the administrator of physical education will work directly. A physician and nurse will deal with the health services of the school. There will be a nutritionist in charge of the food services. Guidance may be offered by several counselors working under the supervision of a school psychologist. The custodial engineer is in charge of all plant and ground services.

Because all these areas are concerned in some way with student health, a committee of officers representing these areas, and of others from the administration, from physical education, and occasionally from parent organizations, acts as an advisory, planning, and coordinating body. The school is the only agency to be uniformly interested in the health and welfare of all children, and its attention to these services is of central importance. Furthermore, because the school as a matter of policy does not provide many of the health services which children should have, the functions of a coordinating committee which includes representatives of the community among its members is essential if there is to be a follow-up on the work done initially by the school.

The administrator of the department of health and physical education may serve as chairman of such a coordinating committee. If the committee serves several schools, it may employ a health coordinator. A representative of the department of physical education should be on a health council or a coordinating committee, whether he serves as chairman or not.

The organization and administration of the school health services has received extensive treatment in several texts. In this discussion the significant fact is the close relationship of the physical education administrator to other personnel working in his area.

College: Research. Engaging in scholarly research has always been a characteristic of teachers in institutions of higher learning. Until the last twenty-five years, however, colleges and universities did not engage in institutional research to any marked degree. World War II demanded cooperative research and turned to higher education for the people trained to plan and conduct it. Since World War II institutional research has grown with the support of the federal government, as well as grants from businesses and industry. So great has been the expansion of federally subsidized research that university administrations have expressed concern lest the federal government dictate the direction and limitations of all university research. Individual research continues alongside institutional research.

The administrator, whether he is head of an institution or chairman of a department, is obligated constantly to encourage scholarly investigation by his teachers. Only in institutions and departments where this kind of professional activity takes place can there be the atmosphere of looking ahead, of testing the old, and of better understanding the present. Research serves the administrator by helping him gain knowledge for solving his problems and for improving his planning. The results of this type of research supply information upon which the administrator may act and from which he gains authority for his actions.

Today large universities may have an officer whose job it is to secure and administer funds for research. Presidents or deans of faculties in smaller institutions usually perform this task. The departmental chairman will wish to know about research that is going on, the people who are doing research, and the availability of specialized personnel and funds to assist him in any research projects which he plans to conduct.

School: research. Schools below the college level were not established for research purposes. Teachers have had neither the time nor the encouragement to do research, although in the past a small number have carried on planned investigations. Today, however, research in public education is important. The classroom teacher does very little research, but school districts and city systems have units which conduct studies and surveys aimed at securing accurate information about features of the schools. Occasionally they promote individual projects. School teachers may become involved as sources of data for projects being conducted by colleges and universities.

The administrator of physical education will benefit from investigations of an evaluative nature. He and his staff also may suggest problems to be studied and, of course, they may work on a project with the research unit.

Public relations: College and School. In an institution of higher education, or a school system with a designated public relations director or counselor, the chairman will be expected to meet two requests. The first is to cooperate fully with the public relations officer on items or events which he is preparing for release. The second will be to inform him promptly of items or events which have public relations values.

Because the area of public relations embraces considerably more than the older one of publicity, the matter will be treated more fully in a separate chapter. Chairmen of departments which include the intercollegiate and interscholastic athletic programs are aware of the importance of careful planning in the conduct of their public relations.

SUMMARY. There are a multitude of administrative functions in colleges, universities, and schools each of which is the responsibility of some member of the organization. The officers named in this part administer functions found in almost all higher institutions and public schools. The administrative organizations do vary, and it is important that the student recognize this in order not to guess but to find out who are the administrative personnel with whom he will work as a departmental chairman.

A final word needs to be said on the lengthy discussion given to the question concerning officers of administration to whom the chairman is responsible. Responsibility to an administrative officer in the sense of subordination to him can be determined only in the light of the function being considered.

In the preceding discussion of a function it appears that one administrative officer, e.g., the dean of students, may have authority over actions of a chairman, while in regard to another function the chairman may share authority equally with the dean of students. The chairman will inquire about these matters and also will be sensitive to the distinctions that fall outside the light of ready definition.

INSTITUTIONAL RELATIONSHIPS

WHAT ARE THE RELATIONSHIPS OF THE INSTITUTION TO THE COMMUNITY?

IMPORTANCE TO ADMINISTRATION. Institutions of higher education have grown increasingly sensitive to the field of public relations. A desire to be better understood has motivated colleges and universities to make determined efforts to inform the community about their ideas and work. Community understanding and support are important to colleges and universities. Public institutions require increasingly large amounts of money for their operation. An understanding and sympathetic public will provide these funds through taxation. Private institutions also seek additional contributions and will secure them from people who believe in the work of these institutions.

GENERAL PRACTICE: COLLEGE. A public which does not understand the philosophy of education, especially of college education, may be critical of anything not yielding monetary return to the student. A belief in learning for values which are not solely vocational, important as these are, is essential to the support of higher education. A renewed emphasis upon liberal education for all college men and women indicates the kind of public attitude which creates a better atmosphere for college growth. Business and industry, which heretofore have been willing to put money into useful research, are giving increasing support to so-called theoretical research. These elements of our economy also contribute to the support of colleges and universities without earmarking their contributions for particular purposes.

Colleges and universities are the historic centers wherein ideas, beliefs, and knowledge are questioned, tried, examined, and sometimes discarded, and where the urge is to seek new concepts or to improve the understanding of old ones. At times this function leads segments of the public to accuse the institution of misdirected effort, of attempting to upset the social order, and especially of attacking particular beliefs. A college or university worthy of its name cannot forego its historic role, but it can create a better atmosphere in which to perform it.

The chairman of a department of physical education may find that his subject is not well understood in the surrounding community, although he may have more opportunity for contact with the community than any one else on the faculty. Because of his training he may be called upon to work with community agencies in the fields of camping and group work with youth. Where his department has the facilities, he may plan for limited recreational use by the community. Community members interested in athletic events can be invited to attend them. Special programs growing out of departmental activities, e.g., dance exhibitions, festivals, sports clinics, may be open to the public. Members of the staff may be active in community projects and organizations and also may address groups in the community. Regular news stories about activities of the department keep the community informed. All these events present the means for increasing mutual understanding and respect between the community and the college.

When one accepts administrative responsibility, he will inquire about the public relations program of the institution and the policies which the administration wishes to follow in this matter. He will also learn from the administration, from his colleagues, and ultimately from members of the community the attitude of the community toward the college and especially toward his own subject area. With information from these sources he can decide what steps to take to maintain or to improve relationships with the community.

GENERAL PRACTICE: SCHOOL. In a sense the public schools have taken for granted that their community relationships are satisfactory. When the voters in one school district after another in one New York county began to question the school budgets and in many cases to turn down proposed budgets including requests for funds to construct needed buildings, the school administration realized that much was needed to improve their community relationships. During a conference of superintendents held in 1958 it was reported that "two of the most common [community problems] are problems of financing and better community relations . . . . The superintendents tended to agree that if educators, as individuals, could do more to sell the community on the value of school programs and the need for support, it would be easier to get more adequate school budgets."[3] Another story in the same issue discussed the negative actions of voters concerning their school budgets. The need for more public information about the schools was indicated. "In some cases where budgets were rejected and later adopted the principal underlying reason was an absence of full discussion. It appears that voters in school districts are now demanding to know exactly what they are being called upon to accept."[4]

As evidence of recognition of the need for maintaining good pub-

[3] Loren B. Pope, "Education in Review," *The New York Times,* July 13, 1958.
[4] "School Budgets Face Resistance," *The New York Times,* July 13, 1958.

lic relations, the AAHPER approved in April, 1946, the publication of a statement entitled, *Together Let's Build Good Public Relations!* The text of the pamphlet indicates that pupils, parents, civic leaders, citizens in general, colleagues, and school administrators be informed by "every possible means" about all phases of the program of health and physical education. There can be no doubt about the necessity to develop and maintain intelligent and friendly communication between the school personnel and the community. It will be one of the tasks of the physical education administrator to ascertain the status of these relationships when he enters upon his job and then to move for their improvement, if this is indicated.

WHAT IS THE PHYSICAL EDUCATION REQUIREMENT?

IMPORTANCE TO ADMINISTRATION. The person entering upon a new task should know the nature of the physical education requirement. The official college bulletin describes the requirements which the student must fulfill for graduation. In public education the state, through its laws or the regulations of its department of education, usually states the subjects which the schools are required to teach. If the curriculum of the secondary school, for example, is determined partly by the local school districts, the state may recommend that selected subjects be included in each school curriculum. Local schools may be given latitude in the degree to which they meet a requirement for teaching physical education because of the variation in the physical education facilities. On the other hand, it should be noted that lack of adequate facilities does not release the school from its obligation to meet state requirements in academic subjects which are necessary for the diploma. In general, too, the state requirement is a minimum, not an optimum. There will be few if any local schools which cannot meet the minimum requirement.

The chairman may wish to know whether or not the present requirement is a change from previous years, as well as the faculty attitude toward the requirement. In an accredited college, which has been visited within the past few years by representatives of the accrediting body, the chairman may wish to read the report made by this body concerning the status of physical education in the institution.

When securing the above information, he may decide also to make a tentative evaluation of the suitability of the requirement for his institution. The person beginning a new job is not likely to institute marked changes in the curriculum of the institution unless he was specifically instructed to do so as part of his duties. He can, though, enter the adequacy of the physical education requirement on his list of matters for study at a future date. If there is no requirement in physical education, the question of whether or not there should be one will concern him, too.

GENERAL PRACTICE: COLLEGE. In colleges and universities, physical education generally is required of students and usually is a requisite for graduation. In 1954 Errett Hummel reported the results of a survey of physical education and hygiene requirements in 59 colleges and universities. Of this number 50 reported that they do have a physical education requirement which students must complete before receiving a baccalaureate degree. The amount of the requirement was reported as follows (some schools were counted twice because of different requirements for men and women):

26 require 2 years
17 require 1 year
3 require 1½ years
1 requires 3 years
1 requires 4 credits
1 requires 2½ years
1 requires a 2-unit course
1 requires 2 credits[5]

A later study made by Cordts was based on the replies received on a questionnaire from 79 women's colleges and 105 men's colleges. In 67 percent of the colleges and universities reporting, physical education was required of all students. Although the author does not explain the difference between the two figures, he reports that "Undergraduate men are required to complete from one to two years of physical education in 73% of colleges and universities, and a similar requirement is made of women in 83% of these institutions."[6]

[5] Errett Hummel, "Report on Physical Education Requirements," mimeographed statement contained in a letter to the author, April 26, 1954.

[6] Harold J. Cordts, "Status of the Physical Education Required or Instructional Programs for Men and Women in the Four-Year Colleges and Universities of the United States," *Sixty-Second Proceedings*, College Physical Education Association, December 28–30, 1958.

Similar studies made from time to time also show that a physical education requirement of two years is typical for colleges and universities.

GENERAL PRACTICE: SCHOOL. Physical education requirements vary from school to school. Although some schools require a daily period, the more common practice is to require two or three periods per week. If scheduling problems are to be minimized, the length of the physical education period should be the same as that for other subjects; or be a multiple of the regular class period. The general belief of teachers and administrators of physical education, and of school administrators as well, is that the pupils and students should have daily physical education classes and that the length of the period, in some instances, should be longer.

Larson and Hill write that "many states have set a minimum requirement of twenty minutes per day for instruction in physical education for the elementary-school child; however, this time is too short for the upper-grade child. It is recommended that the daily physical education period be at least twenty minutes in length for the primary grades, and thirty to forty minutes in length for the upper grades. This time should be the actual participation time and should not include that spent going to and from the activity areas."[7]

Hall states that "a daily program of approximately an hour throughout each year of the secondary schools is highly recommended for consideration."[8] He continues by pointing out that one period of physical education a day for a year should earn a unit of credit, just as one period daily of English throughout a year is given the value of one unit of credit. If this were done, the total units required for graduation should be increased to twenty. There are moves to increase the unit requirement for graduation as a result of the intense emphasis upon mathematics and science in the program of secondary school students. Physical education should receive consideration for the daily period and equivalent unit credit in any proposals for curriculum change.

[7] Leonard A. Larson and Lucille F. Hill, *Physical Education in the Elementary School,* Henry Holt and Company, 1957, p. 143.

[8] Joe Hall, "The Role of the Superintendent," *Current Administrative Problems,* American Association for Health, Physical Education and Recreation, 1960, p. 17.

The State Curriculum Committee of the Maine State Department of Education prepared a statement of philosophy and recommendations for health and physical education in the secondary schools. Their opening statement follows: "We believe that the secondary school should provide for all pupils adequate programs in physical education, health, and safety education, because good health is essential to effective living and consequently is an important goal of education. To accomplish this objective we believe that five 50-minute periods each week should be provided for each pupil in grades 7–12."[9]

WHAT IS THE ATTITUDE OF THE FACULTY TOWARD PHYSICAL EDUCATION?

This discussion deals principally with the college and university situation. Faculties of institutions of higher education have a large measure of control over the curriculum. They can, and often do, change the requirements in physical education which a student must complete for his baccalaureate degree. Teachers and administrators in public schools face other types of pressures and controls. One can say also that in general there is a greater interest in physical education on the part of the school's community than there is among college and university faculties. Furthermore, the local school is insulated to a degree by the state education department from capricious changes in its program. The administrator should take no refuge, however, in the seemingly larger measure of stability in the public school curriculum. All that is written in the following paragraphs concerning his responsibility for developing and conducting a program of physical education which meets the highest standards set by the profession applies with just as great force and meaning to the public school administrator and teacher as it does to the college administrator and teacher. If the school administrator of physical education winces when a community group discusses eliminating the frills in the school curriculum, he is vulnerable to the criticisms which are set forth below.

IMPORTANCE TO ADMINISTRATION. The fact that physical educa-

[9] "Health and Physical Education in Maine Secondary Schools," *Journal of Health, Physical Education, Recreation,* November, 1960, pp. 32–33.

tion is a department in the college and that its courses are offered as part of the college curriculum indicates that the faculty favors the subject to some degree. The chairman may wish to know whether or not the status of physical education is one of grudging acceptance or of wholehearted approval; he will take steps to assess the attitude of the faculty toward his department and its work. A uniform faculty attitude toward any subject is unlikely, but there will be a general, predominant point of view which influences faculty action where physical education is concerned.

Administrators and teachers of physical education occasionally suffer from feelings of inferiority because their subject is not accorded as high a status as certain other subjects in the college. If one is observant, he will find that there are various levels of prestige in a college and that physical education is not the only subject which may be accorded a status below the highest. The only point which should concern a teacher of physical education with regard to his standing in the institution is that his work is of a calibre commensurate with that of his colleagues.

In discussing the matter of relationships with university faculties, C. H. McCloy introduced an historical note which will be helpful to the teacher and administrator. He commented as follows:

> We in physical education suffer from the fact that our subject in many, if not most universities around the world is not considered what the Germans would call "a wissenschaftliches" or "scholarly" subject. From the history of education, it will be recalled that early in the century, the same was true of many of the sciences, such as chemistry, and later was true of sociology, of political science, of economics, and of many other subjects: they got in one by one over the protests of the humanists. Physical education suffers much more acutely from the same phenomenon.[10]

In recent years professional organizations in physical education have become alert to the attitudes of faculties and, as a result of some disturbing experiences, have given attention to the weaknesses in programs and to criticisms which colleagues in other subject areas have voiced about physical education. In later sections of this text the significant matters will be dealt with in detail. At this point

[10] C. H. McCloy, "Suggestions on Selling the Required Physical Education Program to a University Faculty," *Sixty-First Proceedings,* College Physical Education Association, January 3, 1958, p. 228.

common attitudes of university and college faculties can be touched upon to indicate the outlines of the problem.

GENERAL PRACTICE. College and university faculties expect that a department will meet the claims which it makes for its subject. When unwarranted claims are made, or when desirable outcomes are claimed but not achieved, the faculties have reason to question the professional integrity of the department. Because the principal outcomes of a college are gained through teaching, the faculties expect that the best teaching practices will be followed, and above all that teaching will be carried on. McCloy, in suggesting ways to gain faculty approval for physical education, states that much of the opposition by faculty people to physical education arises from the poor programs which they experienced themselves as students or the unimaginative and indifferently conducted ones which they observe in the college. Faculty will appreciate and praise professionally conceived and conducted programs aimed at the best in the educational level with which they are concerned.

Collegiate subjects require concentrated effort, including study and class participation by the students. Whenever a subject requires neither of these to any degree, the faculty feels that both the time the student spends and the money which the institution expends are wasted. The faculty expects that there will be instruction, study, and practice in all college courses. Otherwise, a subject or program does not belong in the instructional curriculum of the college.

The program of intercollegiate athletics may be misunderstood. Faculty members who have worked in institutions where the intercollegiate athletic program was run almost as a separate entity and violated the ordinary rules applied to nonathletes regarding admissions, scholarships, standards for retention in college, and requirements for class attendance, may associate all persons in physical education with such practices. In other words, the faculty anticipates that a new administrator may belong to the group who seek privileges and it will be prepared to resist such advances. One should recognize, too, that some members of the faculty may think that athletics should be specialized entertainment and will have little or no objection to the special privilege approach. The writers of this text do not support this latter approach. The place of athletics in a physical education program has been described in Chapter 3.

There will be a number of faculty members—and the size is an unfortunate commentary upon physical education programs—whose own experience in physical education classes was unpleasant. They may think of all physical education as similar to that which they experienced in their earlier days. These people can be brought to better understanding of the program.

The narrow-thinking academician may view physical education as a frill. In fact, anything to do with the body may seem out of place to him. Today, however, even this strict mental disciplinarian finds that the evidence supporting the integrity of the entire individual is too great to be ignored. He may be seeking active recreation himself. Physically weak men cannot be used in experimental space travel.

The most prevalent attitude of faculties will be that physical education has a place in the education of young men and women and that the values which the profession claims for its work are worth seeking in college. This attitude has influenced the development of physical education as a required subject in colleges and universities of this country. The profession can do no less than meet its obligation to keep faith with the faculties by organizing, conducting, and maintaining the best possible programs of physical education in our colleges and universities.

From time to time studies are made of the nature of the physical education requirement in colleges and universities. The following table is taken from the report of a survey made by Paul F. Cieurzo, Jr. Questionnaires were sent to the registrars of 685 colleges and

	Private	*Public*	*Combined total*
No. of institutions replying	392	257	649
No. of institutions requiring basic physical education	328 83.6%	245 95.3%	573 88.1%
No. of institutions requiring basic physical education granting academic credit for courses	224 67.6%	215 87.7%	439 74.8%
No. of institutions counting basic physical education toward honors	152 46.3%	173 68.3%	325 55.9%

SOURCE: Paul F. Cieurzo, Jr., "College Physical Education Survey," mimeographed report presented to the annual meeting of the College Physical Education Association, 1954.

universities. There were 649 replies. Replies to the inquiry show a wide acceptance of physical education, not only as a course for credit in the college or university, but as one required of all students for graduation. One note of special interest is the high percentage of institutions, both private and public, which accept grades earned in physical education in their bases for computing academic honors.

Errett Hummel completed a survey in 1954 on a smaller number of colleges and universities. In his findings, "of the 59 schools reporting, 50 do have a physical education requirement that students must complete before receiving a baccalaureate degree."[11]

These two reports strengthen the belief that college and university faculties and administrations think of physical education as belonging in the curriculum. Curricula are under study, however, and the chairman of the department of physical education should take part in any such study made in his institution. New demands and changing circumstances place new values upon courses. Growing enrollments in colleges and universities cause tremendous increases in costs. In trying to meet the demand for higher education without reducing standards and services, institutions are forced to examine every aspect of their work to see where unnecessary costs can be eliminated. Current emphasis upon a subject area, such as science or mathematics, may cause an institution to allocate more of its resources to these areas at the expense of others. The chairman of physical education, therefore, must participate in educational planning for the entire institution and must constantly be evaluating the program of his own department in light of the changing emphases in his institution.

Esslinger has made the following pertinent observation: "If the increase in enrollment is not accompanied by a proportionate increase in facilities something must give. The only thing which can give is the program."[12] He lists seven modifications as examples of changes which may be forced upon the department. None is a new development; all have been tried to some extent by various college and university departments. The one which the department itself

[11] E. Hummel, *op. cit.*, p. 4.

[12] A. A. Esslinger, "Problems of the Physical Education Service Program," *Sixtieth Annual Proceedings*, College Physical Education Association, 1957, p. 218.

would not wish to initiate is the reduction in the physical education requirement. If unwanted modifications are not to be imposed upon the department, the administrator and his staff must assess more thoroughly than ever before the fundamental considerations upon which their collegiate programs are based. This strong challenge to the college physical education staff can be issued with equal force to the administrators and teachers in the schools.

The person taking up a new post will learn a good deal from the president of the institution about faculty attitude toward physical education. He will add to this information as he becomes acquainted with members of the faculty at lunch, at committee meetings, and on other occasions where informality permits free expression of opinions and ideas. Actions which the faculty may have taken in the past on matters concerning physical education will reveal further information about the place of this subject in the curriculum of the institution.

DEPARTMENTAL ADMINISTRATION

The subjects considered in the previous pages deal with the general administration of the school or college as it relates to the departmental administrator and his responsibilities and working relationships with the general administration. The administrator will also need to secure information on several subjects pertaining to his department before he can proceed to the job of planning and conducting a program. It should be repeated that this is written from the viewpoint of a person beginning a new position. For one who is already accustomed to his position, the topics dealt with may serve as an outline for a review or survey of his own departmental organization and operation. What does the administrator need to know first about his department?

What Facilities Are Available?

IMPORTANCE TO ADMINISTRATION. The facilities available for departmental use determine to a degree the activities which are in the instructional program of physical education. Before the administrator can plan his program in detail he will have to know what facilities are available or can be acquired. Although the person entering a situation of limited facilities must try to secure additional ones, he will start with what he has and build from that point onward. One should note that while the limitations of facilities may restrict the variety and kind of activity which can be taught, this does not mean that facilities determine the nature of the program.

GENERAL PRACTICE. The practice is to assign those facilities which are designed to accommodate physical activities to the physical education department. The control, supervision, and operation of the facilities usually fall under the physical education administrator. Practice in both schools and colleges places the administrative supervision of all educational facilities under one officer. Although responsibility for managing the facilities throughout the year is delegated to the department concerned, it is possible that their assignment for other uses will make them unavailable to the department. Policies governing this administrative control should be known to the administrator of the department of physical education.

SUGGESTED STEPS FOR SECURING THE ANSWER. It is not difficult to answer the question of availability, because facilities for physical education are readily found when one visits a school or a college campus. The answer should state the number of teaching stations which the facilities provide and the size of classes which each can accommodate. A small gymnasium normally may provide one teaching station, but under special conditions it may provide for two stations when the activities to be taught are chosen with the limitations in mind. Field areas may provide one or more stations according to the activities which are taught and the class size assigned to the station. A single large field may serve only one class of twenty students in golf instruction and practice, whereas it has space for two or three classes of thirty-five students each in fundamental skills of sports and games. A swimming pool normally will permit teaching a class of twenty-five to thirty students, but under conditions of heavy demand two smaller classes with a total registration of forty or forty-five students can be given certain types of instruction and practice in swimming. The administrator may assess his facilities in terms of the most desirable use and then prepare a second assessment showing the maximum usability under crowded conditions.

The administrator may find space which has not been used previously but can be adapted to classes in physical education. Perhaps simply noting that these spaces exist will be sufficient during the initial survey. When program planning indicates a need for extra space, he may act to try to secure the additional areas. Also, the administrator will inquire about the college and school use of community facilities. Public park facilities nearby may be available; lakes, public swimming pools, or other water facilities may be open for college and school use; golf courses may permit limited class use. The kind of community facilities available depends upon the location of the institution as well as upon the degree to which such facilities have been developed by the community. In any event, the chairman will make as full and as careful a survey as possible.

Increasing college and school enrollments are creating class loads beyond the capacity of the facilities. Among the suggestions which have been made to institutions for meeting this increase is one by Esslinger, urging use of off-campus facilities. He states, "While it is advantageous to use departmental facilities there is nothing sacred about it. Municipal facilities for golf, tennis, and swimming may be rented or borrowed. Commercial bowling alleys and swimming pools may be used. Social agencies have facilities which might be leased. Many colleges are currently taking classes to ski areas, and lakes, and rivers. Student unions are providing increasing facilities for physical education activities which can be used for teaching stations."[13]

To take high school students away from the school building for class instruction presents problems. The available time may be short, hazards of moving the group may be considerable, and the students may be expected to bear the additional costs of some activities. On the other hand, school administrations are permitting classes to meet away from school for instruction. The development of interest in outdoor education leads to off-campus activities. An extension of the school day and the use of Saturdays for the conduct of off-campus classes are additional ways to make use of community facilities for physical education classes. Unfortunately, institutions located in heavily populated metropolitan areas seldom have adequate field space of their own and must depend upon municipal field and court facilities for their outdoor program areas.

[13] A. A. Esslinger, "Problems of the Physical Education Service Program," *Proceedings,* College Physical Education Association, 1957, p. 219.

The relationship of class size to effectiveness of instruction is determined by several factors. Prominent among these are the purposes to be achieved through class instruction, the nature of the subject, the methods of teaching employed, the skill of the teacher, and certainly the characteristics of the pupils and students. There often is a direct relationship between the facilities which one has and the size of his classes. For purposes of determining the usefulness of a facility he can estimate the total number of students who can be accommodated for purposes of instruction and practice and then adjust his computations according to the optimum size of the class.

HOW MUCH TIME IS ALLOWED FOR PHYSICAL EDUCATION?

IMPORTANCE TO ADMINISTRATION. Courses of instruction will be planned according to the amount of time which the college or school curriculum allows for each course. If physical education is required for all students, the college will specify both the amount of time per week given to this program and the number of terms or years which the student must complete to meet the requirement.

The school requirement may be set by the state and described as a minimum number of minutes per week in class. The local school prepares its own class schedule and it may, if it wishes, exceed the minimum time set by the state. The amount of time which the school or college allows for the courses of instruction in physical education determines the extent of the instructional program.

Studies of the nature of the physical education requirement in colleges and universities are made from time to time. Two recent ones, referred to earlier, show a range of requirement from one year (two semesters or three quarters) to four years (eight semesters or twelve quarters). The requirement most frequently mentioned was for two years. The reasons for the differing lengths of requirement are not given in the studies. The frequency of the two-year requirement probably is explained by the fact that colleges tend to emphasize basic preparation during the student's first two years in college and physical education is one of the courses belonging in the basic general education or liberal studies program of the college.

Studies have been made of the need for physical education in the schools below the college level. There is general agreement that the high school student should have at least one period a day in physical education. Junior high school and elementary pupils need more. There is no such general agreement among college teachers, because the purposes which the college physical education courses seek are not as consistent in college as in the lower schools. It was pointed out in the earlier chapter on objectives that the individual college has its own purposes which also serve as the major goals for the physical education program. There is less clarity on the precise nature of collegiate physical education because heretofore colleges have been trying to complete the job which should have been done at the secondary level.

Whatever the general practice is among colleges, the chairman will plan his program according to the time allotment of his own institution. There is usually flexibility in the way in which the weekly time may be used. Whether a course is scheduled for three periods of one hour each or two periods of one and one-half hours each may be optional. Such flexibility is limited, however, by the practice followed in scheduling other courses. Physical education courses should not create conflicts in the schedule.

HOW ARE PHYSICAL EDUCATION COURSES SCHEDULED?

GENERAL PRACTICE: COLLEGE. The obvious answer is that physical education classes are scheduled in the same manner as other classes in the institution. The point is precisely that these courses should be scheduled as part of the student's total program. Usually the department offers these courses throughout the day so that the student can complete a satisfactory program and the staff can be used most effectively. In some cases all physical education classes meet in the afternoon after the majority of the other classes are finished. This kind of arrangement presents administrative problems and probably taxes the ingenuity of the administrator to arrange a program which fully meets his objectives. Unless the student body is small and the physical education facilities and staff more than ample, the chairman will be pressed to schedule all courses within the limited period of the late afternoon hours.

It is desirable that students register for physical education courses as they do for other courses and that the department be prepared to manage this type of registration.

GENERAL PRACTICE: SCHOOL. Scheduling of classes in schools is generally carried out in the administrative office. There is not the flexibility of schedule which is found in the colleges. All students complete their daily programs within a specified period of time. There is a school day, which can be likened to a work day. Scheduling programs for students in schools, especially in the high schools, is not easy and often cannot always allow for the satisfactory grouping of students in physical education classes.

It is believed that physical education scheduling will best suit the needs of the departmental curriculum when the administrator and his staff have stated clearly their objectives, the means to be used to achieve them, and the measures upon which appraisal and evaluation are to be made.

HOW MANY STUDENTS MUST THE PHYSICAL EDUCATION COURSES SERVE? HOW MANY WILL PARTICIPATE IN OTHER ACTIVITIES CONDUCTED BY THE DEPARTMENT?

IMPORTANCE TO ADMINISTRATION. The number of students registered in courses and taking part in other programs offered by the department bears a direct relationship to the number of persons on the departmental staff. Institutional practices have varied somewhat in the way in which the relationship is interpreted, but the increasing costs of all education are forcing the college and university administrations to expect greater productivity on the part of their staff without sacrificing desired personal contacts between teachers and students and without increasing the already heavy load of the teaching staffs. One way of keeping costs in line with productivity is to maintain an optimum ratio of students to teachers in the courses of instruction, a practice which leads to more careful scheduling of classes, elimination of small sections, alternate scheduling of courses with limited enrollments, and employment of teachers in direct proportion to the need as demonstrated by the number of students registered in courses.

Only in localities where temporary teachers can be employed, either for a full term or on a part-time basis, can last-minute adjustments be made in staff so that only that number of teachers is employed which is needed to handle the student registration. Schools and colleges located in large metropolitan areas or close to sizable graduate schools have an advantage in this respect. Other institutions must plan for staff on the basis of the best estimates available prior to the opening of the school year and then make necessary adjustments according to the capacities of their staffs.

In the school there is little likelihood that the administrator will have to drop small sections—there are none—or that he will offer courses in alternate semesters. His department has all the students every term. His problem will be to plan ahead in order to recommend to the school administration the number of teachers needed in the next term and the next year. School budgets are prepared on an annual basis. Once they are adopted, there is little leeway for increasing personnel expenditures.

General practice. Where physical education is a required college subject, a rough estimate of the number of students who will be registered in physical education is based on the number of students in the classes affected by the requirement. More exact numbers will be based upon registrations actually made in the courses at the beginning of the semester. Because registration itself takes place too late to permit the college and its department to plan for staffing and other needs determined by the number of students enrolled, institutions often have a presemester election, or even actual registration, for courses for the following term. Figures secured from this presemester election form the basis of departmental planning for the number of sections of each course to be given and the number of staff members needed to carry on the program. If it is not possible to increase staff in proportion to enrollment, the department has to adjust in other ways to meet unexpected increases in enrollment.

In order to plan for their needs the schools estimate their enrollments for September on the basis of school registrations and course registrations made in the previous spring.

Regardless of the procedure used to register students, the chairman will plan his courses according to his program goals and in the light of previous enrollment data. The number of students who register in the courses will influence immediately the allocation of facilities, class size, and staff assignments.

Suggested steps for securing answers. The number of students to be enrolled in courses of instruction can be determined from early registration data and from estimates based upon previous enrollments. The number of students served by the department in other than courses of instruction will depend upon the kinds of non-class programs which it conducts. One thinks immediately of intramural athletics as a program usually promoted and conducted by the department. If the intercollegiate or interscholastic athletic program is one phase of the department's operation, the number of teams involved will determine the additional load upon its facilities, staff, and financial resources. Other activities may include clubs, organized recreational services, and special events which are part of the regular college calendar.

Where programs in these areas are already under way, one can determine the number of students taking part from records of the entries in intramurals, from the rosters of squads in intercollegiate and interscholastic athletics in reports prepared by clubs, and from those responsible for special events and organized recreational activities. If new programs are to be introduced in these areas, the chairman and his staff will determine the extent to which the department wishes to commit itself and will estimate the number of students to be served. In this case the number of intramural events, or the number of intercollegiate, and interscholastic sports teams to be supported, are the determining factors rather than the number of students to be served.

The total obligation of the department with regard to the students taking part in its various programs will be found from the data on course registrations and on the number and extent of the nonclass programs. The chairman will recognize that his primary function is the effective conduct of the instructional program of the department. The magnitude of this function determines departmental needs in terms of funds, staff, and facilities. Institutions occasionally allocate proportionately more of their resources to nonclass programs, such as intercollegiate athletics, but the function of an institution is satisfied first through the instructional program, and this must be one of strength and professional excellence.

It should be repeated that it is essential that the department goals be clearly stated and that they be consonant with those of the institution as a whole, so that staffing will not become solely a matter of meeting student registrations from term to term, or, worse, of catering to so-called popular demand, which is seldom a demand, or popular, or aimed at any substantial educational goal.

HOW MANY PHYSICAL EDUCATION TEACHERS ARE AVAILABLE?

Ordinarily the answer to this question is simply the number of teachers who are members of the departmental staff. If one enters a department which has been established for some time, the staff listing in the college bulletin will give the names and instructional ranks of the teachers. In a school the principal can supply the list of persons who are teaching in any phase of physical education. If one is starting a new department he may be the only teacher, or he may employ one or more persons to work with him in the new department.

The practice of employing a teacher from another subject area to do specialized teaching in physical education is disappearing. If one should find this practice in a prospective situation, he can learn of its extent from the faculty administrative officer who maintains a record of the teachers of courses offered by the institution. One may find occasionally that a member from another department is employed to coach an intercollegiate or interscholastic athletic team. In his capacity as a coach of a sport team this person is a member of the departmental staff.

One may wish to know the length of service of members on a departmental staff, any special department responsibilities which they may have had previously, and the particular competency in physical education of each. Other information about staff members is important, too, and will be dealt with in the section devoted to staff matters.

IS THERE ANY DIRECT STATEMENT OF EXPECTATION OF THE NEW ADMINISTRATOR?

When a college president or dean or a superintendent of schools employs a person to head a department, he is satisfied that the employee possesses the qualifications required for the job. Often in the interview preceding employment the candidate is given a clear description of the needs which the institution wishes to have met.

The urgent needs may be set forth at this time. Occasionally, a specific problem will be uppermost in the situation and the president, dean, or superintendent seeking a solution will indicate its importance to the candidate.

If the prospective employee does not receive a clear indication of the expectations which the institution holds for him, he should make tactful inquiries before he accepts the job. One wishes to work in a situation where there is opportunity to express his own ideas, and also where the requirements of the job are in harmony with his own professional ideals.

It goes without saying that one cannot accept a job, aware of the expectations, and, once employed, ignore them. Reactions to this kind of conduct are drastic.

ARE HEALTH SERVICES A PART OF THE DEPARTMENTAL ORGANIZATION?

College health services may be part of the organization of the department of physical education (health and physical education), or they may be administered as a separate division. The latter is more likely to be the case. Because of the necessarily close working relationship which must be maintained between physical education and health services, the chairman of physical education must learn the lines of responsibility affecting both units and the policies and practices which are in force between the two. If physical education is a new program in the institution, these relationships will require cooperative development. If these services come under the department, the chairman will need to make a careful study of policies governing the conduct of the health services and the coordinating lines of responsibility within the department.

WHERE AND HOW WILL THE ADMINISTRATOR SECURE THE INFORMATION NEEDED TO CARRY ON THE JOB?

In the text following each of the previous questions, sources of information have been given to which the chairman may go for assistance. Before proceeding to discuss the program of physical education itself, it will be helpful to summarize the importance to the administrator of knowing what these sources are and how to use them in his work. Sears refers to them as the "forces that energize administration."[14]

State laws, or in the case of the college or university, provisions of the institution's charter and legislative acts of the faculty, define the limits of authority. In these formal documents the chairman finds the general description of the educational duty which his department is to perform, as well as the authority given him, or to him through the faculty and the administration, for developing, operating, and maintaining his particular educational unit. It follows, therefore, that the chairman should know his legislated powers.

The education of children and youth is a goal which our society deems important. It has, therefore, made it possible for the schools, colleges, universities, and specialized educational institutions to become established and to flourish in the United States. Society cannot manage the individual institution; therefore, the professional educator is charged with the responsibility for conducting the educational program. To do his job well he needs a good deal of knowledge about the students and their abilities, interests, health, and capacities for learning, about the subject matter, the emphases required by a changing society, and many other matters pertaining to teaching and learning. Furthermore, there are administrative aspects of his work which he must understand. In order to acquire this knowledge the administrator will observe the actions and processes in his institution, study subjects of significance to his job, and provide for investigation of problems demanding solution if the work is to progress effectively toward established goals. He may even reevaluate the goals themselves. Research, scholarly study, and constant, directed observation characterize forward-looking administration.

Educational programs reflect social aspirations and attitudes. The cultural pattern of the group influences the way in which educational administration functions. It is necessary to distinguish between the apparent cultural patterns, which in reality are temporary symbols of cultural factors, and the deeper, persisting cultural beliefs. Social usage also is reflected in educational practices and may be found in codes of ethics followed by the teaching profession.

[14] Jesse B. Sears, *The Nature of the Administrative Process,* McGraw-Hill Book Company, Inc., 1950, p. xi.

Desirable standards of educational practice are suggested in the literature prepared by regional accrediting agencies. Whatever the evidence may be, the administrator will take into account the nature of the society in which he is working.

The three large areas from which the administrator may secure information and knowledge concerning his job have been given. They are laws, knowledge and research, and social usage. The administrator must draw upon them regularly if he is to perform his educational function effectively.

Chapter 6

THE BUDGET

EDUCATIONAL institutions, like business and industrial establishments, operate financially according to a budget. Teachers are rarely instructed in the values and uses of educational budgets, although the extent of their work is influenced by the budget, that is, the manner in which available funds are allocated.

A departmental administrator must know enough about budgeting procedures to prepare his own budget and exercise effective management of his resources. The following discussion aims to prepare the administrator to meet this requirement.

PREPARATION AND ADMINISTRATION

WHAT IS A BUDGET? WHAT IMPORTANT FUNCTIONS DOES IT SERVE? HOW IS IT PREPARED, APPROVED, AND ADMINISTERED?

There are several definitions of the term *budget*. One writer states that the implication is primarily that of limiting expenditure, and it is likely that many people think of this when they hear the word. A dictionary defines budget as "a statement of probable revenue and expenditure and of financial proposals for the ensuing year as presented to or passed upon by a legislative body." Bartizal states that "A budget is a forecast, in detail, of the results of an officially recognized program of operations based on the highest reasonable expectation of operating efficiency. What may be the 'highest reasonable expectation of operating efficiency' is a matter of management policy, but a forecast should not be regarded as a budget unless it is concerned with the correction of conditions which result in preventable waste or excessive cost."[1] Although this last definition refers to budgeting in business, its meaning can be applied to educational enterprises as well.

Perhaps a simpler definition is that a budget is a plan for spending money. There is merit in this definition, too, because it immediately raises a question concerning the purposes to be achieved by spending money. In a business concern the purposes may be to make a profit, to develop a new product, and to increase production. In an educational institution goals to be achieved by spending money must be set forth, too. Chapter 3 discussed the nature and importance of goals. Often they are ignored when budget-making takes place, because the procedure is habitual, traditional or restricted by a limiting definition. Emphasis upon a budget as a plan for spending money encourages the administrator to consider the entire plan of his department or institution and to appraise the needs in terms of the amount of money required to meet them. A budget, therefore, demands that its maker look ahead for a definite period of time and endeavor to outline or visualize the goals he wishes to achieve during that time. His budget then reflects his estimate of the amount of money which will be required to meet his goals.

IMPORTANCE TO ADMINISTRATION. The importance of the budget to an institution is stressed in the following quotation relating to the work of the business office.

> Of unusual importance in relation to the business office is the matter of budget preparation and control . . . the important matter . . . is the procedure to be followed in the preparation, adoption, control, and adjustment of the budget during the actual period of development. The procedure itself, in my judgment, is of transcendent importance because the budget mechanism is the only effective way yet designed for periodic audit and review of all operations of the university. It is the means by which the balanced institution can be planned and developed, the means by which

[1] John R. Bartizal, *Budget Principles and Procedures,* Prentice-Hall, Inc., 1940.

a complete understanding of the university goes down to the individual staff member and up to the president and the board members, who ordinarily cannot be familiar with the operating details during the fiscal period.[2]

Important values for the department as well as the institution are attached to the process of preparing and administering a budget. If the departmental chairman is to make the maximum use of the funds available to the institution and, through allocation, to the department, he must recognize these values. The following enumeration suggests the importance of budgeting to the department.

1. Budget-making stimulates planning for the present as well as for the future. It requires that decisions be made with respect to where money shall be spent, and when it shall be spent on any item or project. There is seldom, if ever, enough money to support every need and desire; therefore, the chairman must decide, usually beforehand, on which items the money is to be spent. For example, will funds be allocated to support intramural athletics at the expense of adequate supplies for instructional classes? Should the budget include an item for an expensive anatomical model which will use up all equipment money for one year? Will the budget items for equipment and supplies be held to practically nothing for one year in order to employ the number of teachers to make it possible to maintain small classes? These are a few types of the questions which will arise in planning expenditures.

2. The budget requires a review of operating costs for the program. Such a review shows where money has been spent, the items which are receiving the larger share of the funds, and those which may need more money. Occasionally, items appear in this kind of review which should be dropped from the budget for reasons of obsolescence or of too great a cost in relation to their value. This review leads to the third point.

3. The budget permits determination of the worth of outcomes in terms of goals being sought and the cost involved in reaching them. In business this determination is shown in a statement of profit and loss for a given period of time. An educational institu-

[2] R. B. Stewart, "The Office of the Business Manager," *Administration of Higher Institutions Under Changing Conditions, Proceedings, Institute for Administrative Officers of Higher Institutions,* The University of Chicago Press, 1947, pp. 68–69.

tion cannot show its profit and loss so readily, but there are criteria which may be applied to the operation to help decide its worth. Planning for expenditures demands evaluation of outcomes.

The chairman of a physical education department will do well to have his information on this point up to date and at hand. Subject matter instruction is costly, and physical education instruction is no exception. Furthermore, physical education requires adequate, specialized facilities which may not cost as much to construct as do other types of buildings and outdoor areas, but which do have to be maintained properly if they are to be continually serviceable. A large amount and variety of supplies are used in physical education. Because the increasing pressures upon educational institutions at all levels raise operating costs higher and higher, every program utilizing educational funds will be not only expected but required to demonstrate its productive worth in the total program of the institution. Physical education administrators should look upon this as a desirable challenge rather than a terrifying threat. If a program makes no substantial contribution to achieving the goals of the institution, it should yield its place and its resources to others which do. Perhaps, before being abandoned, a program can be modified so as to make a valued contribution. It is important, therefore, for the chairman to know not only his costs but also the worth of the outcomes of his physical education program.

It should be said that the financial picture is not entirely favorable to physical education. Often the classes are two to six or seven times the size of those assigned to a classroom subject. The physical education instructor typically has a teaching schedule twenty percent heavier than that of his colleagues in other subjects. In addition, he must supervise extensive facilities, be present after school for special activities, work on Saturdays and some holidays, and in other ways give service considerably beyond that expected of the classroom teacher. Furthermore, physical education facilities receive much greater use than do those of other subjects, especially where students are given relatively free access to those facilities during their out-of-class time. Except for the college library, probably no other departmental facilities receive the heavy out-of-class use given by students to physical education facilities. Nevertheless, these matters may be overlooked by college and school administrations which see value only in printed subject matter, unless the chairman himself knows and can demonstrate their worth.

4. The budget controls program development according to an institutional rather than a departmental pattern. In a college or university where the department of physical education considers itself an integral part of the institution's total educational program, money which is made available for program development will be allocated in the best interests of the entire institution. A similar policy should apply in the schools.

The same principle applies within the department. Wherever the department itself has both the obligation and the opportunity to study the financial planning for the year ahead, its professional staff should achieve a desirable plan for balanced program development. If the reader will refer to the preceding item (3), he will recognize the connection between it and this point on balanced program development. Program balance does not mean equality in all aspects. The instructional program may take first priority and receive the largest amount of money, but retain a correct emphasis in relation to the remainder of the program. Often intercollegiate athletics in colleges and universities, are supported by funds which are separate from those used to maintain all other phases of the physical education program. If the money for the entire program comes from one fund, the practice frequently observed in colleges of spending the major share of money on the intercollegiate athletic program would be recognized as disturbing the proper balance between this aspect of physical education and all the others. In some institutions, however, such an allocation of money is consistent with the goals of the institution.

5. The budget encourages the use of efficient business practices in the department. Making expenditures within the amounts allocated through the budget, seeking to find the greatest value for the money expended, maintaining records of all transactions, noting where more or less money is needed, and becoming aware of unit costs are all designed to improve the financial operation of a department and to carry out more fully the intentions of budgeting practice.

6. Finally, the budget makes it possible to secure more of the items and services which a department needs, because it provides

the means to acquire them in its plan for spending money. Capricious spending and wasteful buying are more likely to be avoided.

PREPARATION OF THE BUDGET. Budget preparation follows a definite pattern which may be suited to the institution concerned. Although one pattern would be to have the budget prepared completely by a central office or officer, the better procedure is that of initial preparation by the using agent. The persons involved in this latter procedure and the steps to be followed will be discussed after the structure of the budget is described.

In order to know how to ask for money to support the many-sided departmental program, the chairman will need to understand the organization of a budget and the major categories under which money is allocated. Local practice may vary from the following list, but generally a budget is divided into two major categories: (1) an operating budget and (2) a capital budget. Within these two categories there may be several subcategories designed to fit the particular requirements of the individual institution.

An operating budget covers the costs of conducting the functions of an institution for a given period of time, usually one year. The capital budget covers the costs of building and land development, major repairs or renovations to facilities, and acquisition of new facilities other than buildings. Items in the capital budget are sizable, requiring the raising of money by bond issues, special taxation, development fund campaigns, and the solicitation of large gifts. The departmental chairman will be concerned with capital outlays as he plans for new facilities and for major alterations and renovation of present ones. He will need to look a number of years ahead to anticipate demands for additional enrollments, changes in program, and depreciation of present structures. Planning for capital expenditures is done on an institutionwide basis. The department chairman must visualize his needs in the framework of the total college or university and its growing and changing programs.

The chairman will be required to prepare an annual operating budget for the forthcoming year. It is not uncommon practice to require planning for two years ahead. In other words, one may prepare a budget request in July to be effective for the year beginning July two years later. A typical procedure for preparing the initial or *asking* budget follows.

Each of the units within an institution which uses funds for its operations prepares its requests for the specified period. The unit may be the department, an administrative office, a service office, such as a dean of students or a health service, or any other unit or division not included in the above list. If the institution is a small college, the initial budget requests may be reviewed by a dean of administration, a faculty committee, or a fiscal officer designated by the president to do this job. In a large college or university the deans of the colleges may review the requests from their respective college departments and then present them to the officer of the university who is responsible for financial matters. At this stage the determination is made as to what size of budget may be presented to the governing board with a chance of being approved. In institutions where the total amount of money to be made available is known before the budget-making starts, this stage may actually be close to the final one. In publicly supported institutions there is always the question of how much tax money will be allocated to them. The size of the budget request, therefore, is related to the amount of the previous budget, current increases related to growth in enrollments and other readily determined factors, and to the willingness of the legislative body to levy taxes which will return the money required to support the budget request.

Revisions are made at the stage when budgets from the various units are assembled and reviewed from the point of view of the total institution. The chairman may be able to suggest the revisions which he prefers, or the revisions may be made by the college or university administration.

The importance of the president in the budget-making process is described by Stewart.

> When the material has been transmitted to the president, he, in turn, should review the budgets, department by department, and should confer with all deans, directors of divisions, and such other departmental officers as may be necessary to enable him to make valid judgments and reach definite conclusions regarding the requests which should be recommended for approval, those which should be indefinitely postponed, and those which

should be presented for consideration at a later time. It is the president's first function to see that such a balance is maintained among the several departments and divisions as will effectuate sound educational policies and long-range programs, and as will assure a uniform treatment of personnel throughout the institution, to the end that all activities may develop in proper relation to one another, thus avoiding a lopsided institution. This over-all review is extremely important, not only in developing sound fiscal and educational concepts, but in bringing about a sense of mutual interest, participation, and helpfulness in the work of the university among all the staffs.[3]

The completed budget request is then submitted to the governing board for its consideration and approval. Where the funds for support of the budget are derived from taxes, there may be public hearings on all budget requests, and representatives of the institution are free to argue for their needs as are representatives from other branches of the government. If the budget request is approved as presented, which is rare, the president of the institution is then empowered to administer the funds allocated to the various budget categories.

If the budget is modified and then approved, the president of the institution is empowered to administer the budget but he will need to advise the various units of the revisions which affect them. Decisions as to how the money for an item, such as educational supplies, shall be allocated within the institution when the total request has been cut ten percent may be made by one person, e.g., the business manager or the dean of administration, or they may be based upon advice from a committee made up of members of the faculty and the administration. Although the chairman of the department may have itemized his request for supplies, when he receives an allocation of funds less than he had requested, he usually will have the authority to decide as to which of the items he wishes to purchase.

The writer has gone beyond the subject of budget preparation into the field of budget administration. Even in this area, however, the act of preparation is still functioning because the chairman must be prepared to select those items to be retained in the final

[3] Stewart, *op. cit.*, pp. 68–69.

budget whenever he does not receive money sufficient to support his initial request.

Budget preparation in schools should follow essentially the same steps. The school principal is the local administrative officer who prepares a budget request based upon the personnel, services, equipment, supplies, and materials required to operate his unit. In addition he will present requests for new programs and new projects.

These requests are sent to the superintendent, who combines them according to the requirements of the board of education's business practices into a budget for the district or the system. The steps from this point on are identical with those already described.

Obviously the number of persons who take part in the preparation of budget depends upon the size and complexity of the system. In a large city the superintendent of schools will have a business officer who actually prepares the budget data; however, the superintendent will make the decisions as to the items to be included in the budget request. It is important to recognize the function of the departmental administrator in preparing the basic data from which a budget must be prepared.

BUDGET STRUCTURE. Accounting and business practices in an institution determine the divisions within an operating budget. The divisions, or classes, are designed to group together similar types of items in order that costs can be more properly determined and to improve the operating efficiency of an office, such as that of purchasing.

The following operating budget divisions are those used in the budgets of institutions under the Board of Higher Education of New York City. They demonstrate the major divisions, as well as the categories under a major division. The budget is divided into funds for personal service and funds for nonpersonal service. The following categories are listed under personal service:

Administration—includes all persons employed in the offices of the president, the business manager, and the registrar.

Day Session—includes all persons employed in instructional capacity, all clerical staffs, laboratory staffs, and medical staffs serving the daytime student body.

Evening Session—(same as day session).
Summer Session—(same as day session).

Library Services—includes all persons employed as professional librarians, all clerical staff and attendants.

Maintenance and Operation of Buildings and Grounds—includes all supervisory personnel, all custodial and maintenance persons, and special categories of workmen, such as carpenters, electricians, engineers and plumbers.

Under nonpersonal service the following categories, or budget codes, are listed:

Supplies—includes all consumable items. There are fourteen subcategories under this code.

Materials—includes construction materials, repair materials, and other operating and equipment materials.

Equipment—includes all items which have a relatively long life in comparison to supplies. There are ten subcategories under this code.

Contractual Services—includes service items for which the college makes a contract with an off-campus agent. There are eleven subcategories under this code.

Fixed and Miscellaneous Charges—includes surety bond premiums.

Because a budget is designed to assist an operation and not to hinder it, if the situation arises in which an item or service is needed which cannot properly be placed under one of the existing codes, a modification in the budget should be made. The listings given above permit considerable flexibility and have been used long enough to serve the diversity of needs presented by institutions of higher learning in the City of New York.

De Young states that budget items for public education may be classified in five different ways, namely, (1) character, (2) organization units, (3) objects, (4) functions, and (5) funds.[4]

[4] Chris A. De Young, *Introduction to American Public Education,* McGraw-Hill Book Company, Inc., 1955, p. 509.

An example of the major headings under the character classification is given.

Major Division	*Example of Item*
General Control	Superintendent's salary
Instruction	Teachers' salaries, school supplies
Auxiliary services	Transportation
Operation of plant	Janitors' salaries, fuel
Maintenance of plant	Upkeep on buildings and grounds
Fixed charges	Fire insurance, rent
(The following items are part of a capital budget)	
Debt service	Principal and interest on loans and bonds
Capital outlay	Purchase of sites, buildings, equipment

The departmental administrator will follow the procedures used in his school to direct the preparation of a budget.

Two questions may trouble the chairman as he prepares his budget request. In the first place should the request represent as accurate an estimate of needs as one can make, or should it be padded in order to anticipate the cutting which often takes place? The writers prefer making an estimate as accurate as possible with no padding. This kind of estimate presents a clear, straightforward picture of needs which can be considered on the basis of evidence and argument. Furthermore, where the relationship between the one who prepares the budget and those who pass upon it is close, in time a feeling is built up that the proposed budget cannot be altered at will but must be studied carefully to see what effect any alteration will have upon the educational program of the institution.

Although the writers prefer an accurate estimate of needs, it is recognized that local prevailing customs and attitudes may dictate that excessive requests be made in order to receive in the final budget the minimum of funds required to maintain one's program. Boards of control or governmental bodies which encourage this kind of approach to budget preparation can never know realistically the actual needs for which money should be appropriated.

The second question concerns the form in which the request is written. Should each item be listed or should items be grouped and only a lump sum request be made? Part of the answer is that in preparing his budget the chairman must deal with each item in order to know precisely what he needs. Unless this kind of thinking is done, the chairman has no way of knowing whether his request, if granted, will meet all his needs or not, nor will he be able to predict accurately the costs of instituting new programs or projects. Furthermore, a careful itemization places some responsibility upon the final board, when it decides that a request must be reduced, to note just what services, supplies, or other needed items are to be eliminated by the reduction.

It may be argued that a detailed listing of needs opens the request to picayune criticism by those in authority. On the other hand, there may be members of a governing body who do not believe that money should be spent for certain items and who would criticize an institution for including such items in its budget request. The problem is one in which differences of opinion on how educational funds are to be used must be resolved through careful preparation of the data to justify requests for money. The chairman must know his institution and its practices if he is to prepare the budget request in the form most likely to be accepted. In no event should he conceal from himself any detail essential to the effective functioning of his department.

Preparation of an actual budget is based upon information which the departmental administrator should possess. The physical education program is the central as well as the broad platform for which budget support is required. Teaching, administration, supervision, planning, facilities, equipment, supplies, and services are required by the program. To estimate his needs in each of these categories, the administrator must use the facts of his own school situation.

The following example of budgeting will assist an administrator in his own efforts. A high school situation with the following characteristics will illustrate the point.

Total enrollment in physical education	1000
Number of periods per week required of each student	3
Number of periods in school day	8
Average class size in physical education	32
Physical education teacher's weekly class teaching loads periods	27

The number of students (1000) divided by 32 (average class size) gives 31.2 sections or classes required to accommodate the student enrollment. The number of classes (31) multiplied by the number of weekly meetings for each class (3), produces 93 class periods required per week. When 93 is divided by 27, which represents the number of classes one teacher can meet weekly, the result is 3.4 (or 4) as the number of teachers needed to carry the instructional load.

A simpler procedure for determining the number of teachers needed may be used whenever a ratio of one teacher to a specified number of pupils is followed. For example, if one teacher is expected to instruct 150 students each week, six or more teachers would be needed for 1000 students. In physical education the ratio is likely to be higher, perhaps 250 students per teacher, and the number of teachers required would be four. This figure corresponds to the one secured by the first procedure.

Instructional and supervisory responsibilities which the staff carries in addition to scheduled class teaching will be itemized. Usually the total teaching load includes time for other than classroom work. If a teacher's out-of-class requirements are heavy, classroom teaching loads will be reduced so that the total load will be within the prescribed limits.

Determination of personnel needs to carry on activities other than class teaching should be based upon established policy for assigning teaching credit. Frequently a physical education teacher will be assigned to coach an interscholastic team as part of his total teaching load. How much teaching credit should be given for this work? The answer depends upon the importance given the assignment. In school systems which pay for coaching as an extra assignment, the amount of the payment indicates that the task is equivalent to one tenth to one third of the teacher's load, with the variation determined by the specific sport involved. The administrator should prepare a schedule of allowances for the various nonclass duties to use in estimating personnel needs for budget purposes and in calculating the load for each individual teacher.

In the example given there may be a requirement for planning, conducting, and supervising intramural athletics. If it is estimated that a teacher will spend five to six hours per week on this job, assuming that each classroom hour represents at least one additional hour of preparation and evaluation in physical education, an assignment of two to three teaching credits could be made. This will require one fifteenth to one tenth of a teacher's time. If two teachers each have coaching assignments in two sports a year, the teaching allowance may be one fourth of their schedules. The administrator may be awarded teaching credit for his work, and this may represent one third of his teaching schedule.

If all these needs are listed in summary, the budget request for instructional personnel will appear as follows:

Class instruction	3.4	teachers
Supervising intramurals	.1	"
Coaching interscholastic athletics	.5	"
Departmental administration	.3	"
Total	4.3	teachers

Since teachers are units, the request will be made for four or five teachers, or for four full-time teachers and one part-time teacher.

A straight arithmetical representation of instructional personnel requirements implies that schedules in the school and teachers' competences are such that both can be utilized completely. This may not be possible. If it is not, adjustments can be made by employing additional personnel, by adjusting schedules to fit the loads of the number of persons to be employed, by reducing the department's program responsibilities, or by increasing class size.

Other than instructional personnel can be requested according to the demands of the job. The administrator may require a clerical assistant for the departmental office and a person to operate and maintain the swimming pool and outdoor play areas. These would be listed as,

Clerical assistant, departmental office	1
Maintenance person for fields and swimming pool	1

Preparation of other than personal service requests depends upon the nature and extent of the program and upon the budgeting practices followed by the school.

A physical education program of sports, games, and dance will require supplies such as balls, racquets, bats, foils, stop watches, recordings, bases, masks, and so on, in quantities sufficient to meet the instructional and practice requirements of the program. Each required item should be listed in the quantity desired. For example, if softball is an instructional activity the teacher in a class of thirty-two students may require ten softballs, eight bats, one catcher's mitt, one mask, and nine baseman and fielder's gloves. If more than one class is to be scheduled for the same period, the quantities should be duplicated. An additional quantity should be included to care for loss and depreciation.

An example of a listing for supplies appears below.

Softballs, each	30
Softball bats, each	20
Catcher's mask, each	2
Catcher's mitt, each	2
Softball gloves, each (22 righthanded, and 2 lefthanded)	24

This procedure is followed for each activity to be offered in the instructional program.

Items of equipment which are to be used in the program are listed separately from the supplies. The department may plan to include trampolining in its program. A diving board for the swimming pool needs replacing. A piece of heavy apparatus, such as a set of parallel bars, also is needed. These items will be presented in a similar manner.

Trampoline, each	2
Parallel bars, sets	1
Regulation diving board, fiber glass, each	1

Departmental budget requests in schools will be unlikely to include other categories. In colleges and in offices of city heads, such as a city director of physical education, other items will be listed.

In addition to presenting a budget request for the specific items already listed, the departmental administrator will show those items which he needs and which are purchased by another department or by the school's central office. Requests for library books should be indicated, and specific facility maintenance, renovation, and remodeling should be set forth as part of the budget request.

Bringing all the previous items together forms a sample budget request for a department of physical education in a school.

DEPARTMENT OF PHYSICAL EDUCATION
BUDGET REQUEST FOR 19__ TO 19__

ITEM	QUANTITY	ESTIMATED AMOUNT[a]
Personal Services		
Instructional		
Annual full-time teachers (includes instruction, supervision of intramural athletics program, coaching of interscholastic teams, and departmental administration)	5	$35,000.00
Noninstructional		
Clerical assistant for departmental office, full-time	1	4,000.00
Maintenance man for fields and swimming pool, full-time	1	4,200.00
Total, personal services		$43,200.00
Equipment		
Trampolines,	2 @ $300	$ 600.00
Parallel bars,	1 set @ 500	500.00
Diving board, regulation, fiber glass,	1 @ 225	225.00
Total, equipment		$ 1,325.00
Supplies		
Softballs	30 @ $1.50 ea.	$ 45.00
Bats, softball	20 @ 2.00 "	40.00
Catcher's mask, softball	2 @ 5.00 "	10.00
Catcher's mitt, "	2 @ 6.50 "	13.00
Softball gloves	24 @ 6.00 "	144.00
Total, supplies		$ 252.00
Library Books, estimated		$ 75.00
Repairs and Remodeling		
Install fluorescent lighting in girls' locker room		

ITEM	ESTIMATED AMOUNT[a]
Rebuild steps at east entrance to gymnasium	
Build spur on west side of track to provide a 220-yard straightaway	
Summary of Budget Requests	
Personal services	$43,200.00
Equipment	1,325.00
Supplies[b]	252.00
Library books	75.00
Repairs and remodeling[c] (to be estimated by building engineer)	
Total request, 19__ to 19__	$44,852.00

[a] Figures given are for demonstration purposes only and are not set down to represent a specific salary or cost in any particular vicinity.

[b] It should be obvious that a departmental program will include more than instruction in softball. The list of supplies is an example of procedure.

[c] The departmental chairman should be consulted on construction of specialized facilities, such as a track. He will submit his specifications prior to or at the time of his budget request. Usually major construction plans develop over a period of time and in conference with the school administrator and school architect or engineer. When a budget request is made, the matter will have received prior consideration as to its extent and probable cost.

Preparation of a budget request for a college department of physical education follows the same procedure. Basic data will be different; for example, the teacher's class load will be smaller, and there will be greater latitude given to the departmental chairman in the assignment of various duties to members of his staff. The college departmental administrator may be expected to consider more of the factors which the institution must pay for to maintain its physical education program. These differences do not alter the procedure which one follows in preparing a budget.

ADMINISTRATION OF THE BUDGET. After the budget request is approved by the agency which has the authority to allocate funds, it becomes the budget and governs the expenditure of money during the period specified. The president of a college and the superintendent of schools are responsible for administering the budget in their respective organizations. According to the size of the institution or school system, there will be one or more officers whose job it is to perform the actual operations concerned with spending the money.

The chairman will need to consult his own administrative officer as to the policies and procedures to be followed in his school or college.

MODIFICATION OF THE BUDGET. Because a budget is the best estimate that can be made at the time of its preparation, as time passes situations will arise which demand some variation in the budget as it was originally approved. One may need fewer instructional personnel than planned, but require additional administrative assistance. When planning the budget the chairman may have anticipated that the consumption of an item such as badminton rackets would be heavy. In actual use the rackets lasted longer than was anticipated, but there was greater than usual breakage in fencing foils. Modifications of this type are made by the chairman within the total funds allocated to the purchase of supplies. In the matter of personnel, if the budget is made up according to specific positions, modification may be difficult but not impossible.

Institutions may control the expenditure of funds by allowing the using agent a portion of the funds for each quarter or half year. Institutions commonly will review their financial status with respect to expenditures periodically during the year. At this time modifications in the budget may be made most readily. Stewart states that "in a well-developed plan of budget procedure there is no particular beginning or end. Proper provision for study and review and conferences among the several levels of university staffs and officers is important. . . ."[5] This policy applies to schools also.

SOURCES OF INCOME. One definition of budget given at the beginning of this discussion was that it is a statement of probable revenue and expenditures. College and universities derive their incomes from a variety of sources. There is some relationship between the number of students enrolled and the income available to the institution, but this relationship is not constant from one college to another because of the differences both in total resources and in educational and administrative policy with respect to the amount of money to be spent per student. The emphasis in this discussion, therefore, has been upon the planning for spending, rather than upon an attempt to estimate the probable income.

Obviously, spending cannot exceed income except in rare instances

[5] Stewart, *op. cit.*, p. 68.

when delayed income will make up an incurred deficit. Budget-making in an institution will be guided from the beginning by an indication of the limits within which spending can be planned. One of the important criteria, however, is that educational planning is the basis for budget-making and that limitation of funds poses only one of the problems which educational administration seeks to solve in carrying out desirable plans. It seems paradoxical, but one must prepare a budget within the means available while at the same time he must make forward-looking plans whose fulfillment may require more funds than are currently available.

Where a department of physical education is responsible for the conduct of intercollegiate athletics and income is derived from gate receipts, guarantees, and other sources connected with this program, the chairman must include this income as part of the money to be used in meeting his budget. Because the program of intercollegiate athletics demands almost as much consideration administratively as that of a department, no detailed consideration will be given here to that program. For purposes of this discussion, it will suffice to make a few points. If the program of intercollegiate athletics is an integral part of the educational program of the department of physical education, any income derived from such a program becomes part of the institutional funds and may either be earmarked for use in the continued support of the program or deposited in the institution's general account. The budgets for intercollegiate athletics will be presented along with other departmental requests and will be reviewed as part of the total obligation of the institution. Income derived from intercollegiate athletics will not be required to support the program but will augment funds allocated by the institution to athletics.

If the program of intercollegiate athletics is administered under the department of physical education, but financially it must pay all or a major share of its costs, separate budgeting and accounting must be instituted, and the program must operate within the limits of its income. Modifications of this plan are more likely to be the rule, i.e., the income will not furnish the total support of the program but will have to be sufficient to carry certain costs. In this case, too, separate budgeting and accounting are used to maintain financial control of this program.

Public school athletics usually are required to support themselves from their income. State legislation may specifically prohibit the use of tax funds for the purchase of athletic costumes, insurance, transportation, and other materials and services which are directly a part of the interscholastic program. On the other hand, instructional personnel whose duties include coaching may be paid from tax revenues.

Management of the finances of interscholastic athletics involves applying the same principles to the preparation and administration of the budget as have been enumerated for the general departmental and school budget. To the budget planning for interscholastic athletics the administrator adds the item of estimated income from whatever sources it is to come. Planning in this situation may require the development of alternate budgets, one based on receiving the amount of money that was estimated, and the other on receiving less than was estimated. It is good practice to build up a small reserve which can be drawn upon when unforeseen drops in income occur.

More detailed description of the items to be included in the budget for interscholastic athletics can be found in texts dealing with the administration of athletics.

SUMMARY

The budget for a department should reflect the plans, goals, and policies of the department. The chairman, in preparing the budget, will be mindful of the amount of money which he will have and will plan for its most effective utilization. He also will look ahead in order to initiate processes by which additional funds can be secured to meet goals which his department and the institution agree are worth achieving.

Chapter 7

DEVELOPING THE INSTRUCTIONAL PROGRAM

PREPARATION for putting a program into operation is a demanding and important undertaking and requires more study than one might think when he begins his role as administrator in a new position. All that has been written up to this point concerns itself with background information or with the working knowledge which the administrator will need as he does his work from day to day throughout the year. With the necessary background and working knowledge the chairman may now consider the program of physical education, which will be his major concern. At the beginning of Chapter 5 it was stated that the approach would be to consider that the reader is entering upon a new job in which he will have to develop a program of physical education. The materials which follow may be suited also to a department which has been in operation for some time, because the questions raised and the points discussed deal with matters of importance not only to the new department but also to established departments.

Because the program of physical education in schools and colleges is centered in the instructional courses, sometimes referred to as the required program or the *service* program, the ensuing discussion will concern itself with these courses. In a sense the program being described is that group of courses normally included in the requirement for a college degree, or the courses required of pupils and students in the lower schools, or, if the courses are not required, those courses in physical activities which students may offer for credit toward the basic education requirement of the institution.

Although there is no entirely adequate descriptive title for this program of courses, a term which has come into increasingly frequent use identifies most accurately the instructional program of physical education in all levels of education and in the various types of institutions. The term is *basic instruction,* and it will be used when reference is made to the instructional program in schools and colleges.

As one studies the following material, he will soon conclude that this is subject matter of concern to more than the department administrator. Each question can be asked by every teacher in the department, and the answers must be found by those same teachers. The administrator's task is to see that the questions are asked and that steps are taken to secure answers which will guide the entire department toward organizing and conducting an excellent educational program. He, or she, will realize that there is seldom just one answer to a question, hence the teacher or the department as an instructional unit must select that answer which is judged most effective for the pertinent situation. In the writing, therefore, no reference will be made specifically to either the administrator of the department or the teacher; it will be assumed that these are matters of significance to both and that only the responsibility for seeking action may differ for the administrator and the teacher. Even this difference may not always exist.

GOALS OF THE BASIC INSTRUCTION COURSES

In Chapter 2 the importance of consistency between departmental goals and those of the institution was discussed. The goals to be achieved through the required courses must be identical with those of the institution, or must contribute to their achievement. Whatever purpose the school or college has, instruction and learning in physical education must conform to it. All of this has been said emphatically and will not be repeated in this discussion.

Has the department taken the nature of the individual into account in setting up course goals? If the individual is a college freshman, is allowance made for the problems of transition from the youth just out of high school to the young college man or woman? If the department includes both men and women students, have the differences in maturity of these groups been recognized in the selection of goals? What are the personality needs of the individual which can be met, in part at least, through the physical education experience? Does he need self-assurance, the ability to subordinate self-interest to the interest of the group without losing his own identity? Has he the ability to face a difficult situation with willingness to go ahead, even though a successful outcome is not a certainty? Has he skill to define a learning problem, ability to see the steps leading to its solution, and perseverance to follow these steps? Personality needs are almost unlimited in number.

Children, youth, and adults spend much of their leisure time in active recreation. What needs do the individuals have for learning recreational activities which they can practice in their free time? Also, what social values are there in the recreational opportunities created through participation in sports, games, dance, and outdoor activities?

One of the unique and important contributions of physical education is made to the physical and physiological development of the individual. What are the characteristic physical needs of students or pupils with whom you are dealing? What are the specific needs of the individual students in your institution? To what extent will the program aim at achieving national objectives of physical fitness for your students?

Periodically attention in the United States is focused upon the physical fitness of children and youth. Each time there are those, often not professionally qualified in either education or physical education, who proclaim loudly the poor physical condition of the people and the cure for their deficiencies. Because these proclamations are based on a motive of self-aggrandizement, and only incidentally upon an interest in improving the status of children and youth, and because the programs generated by these periodic outbursts take into account neither the actual needs of the individuals nor their own interests in the matter, the programs accomplish nothing. The unfortunate aspects of these experiences are the actual failure of the programs to bring about any marked improvement in the fitness of children and youth and the failure of the profession itself to incorporate in its basically sound program those features which can make improvements in physical fitness.

Research into the nature of physical fitness, how to measure it, to describe it, and to attain it has been increasing each year. One can follow the outcomes of research through a study of the *Research Quarterly,* through the professional journals in related fields, such as biology, physiology, and medicine, and through reports on research in publications, such as the *Proceedings* of the College Physical Education Association.

In establishing the goals for basic instruction, one will wish to study carefully those which are to be included in this area of physical and physiological outcomes. It cannot be assumed that all children and youth enrolled in physical education courses need to improve their physical fitness. One can say that certain standards are desirable and that those who have not met them should engage in activities selected because of their important contribution in this area. Physical education departments will select the most useful activities and will establish meaningful standards. Since this will be one of several goals guiding the program of the department, the activities making up the courses of the department will coordinate the work leading to its achievement with a program which keeps in balance the achievement of all goals. It must be repeated that the nature of the individual must be acknowledged whenever the matter of goals is under consideration.

The student will recall the discussion of goals which the profession of physical education itself has determined as the major objectives for its program. Reference should be made to Chapter 3 for a statement of these objectives. The administrator of a department will accept the major purposes of the field as those which give direction to his own program. To do otherwise is to introduce additional kinds of learning under the guise of physical education, an action which may pass scrutiny in a local circumstance, but which will create misinterpretation of the field of physical education among students, faculty, and others who come in contact with the program.

When one is planning his program, or is restudying it with a view to making changes, his own goals should take cognizance of the purposes of the field itself. Although too much repetition lessens effect, it should be said again that these formulations of goals must also be consonant with the institution's goals. The discussion of goals in this section is aimed at directing attention to those characteristics of the students and of the institution's educational program which are to be taken into account by the departmental administrator and his staff when they set the goals for their own educational program.

OPERATIONAL AND ULTIMATE GOALS

Foshay gives added light to this problem when he shows the relationship between ultimate goals and operational goals. He writes as follows:

> The first question we need to consider, therefore, is, What is the nature of the man we wish the school curriculum to imply? Which analysis of man's nature is the most helpful? We should be giving this matter continuous and extended consideration.
>
> I have referred several times to the tendency to confuse ultimate goals and operational goals. I do not, of course, mean to imply by this that a consideration of ultimate goals would be sufficient. One cannot organize a curriculum around ultimate goals; one must have in mind a series of steps—means, if you will,—toward such ultimate goals. These steps are operations; achieving each of them is an operational goal. To state such operational goals as steps toward the ultimate goal of making a man is to achieve a sort of translation, for we educators are among those who are most certain that ultimate goals have no meaning until such a translation ("implementation" we usually call it) has been made. The trick is to keep the implementation consistent with the ultimate goal; or, if you please, to make a genuine translation, so that the spirit of the original is not vitiated.[1]

Because the ultimate goals of education are statements of values in which society places importance, such statements become platitudes unless they are converted into action by students in our schools and colleges. It is important, therefore, that the administrator and the teacher plan to translate the ultimate goals into steps leading to their achievement. Two observations must be made. In the first

[1] Arthur W. Foshay, "Educational Goals," *Educational Research Bulletin*, February 13. 1957, pp. 32–33.

place, an educational program is possible only when all the energy of the curriculum is devoted to achieving the ultimate goals. In the second place, once the operational procedures have been effected which lead to achievement of the ultimate goals, periodic review of the procedures is essential in order to avoid their becoming the goals and to keep the procedures themselves from becoming routine to the point that the student is overlooked in the teaching process.

Perhaps the difficult, complex planning required to prepare comprehensive courses of study in physical education activities aimed at achieving all the professed goals discourages administrators and teachers, who find it easier to work for accomplishment in just one or two areas. Achievements in motor skills are obvious; similarly, improvement in physical fitness can be measured by one or several tests described in professional literature. One can establish standards toward which the students are to work and can point with pride to their accomplishments in these areas. What significance do these have for the ultimate goals? How pertinent are the standards to the ultimate goals of the institution, the society, and the individual himself?

The danger of stating an ultimate goal without checking to see that steps are taken to achieve it is illustrated in a study reported by Kistler. One of the social values which members of the profession of physical education have stressed as an important outcome of participation in games and sports is sportsmanship—a quality involving courtesy and consideration for the opponent, strict adherence to the rules, refusal to take an unfair advantage of an opponent. Kistler asked young men and women enrolled in required courses in physical education at Louisiana State University, and a small group of adult males living in the university community, to react to a series of behavior situations in sports which were described in written form. The students and community members were asked to state whether or not they approved the described behavior and to give reasons for their answers. The entire study cannot be repeated here but excerpts taken from the report will demonstrate a point.

(1) *Booing of visiting team basketball players as they attempt to make free throws is not considered poor sportsmanship by an appreciable percent of men and women.* Twenty-three percent of the college men and thirty-

six percent of the college women did not consider it such. Fourteen per cent of the adult men indicated that they thought the practice is not evidence of poor sportsmanship.

(2) *Approximately fifty percent of the college men, about one-third of the male adults and fifteen percent of the college women approve of the practice of deliberately taking advantage of a situation in sports and putting it up to the Official to catch them doing so.*

Most of the reasons given in support of the practices indicated were to the effect that it is the official's business to make the decisions and that it is "smart" play to take any advantage that can be gotten due to failure of the officials to make decisions preventing such practices.

(7) *Sixty percent of the college men and forty-five percent of the male adults approved of deliberately breaking rules when it appears that something might be "salvaged" out of a bad situation by so doing.*

The above percentages approved of deliberate fouling on the part of a guard on defense in basketball when he finds himself outnumbered three-to-one by offensive players bringing the ball down the floor for a shot.[2]

The data are presented to call attention to the number of people who approve unsportsmanlike conduct. It can be argued that there are sizable percentages who do not approve unsportsmanlike conduct. One of the disturbing findings reported by Kistler was that students who had had high school athletic experience more often approved unsportsmanlike behavior. One study does not make a complete case, but indications from other events suggest that the value placed upon sportsmanship has diminished greatly among a large percentage of the population which has had schooling, presumably in situations where sportsmanship was a goal being sought.

Whether one likes it or not, the values sought in interscholastic and intercollegiate athletics are not those ascribed to them in the professional literature of physical education and athletics. It may be that those responsible for the administration and conduct of athletics have substituted the current values for those which have been written about earlier. The present commentary is not a critical review of the values in athletics today, but an appraisal of a situation in which the professed goals are not the real ones because

[2] J. W. Kistler, "Attitudes Expressed About Behavior Demonstrated in Certain Specific Situations Occurring in Sports," *Proceedings*, College Physical Education Association, 1957, pp. 55–57.

those who conduct the programs have not related their practices and procedures to the stated goals. While physical education courses are not interscholastic or intercollegiate athletics, the public acclaim given to athletics has attracted the teacher of physical education and he has accepted the values of the popular program. Coaches of athletic teams also teach physical education classes and quite naturally introduce their values into sports and basic instruction courses alike.

Whatever goals are chosen, it is important to align the instructional materials, methods, and situations with them. Appraisal of outcomes in terms of the goals is then possible. More important is the fact that the administrator has planned and is conducting a program of physical education which has educational integrity.

ESTABLISHING GOALS

An administrator beginning a new position may have to set forth initially the goals which are to serve the curriculum. If he has other staff members at the beginning, the establishing of goals which direct the basic instructional program is a function of the entire staff under the leadership of the administrator. If he is the only member of a department, he may consult with interested colleagues, teachers, and administrators of physical education in nearby schools and colleges. There are, of course, the rich sources of ideas and experience to be found in professional literature. If he takes a position in a department whose program has been established for some time and he believes that the curriculum should be critically reviewed, he should utilize the department staff fully in this process. Such a review necessarily considers the goals of the instructional program.

The instances in which a person starts his work with the initial opening of an institution are rare, although the building of new schools and the expansion of institutions of higher education provide many new positions in new institutions. Whether one starts a new department or takes a position in an established institution, eventually he will wish to review his departmental curriculum. At this time his department will have acquired a staff, there will be students in the physical education program, and there will be colleagues in the institution who are interested in the departmental program. Curriculum review, which includes a study of goals of instruction, can involve persons from each of these groups.

Democratic practices pertinent to staff organization and conduct will be discussed in detail in a later section. Staff participation in setting and reviewing goals is one instance of democratic practice. On this point Hughes and French state that "democratic representation and participation includes the *determination of policies* as well as attention to the details involved in putting them into practice."[3]

Nash emphasizes the importance of cooperative action in planning goals. He writes:

> The concept of democracy as an evolutionary process, with continual re-evaluation of goals and issues, takes cognizance of both the human desire for goals and standards and the inevitable change and growth process which is fundamental to life.
>
> Not only does democracy provide for change and development through flexible planning, but it also assumes that this planning must be a cooperative effort. The citizens as well as the leaders must have a part in the planning. Not only the administrator and the supervisor, but also all their associates must have a voice in this planning.[4]

Some colleges invite students to take part with the faculty in considering purposes and curriculum. Hughes and French state that democratic representation, in general, means that every individual affected by an administrative principle or policy should have some part in its formulation and adoption. In commenting on the possibility of improving student social behavior through the physical education program, Nordly says that "agreement among staff members on a statement of values for direction of college physical education could be highly desirable. Involvement of students and other faculty members in the process is indicated as such goals are defined.[5] Scott points out that "the primary responsibility of mid-twentieth century physical education is to aid students in planning, selecting, and participating in motor activities through which the

[3] William L. Hughes and Esther French, *The Administration of Physical Education for Schools and Colleges,* A. S. Barnes and Co., 1954, p. 6.

[4] J. B. Nash, Francis J. Moench, and Jeannette B. Saurborn, *Physical Education: Organization and Administration,* A. S. Barnes and Co., 1951, p. 179.

[5] Carl L. Nordly, "The Improvement of Social Behavior in the Physical Education Program for the General College Student," *Sixty-First Proceedings,* College Physical Education Association, 1958, p. 51.

goals of general education are achieved." He suggests that students "should be helped to explore their own levels of aspiration in physical education and formulate their own goals in the light of these aspirations."[6]

In two universities where the physical education requirement was under study by the faculty who intended to modify or eliminate it, the departments were able to argue successfully for its retention. Among the data submitted in support of their arguments were the results of student opinion polls, and in both instances it was believed that these data were most helpful. One report stated that "this document served a useful purpose in defending the requirement and, as well, served as a guide for curriculum planning in the required program."[7] Students had not taken part in selecting the goals for the courses in either case, but their reactions to the program and its purposes impressed the general faculty and in one university indicated that the students may make worthwhile contributions to the planning of the program.

Participation by students in the process of planning for their education may yield several benefits if the process is conducted with skill and with thorough knowledge of its limitations as well as its possibilities. Intelligent planning demands a knowledge of values and possible outcomes to be achieved through courses of instruction. It also assumes that the participants are studying the broad picture of education rather than a narrow one of capricious interest. Finally, its effectiveness depends upon mutual respect and trust between students and faculty. The administrator and his staff cannot abdicate their responsibilities for providing the best education which they are professionally prepared to give; hence the participation of students acts principally as a leavening factor in the planning process. In colleges and universities, acceptance of students as co-workers with faculty in considering the goals of physical education instruction has met with favor. Each administrator and his staff

[6] H. A. Scott, "Physical Education as a Phase of General Education," *Proceedings,* College Physical Education Association, 1957, pp. 304–305.

[7] R. A. Snyder, "Interpreting Physical Education to the Several Faculties, The U.C.L.A. Story," *Proceedings,* College Physical Education Association, 1958, p. 236. *See also,* H. E. Kenney, "The Defense of the Physical Education Requirement at the University of Illinois," *Proceedings,* College Physical Education Association, 1958, p. 225.

will decide whether or not they wish to invite students to work with them and also whether or not the circumstances in their institution indicate that students and faculty can hope to establish a working rapport.

After this rather lengthy discussion on establishing goals in the local department, the summary is brief. The department must state its goals clearly in order to choose the curriculum best suited to the goals and to provide a definite basis for evaluating the effectiveness of the curriculum.

MEANS FOR REACHING GOALS

Departments of physical education may differ somewhat in the expressed goals which they choose, but the means for reaching them are generally alike. Physical education implies education of individuals primarily through big muscle activity. The *Dictionary of Education* defines physical education as "the program of instruction and participation in big-muscle activities designed to promote desirable physical development, motor skills, attitudes, and habits of conduct."[8] Williams' concept of physical education as education through the physical means has provided the basis for his statement that "physical education is the sum of man's physical activities, selected as to kind, and conducted as to outcomes."[9]

J. B. Nash describes the meaning of physical education in detail. He writes:

> Physical education is a fundamental teaching or administrative division of the total school organization. It utilizes and extends the use of vigorous neuromuscular activities which are the basis of education. Physical activities and the drives behind them are age-old play urges for man, and as such, a means to express himself through total body coordination, and this means of expression predates all recorded language. Physical activities today are centered around the play lot, the playground, the athletic field, the gymnasium, dance floor, swimming pool, ice rink and the ski trail.
>
> Physical education, in terms of outcomes, is the sum of the changes in

[8] Carter V. Good, Ed., *Dictionary of Education,* McGraw-Hill Book Co., Inc., 1945, p. 298.

[9] Jesse Feiring Williams, Clifford L. Brownell, and Elmon L. Vernier, *The Administration of Health and Physical Education,* 5th ed., W. B. Saunders Company, 1958, p. 10.

an individual caused by experiences centered around these total body activities.

Physical education, as an activity, is a tool with which the leader works. Health and recreation are outcomes. The area of physical education contributes to these outcomes, but so do all other areas of education.[10]

The leaders agree that the activities typical of a physical education curriculum are not the ends but are the means by which the goals of physical education are achieved.

RESOURCES OF PHYSICAL EDUCATION

An observer of certain physical education classes may conclude that learning how to perform the physical activity is the primary and major end of the teaching and learning program. He may find that achieving a batting average of .300 in baseball and a time of 10 seconds in running the 100-yard dash are the principal goals. As difficult as it is not to set these up as major aims, the professional teacher must keep forever in the front of his mind that neither a batting average of .300 nor a time of 10 seconds in the 100-yard dash is a major aim of instruction in physical education. Baseball and track are two activities in which boys and girls, young men and young women take part; quite naturally they study and practice to improve their performance in the activities. Through their work and study, however, in a carefully planned program of physical education they will achieve the major goals of physical education.

Large muscle activities make up the major resources of physical education. In selecting the subject matter of basic instructional courses in physical education, one should look upon these resources as the central content of the courses.

It has been stated that resources should be chosen whose use will make possible the optimum achievement of the goals. The significance of this statement must be impressed upon the administrator and the teacher so that they will center program planning upon the important job of teaching for goals rather than emphasizing the means. Striking examples of the futility of ignoring the relationship between resources and goals can be found in many articles and in

[10] Nash, *et al., op. cit.,* p. 3.

convention and conference sessions which have debated the subject of formal versus informal sports, or gymnastics versus games and sports. In one city the teachers have commented that the director of the program for the city schools, desiring to seem in step with the movement toward a broader program of physical education, had not permitted the replacement of worn pieces of apparatus. The result was gradually to eliminate apparatus activities from the program. The protest against games and sports embodied in the cry of "Let's have some muscle," and followed by a plan which suggests that muscle can be developed through only one kind of activity, represents an interest only in certain resources, not in the goals. All these controversies are pointless until one judges which resources are most suitable for achieving the chosen goals. Each resource has a contribution to make to some goal. Judging which resource is most effective in the situation is the function of the administrator and his staff.

Careful selection of resources richest in the learnings being sought encourages the administrator and his staff to review their program frequently, to make changes from time to time, and to develop evaluative measures which have meaning for them and for the students taking part in the program. When the goals of a program become the guides which the administrator and his staff follow as they plan course content, situations which are meaningless, relatively barren of new learning opportunities, and often narrow and repetitive in content will be eliminated. A teacher going into a junior high school found that the program for girls for three years was basketball! Apparently the only guide which the administrator had followed was to provide an activity with a high pupil interest value, low in cost, and easy to supervise. In contrast, a program which utilizes a variety of resources, each chosen for its unique and effective opportunities for purposeful learning, which knows and acknowledges the characteristics of the varying age groups, as well as the differences between individuals, which leads on from one level of learning experience to a new and more mature one, and which expects excellent teaching is the one which has been planned according to carefully chosen and clearly defined goals. One may add, too, that the planning has been done by an educator whose own ideals include professional scholarship.

PHYSICAL EDUCATION FACILITIES

Programs must be planned according to the facilities which are available. The goals chosen may give direction to a program regardless of the facilities, but the selection of resources has to be made initially according to the availability of facilities, time, qualified staff, and supplies. By focusing his attention upon the goals rather than upon the facilities when planning his program, the administrator or teacher determines what variety of resources, suited to the facilities, time, supplies, and staff, will lead to optimum achievement of the goals.

When the facilities consist of one medium-sized gymnasium-auditorium, a small locker-dressing room, with one or two showers in an adjoining shower room, and a small rough field next to the school, is it possible to offer softball in the fall and spring, and basketball and volleyball throughout the winter months, year after year? Can one utilize not only these activities (resources) but others which may be more suited to achieving some of the goals and which may provide better learning situations for certain age groups? Within the facilities and available staff, whether abundant or meager, the means for achieving worthwhile educational goals through physical education are present. Careful study of one's goals and imaginative use of facilities for the conduct of the courses result in a program of instruction leading to the successful accomplishment of the chosen goals.

RESOURCES OF PHYSICAL EDUCATION FOR COURSE CONTENT

A listing of all known activities would be a volume in itself, especially if one were to include activities for all age levels. Writers in the field of physical education have listed many activities, grouping them into categories roughly based on the principal characteristic of the activity. The following represents a grouping of activities according to their content. The lists given are not exhaustive.

Gymnastics: calisthenics, Danish Gymnastics, apparatus, marching, special exercises, fundamental skills, trampolining, weight lifting.

Rhythmics: singing games, folk dances, square and circle dances, ballet, modern dance, ballroom (social) dances, clog and tap dances.

Relays, stunts and group games: Basket Toss, Rescue Relay, Do as I Do, Follow the Leader, Ankle Walk, Hop and Turn, Cart Wheel, Duck Walk, Bombardment, Blind Man's Buff, Prison Ball, Tag games, Red Rover, Kick Ball, Indian Club Snatch.

Aquatics: swimming, diving, lifesaving, boating, canoeing, sailing, water skiing, skin and scuba diving, water polo, synchronized swimming.

Individual sports: golf, tennis, handball, squash, bowling, table tennis, horseshoes, quoits, paddle tennis, tennikoit, archery, badminton, skating, riding, skiing, hiking, cycling, track and field, squash, racquets, camping, fishing, hunting.

Combatives: boxing, wrestling, fencing, judo.

Team Games: basketball, softball, speedball, touch football, football, volleyball, baseball, lacrosse, field hockey, soccer, ice hockey, rugby, fieldball.

The foregoing discussion of primary resources should not exclude from consideration other resources through which learning occurs in physical education. Occasionally the means for primary teaching will be found in other resources. More frequently the supplementary resources provide means for enhancing the learning or for enriching the teaching. Books, magazines, pamphlets, film strips, slides and motion pictures, drawings, diagrams, posters, demonstrations, field trips, visits to other schools, and special events provide materials and means for teaching physical education. Although the primary resources are the physical activities, one will remember that skill in the activity is not the only end to be sought through teaching and, ultimately, is not the primary end of the teaching. By means of the physical activity, however, the student learns valuable lessons in personal conduct, standards and ideals, in social values, group behavior and group responsibility, in knowledge of physiologic needs of the body and the ways to meet them, and in worthwhile use of leisure.

Through physical activities the student learns many related ideas and bodies of knowledge. Often these related learnings are really given direction and integrated into the student's acquired knowledge through the use of one or more of the resources referred to above. A student learning to play tennis may also learn how to choose a racket and become aware of the several international tournaments and the functions of the United States Lawn Tennis Association in amateur tennis. Another student may complete a course in gymnastics and apparatus and at the same time learn about the nationalistic origins of the major gymnastic systems. The fact that there is less interest in these activities in the United States than in Germany, Sweden, and Russia today may be explained in terms of societal differences. The student will learn that peoples throughout recorded history have expressed their feelings, emotions, ideas, and hopes through contests, dances, exhibits of physical prowess, and even through the development of the body itself, if the teaching situations include study of these matters as an integral part of their plan.

In the same way the student needs to experience the exhaustion which attends an all-out effort before he can know the satisfaction which comes from making the effort and from knowing that he was capable of such an exertion. A new appreciation of himself grows out of this kind of experience. Furthermore, the individual who tires at the thought of muscular work can better assess his physical condition when he is faced with the results of a poor performance at a modest task. Perhaps the value which he has placed upon lack of condition is now seen in clearer perspective, with the result that better physical condition becomes a goal to be sought rather than shunned.

The teacher may assume that these interpretations of the results of taking part in activities will be obvious to all, even the student participants. Unless the teacher calls attention to them, however, directly as well as through supplementary resources, the student may either ignore or not recognize the significant interpretations, or he may place high importance upon outcomes of relatively unimportant value, or he may see value in possible undesirable outcomes. It is obvious that the value is that quality ascribed by the individual himself, but education's obligation is to point out those values which are held in high esteem by society. In a game a player may place value upon winning to the point that the means, any means, are justified if they lead to victory. Under instruction in the same activity he can retain his intense desire to win while working for his goal within rules and ethical practices which are more valuable to society and to him, in the long run, than winning.

TEACHING METHODS AND THE ACHIEVEMENT OF GOALS

The content of a subject and the method employed in teaching it are bound together to produce a unified experience for the learner. Without the substance of extensive and deep subject matter, method becomes a superficial exercise devoid of direction. Concentration upon the subject matter alone, disregarding the rich knowledge about methods of teaching and learning, wastes student and teacher time, results in limited learning when there is possibility of abundance, and overlooks the necessity of educating in matters equal in importance to subject matter if the benefits of learning are to be continually sought. In physical education the methods which teachers employ are vitally important to the achievement of the goals of the program, especially those outcomes which must be secured through the primary resources but which are not given direction by these resources. For example, one may teach students how to be expert tennis players, mastering all the skills of the activity. These are the primary resources. Unless direction is given to attitudes and conduct while the students are learning the skills of the game, there is no way to predict that any of them will obey the rules, play with consideration and respect for both partners and opponents, train adequately for strenuous play, or acquire any other learnings thought to be of value. Certainly relating the learnings in tennis to the cultural characteristics of a society does not just happen when the method used concentrates upon teaching the primary skills.

Oberteuffer states that "method, to some, is narrow and is concerned only with getting an activity taught. The broader interpretation of method is concerned with the many values which are at stake in any learning situation and thus seeks not only the accomplishment of skills in the activity but also results in the development of values, and in attitudes and character."[11]

[11] Delbert Oberteuffer, *Physical Education,* rev. ed., Harper & Brothers, 1956, p. 301.

Earlier sections of this text have developed the thesis that physical education must conform to educational purposes and follow the best in educational practices. This criterion applies to the methods of teaching as well as to the kind of goals chosen and the subject matter selected. Again Oberteuffer sets forth the fundamental conception of the physical education program and the relationship of method to achievement of the goals of such a program.

> In essence we confess to basing the program upon one fundamental fact of man's life, namely, his unitary (rather than atomistic) nature; and upon one basic assumption concerning the purpose of education—that the purpose of education, at any level, is not the cultivation of the intellect or mind alone but is the development of the man, the citizen. This fact being true, and this assumption being reasonable, then the ultimate test of a modern program of physical education will be found not only in the acquisition of the skills and knowledge of sport and dance, but more fully in accretions to personal development which are reflected in the quality of one's life and living.[12]

Clearly the method of teaching is part and parcel of the subject matter used for achieving the goals of education or of physical education. In a sense it is unwise to identify a method of teaching, because the act of identification tends to attribute special and separate qualities to method. The teacher may think only of the procedures for calling a class to order, or for taking attendance, or giving a test. Although these are necessary and usually important aspects of class management, they are not the methods of instruction. The use to which such procedures are put in achieving educational goals is the method. Perhaps methods integrated with the various resources and suited to the nature of the individual as a learner, became the means for achieving one's goals. If this is possible, one will recognize that methods are suited to the resources as well as to the goals in mind. Methods also are related to the learner and the teacher. Edgar Dale writes that "to set up an educational philosophy is to note ends, that is, desired effects. But to note ends and be unconcerned about the means is to commit folly, be sentimental, not realistic."[13] Not only must the administrator and teacher be concerned

[12] *Ibid.*, p. 467–468.

[13] Edgar Dale, "Educational Means," *Educational Research Bulletin*, February 13, 1957, p. 36.

about the means, but he or she must be willing to select or devise means which are effective. "A sound educational program requires us to match ends with means. Otherwise we waste time, talk froth, fall into the trap of many who talk fruitlessly about liberal education, good citizenship, tolerance, critical thinking, and the like."[14]

If methods are a part of the means, bonded with the various resources as a dye becomes part of a fabric, it behooves the teacher to think carefully about the kind of method which is to become a part of any means. Is achieving democratic behavior an important goal? If the answer is yes, the means must provide for practicing this kind of behavior, not just learning about it. A speaker recently stated that one of the greatest needs today was to give people a basis for recognizing and opposing demagoguery. Are there means in physical education, especially in athletics, to assist in achieving such an end? If respect for the worth of the individual is a major goal of education, cannot physical education, through its resources and the way in which they are employed, create understanding of this concept far more effectively than can be done through reading about it? Naturally, reading and doing together make for a richer, broader knowledge.

The administrator, in planning to achieve the goals of the program, will utilize the best resources and the most effective means. A program of physical education is described broadly by its purposes, resources for teaching and learning, and the methods of teaching which are to predominate. A physical education curriculum is an orderly presentation of these matters which serves as a guide for the organization of learning programs in specific situations. An administrator will require further information, however, translate the curriculum into an organization of pupils and students in his school or college for the purpose of instruction in physical education. The section which follows deals with the factors of classification of individuals, the time available for classes, and the need for progression in subject matter. These factors influence the organization of an instructional program in an existing institution. Whether the nature of these items is already determined before the administrator enters his position or it remains to be decided after he arrives, the

[14] *Ibid.*, p. 36.

administrator must reckon with each of them as he plans his actual program.

CLASSIFICATION AND GROUPING OF STUDENTS

In planning his program of instruction the administrator will be sensitive to the literature which emphasizes the need for grouping students in ways which promote their optimum learning. Educational literature has long held that individuals differ, hence that they cannot all be treated alike in the learning situations. Classification and grouping procedures attempt to place together for teaching and learning purposes individuals who are similar with respect to their needs, abilities, and previous learnings.

Schemes for classifying students have been developed in the field of physical education in order that persons of like qualities can be grouped together for teaching or for participation in contests and games. Their use, which has not been extensive, has been in the elementary and secondary schools more than in the colleges and universities. In schools which do not group their pupils for other subjects, grouping for physical education classes may be impractical or at best difficult to arrange. In schools which group their pupils for other subjects, assignment of pupils to physical education probably will be according to their grouping in these other subjects.

In colleges and universities, because of the greater flexibility which these institutions allow in the scheduling of courses, there is no pronounced administrative obstacle to the classification of students for physical education. Because of limited staff and facilities, an individual institution may find that it is not possible to classify students for physical education except in the gross manner of course content readiness or class standing in the college.

PURPOSE OF GROUPING STUDENTS

The administrator will wish to know the values ascribed to the classification and grouping of students and will need to decide whether or not he can and should utilize classification procedures in his program. What purposes are achieved by classifying and grouping students in physical education?

In the first place, one must know what he is trying to achieve through the teaching situation. He must know his goals. For our purposes it is assumed that the administrator has his goals. Also he must know by what measure he can state that any individual has achieved the goals or at least has reached an acceptable station along the road to the goals.

With these matters decided, it can be said that one function of classification and grouping is to improve the effectiveness of instruction by knowing the kind and amount of learning which the students are expected to acquire. To know where a pupil stands at the beginning of an instructional term supplies the teacher with a rough indication of his distance from the goal. The steps along the way can be planned so that only those which actually lead the pupil on are taken. If pupils with like distances to travel are placed in the same group for instruction, the efforts of teacher and pupils alike can be effectively directed to the same study and learning, because it is supposed that students with like needs will learn together more rapidly than those of widely differing needs.

A second function of grouping is to extend the upper limits of pupil learning by eliminating unnecessary work and by having a class in which all members may go on together from a common starting point. Students with like qualities with respect to a known educational goal should not repeat the steps which they have already learned. The time saved should be considerable, and the motivation of the student should be greater because he faces new challenges, rather than old tasks already performed. Furthermore, if the department intends to reach as high an achievement level as possible, the particular goals set for a group may be more ambitious than those set for another group because of differences in their standings at the beginning of the instructional term. This latter is the major argument for grouping gifted children together in certain school subjects. The trait upon which classification and grouping are based in this instance may be predicted intellectual capacity rather than previous achievement. Both factors should be considered, however, if correct grouping for instructional purposes is to be carried out.

Finally, grouping of pupils may permit more reliable evaluation of their work. Because the individuals in a group may be expected to perform nearly alike with respect to the qualities upon which their grouping was based, the evaluative instrument or means can be designed to fit this particular need, and the interpretation can be made directly in terms of the basis for grouping.

METHODS OF CLASSIFYING STUDENTS

Before discussing critically the above values claimed for grouping, a review of the methods and devices available for the purpose of classifying students in physical education will supply examples which give meaning to the entire discussion.

In any educational institution one recognizes immediately that individuals are grouped by grade level, which usually is closely allied with the pupils' ages. Furthermore, in some activities the individuals may be grouped by sex at certain ages or after a certain age has been reached. In schools, classification by grade, usually by age, and sometimes by sex, is commonly the rule. Because such measures are not sensitive enough to select individuals who may differ widely in other ways which have real bearing upon their ability to learn, and hence upon their needs in the learning situation, other classification devices are used.

Essential to all physical education, regardless of the organization of classes, is the classification of students based on the physical, or medical, examination. The results of this examination will produce at least two groups, namely, those who may be permitted to engage in any activity offered in the program, and those who need to adapt or restrict their activity in some way. These large, relatively homogeneous groups are really quite heterogeneous with respect to other factors, such as individual size, strength, motor skill, and previous experience. Further classification is possible.

The classification of new groups entering a school or a class may be achieved rapidly by the use of an appropriate classification index. Measures of age, height, and weight provide the values from which a classification index can be obtained. Indices have been developed by several investigators over the years. McCloy, who had studied the work of others, carried on his own investigation of methods of classifying children and youth in relation to their participation in physical education activities. McCloy's Classification indices are:

Where A = Age
H = Height
W = Weight
Classification Index I = 20 A + 6 H + W (high school)
Classification Index II = 6 H + W (college men)
Classification Index III = 10 A + W (elementary school)[15]

The predictive value of each factor varies from age group to age group, hence the weightings also vary. Also the indices do not provide as valid a classification for high school girls as for boys. In high school and college groups age is no longer an influential variable after the age of 17. McCloy states that "the classification index, as such, is of no greater value than age alone in the classification of girls, and that age is of value as a classifier only up to and including thirteen and one half years of age."[16]

These indices have limited value when classifying for instructional purposes, although they could provide a basis for initial grouping. McCloy states that after such "preliminary classifications have been made, a number of exceptions will be found. Elements such as speed, information about the event, motor educability, and such character qualities as interest, persistence, and courage are entirely unmeasured by these devices, and variations in these and other traits will necessitate adjustments after the group has been classified as to size and maturity by the Classification Index.[17]

One may choose to classify individuals according to their developed motor abilities. Because the number of these abilities is large, the teacher will select the test, or battery of test items, which measures the qualities or abilities to be developed in his own program. Mathews states that "such testing is worthwhile, for, knowing the motor ability of the pupils, he (the teacher) may classify groups according to proficiency for participation in physical education classes. It stands to reason that if the physical education program

[15] Charles H. McCloy, *Tests and Measurements in Health and Physical Education,* F. S. Crofts and Co., 1939, p. 40.
[16] *Ibid.,* p. 54.
[17] *Ibid.,* p. 55.

is made up mostly of skill activities it is logical to place pupils of nearly the same general athletic ability together."[18] He cites an example of the application of this grouping plan:

> Let us consider for a moment the value of placing pupils of like ability in the same group in terms of teaching efficiency. Were you to conduct a single tennis class made up of beginners, intermediates, and advanced players, one lesson plan could not possibly satisfy the situation. For example, you wouldn't spend a great deal of time on basic fundamentals with the advanced players, nor would you begin discussing theory and strategy of play with the novice group. Instead, the lesson would be planned with reference to the strengths and weaknesses of the individuals. In other words, you would plan your lesson to meet the individual needs of the pupil. Thus, if you were teaching all advanced or all beginners (homogeneous groups), your instructional program would be greatly facilitated.[19]

Tests of motor ability have been devised for the various grade levels from elementary school through college. McCloy has developed a motor ability test with forms for use with boys and with girls. Cozens developed a test of general athletic ability to be used in classifying college men for physical education instruction. The results of the test serve as a guide for assigning the student to a definite type of activity.

The Scott Motor Ability test may be used to group high school and college girls for class instruction, for team competition, or to predict expected level of achievement. The test is composed of five items: (1) obstacle race; (2) basketball throw; (3) standing broad jump; (4) wall pass; (5) 4-second dash, which may be used in place of the obstacle race. A table of T-scores is available for each event. The girl's score is the average of the T-scores earned on the three or four tests taken. It should be mentioned that item (4) may be given if time permits, but that the test score may be based on the results of three events.

If one wishes to follow the school practice of grouping students according to innate ability, he may use a test of motor educability for this purpose. In 1927 Brace published a test which attempted to measure motor ability as an innate quality. Subsequent study of

[18] Donald K. Mathews, *Measurement in Physical Education,* W. B. Saunders Company, 1958, p. 117.

[19] *Ibid.,* pp. 117–118.

this test by other investigators has resulted in some modification of the items selected for administration to various school age groups, and also has brought into use the term *motor educability* as more appropriate to describe the trait being measured. In 1932 Johnson published a description of a test of motor educability to be used for grouping pupils in physical education classes. Both the Brace test and the Johnson test are of the stunt-skills type. Individuals are tested upon their ability to perform relatively unfamiliar stunts of varying degrees of difficulty and are scored upon their success in doing this in one or two trials. No practice is permitted.

Tests of motor educability are supposed to measure the capacity of the individual to learn motor skills, whether he has had experience in physical activities or not. Tests of motor ability, as they are now defined, are supposed to measure the general development of ability in the area of physical activities. Either test type can provide general ability groupings, although the one made up of motor ability items may yield the finer classification of individual abilities.

In programs of physical education which teach games, such as basketball, volleyball, and tennis, and individual activities, such as swimming, track and field, golf and the like, the teacher also may wish to group students according to the level of learning in the particular event at the time they enter the term or prepare to register for the class. Information about the previous experience of the individual in any chosen games or sport should be known before the person selects his activity, or before the teacher or administrator makes assignments to classes.

If the information is not obtained until after the student appears in class, either the grouping will have to take place within the limits of the class itself, or the program will have to have exceptional flexibility to permit the shifting of students from one class to another after the term is under way. On the other hand, in programs which allow some latitude or choice in the activities which the student may elect, it would be administratively impractical to accumulate all the information which might be needed about each student. For this reason a more general measure, such as one of motor ability, which can be given to all individuals prior to their entrance into class activities, supplies the information upon which basic groupings can be made. If it is found necessary to make additional groups within a class, tests of achievement in the game or sport itself may then be given. It is common practice to include a test of swimming ability as one of the preterm classification measures. Generally, however, individual game or sport skills are not tested prior to the opening of the school or college term.

Occasionally measures of proficiency in certain games and sports are used to determine the individual's need for further participation in physical education. The reader may refer to an earlier description of the program of physical education at the State University of Iowa. Students were tested on swimming, strength, endurance, and agility. Those who achieved at least an average score on these events are permitted to take skills tests. In the skills area the student must show a knowledge of at least six skills and be successful in performing them. If the student meets the score requirement on the physical fitness tests and shows a knowledge of six skills activities as well as ability to perform them satisfactorily, he meets the requirements of the department for physical education and is recommended for exemption from further required participation.

Although tests of general motor ability include events which are a partial measure of organic endurance and muscular strength, none determines these items as thoroughly as do tests whose purpose is the measurement of strength and physical fitness. Where the department program emphasizes these qualities, tests designed to measure strength and endurance may be incorporated into a program for classifying students. Among these measures, the Strength Index, a gross score obtained from measures of lung capacity and performance on six strength tests, has been studied more extensively than any other. There are tables of norms for boys and girls, men and women. The procedures have been described very carefully in order to eliminate chance errors. Correlations with other factors, such as general athletic ability and changes in health status, have suggested both predictive and diagnostic values to the test. There is one drawback, namely the expense of the equipment needed to administer it.

The Kraus-Weber battery of tests, which has become popular within recent years, contains six items which can be administered with a minimum of equipment. This battery has been given primarily to elementary and junior high school children. The items attempt to measure the strength of the trunk muscles and the flexibility of the hamstrings. Measures are relatively crude, but they do indicate those who are definitely weak in the trunk musculature.

As part of the program to promote an interest in fitness a battery of fitness (really physical fitness) tests was developed under the leadership of the Research Council of the American Association for Health, Physical Education and Recreation. The battery of tests is designed to test elements of fitness of both boys and girls in grades 5 through 12. The items included in the battery attempt to measure the individual's efficiency in running, throwing, strength, agility, and endurance. The ten items include the following events: (1) pull-up, (2) sit-up, (3) shuttle run, (4) standing broad jump, (5) 50-yard dash, (6) softball throw for distance, (7) 600-yard run-walk, (8-10) aquatic tests.

Several uses have been designated for the test.[20] It is suggested that the results of the test battery be used to counsel the student with respect to the kinds of physical activities in which he should take part. If the student understands his performance level on the test battery, he may more readily see what is necessary to improve his performance. "Through the use of the Personal Fitness Record, which includes a Profile Record Form, developed by the AAHPER, each pupil can study the results of his own achievement on the test. With the help of the teacher, plans can be made and activities provided to help the pupil improve his performance on the tests. Such individualization helps the pupil better understand the goals of physical fitness and learn how to overcome his weakness."[21] Grouping or classification of pupils for purposes of more direct instruction according to their needs in fitness is not emphasized.

The physical fitness battery of tests can be used for the purpose of grouping students in programs which give primary emphasis to the achievement of standards on these or similar tests. The tendency to consider physical fitness as the principal goal for a program of physical education has diminished to the point where the renewed interest in this quality has not brought a marked reversion to

[20] *See* Helen M. Starr, "How to Fit in Fitness Testing," *Journal of Health, Physical Education and Recreation,* March, 1959, pp. 18–20.

[21] *Ibid.,* p. 19. A complete description of the tests and scoring procedures is given in *Youth Fitness Manual,* American Association for Health, Physical Education and Recreation.

strictly exercise programs. Suggesting that test results be used as the basis for counseling and guidance of students with respect to their physical education program implies that the individual must achieve the higher levels of fitness within the more extensive instructional program of physical education. Furthermore, one may interpret Starr's discussion on this point as meaning that individuals whose performance levels are low are expected to work on their own to improve their ability and to develop a higher level of fitness. One can visualize an instructional program suited to the age levels of a school population as an ongoing affair within which the individual is measured on his fitness and through which he is expected to improve his level of performance, if that is needed, and to maintain an acceptable level when he has achieved it.

School and college organizations do not normally permit as much individualization as the previous discussion suggests. Also, physical fitness of some level is required if one is to be able to benefit from instruction and practice in physical activities. There will be those, however, who do not possess even this level of physical fitness. Special programs devoted principally to improving the strength, stamina, and agility of this group may be necessary before any significant learning in motor skills can be expected.

Comment on Use of Classification Procedures

Classes of instruction in games, sports, dances, and other motor activities may be better organized if students are grouped according to their knowledge and skill in the activity at the beginning of the class term. Application of measures of pupil and student status in an activity yields information about them and their needs which will help the teacher and pupils to identify their needs with respect to the course of study and to see more clearly the steps to be taken to meet them.

When the teacher or administrator thinks of using classification measures in order to group pupils and students, he will have to choose the purposes to be served by grouping procedures. That there are many arrangements from which one can choose a plan is obvious to the reader of literature on testing. How important is it to group students in particular ways for physical education? Does the student learn more effectively in an homogeneous group than in an heterogeneous one? After studying the following material, one who decides to classify his students for purposes of grouping will be aware of the limitations of classification as means for improving the educational process.

Good and Scates discuss classification as one of the descriptive methods of research. They have written a general and critical analysis of the method which serves as a basis for the teacher or administrator who is considering the arguments for and against the classification of pupils and students. Although they are writing from the viewpoint of one planning a research task, their analysis may be applied to the entire idea of homogeneous grouping, or to classification for the purpose of arranging similar groups. The portion of their discussion which is particularly valuable at this point is somewhat long for quotation, but it is not completely meaningful unless the entire passage is given.

It is perhaps commonplace to think that objects which are well known fall naturally into groups, on the basis of characteristics which are rather evident, and that these groups are essentially inherent and inflexible. Such beliefs characterized the thinking of the classical scholars, whose desire to find absolutes, such as rigid categories with no borderline cases, led them to warp their conclusions into the desired mold, in spite of abundant evidence to the contrary. There is always the tendency to let one's thinking fall into the easy pattern of the dichotomy—to see things as "all or none," as "white or black." This tendency toward absolutes was so strong that, for Plato to speak of "the good" was presumably to indicate as definite a category as to speak of persons who are between 5 feet 11 inches and 6 feet in height. There are still occasional evidences of the persistence of these notions of rigidity for even loose verbal categories, and of the fixity of typical characteristics. The very elaborateness of such classification schemes as those in botany and zoology may suggest a certain amount of finality and possibly (as with Aristotle), even an element of determinism.

Modern scholarship does not support these notions. Perhaps scientists of the present century have learned not to let their preconceptions close their eyes to exceptional cases which actually occur. For example, in biology there are probably no more sports ("spontaneous" deviations from types) today than before, but biologists have stopped ignoring them. The statistician, with his insistence on counting cases in various categories (instead of only two categories), has made it impossible in most instances to think in the old terms of discrete categories. Everything varies, and any "class" of objects in nature will be found to have so many variations, both quantitative and qualitative, that genuine difficulties arise as to what belongs in the class. We can set up neat systems of thought, but nature is not so neatly ordered.

Difficulties occur in both simple and complex classification schemes. In a classification scheme that exists on only a single level of ordination (that is, the categories are not further subdivided by subclasses, nor integrated into larger supergroups), actual cases are likely to be found which cut across any dividing lines that may be drawn—that is, if one searches widely and does not close his eyes to actual variations. Such cases may combine in all possible proportions the characters of two or more classes which may be set up, so that, theoretically, an infinity of categories would be necessary to accommodate the cases. In practical situations we may not care about making special provision for many of these borderline or overlapping cases. That is, for convenience, we may make and use fairly simple categories, such as for sex; but as a matter of principle we must recognize that exceptions occur.

Actuality is rarely as simple as our thought about it. In a questionnaire study, for example, it would seem a perfectly simple thing to count the number of questionnaires returned and the number not returned. But in such a dichotomy where will one count those returned by the post office for lack of current address? What about those returned which are only partly filled in? Such incompleteness may range by degrees from a minor omission, all the way to a return that is wholly blank. How would one count (within the frame of two classes) a questionnaire that was complete, but which gave evidence that placed the reply under suspicion? Or a questionnaire filled in by someone who was not supposed to receive it? Or one which was partly or wholly illegible? And so on. The category "number returned" may be restricted to "number of usable returns"; practically, this may be an improvement, but it will be evident that the limits of such a category are matters of judgment and, therefore, arbitrary. Such a simple set of categories may be sufficiently accurate for most purposes, but they are to some degree forced and cannot, therefore, be thought of as absolute.

Problems of the foregoing type are accentuated when categories are to be formed by dividing up a scale of magnitudes. For example, at what specific height is a person tall? At what point on the intelligence scale does a person become "bright"? At what moment does adolescence end? If limits are fixed for such categories (they would have to be defined rather definitely if used in research), it is clear that such limits would be wholly man-made whether arrived at by agreement, tradition, statistical calculation, or other means. The point is, again, that natural qualities of cases cannot be depended on for the setting of limits to categories.

It might be assumed that the problem could readily be met by making the classification scheme more complex—by providing for a hierarchy of subclasses on whatever number of levels may be called for. Such a scheme, however, only adds new problems to the old. Instead of having only the problem of where to draw limits, one now has the problem of subclasses which violate the major definitions for higher levels, usually by combining several critical qualities. If one seeks to solve the difficulty by moving the disturbing class to a higher level, he may find that other groups will not "go along"—that new problems of the same type are created. These problems are not merely matters of immature thinking; they may be logically insoluble in terms of any reasonably systematic schemes. Consider, for example, the problem (or the impossibility) of differentiating in consistent terms between plants and animals. Of course the "man on the street" can tell the difference; his knowledge does not extend to the complicating cases. But certain groups of living things exist that have (or lack) one or more of the properties accepted as essential plant properties and also one or more of the properties accepted as essential animal properties. Thus, the genus of life known as Euglena is claimed by professional botanists as being in the plant kingdom, and by professional zoologists as being in the animal kingdom. In this instance there does not seem to be any uncompromised basis for a decision one way or the other, since either decision would violate more general decisions already made.

It may be somewhat surprising to realize that there is no way to tell where the genus Euglena actually (inherently) belongs—but there is no such thing as essential objective categories. What is a plant and what is an animal is something that man determines. That is, he decides what qualities he desires to apply the term *plant* to, and what qualities he desires to apply the term *animal* to. (Apparently man's thinking at this point is too simple. It becomes obvious that not all living things can correctly be accommodated by the choice, "plant or animal"; however, under the influence of tradition based on hundreds of thousands of years of rather superficial experience with living things, man continues to try to make the convenient dichotomy do.) The important point is that these categories grow out of man's reactions to nature and reflect his (crude or refined) observations. Apart from man's thinking there are no plants or animals; the corresponding objects exist, but not in these categories. As Charles H. Judd used to say in his lectures, "There are no vertebrates in nature. There are animals having backbones, but it is man who created the class (the idea) 'Vertebrata.'" Any classification represents the investment of observations with an idea.

These statements are not meant to imply that one is free to make class concepts in any fashion he may choose. It is assumed that the researcher's concepts will be formed in the light of his disciplined perception, will be tested by further observation, and be evaluated by all the critical faculties at the disposal of scientific workers. Physical and biological scientists have invented a large number of concepts which they have had to discard, because subsequent research failed to support them. It is, however, important to realize the extent to which classes are mental; they do not exist in nature apart from man's mind; they represent man's views of the world. *Nature provides the objects, man provides the classes.*

With the foregoing background, it is possible to view classes in terms of their essential purpose, which is to serve some interest of man. The person whose thinking is swayed by a mechanical conception of objectivity will likely say, Man didn't make things similar; they exist that way. Quite true, but one cannot avoid the immediate question, Similar with respect to what? Any set of things which are similar are similar only in certain respects; in certain other respects they are different, and it may be that in all other respects they are different. One must not become so obsessed with the particular character or characters in which he is interested that he loses sight of the fact that these are, objectively, of no more importance than any other characters—than the multitude of characters on which the things are different. It is only when certain characters become the object of one's interest that these particular traits become important—important for him, and possibly for other persons. But why do these qualities become of interest to him? Particular characters are selected for attention in the belief or hope that they will serve some purpose—to order the data, to describe the cases, and so on. In other words, classification is simply *selective association,* and for this selection to have any value, it must, sooner or later, serve a purpose.

When one determines the basis of the classification he expects to use and sets the limits for each category, he determines what cases will be regarded as similar; that is, what cases will form a class. If one argues that these cases not only *will be regarded* as similar but that they actually *are* similar, the answer is that he is quite correct, for in some sense or other everything is similar to every other thing. But such generality is meaningless and unprofitable. It is only when the similarity, or association, is selective, and selective with regard to some purpose, that the similarity is of any importance. Further, it should be noted that any certain number of persons who might be placed together into a group . . . might, on some other basis, be scattered into several different groups. *Cases form a class only when looked at in a certain way.* The way one decides to look at objects or events is a matter of choice, a choice to be made in the light of the purposes to be served.[22]

One may summarize the ideas and the schemes for grouping in a few short paragraphs. Of first importance is the obvious fact that knowing students' abilities, interests, previous learnings, personal traits, maturity levels, and whatever other pertinent facts may exist helps the administrator and the teacher plan for more effective learning through the school curriculum. Classification devices, ability and capacity measures, tests of learned skills, inventories, check lists, rating schemes, questionnaires and other instruments which may be used to secure the necessary information can be used to learn about the nature of the pupil. Before taking the final step in an important decision, one must consider the child and youth as a single entity, not as a series of test scores or checks on a rating sheet.

The purpose of grouping is to facilitate learning by placing together pupils who have selected characteristics in common, but this does not necessarily achieve the major goals of education, because homogeneity actually is not assured through such groupings. This may be called an imposed grouping, because the basis is something less than the total complex of the individual. On the other hand, placing together students who have consciously expressed similar needs and are ready to learn how to meet them may facilitate learning at a more uniform rate and more nearly realize the potential of each individual. Because no class can be considered completely homogeneous, any grouping procedure will require the teacher to concern himself with the individuals, because they vary one from another in spite of being similar in selected qualities.

Physical education teachers and administrators often face extremely difficult teaching situations because pupils are assigned to their classes on the basis of convenience to the remainder of the school. A high school teacher may have students in one class ranging in age from fourteen to eighteen years. In other qualities these students will vary even more. Putting together students who differ widely in capacities, interests, and previous learning does not pro-

[22] Quoted with permission of the publisher from Carter V. Good and Douglas E. Scates, *Methods of Research,* Appleton-Century-Crofts, Inc., 1954, pp. 496–500.

vide the easiest nor the best learning situation. Where such a situation exists, however, organization of the class into groups, utilization of the maturity and skills of the older and more advanced students to help the less able and younger ones, planning with the class and the groups on the important goals and on the effective use of the instructional and practice time, and skillful course planning and teaching can create a favorable learning situation. One should add that heterogeneity does not necessarily mean large classes. If classes are large and heterogeneous, the need for more than one teacher is imperative in the lower grades. In high schools and colleges student leaders may assist in the conduct of the instructional and practice period, but they should not be expected to do more than assist, nor should they fill the need for additional professionally prepared personnel.

TIME ALLOTTED TO THE TEACHING OF PHYSICAL EDUCATION

In the elementary and secondary schools the minimum time assigned to a subject usually is included in the state's regulations governing the curriculum of the schools. For physical education this may be given as the number of minutes per week which each pupil or student is to spend in physical education classes. In 1948–1949, the total per pupil enrolled for all grades and for cities of all sizes was 122 minutes per week. The range was from 97 to 133 minutes. These figures represent actual time devoted to physical education.[23]

If the recommendation of a daily period of physical education for each pupil is followed, the average class length may be too short to allow for the achievement of worthwhile outcomes according to the time indicated in the preceding paragraph. To provide a class period of desirable length for teaching purposes, the administrator will have to plan on fewer periods weekly. If the school allows 120 minutes per week, the administrator can plan for three periods of 40 minutes each or two periods of 60 minutes each. Both arrangements are used, but neither meets the minimum of one period per day for each pupil in the school.

Brownell states that "a vigorous physical education program for

[23] National Education Association, "Personnel and Relationships in School Health, Physical Education, and Recreation," *Research Bulletin,* October, 1950, p. 92.

elementary school children is essential to normal physical, emotional and social development," and that the trend toward "ever increasing mechanization and urbanization of modern living" is placing greater responsibility for this development upon the school. "The school must provide some part of the two to four hours of vigorous physical activity that is recognized as essential for each child daily."[24]

One starts his planning with a standard in mind. With respect to the time required for adequate instruction and practice in physical education activities, the standard is one hour per day as a minimum. Junior and senior high school youth should have more. The actual arrangement of periods and their length will be determined, however, by the schedule which is followed by the entire school.

At the college and university level the class hour usually is fifty minutes with ten minutes allowed for changing classes. It is possible to offer single or double period classes within the framework of the college class hour schedule. In the majority of institutions the classes in basic instruction meet three times per week. Variations found in a small percentage of the colleges are two, four and five periods per week. If the class periods in physical education are treated as instructional hours in which the students learn skills and other knowledge which motivates them to participate actively in out-of-class time, the three hours of instruction may provide sufficient time to accomplish the important goals of physical education. If all the student's physical activity occurs during the three class periods, the time allotted is insufficient.

The class period in physical education usually allows time for the student to take a shower following activity. The shower bath following a period of exercise is not only refreshing but an important aspect of the physical education experience. Because of the time required for showering and dressing by the student, the class period in physical education should not be less than fifty minutes in duration. Longer periods may be more desirable only if the frequency of student participation in activity is not decreased to a point where each week seems like a new beginning.

Recommendations that students take showers following exercise

[24] Clifford Lee Brownell, *Report to the Profession,* a report given at the Opening Session of the 58th Convention, American Association for Health, Physical Education and Recreation, New York, April 19, 1954 (mimeographed).

apply to both sexes. The use of the shower after exercise is part of the learning which goes on under the skilled teacher. The teacher, therefore, plans for the development of an attitude which favors taking a shower after exercise.

A textbook cannot settle the matter of class schedule. The administrator must establish a period long enough to accomplish some worthwhile goal. He should also secure frequent periods of instruction and practice, especially in the high school and lower grades, because the need for activity is great both as to amount at any one time and as to frequency and regularity.

PROGRESSIVE GRADING OF INSTRUCTIONAL MATERIALS

The school system or college faces the problem of providing for the continued growth of its students in the material of education. To accomplish this growth, courses of study are prepared for subjects which intend to advance the students' learning at any level over his learning at a previous level. In general, one can say that educational programs must carry the student to new levels of knowledge and achievement to justify their cost in money, time, teacher and student effort, facilities, and other items of expense.

Among his fundamental principles for planning the curriculum Oberteuffer states that "the curriculum should be planned to allow for progression in learning, with a minimum of repetition of activities . . . . It is to be a *learning* experience in which, through the medium of motor activities, a child is moved along from one stage in his development to another more advanced stage farther on. He need not spend his time running in place, academically speaking. He should get somewhere."[25] Oberteuffer further emphasizes that progression in learning is an essential of education. "If physical education is to be fully educational in character, it must seek—and get—progression, using repetition only when it is helpful in learning and for recreational purposes."[26]

Progression in the elementary and high schools relates to age and grade changes of the pupils. Arranging the curriculum of physical education so as to provide increasingly richer and more difficult

[25] Oberteuffer, *op. cit.,* pp. 291–292.
[26] *Ibid.,* 292.

materials for the pupils as they proceed from grade to grade is accomplished by selecting resources which are suited to an age level or which have elements that can be taught in sequence, leading to the learning of the complex, complete activity. Primary age children may learn singing games and basic rhythmical movements, such as skipping and hopping, and then proceed to simple dances. Older children will learn more difficult dances and steps leading to the square and social dances of high school and adult ages.

Likewise, games and drills involving learning and practice in skills fundamental to sports will be a part of the curriculum for the younger children. Games of low organization are suitable for older elementary children. More highly organized games are taught in junior high school, especially with the view to introducing new skills and to acquiring the personal and social attitudes and behaviors essential for satisfying team play.

Because children at every age differ one from another in physical, social, and personal maturity, and because the school curriculum is expected to recognize these individual differences, a curriculum progression either will be arranged with the greatest possible flexibility to meet these individual needs or will be arranged to suit the median characteristics of the group, with allowance being made for those individuals who vary greatly from the median.

If the physical education curriculum is related to a core school curriculum or is organized into units around a central theme, progression is attained when the themes for the units fit the interests and needs of the age groups and contribute to the achievement of the objectives of the school. The unit type of organization allows for greater adaptability to the individuals in the group. It does not, however, lend itself well to a closely organized progression from the first grade through the high school.

Although college students at the beginning of their freshman year are not alike in their maturity, their qualities are similar enough so that planning for progression according to age and grade changes does not seem feasible. The college program, too, must be educational and should avoid uncalled for repetition of subject matter. At the same time it will necessarily, utilize activities which have been included in high school programs. Progression in the college, therefore, is completely related to the objectives which the college and the department of physical education have chosen. The variety of maturity levels which the entering students present with respect to the objectives will direct the selection of program content for purposes of establishing progression in learning. Their ages, except as students vary in age away from the mean for their class group, and their grades (classes) in college will be of little significance in setting up the progression.

College physical education courses should be planned in the same manner as any collegiate course of instruction in any subject. The purposes to be achieved are to be clearly set forth and the means used to achieve them described. Progression then is determined by choosing the order in which the parts of the course are to be presented. Those parts which must be mastered before the student can move ahead will appear first in the course.

Organizing subject matter into a series based on the assumption that all individuals of a certain age or grade will be ready and able to learn a designated block of knowledge presents limitations to learning. On the other hand, establishing the minimum learnings for each age or grade group assures that there will be adequate achievement by the majority of pupils in each group. It will also serve to direct attention toward the objectives throughout the school.

In both schools and colleges the arrangement of subject matter should be that which most effectively leads to the achievement of objectives. Such a principle can be practiced only if there is frequent and meaningful evaluation of student achievement and of teaching effectiveness. Without this kind of evaluation, progressively arranged subject matter may be useless as far as the pupils are concerned.

The administrator will have his complete program written in the form of a curriculum. The objectives of the program, their relationship to the objectives of the school or the institution, the resources which are available, methods of evaluation which may be applied, and suggested emphasis upon methods of teaching will be a part of the document. In addition, he will have a course of study, or syllabus, prepared for each grade, year, and subject. The syllabus will state the objectives to be achieved, the subject matter and a suggested order of presentation, suggested methods of teaching, and evaluative procedures.

The individual teacher, working with a syllabus and with a known group of students, can make his daily lesson plans suit both the major objectives of the syllabus and the particular capacities and needs of his group. Such modification is necessary if teaching is to have meaning for the group which the teacher faces. Both curricula and syllabi require frequent review and revision. The administrator and his staff will see to this.

Because physical education is usually a required subject in the curriculums of schools and colleges, all pupils and students, except those specifically exempt, are expected to complete the courses satisfactorily. The administrator will receive requests from time to time to modify the requirement for an individual or a category of individuals. The usual types of requests are discussed in the following section.

SPECIAL MATTERS RELATING TO ADMINISTRATION OF THE INSTRUCTIONAL PROGRAM

The administrator of physical education will encounter the following matters for which he will be expected to establish policy: requests for exemption on account of military service, requests for exemption because of age, evaluation of transfer credit, waiver of the requirement by examination, credit for physical education based on intercollegiate athletic participation, and administration of the physical education requirement for graduation. All except the last are related principally to the college program of physical education. The following discussion describes the nature of the problem which the administrator faces and suggests policies which he may institute to deal with each situation.

REQUEST FOR EXEMPTION BECAUSE OF MILITARY SERVICE

Identifying the aims of military training with those of physical education has been characteristic of a few universities and the thinking of some educators. Such thinking is not common today and probably exists only where physical education programs themselves follow the pattern of basic training for military service. During World War II college and university programs were modified to include more vigorous physical conditioning activities for men about to be inducted into military service. The value of these modifications for purposes of military preparation was largely lost as the preservice male populations diminished almost to zero during the latter years of the war. At the same time the American Association for Health, Physical Education and Recreation developed a program known as the Victory Corps Physical Fitness program which was aimed at improving the physical fitness of high school and younger youth.

When the ex-servicemen began returning to the colleges and universities after the war was ended, they were treated in several ways with respect to their physical education requirements. In those institutions which had maintained their programs of physical education as an integral part of the total educational program of the student, the returning ex-serviceman was treated as any student who either was entering college for the first time or was entering with previous study which could be offered for credit toward his college degree. His military experience was evaluated the same as the study and experience of a student transferring from another institution of collegiate rank.

Furthermore, instead of treating physical education as something to be avoided if at all possible, several institutions presented their programs as opportunities to meet special needs of many ex-servicemen who were seeking physical rehabilitation, active recreation, or social and personality reorientation. The student was judged according to his previous learnings and his individual needs, which could be fulfilled, in part at least, through his participation in physical education courses.

For some unknown reason, physical education was accorded a different status from other subjects by a number of universities and by the American Council on Education. The ex-serviceman not only had his requirement in physical education waived completely, but he often was given college credit in physical education because of his military service. No real justification existed on educational grounds for these actions. Probably the action of the American Council on Education in recommending that "physical education experiences during military service of at least six months duration" be accepted in lieu of requirements in physical education and health education at both the high school and freshman-sophomore levels of college influenced colleges and universities to grant both exemption from the requirement and credit for the military experiences.

As early as 1945 the College Physical Education Association took action to offset the effect of the above recommendation. A substitute recommendation was prepared and sent by letter to presidents, examiners, and registrars of American colleges and universities, as well as to college health and physical education administrators. The substitute recommendation sought to establish equivalence as the basis for college credit and to urge colleges to recognize the individual needs of returning servicemen.

Subsequently the College Committee on Physical Education and Athletics, representing the College Physical Education Association, the National Collegiate Athletic Association, and the American Association for Health, Physical Education and Recreation, issued a statement concerning not only military service, but also collegiate military training programs and physical education. The full text of this statement follows:

1. It should be clear to all in college physical education and in colleges generally, that military science and physical education are not synonymous. They are two different programs employing different techniques, seeking different outcomes, and existing for different purposes. Leaders in both areas recognize these differences.

2. On campuses where both programs are offered there should be developed a spirit of cordiality and cooperation without infringement, precedence, or domination of one over the other.

3. The College Committee fully subscribes to the recommendation of many other groups to the effect that a course in military science is not a proper substitution for physical education.

4. Likewise, the College Committee strongly urges faculties to establish the principle of equivalence when accrediting military experience with reference to physical education. This problem loomed large following VJ Day and the Committee feels that some considerable injustice was done many veterans by eliminating them from recreational or therapeutic physical education so necessary to their continuing adjustment to the college or community environment. The best results were obtained on those campuses where credit was given for physical education as it was for other areas of learning; that is, on the basis of experiences in the services equivalent to the kind and quality of instruction receivable on the campus. The Committee recommends that where blanket or indiscriminate credit for physical

education was given just because the student was in military service, the practice be now discontinued and experience in physical education from any future military service be evaluated for quality the same as experience in other fields.[27]

The preceding statements are part of a longer report concerned with physical education at a time when the Korean War was developing. Earlier, the Third National Conference on Health in Colleges had included the following statement and recommendation in its report:

> The policy of excusing veterans from physical education or giving them blanket credit for military experience has been a serious mistake in the postwar period. The nature and emphasis of programs in the armed forces were not comparable to the objectives of modern physical education programs. Of even more significance, for purposes of this report, is a recognition of the need for continuing experiences in physical education which will maintain the health and total development of veteran students.
>
> Therefore, it is recommended that a policy of evaluating military physical education for equivalence should be established and limited credit granted accordingly. Where blanket credit has been given, the policy should be voided as soon as possible. In other respects, requirements for veterans should remain the same as for non-veterans.[28]

In the mind of the professionally prepared physical education administrator, physical education has its own goals, content, and methods, and these are not interchangeable, not even similar in most instances, with those of the military services. The administrator, knowing this, must be sure that others in school and college administration understand it, too. One way to transmit the ideas is to state publicly one's goals and to demonstrate through his program both the content and methods used to achieve the goals. There is no competition with the military services in this matter. Officers placed in charge of training men, whether it be at military installations or on a college campus, are not seeking to teach physical education. Their own subject matter is complex and elaborate and requires all the time allotted to them to teach it.

[27] College Committee on Physical Education and Athletics, "College Physical Education for Peace and Defence," *Fifty-Third Annual Proceedings,* College Physical Education Association, 1950, pp. 134–135.

[28] Report of the Third National Conference on Health in Colleges, *A Health Program for Colleges,* National Tuberculosis Association, 1947, p. 60.

In summary, one can state that neither exemption from required courses in physical education and health instruction, nor the granting of blanket credit for these subjects on the basis of military training and service should be allowed, except in those instances where the military experience is equivalent in kind and quality to that offered by the school or college.

REQUESTS FOR EXEMPTION BECAUSE OF AGE

In the past a number of the colleges and universities have exempted students over a certain age from the physical education requirement and have permitted them to substitute credits earned in other courses for those ordinarily earned through physical education courses. Twenty-five years ago the number of students receiving this exemption was small. Changes in the college population since 1950 have altered the magnitude of the problem and made it necessary to review the older policies which have been followed in this matter.

Men returning to college from military service in World War II usually were older than prewar graduates. Men and women who had had little interest in higher education prior to their military service learned new values for college education and enrolled in colleges at the close of the war. The financial benefits offered to ex-service personnel made it possible for many of them to go to college. Today women whose families have grown to the age when they are in school a greater part of the day are seeking to complete their education in preparation for a vocation. Other factors also are acting to increase the number of women in this group of college students. Finally, there are those who started to work before entering college, or after only one or two years in college, and now, because they need the advanced education and can afford it, are returning. The number of ex-servicemen has diminished, but the other groups maintain their numbers. It is clear, of course, that the admissions policy of an institution will affect the number of older students.

The question is whether persons older than 23 or 24 should be expected to meet college requirements in physical education. In the past some institutions automatically waived the requirement for anyone twenty-five years of age or older! Is there any age at which the person should be exempt from the requirement?

The answer should be given not in terms of chronological age but according to the educational value of the courses. It is clear, but often overlooked, that the individual who enrolls in a college agrees to meet the conditions specified for the degree. He cannot avoid this fact. If physical education is stated as a part of the college curriculum, and if the courses offered can contribute to his education, then the student must include them in this course of study. Age alone has no particular bearing upon the matter except as it modifies the individual's goals and needs. The major necessity is to be certain that requiring the individual to take part in physical education is furthering his college education.

While individual consideration is important in planning physical education course placement at all age levels, it is essential that assignments and requirements for the older adult be made individually. Although the ultimate placement may be in a regular class activity, and usually will be, the decision to enter that activity can be arrived at satisfactorily only through individual conference. The administrator does not force individual conferences upon all adults, because many of them will be only too pleased to follow the usual program pattern. One must provide for the individual who seeks an exception and must act according to the particular circumstances.

What are some reasons why older adults do not want to enroll in physical education courses?

1. They do not understand the program and what it is trying to do. They think of it as a children's program. Some believe that housework, walking to the bus or the garage, or washing the car occasionally gives them the exercise they need. Some texts used in freshman hygiene courses repeat this unsupported belief!

2. Adults, especially those in their thirties or older, are frightened at the prospect of being placed in classes with younger adults. If they have not been active in games and sports in their earlier years, they fear being embarrassed by their motor inabilities in the class with younger persons. The fact that they take all their other classes with younger persons does not seem to affect this feeling about physical education. These people can be reassured by examples of previous adults who have taken part in the program with real pleasure, and by the fact that younger people are too busy trying to overcome their own inadequacies to observe anyone else's performance. This

adult emotional factor cannot be ignored, however, and the initial physical education experiences must allay rather than reinforce it.

3. The adult is in a hurry to finish and does not wish to "waste time" on physical education. This attitude grows out of unfamiliarity with a sound program. The idea of hurrying through college is not widespread. Where students may accelerate their progress, definite procedures are open to them. Physical education, too, can be part of such an accelerated program, with the student receiving the same consideration as he does in other courses.

4. The adult feels that exercise is not important to his age group. At one time, of course, there was a firm belief that after the age of forty one should do no exercise beyond that required to move the body from one chair to another. This view, which the physical education profession never accepted, and by example constantly disproved, has been completely cast aside today. Evidence continues to accumulate that men and women not only feel and live better, but actually are healthier, when they continue regular exercise throughout their lives. Obviously, exercise must be chosen according to the person's capacity to engage in it. The dictum of "no exercise after forty" is dead.

Physical education programs at the college level must suit the needs of the individuals attending the college and at the same time fulfill an educational function in the college. If these conditions are met, the older adult will find that he, too, can secure valuable educational benefits from his physical education courses just as he does from his other subjects. For the adult in college, who is likely to be highly vocationally minded, physical education becomes one of his more liberal studies.

TRANSFER CREDIT

The term *transfer credit,* refers to the credit value of courses which students have taken in other institutions of similar grade level. These students who transfer from one school to another within the same state will find similarity if not identity in the below-college grades in the curricula of the various schools. Where differences do exist, students who are deficient in the course requirements will be expected to make them up by staying in school for a longer period or by going to summer school. Students who move from one state to another may find distinct differences in requirements for graduation. Where physical education is involved, the administrator should work out with the school administration a policy which will guide the evaluation of achievement records that students present when they apply for admission to the new school.

Colleges regularly admit a sizable number of students who have begun their collegiate education at other institutions. Because college requirements for graduation vary widely with respect to specific courses, and because courses with similar numbers and titles may not be alike, the evaluation of student transcripts is an important duty of the departmental administrator. Courses in physical education which the student has taken elsewhere must be evaluated with the same care as courses in any other subject. The following items should be taken into account in evaluating a transcript of courses taken in physical education. One compares the courses submitted with those given in his own institution in terms of purposes, content, class time allotted to the courses, and college credit awarded. Where courses taken elsewhere by the student are essentially identical with courses given by the college to which he is applying, full credit can be given for his previous work. Where the courses are not sufficiently similar and they make little or no contribution to the goals of the institution to which the student is applying, no credit should be given. In the latter case, when a student has completed course work which is accepted as being of collegiate calibre but does not meet the requirements of the institution to which he is transferring, blanket credit toward the degree may be awarded without in any way affecting the course requirements which he must meet.

A student may have completed courses equal in number to those required by the institution to which he is transferring without meeting specific subject matter requirements. For example, an institution may require credit for four semesters of physical education toward graduation, with one of the courses to be in swimming or dancing. A student presenting credentials from another institution may have completed four courses in physical education without having taken one in either swimming or dancing. The departmental administrator can award the student credit for three semesters and require the fourth one in the specified subject at his institution, or he may award credit for three courses assigned specifically to courses in his institution, give blanket credit toward graduation for the fourth semester, and require the student to complete the specified course prior to graduation.

Careful evaluation of transcripts is important, because students may come from an institution with credit for several semesters of work in physical education. Upon investigation of the record, and occasionally in conversation with the student, the administrator learns that the student earned his credits on one intercollegiate athletic team or that he spent three semesters in the same recreational activity. Unless these experiences are bases for credit in the new institution, an appropriate adjustment must be made in the student's requirements for graduation.

Because college transfer credit is assigned to specific courses in the institution, and because course numbers and titles on transcripts rarely are adequate course descriptions, the administrator will have to secure additional information about courses offered at other institutions. One source is the bulletin of the institution, which gives official course descriptions and credits. Another source is the student himself, who can supply brief descriptions of the actual work of the course. One can get not only this kind of information but also a fairly clear idea of the quality of instruction and the standing which the course has, at least in the minds of the students. If one is well acquainted with the institutions in his region, or on a national scale, he can use this knowledge to augment that which he gains from bulletins and from students' comments.

One other aspect is the credit value given to courses by the original institution. If the institution grants positive credit, there is no additional problem. If, however, the institution requires physical education for graduation, but does not grant credit for it—a kind of negative credit idea—the administrator may, if the courses are equivalent to those offered in his institution, exempt the student from the parts of the requirement which he has met, but may or may not award credit, as he sees fit. Because the institution which holds the student to a physical education requirement without credit usually has a total credit requirement for graduation lower than that of the institution which grants credit for physical education courses, in a sense that institution is granting credit for the courses.

College credits may be in semester units or quarter units. A semester credit is the equivalent of one and one-half quarter credits. A quarter credit is the equivalent of two thirds of a semester credit.

College credit can be awarded only where there is a basis for assigning transfer credit. One cannot create credits unless previous work has been performed. As a rule the term *previous work* means regular collegiate level courses.

Finally, the college to which the student is applying is not obligated to award credit for work taken elsewhere. In considering the educational welfare of the student it may decide to grant him neither credit nor waiver of requirements on the basis of previous college work. The local institution has complete jurisdiction over the granting of its credits and degrees.

WAIVER OF REQUIREMENT BY EXAMINATION

The use of achievement or proficiency examinations to determine the degree to which a student meets the requirements of parts of the curriculum leading to a degree, although not uniformly applied, is well established in college and university practice. Institutions may, as did the University of Chicago, rely heavily upon this kind of examination procedure to determine the student's eligibility for admission, his standing at entrance, and his progress toward the degree. Placement tests, which are a form of proficiency examination, are used widely by colleges for purposes of directing students into courses for which their previous preparation has fitted them. Where these courses are more advanced than those for which he normally would have registered, the student has in effect met part of his collegiate requirements by examination.

Physical education departments use proficiency tests to a limited degree. In a report made by Hunsicker[29] in 1953, eight percent of the institutions studied granted credit or waived the requirement in physical education on the basis of satisfactory performance on a proficiency test. Generally the purpose of proficiency testing is to

[29] P. A. Hunsicker, "A Survey of the Service Physical Education Programs in American Colleges and Universities," *Proceedings,* College Physical Education Association, 1954, p. 30.

acknowledge the learning which the individual has made, in order to avoid his duplicating course work in which he is already proficient and to accelerate his progress toward the college degree. Oberteuffer states as his first principle that "the curriculum should be planned to allow for progression in learning, with a minimum of repetition of activities." He emphasizes further that "a repetitive experience is hardly worthy of academic credit year after year."[30] At the college level students enter with backgrounds of experience in physical education. Those who have achieved through their precollege experience part or all of the goals of the college physical education program may be given special consideration with respect to continued participation in this phase of their education.

One of the features of the program at the State University of Iowa, which was described earlier, is the opportunity given the student to fulfill all his physical education requirements by taking and passing several tests. In this instance the student who achieves an average or better than average score on the physical fitness tests and who demonstrates knowledge and skill in six activities as designated by the department may be recommended for exemption from the physical education requirement.

Columbia College developed a similar kind of program to meet the special circumstances of the returning ex-servicemen following World War II.[31] Ohio University set up a program of proficiency testing for entering students as a basis for selecting those students whose requirement could be waived.[32]

The use of proficiency testing as a means for giving improved direction to the student's educational effort makes sense. It can be relatively simple and direct, as in the case of the program at the State University of Iowa. Questions are raised about the procedure, however, where the goals of the program include accomplishments in addition to motor skills, endurance, strength, and agility. One group of physical education teachers and administrators included continuing physical activity among the values

[30] Delbert Oberteuffer, *op. cit.*, pp. 291, 292.

[31] Harold E. Lowe, "An Adjustment of the Physical Education Requirement for Veterans at Columbia College-Columbia University," *Proceedings*, College Physical Education Association, 1947, p. 53.

[32] Carl Nessley, "The Required Physical Education Program at Ohio University," *Proceedings*, College Physical Education Association, 1948, pp. 23–29.

to be gained through the physical education program. One may ask how frequently the student will engage in physical activity if upon entering college he becomes exempt from further participation because of his achievements in skill and physical fitness factors?

Another question concerns the level of proficiency testing. Are teachers concerned with a minimum level, or should they hope to lead students to levels above the minimum? If the student who has achieved this minimum level is exempt from further participation in physical education, is he adequately educated in the field of physical education? The advocate of proficiency testing may well point out that the level of acceptable proficiency is set at the discretion of the testing department. This is quite correct. Once one has decided to set levels above a so-called minimum, he finds that the steps between this point and real excellence are vague and he must establish a much higher level of proficiency. If this is done, those students who can achieve it will be so few that the students as a group may feel that registration in the courses is to be preferred to taking the tests. Certainly establishing proficiency levels is more than a statistical procedure.

A third question concerns the narrowness of the proficiency tests themselves. Comprehensive tests which will suit the needs of many colleges are not available. As previously indicated, the proficiency tests now in use measure accomplishment in certain physical fitness items and in motor skills. If the administrator wishes to learn about the student's achievement as a team player, or about his social and ethical practices in sports and games, he faces an obstacle which cannot be easily surmounted at the present time. Perhaps, though, this difficulty is not so much a criticism of proficiency testing as an expression of deficiency in both this phase of testing and teaching in the basic instructional program. In any event, the proficiency tests now in use do not cover all the professed objectives of physical education.

Hughes states the problem as follows: "Success in passing a proficiency examination or achievement test in . . . [several] listed areas meets only one of the major objectives of physical education, that is, the development of recreational skills. Students who pass such a test may have failed to develop fitness, or a play attitude, or sportsmanship." Instead of exempting students from further participation in physical education, Hughes suggests that "they should not . . . be excused from the program just because they have developed skills. The highly skilled students may be permitted wider choice in electing activities, but this means they are required to elect something and to participate."[33]

If proficiency tests are to be used at any point along the educational path, they should be developed carefully with respect to the purposes of the department and the institution and with the best interests of the student in mind. They should be administered thoughtfully, so that there are provisions for the student to continue his education more effectively. The idea of such testing should not be to "get rid of the student," but to make his work in the institution more meaningful.

CREDIT FOR INTERSCHOLASTIC AND INTERCOLLEGIATE ATHLETIC PARTICIPATION

In high schools, where physical education is a regular part of each student's program, and in colleges which require courses in physical education as part of the student's degree program, the question arises as to whether participation in interscholastic and intercollegiate athletics should receive credit. The following statement may suggest a general policy to govern the matter. Where programs of interscholastic and intercollegiate athletics are conducted primarily and principally for educational purposes, where the various teams are instructed by professionally prepared teachers of physical education, and where the policies governing the programs demonstrate that such programs are integral parts of the school and college, these programs should be treated as any other course in physical education.

The nature of athletics and the manner in which students take part present several special problems. In the first place, a student who starts on a team in his first year may play on the same team each season throughout his career in the institution. Although he may improve his performance each year, in a sense he is repeating much of what he learned in his first season. Credit should not be

[33] W. L. Hughes and Esther French, *op. cit.,* p. 69.

given for participation in the same sport for more than one season of play.

Departments of physical education which require variety in the courses which students take and progression within subject areas will present the athletic team member with the possibility of enrolling in a course in the basic instructional program during the season of his athletic sport. It is desirable to avoid this situation if scheduling flexibility permits. In high schools there seems to be no alternative but for the student to take part in both courses. The college student may alternate his courses in basic instruction with the sport season, although for sports whose seasons cover parts of two semesters there is no way to avoid dual enrollments for one semester at least. No apology needs to be made for this situation. Student participation upon athletic teams is usually voluntary. There is not reason to expect courses in physical education to give way simply to accommodate either the individual student or the coach.

If the department has developed proficiency tests in which it has confidence, it may encourage the student who is on an athletic team to meet selected objectives by demonstrating satisfactory proficiency. Let it be repeated that actions based upon such testing need careful planning to be appropriate to the educational purposes of the institution.

Athletic team experience which is to be accepted as a course in physical education should be judged as any other learning experience. Procedures used to evaluate students' work in basic instructional courses and to assign marks should be applied to students' work on athletic teams.

In the interests of the student the department should not permit his participation in a few sports to fulfill the entire requirement in physical education. Perhaps it is more meaningful to say that all the objectives of a sound program of physical education cannot be met by the experiences which a student has in two or three intercollegiate or interscholastic sports.

Colleges which have a department of athletics separate from the department of physical education encounter a problem of coordination in the matter of credit for athletic participation. This kind of separate organization for athletics usually suggests emphasis upon athletics as entertainment or as income-producing activities. It is doubtful whether student participation on teams maintained for these purposes fits the definition of educational endeavor for which credit should be awarded. The administrator of physical education will decide the policy to be followed and take the steps to implement it in his particular situation.

Sound policy governing the granting of credit for participation in interscholastic and intercollegiate athletics can be formulated if the administrator will keep educational values in the forefront. He must insist upon the significance of the physical education goals and the importance of having all students achieve them. Inter-institutional athletics have a way of dominating the scene unless one holds to the conviction that this type of athletic program is only part, not the entire physical education program. This viewpoint must be professed and supported by the administrator and his staff.

PHYSICAL EDUCATION REQUIREMENTS FOR GRADUATION

The discussion of this item concerns problems created by students who do not follow the usual pattern for meeting course requirements for graduation. In every institution there will be a few students who, for one or more reasons, reach their senior year, even their final senior term, with deficiencies in areas of required work. The examples given in the discussion which follows represent common situations.

Some students are indifferent to physical education or prefer to avoid the courses, if at all possible. These students may postpone meeting the required work until their final year, when they find that they now have three semesters of required courses to complete within one or, at the most, two semesters. What can the administrator do in answer to the student's appeal for permission to take all the work in one semester, or to be excused from a portion of the requirement?

Enrolling in more than one course in physical education in any term defeats one of the purposes of participation, namely to maintain regular activity over an extended period of time. On the other hand, an able student can learn the subject matter of more than one course in physical education if he wishes to spend the time and effort demanded. To condense three semesters of work into one reaches a point of absurdity, however, and weakens the standing of the course. In other words, the courses should be of such a calibre that a student cannot successfully complete that much work in one term if he also is carrying a normal schedule of other courses.

The student may attend summer session to complete a part of his requirement. Also, he may delay graduation until he has fulfilled his obligations to the school or college. In the latter case he may be permitted to enroll in an approved course in another institution if he plans to work in another locality. Finally, if there is some basis in his previous organized educational experience to justify a proficiency examination, it may be possible to waive part of the requirement without credit. If the student does not need the credit for graduation, he may be helped by this means.

Obviously, the best solution is for the student to complete his required work prior to the date for his graduation. If the student has not done this, he should be declared ineligible for graduation until the work is completed.

There is the student who fails his course in physical education in his last semester. The only decision in this case is not to allow him to graduate. He may complete his work by attending for an extra term, either in summer or during the regular school year. A proficiency examination in the subject matter of the course should not be permitted.

The thorough teacher observes the status of his students regularly throughout the term and concerns himself with those who are in difficulty before they reach a point where failure is almost certain. The willing student can be helped. The uncooperative one who really earns his failing grade cannot be given faculty approval for graduation.

Every institution has students who are plagued periodically by ill health or who are temporarily handicapped to the point where they must be kept out of physical education for limited periods of time. The administrator must decide whether or not to waive part or all of the requirement for these students. These students may not be able to take part even in an adapted program. The decision as to the standing of the student should be made in light of the total situation: the amount of time involved, the physical condition of the student, his needs with respect to physical education course outcomes, and the values of the physical education program for him. Wherever it is possible to do so, both the student and the administrator should anticipate the problems to be faced and make tentative plans to meet them. The administrator should note on a student record card or other form the nature of the proposed actions to be taken in the future.

In summary, one can say that physical education requirements for graduation must be fulfilled. Any adjustments or modifications are made according to generally accepted institutional policy.

BIBLIOGRAPHY

Esslinger, A. A., "The Program at West Point," *Journal of the American Association for Health, Physical Education and Recreation,* May, 1951, p. 20.

An adequate description of the physical education program including objectives, schedule of activities, and an expression of the attitude of the Academy officers toward the program.

Stanley, D. K., and Norma Leavitt, eds., "Basic Issues," *Journal of Health, Physical Education, Recreation,* February, 1960.

Helpful answers are given to the question, "How may physical education programs best be adapted to the problems created by too many students and not enough teachers or facilities?"

Trump, J. Lloyd, "An Image of a Future Secondary School, Health, Physical Education, and Recreation Program," *Journal of Health, Physical Education, Recreation,* January, 1961, p. 15.

Suggestions on the organization of instruction indicate the changes which administrators and teachers must contemplate as they plan for their own future programs.

Weiss, Raymond A., *et al.,* "The Contributions of Physical Activity to Human Well-Being," *The Research Quarterly,* May, 1960.

Wessel, Janet A., John A. Friedrich, and Dorothy A. Kerth, "A New Approach in the College Required Program," *Journal of Health, Physical Education, Recreation,* November, 1960.

Chapter 8

MEASUREMENT, EVALUATION, AND GRADING

THE TEACHERS and the administrator who have prepared a program of instruction in physical education will desire to know how fully the program is accomplishing their purposes. The principal participant, the student, will have his own goals which he has chosen from the opportunities presented by the program of instruction. His accomplishment is the measure of program effectiveness.

MEASURING PROGRESS OF THE STUDENT TOWARD HIS GOALS

Reference to the participation of students in the selection of goals to guide their study and learning was made earlier. There are many ways in which goals may be reached. Because the student desires to select the steps which he needs to take, there is every reason to encourage his participation in defining the steps which he wishes to follow.

Measurement and appraisal are necessary to help the student define his goals clearly and to test his progress toward them. Measurement of individual standing in traits affected by physical activity provides the starting point from which the student projects his needs. Periodic measurement determine the rate of change as well as the direction taken by the student as he pursues the physical education learning experiences. The teacher, or the administrator and his staff, supplies the matrix of learning opportunities within which the student moves from his initial stage to later chosen ones.

The purpose of this section upon measurement is to study the kinds of measuring or evaluative devices which can be used to describe the student's initial status and the changes resulting from his participation in an educational program. This section is not a review of tests and measurements in physical education. For further study in this more extensive and specialized area the student is referred to the list of texts appearing in the bibliography at the end of this chapter.

THE NECESSITY FOR MEASUREMENT

Teachers of physical education, as well as teachers in other subject areas, are often reluctant to use tests. Comments that "they take too much time," or that "no good tests exist," or that "the results don't mean anything anyway," are given as reasons for not using measuring instruments freely in the teaching of physical education. According to the authorities in the field, none of these reasons is valid. Clarke states:

> The scientific or measurement approach to program planning is the only way that the teacher has of insuring himself against waste. It is safe to assert that the physical educator who does not measure wastes 50 per cent or more of his efforts. If he does not test to determine the physical needs of individuals, how can he plan a program to meet those needs, and how will he know that they have been met? Can he show that his teaching is benefitting his pupils in any way whatsoever? How? In what ways and how much? Can he prove that certain phases of his teaching, if not all of it, are not definitely harmful? Can he demonstrate how well an activity has been learned? Could he defend it against an investigation by administrative officials—except verbal rationalization, a mere burst of "oratory"?[1]

Clarke states further that to prepare an *adequate* physical education program, teachers must measure, for measurement is indis-

[1] H. Harrison Clarke, *The Application of Measurement to Health and Physical Education,* 3rd ed., Prentice-Hall, Inc., 1959, p. 12.

pensable to an adequate program as measurement is impossible without an adequate program."[2] The usefulness of testing and measuring can be negated when testing is done for its own sake without relevance to student or teacher goals.

Glassow and Broer write: "But measuring or testing is not in itself a vital and indispensable part of teaching. It is valuable only because through its wise application teaching can be improved to a degree which is impossible without measurement."[3] If one is interested in making his teaching as effective as possible, he will apply measurement to his work. Williams places great emphasis upon measurement. He states: "Occasionally an administrator or teacher contends that the practical affairs of his work leave no time for attention to *evaluation.* In a sense evaluation is like bookkeeping in business; it indicates direction, and shows degrees of accomplishment. The worth of administrative procedures and teaching methods remain obscure or unknown unless their effects are evaluated."[4]

The foregoing excerpts from other writers provide sufficient evidence of the significant place which measurement occupies in teaching physical education. Let those who are enthusiastic about measurement keep in mind that testing and test results do not determine the goals or major directions of the program. Neither do they supply wise direction for the individual student who is looking for purpose in his study and participation in physical education. Those who refuse to use any but the minimum end-of-term measures are reminded that teaching in this manner is like starting on a trip without some kind of idea as to how far one must go to reach a point and how far one has gone after a day of travel.

MEASUREMENT AS AN AID TO INSTRUCTION

Returning to the original question concerning the student and his goal, one can say that the major areas through which physical

[2] *Ibid.,* p. 11.

[3] Ruth B. Glassow and Marion R. Broer, *Measuring Achievement in Physical Education,* W. B. Saunders Company, 1938, p. 9.

[4] Jesse Feiring Williams, C. L. Brownell, and E. L. Vernier, *The Administration of Health and Physical Education,* 5th ed., W. B. Saunders Company, 1958, p. 346.

education makes its contributions give the first criteria for selection of measuring instruments. These are: organic or physiologic development; social learnings; motor skills for leisure and utility; and personality gains, including attitudes as well as desirable emotional and mental characteristics. The student's achievements in these major areas are the events and qualities which the teacher will wish to appraise through the use of appropriate evaluative procedures.

A fundamental policy in physical education is that the student's status with respect to his ability to take part in any kind of exercise program is determined before he enters classes. At all grade levels, and for all ages, this examination is of first importance. The physical or medical examination is made by a physician, and its purpose is to appraise the health status of the individual. On the basis of this appraisal the examiner determines whether or not any modification of the student's educational program, including his physical activity, is to be recommended. In order to protect the individual as well as to promote an improvement in his health through whatever means are available, it is important that the medical examination be given prior to his beginning any educational program.

At any moment in his educational career the individual's capacity to learn new knowledge and skills is based upon his standing in several abilities and acquired skills. The function of measurement is to determine this status. The physical examination obviously is such a measure. Other measures of the individual's standing in those matters with which the instructional program is concerned will be made, and as he proceeds he will be tested from time to time during the term.

Although each measuring event is an appraisal of status, a series of measures provide information about the direction and extent of changes which are occurring in the individual. These changes should be viewed in terms of established values, otherwise one cannot know whether they are worthwhile. Comparison of the measures of status with previous measures, with previously established objectives, with standards, norms, or other suitably selected criteria provides the means for judging the significance and the direction of the individual's learning. If a student who was classed as a nonswimmer entered upon a course of instruction aimed at teaching him to swim and, at the end of six weeks, was still getting accustomed to the water but had made no progress toward floating, propelling himself through the water, or swimming with a fair degree of success, could one say that his progress was below, up to, or beyond expectations? It is necessary to know how much accomplishment in swimming a beginner can be expected to make during any course of instruction or part thereof.

Occasionally measures of initial status are termed *diagnostic tests*. Measures made during the term and at the end of the term are called *achievement tests*. Obviously the term applies to the intent of the tester and to his interpretation and use of the test results rather than to the nature of the tests. Diagnostic tests become achievement tests later. Achievement tests are given at the beginning of a term to diagnose the status of the individual's capacities and achievements.

CONSIDERATION OF COMPONENTS TO BE TESTED

Status in the area or organic fitness, growth, development, nutritional status, and physiologic efficiency may be measured in part by one or more of several tests. A department of physical education is concerned with the changes in status which result from the individual's participation in its program. Attention is given, therefore, to measures of developmental changes, such as endurance, strength, speed, agility, and power. The relationship of individual achievement in these qualities to structural factors, such as height and weight, may be noted and actually may be a part of a multiple item test. The level of performance is, however, the measure of achievement.

It should be noted that the physical education teacher is interested in the factor of growth. Measurement of this item should be a part of the physical examination. Recommendations for physical activity, as well as for other steps related to the growth status of the individual, should be made by the examining physician.

Tests in these areas attempt to predict total present capacity from measures of selected actions. The administrator may choose from strength tests, of which the Rogers Strength Test is a widely known example; endurance tests, of which the step type and those used by the military services in World War II are examples; tests of speed and agility which are found in running, swimming, and the potato race type of event; and tests of power exemplified by throwing-for-distance and jumping events. There are also cardiovascular, pulse-ratio, and organic efficiency tests which are useful principally in the research laboratory because of the time required for their administration and the special testing equipment which is needed.

Measures of status in the area of organic fitness should be made as a regular part of the class program. It is correct to assume that persons who are regularly active physically achieve a degree of organic fitness. To achieve a predetermined level of organic fitness, however, demands that measures of individual status be made at appropriate times during the instructional term in order to appraise as well as measure the achievement. The matter of physiologic fitness will be more meaningful to children, youth, and adults if performance is related to other activities in the physical education program. The use of a test from this area as a diagnostic test and later measure of status during and at the end of the term will supply data with which to compare the student's later status with his starting point and his goals. Furthermore, he can see how he stands in relation to others, if this is a matter of importance.

Attitudes toward a subject influence the willingness of the individual to enter wholeheartedly into achieving the purposes of instruction, and also determine whether or not the individual will continue to practice what he has learned. Richardson[5] has constructed a scale for appraising attitudes of college students toward physical fitness and exercise. The scale, which can be administered easily, may aid the teacher to plan better for the preparation of students to enter programs of physical activity willing to take part in the instruction and practice of the course. Serious individual problems also can be uncovered by such a scale.

[5] Charles E. Richardson, "Thurstone Scale for Measuring Attitudes of College Students Toward Physical Fitness and Exercise," *Research Quarterly*, American Association for Health, Physical Education, and Recreation, December, 1960, pp. 638–643.

MEASUREMENT OF SOCIAL MATURITY AND PERSONALITY

Although modern physical education stresses the significance of its contributions to social maturity, also called social efficiency, very little objective evidence exists to demonstrate changes in the status of students as a result of their physical education experience. Grading schemes rarely refer specifically to accomplishments in this area of social efficiency. Tests and measures are more likely to be concerned with skill, strength, growth changes, and motor performance than with social and personality changes. The reason for the dearth of objective evidence becomes strikingly clear when one studies the available measures of social growth, or social change. The number of measures is small and their validity is not high.

In spite of these current difficulties the teacher must apply the best measures available to determine the status of the individual in social qualities and to mark the changes in this status which accompany his learning in physical education. The available measures are not highly predictive and should not be interpreted closely with respect to the student's status. They are most useful in centering attention upon the student's strengths and weaknesses and upon the goals, in terms of new or changed behavior, with which both the student and the teacher should be concerned. In the earlier years of childhood the measures can help the teacher give direction to the social growth of the child. In later years of adolescence the measures can help in broadening social maturity for the particular age as well as in giving direction and emphasis to additional needs.

Difficulty of measurement in this area arises from the traits which make up social efficiency and the breadth of meaning given to them. There is no clear, universal meaning which can be applied to a trait. Because the trait can be measured only as it is manifested in behavior, the matter of judging the factors in the total situation increases the difficulty of securing reasonably accurate results. Even individual intent is a factor, but it is not measurable.

Some of the traits which contribute to social efficiency are courage, initiative, perseverance, self-control, morality, courtesy, sympathy, loyalty, cooperation, and honesty. There are others. Because a student may manifest one trait to the detriment of others, in a social setting the measure should take into account the acceptable or desirable degree or quality of manifestation. For example, one may have sympathy, a desirable trait, but his sympathetic behavior may lead to lack of cooperation, or to a loss of self-control, or in extreme cases to immorality.

The teacher who plans to inculcate desirable social behavior in his students may focus attention upon conduct in physical activities. Because these activities are rich in opportunities to practice social behavior, the learning itself may also be very rich. Although learning to behave in a socially desirable manner in physical activities contributes to maturity and social acceptability, the relating of these qualities to other aspects of living should also be part of the teaching in this area.

Tests to measure social traits should consider the broader application of the social factor, although measures of behavior responses in physical education activities are available. Three general procedures are used to measure social traits. One method is to rate the student on a prepared scale of behavior traits according to the frequency with which he manifests the listed traits. McCloy,[6] Blanchard,[7] and O'Neel[8] have prepared rating scales of this type.

A second method is to present the student with a list of statements or descriptions of conduct situations and to request a written response to each item. There are many tests in this category.

Lauritsen developed a test designed to measure the ability of the student to apply principles of sportsmanship. The test consisted of three steps; first, a description of a specific situation in a sport was given; second, a list of conclusions or courses of action was provided, from which the student was to select one; third, the student was asked to select from a list of reasons those which supported the conclusion which he had chosen in the second step.

[6] C. H. McCloy, "Character Building in Physical Education," *Research Quarterly,* October, 1930, p. 42.

[7] B. E. Blanchard, Jr., "A Behavior Frequency Rating Scale for the Measurement of Character and Personality in Physical Education Classroom Situation," *Research Quarterly,* May, 1936, p. 56.

[8] F. W. O'Neel, "A Behavior Frequency Rating Scale for the Measurement of Character and Personality in High School Physical Education for Boys," *Research Quarterly,* May, 1936, p. 67.

Haskins[9] has developed a test of concepts of sportsmanship based on problem situations. The test describes an event in a game or other activity situation and lists a number of comments evaluating the situation. The student is to select the item which represents his idea of correct conduct or belief. The test, which can be secured in two forms, is easily administered and can be used as an instructional aid.

In the field of general social adjustment the following tests are suggested as representative of this type of measure.

1. The Bernreuter Personality Inventory for high school and college students, and adults.[10]
2. The Bell Adjustment Inventory for high school and college students.[11]
3. Washburne's Social Adjustment Inventory, which may be used with high school and older ages.[12]

The third procedure is the anecdotal record or description of an incident of student behavior. Records are made by the teacher and are kept over a period of time. A summary statement can then be prepared from the record of anecdotes to describe observed behaviors and form the basis for describing personality traits of the student. An important feature of the anecdotal record is that it is a descriptive note of a student's actual behavior, made soon after the behavior occurred. Memory of the event should be clear. There is less risk of the halo effect influencing this record than in the case of teacher rating scales.

LIMITATIONS IN THE USE OF MEASURES OF SOCIAL MATURITY AND PERSONALITY

The administrator or teacher who uses either rating procedures or the anecdotal record must be familiar with their limitations. In the first place, rating and ranking procedures should be used in a

[9] Mary Jane Haskins, "Problem-Solving Test of Sportsmanship," *Research Quarterly*, American Association for Health, Physical Education and Recreation, December, 1940, pp. 601–606.

[10] Robert C. Bernreuter, "The Theory and Construction of the Personality Inventory," *Journal of Social Psychology*, November, 1933, p. 387.

[11] Hugh M. Bell, *The Theory and Practice of Student Counseling*, Stanford University Press, 1935, p. 117.

[12] John N. Washburne, *Washburne Social-Adjustment Inventory*, Thaspic Edition, World Book Company, 1936.

situation when behavior to be judged is described ahead of time and the rater has been purposefully observing students for their manifestations of these behaviors. In other words, teachers must plan and prepare to rate students long before the actual rating is to be done.

Obviously, although not seemingly so in practice, traits to be rated must be defined or described so that two or more raters judge the same behavior by the same standard. Again, in order to meet this requirement raters must agree ahead of time upon the descriptive definition of behavior. On this particular point, simply recording the behavioral incident without rating it avoids the possibility of an initial error of interpretation. At a later time several judges (teachers) concerned with the individual may review the records and reach agreement as to their meaning.

If changes in personality and social behavior are sought through teaching, it is essential that all students be rated at as nearly the same time and under as similar conditions as possible. To rate two or three students on one trait at one time and two or three on another trait at another time opens the procedure to a maximum of error. The administration of rating procedures is slow at best, hence the teacher must plan carefully for the rating so that errors are minimized. If this principle is ignored, and the teacher grades without uniformly observing all students who are to be rated, the judging will be heavily influenced by the halo effect.

Confidence in the reliability of ratings may be manifested cautiously when at least three ratings made at different times but on the same traits are secured, or when at least three different judges rate the same individuals on the same traits at about the same time. Five judges, or five different ratings, provide considerably more reliability.

Clearly, if one is to use these measures to assess the social efficiency of the student, careful development of a technique that is administratively feasible is a necessity. Otherwise, too much time is utilized in the procedure, or the results are hardly worth the time, however little, taken to secure them.

The anecdotal record demands similar consideration if it is to be used as an evaluative measure. Regular records should be kept for all children, not just those who stand out either favorably or unfavorably. Anecdotes should cover a range of the behaviors sought. They should be made as soon after the behavior occurs as possible, certainly not later than on the same day. When the teacher records the anecdote, he must be faithful to the facts of the situation; in other words, he must not interpret the behavior as he records it. Interpretive comments may be with the anecdote but should not be a part of it.

Both ratings and anecdotal records may become so numerous as to be unwieldy and practically useless. Such records should be summarized at the end of regular periods, recommendations made for teacher and pupil activity, and only those notes retained which have meaning for further teaching or learning. The time of both teachers and students is too valuable to be wasted by permitting either to apply procedures which yield no beneficial, constructive, or on-going results.

The paper and pencil tests which can be answered by one or several classes at one time and can be scored quickly offer a more usable instrument for measuring personality traits. Unfortunately, these tests have their limitations too. In the first place, validity is inferred from their relationship with some selected criterion, which means that there is a degree of invalidity in the test score. In the second place, all persons are measured on test items selected to cover a wide range of traits in a population. Unless the local teacher incorporates learning experiences involving the development of these traits, the tests may not be suited to a particular situation. To say this differently, one would note that the personality which is being tested is limited by the traits which the test items attempt to measure.

A student who is familiar with verbal concepts of personality traits may answer these tests as he thinks he should, rather than according to the true situation. On this point one will note that a test which deals with multiple traits, such as Washburne's *Social Adjustment Inventory,* is more difficult to answer than those focusing on relatively few traits. This weakness of paper and pencil tests usually can be overcome to a degree by seeking student cooperation through stating the purpose of the test and assuring students that their answers will be treated confidentially. If these limitations are taken into account in their use and interpretation, the paper and pencil tests of personality traits may satisfactorily serve the teacher who seeks to measure status and change in his students' personalities during their terms in physical education activities.

The problem which the educator faces with respect to teaching socially accepted concepts of behavior is that he must go more deeply than the student's overt behavior in order to develop the skill, understanding, and willingness to choose behavior which leads to the achievement of socially accepted goals. Any single act of a student may have two or more interpretations, of which only one may appear to represent a socially acceptable action. Behavior, however, takes place in a total pattern which itself is one stage of development in the continuous life activities of the individual. Until the observer, who may be the teacher, knows all or a large part of the total pattern, his interpretation of the meaning of a single act may be far from accurate.

Attempts to measure personality by using typical, or standard definitions of behavior actions will miss the meaning which each situation has for the individual involved. It is probably correct to say that *usually* like behaviors have a similar meaning. The slight dissimilarities and the unusual instances should make one pause in his eagerness to draw parallel meanings from like experiences.

Perhaps the significant function of personality tests is to identify the behaviors whose meanings should be sought. Another useful function of such tests is to point up behaviors which generally are ineffective in society when the individual uses them to try to solve a problem or to satisfy a need. In other words, regardless of the acceptability of one's motive or meaning, some behaviors rarely lead to success in fulfilling the motive. One may desire to belong to a team, but trying to secure membership by being uncooperative, lazy, and abusive of one's fellows generally will not lead to his success. McCloy states that "these ratings (tests) should be used primarily to evaluate and make clear to the teacher the student's present status so far as his conduct, habits, and attitudes are concerned. . . . The teacher should constantly strive to manipulate his teaching program situations so as to give laboratory experience to the student in desirable forms of conduct."[13]

Finally, with respect to the social behaviors in physical education activities, the teacher can distinguish those more favorable in character from those less favorable. In doing this the teacher will help students to learn the ethics of the activity situation, and he may extend the meanings beyond the physical education situation. Furthermore, he may see for the first time the conduct patterns which have developed in his classes without his being aware of them. If physical education is to meet the objective of social efficiency, those who administer and teach the subject must plan their teaching to include the opportunities for learning new behaviors and the means for measuring changes in these behaviors.

Personal and social behaviors are so intimately bound together that the goals sought in personality development are really part and parcel of those sought in the realm of social efficiency. Measures used to evaluate one's social efficiency take into account the personal qualities which one should have in order to manifest socially effective behavior. Although both social and personal qualities were listed separately when goals of physical education were mentioned earlier in the section on teaching and measurement of these learnings, the two groups now become parts of one.

MEASUREMENT OF MOTOR SKILL PERFORMANCE

Measurement of motor skills has been and is today the most practical type of evaluation. There are two reasons for this. One is that physical activity, which involves the performance of motor skills, is the central core of the subject of physical education. The other is that tests for measuring status in motor skills are numerous, relatively easy to administer and interpret, directly related to the teaching of the motor skills, and readily usable in grading. That motor skills are the basis for teaching in physical education is a fundamental principle in the planning and organizing of a program of physical education.

[13] C. H. McCloy, *Tests and Measurements in Health and Physical Education*, F. S. Crofts and Co., 1939, p. 292.

Where the learning of skills is not the central point in the program, meaningfulness for both student and teacher is incomplete. An emphasis upon skills alone, however, also leads to incomplete educational outcomes and overlooks the larger purposes of education and physical education. It is through the learning of skills and their practice in games, dance, and other activity situations that students achieve the objectives of education and physical education.

Unless the individual possesses sufficient skill for satisfying participation in physical activities, he is unlikely to continue them with any regularity. Physical and physiologic fitness, social values found in many activities, and the recreative effects of pleasurable and stimulating play are not achieved when activity is limited in frequency and amount. It is important, therefore, to evaluate the status and progress of pupils and students in their motor skills learnings.

In discussing the goals of physical education, care was taken to distinguish between physical activities as the ends and as the means of achieving significant goals. The teacher of physical education, as the teacher of any other subject, constantly faces the necessity of balancing the value of the skill goals with the value of the larger guiding educational goals. It must be clear, too, that these values do not maintain a constant relationship for all age groups, nor for all schools and colleges, nor for all individuals. With physical activities as the body of subject matter for physical education, there is every reason to choose goals of performance in the activities which are worth working to achieve and which draw into the learning process other knowledge, attitudes, skills, and behaviors which are part of the larger goals of education. There is good reason to teach for excellence in the performance of motor skills; there is equally valid reason for not placing excellence of performance in physical activities as the single major goal of physical education.

The bibliography at the end of the chapter lists references dealing with the various tests of motor skill performance. A discussion of the use of skill tests will point out their place in the program of physical education. Bovard and Cozens suggest the following:

> From every standpoint the measurement of achievement seems to play an important role in establishing an efficient program of instruction. Scientifically constructed achievement scales will be an invaluable aid to both student and instructor. For the student they: (1) stimulate his interest in activities through a fair evaluation of the performance he makes and the improvement he shows; (2) give him a basis upon which he may judge his standing in the group; (3) point out to him weaknesses as well as strengths, thereby assisting him to improve his deficiencies. They are invaluable to the instructor: (1) in showing him the skill status of his classes, so that he may adapt his teaching to their needs; (2) in checking up on his students as to whether or not his teaching is being assimilated; (3) as an aid in further research and experimentation.[14]

Mathews states that "skill tests reflect the ability of the pupil to perform in a specified sport such as badminton, handball, or basketball. By knowing the level of ability of a youngster in a particular sport it then becomes possible to use his skill ability score for such purposes as classification, determining progress, and marking."[15]

In the field of motor skills, and especially sports skills, many tests have been devised to serve one or more of the functions listed above. Individual teachers may make up their own tests to serve their own special circumstances. Tests which are to be used for significant evaluation and student guidance should be constructed according to accepted procedures for the preparation of an acceptable measuring instrument.

Tests have been devised to measure achievement in almost every sports activity. A typical test will consist of several items, each representing a skill taken from the complete activity. A test of basketball playing achievement may include a dribbling event, a basket shooting event, and a modified passing event. A volleyball test may include a serving event, a volleying event, and a jumping and striking event. The individual's score for the test is the combined scores of the several separate measures. This combined score is intended to predict ability to achieve in the total event, that is in the game or sport. This type of test may be called an isolated skills or a simulated sports test. The error of prediction is large

[14] John F. Bovard and Frederick W. Cozens, *Tests and Measurements in Physical Education,* 2nd ed., rev., W. B. Saunders Company, 1938, pp. 166–167.

[15] Donald K. Mathews, *Measurement in Physical Education,* W. B. Saunders Company, 1958, p. 155.

even in the best tests, and the teacher should not interpret these scores as precise measures. Utilizing the performance of separate skills within a battery may be more helpful to the student and the teacher in determining the student's needs for instruction and practice. As gross screening measures, and as general tests of the individual's readiness to move on to a higher level of performance, tests such as these are helpful. An advantage of the skills type of tests over a rating or judgment procedure is its greater ease of administration, because this type of test can be given to an entire class during a class period and can be scored quickly. Furthermore, these tests are generally more objective. All students are given the same kind of test to perform under reasonably similar conditions. In this way all attributes of each student which the teacher may wish to assess are called into play. In judgment procedures, often only the weak or the strong points of certain students are noted.

MEASUREMENT OF GENERAL MOTOR ABILITY

Motor skills items also are used to construct tests to measure achievement in abilities other than those of the game or sport itself. Tests of general motor ability may include running events, gymnastic skills, jumping, basketball throw, baseball throw, and other skills as part of the test battery. Tests attempting to measure the innate motor ability of the individual, a quality which has been called "motor educability," include various stunts, such as jump and turn, forward and backward rolls, balancing on one foot, and others. It is difficult to construct tests of motor educability which do not allow for previous learning. The tests available may be useful as crude screening devices. Tests aimed at estimating the potential of the individual for general motor development are also available. Each of these types has purposes which the teacher may wish to fulfill in his classes. The proper use of these devices and the correct interpretation of results will help to define the starting point and, by inference, the goal, and to measure the changes resulting from instruction and learning.

A TESTING PROGRAM IN OUTLINE

A testing program can include the following steps as integral parts of the total instructional program. Physical examinations and measures of growth status precede other tests and will be given as often as the nature of the student population demands it.

At the beginning of the year:

1. Physical or medical examination, administered prior to the indvidual's entrance (enrollment) in an activity program.
2. For school age children, measure of growth status.
3. General classification tests or general motor ability test to secure indication of individual potential.

or

At the beginning of each term:

4. Achievement tests to secure information on initial status as a basis for defining individual needs and for guiding the planning for instruction. If grouping is used, the results of these tests will be helpful in sectioning. (Sports skills, aquatics, dance, social and personality traits, knowledge about activities.)
5. Strength, endurance and agility tests as a basis for establishing individual needs in these areas.

During the term of instruction:

6. Achievement tests to measure progress and to point out needs for instructional emphasis.
7. Self-tests in events in which the individuals need development in strength, endurance, and agility.

At the end of the instructional term:

8. Achievement measures to serve as basis for appraisal of individual's accomplishments and for guidance for further education.
9. Repeat strength, endurance and agility tests to serve as basis for appraisal of individual's status, and for recommendations and requirements for further practice, if this is indicated.

Both the general classification tests mentioned in item 3 and the tests referred to in items 4 and 5 can be used. The choice is made locally in the light of program purposes, time for testing, and possibility of following the results of the tests in the organization for instruction.

If test score norms are not already available for the school or college, these should be computed when adequate data are available. National norms, if they exist, can also be used. The reader's attention is called to the earlier comment on appraisal and to the later section on grading. Norms are useful only in relation to other criteria for appraising the individual's status.

McCloy summarizes the function of testing and measuring in physical education in the following manner:

> The best educational results from physical education will come only when a relatively large emphasis is placed upon the *needs of the individual.* This involves a knowledge of: (1) his various innate capacities or potentialities for development; (2) the level of skills and abilities to which he has attained, both absolutely and as related to his capacities; (3) a diagnosis of the reasons for apparent specific disabilities or shortcomings; (4) an adequate sectioning scheme which will insure for the pupil an optimum opportunity for educational as well as purely physical development; (5) standards, adapted to individual capacity, for motivation, and for use in grading and promotion—promotion primarily for better educational opportunity, not just as a sort of prize.[16]

PROFESSIONAL USE OF TESTS

A question frequently raised concerns the time demanded by a testing program and whether or not one is wise to take so much time from teaching. If tests are considered solely as measures of terminal accomplishments, the amount of time given to testing definitely should be limited. On the other hand, perceiving the value of testing to be directional, instructive, and a terminal measurement of accomplishment, the teacher finds that a larger proportion of time may be given to measurement because it results in more effective teaching and learning. One must judge his own situation to determine the time allotted to this aspect of the program. The following diagram attempts to demonstrate that tests serve several purposes according to the time in the learning situation at which they are given, and, of course, according to the intention of the teacher who administers the tests. If the instructional period is thought of as having a beginning, an intermediate stage, and a terminus, tests may be used to measure students' status at the beginning, to check their status several times during the intermediate period, and to measure their status at the termination of the instructional period. Each measuring point, however, may become the new beginning, or check stage, or terminus. In a program of physical education which extends over several years of the pupil's life, tests do serve each of these functions.

[16] McCloy, *op. cit.*, pp. 298–299.

Initial status — D
In-between status — C
Terminal status — T

D
C - D
T - C - D
T - C - D
T - C
T

The acceptance of the view of measurement as that means which enables both the teacher and the student to gauge the rate of progress, or the actual point of attainment at any one time in the movement toward the goals of education, leads to the use of tests for guidance rather than for wrapping and tying up for storage purposes blocks of learning which are now completed. A student may view the result of any test and remark, "At this point I have made this progress; what are the next steps?" The teacher may comment similarly upon both the present achievement and that which is now open to further achievement.

Mooney discusses the attitude toward the institutionalization of tests in the educational operation. "Achievement tests and intelligence tests have been easy to make. These evaluate what a child can do as a task-performer and not what he is as a person. Our extensive use of these tests has likely strengthened a conception of education as task-performance, while by default, weakening a conception of education as the cultivation of a valued human being."[17] In an age when many are preaching the great urgency for training more scientists and mathematicians, it is easy to concentrate upon the ability to perform tasks and overlook the real reasons for the tasks themselves. The individual is too readily ignored. Of course, the criticism is immediate, namely that attention to the individual means education goals limited by individual whims. This has never been a method of operation in seriously considered educational practice, because it does not achieve the purpose of full growth and development of the individual, nor does it prepare persons for democratic citizenship.

Cottrell has stated the dilemma which the teacher faces in trying

[17] Ross L. Mooney, "Educational Appraisals," *Educational Research Bulletin*, February 13, 1957, p. 50.

to meet the requirements of teaching for the immediate situation as well as for the ultimate goals. His discussion bears upon the methods of appraisal which the teacher may choose to use, as well as upon his intention in using them.

If each proximate goal of the educational process leads to another goal and to an ultimate one of indefinite scope and time, is the teacher obliged to justify his choice of means for education only in terms of some abstraction? Such a policy would obviously make the educational process unintelligible. The here and now are usually all too impressive realities for the teacher. They make their demands and they carry their own unavoidable, if limited, significance. Even those people who view the present as but a moment in the process of evolution toward another (and hopefully better, more perfect) order of being regard the ends and the means of the present day as necessary and possibly determinant in that process. Thus, while each moment of life and each device used in fulfilling a human purpose may contain in embryo a possible ultimate value, the ultimate value is always and in practical terms only expressed in the moment of now.

The dilemma of the teacher and of those persons who are charged with the design of the educational program is therefore clear. How is one to conduct an educational process in which every activity of the learner is both consummatory and instrumental to the attainment of another activity? Put in this way, the dilemma has a familiar sound, for every teacher knows that today's lessons well learned pave the way for what is to follow. But it is precisely in the consideration of what is to follow, what indeed does inexorably follow, that the responsibility of the teacher becomes breathtakingly exciting, as well as mountainously large and heavy. It calls for great wisdom for the teacher to see each moment both for what it is, in and of itself, and for what it signifies in terms of wider outlook on life and in terms of the possibility of becoming. This dilemma, like many others, is real and ever present, and doubtless is never neatly soluble. But facing it makes the work of the teacher one of the grandest adventures in the world.[18]

SIGNIFICANCE OF GRADING IN PHYSICAL EDUCATION

Physical education has an established place as a regular subject in the school and college curriculum. All members of the administrative and teaching staffs of these institutions may not define physical education as identical with other school subjects, but they

[18] Donald P. Cottrell, "Paradoxes for the Professional In Education," *Educational Research Bulletin,* February 13, 1957, pp. 57–58.

do recognize it as belonging in the educational program. If physical education is a means for teaching and learning within the purposes of the educational institution, the productivity of the program, as measured by student and pupil achievement, must be known. Obviously, the central concern is the education of each individual, but his achievement is also important in relation to others in the same situation. Grading in physical education is essential.

The administrator's concern is not with the question of whether to grade or not to grade, but with the functions of grading, with the means for fairly and efficiently appraising the accomplishment of students in physical education, and with the selection of grade procedures which indicate the results of appraisal. These matters will be dealt with first generally, and then specifically for physical education.

A mark or grade is the symbolic recording of one person's judgment of another. In the school situation the teacher makes judgments concerning the actions, personality, and accomplishments of his students and records these with some sort of mark to represent a composite unit of achievement. A grade always relates to some criterion of group performance or to the status of other individuals within a group. There is no absolute standard against which judgments are made to form the basis for marking or grading.

The function of a marking system is to provide information. Who needs this kind of information about students? Thorndike and Hagen suggest five normal users. "They are (1) the pupil being evaluated, (2) the pupil's parents, (3) some school that the pupil will attend later, (4) a potential employer or similar outside community agency, and (5) the school itself."[19] Although the term *pupil* suggests grades below high school and college level, the list applies equally well to both high school and college students. Each of the above users has specific needs for information about the educational status of the pupil and student at any particular time. Not all have similar needs, hence not all can benefit from the same kind of reporting of achievement or status. The pupil may need guidance in dealing with weaknesses in his learning, as well as in utilizing his

[19] Robert L. Thorndike and Elizabeth Hagen, *Measurement and Evaluation in Psychology and Education,* John Wiley and Sons, Inc., 1955, p. 458.

strengths; he may need motivation; he may seek vocational direction. Parents are concerned about the welfare of their children and wish to know how they compare with what is expected of them and with the other children; they will be in a better position to help the child when they know his needs and his potentialities.

The school or college teachers need information on student status in order to do a better job of teaching and guiding. The institution also may wish to make decisions about the kind of students to be admitted in terms of the achievements expected of them. The emphasis given to a college education, and even to graduate work, suggests that it is helpful to know that students have demonstrated their capacity for doing such work and are prepared at the end of four years of high school, or of college, to enter the next level of education.

Employers may be interested in the general academic achievement. Some may be seeking persons with special skills who are finishing high school. Other information about the student, such as his participation in out-of-class activities, personal maturity, and ability to work with others, may be of equal importance to an employer.

The single grade cannot represent all the information desired by each user. As a matter of fact, it may not represent the information accurately at all. In other words, the mark or grade tells nothing about those personal qualities of the student for which information is being sought. Furthermore, the emphasis in education or curriculum varies with the grade levels.

The principal task of the school is to supply learning situations which offer the elementary child the means of gaining developmental maturity in all ways commensurate with his individual rate of growth and with his unfolding capabilities. Evaluation of the school achievement of the elementary child therefore must measure his progress in relation to these individual factors, and the measures must indicate those means which will further the education of the total child. Furthermore, the measures must be reported to the parents in such a way that they, too, can do their part in supplying the means out of school, as well as for the school itself, for the best development of the growing child.

When the child passes from a nondepartmental program in the

elementary school to the departmental one of the secondary school, he works with more teachers and thus is evaluated almost entirely in terms of his achievement in individual subjects. The secondary school also initiates more general measures upon which extremely tentative predictions are made with respect to the individual's future educational direction. The levels of personal and social maturity which the individual achieves from time to time are important factors in his total education accomplishment. All these factors are represented in the report which the school makes periodically on each student. In addition to serving as valuable information to the student, his parents, and the school as they work toward the best educational outcomes, these several evaluations are useful to higher institutions to which the individual aspires and to future employers.

In colleges the subject matter grade is the central measure of student achievement, although colleges profess to be concerned also with personal and social qualities.

With such a variety of items upon which measures are made in the various educational levels, one may admit to some perplexity as he tries to find a single grade which represents correctly and adequately all the items.

Problems Associated with the Single Grade

Two major problems are faced by the teacher who plans to report student accomplishment by a letter grade or number. The first problem concerns factors which make up a grade. The second problem is that of assigning the grade and interpreting it to those who may need the information which it signifies. If the procedures for selecting the items upon which the grade is based have been realistic and meaningful, the problem of assigning and interpreting is solved because these matters are directly related to the grade itself. Physical education teachers are not in complete agreement as to what constitutes the basis for a grade at any age level. It is essential, therefore, that the basis for the grade be one which is meaningful to the teacher, the school, and other users, especially to the student and his parents.

The first step in the selection of factors making up the grade is to decide what is to be judged (measured). Because the curriculum is designed to achieve objectives toward which each part, or course, contributes, recognition of these objectives and a statement of those aspects of objectives which are to be judged for grading purposes is fundamental. The teacher may doubt that all objectives can be measured, or that each one should be included in the grading procedure. In any event, a carefully chosen statement of items to be judged as part of the grade is the initial step.

The second step is to select appropriate measures by which the items are to be judged and to provide a fair way to combine scores made on the various items. Any or all of the following procedures may be used; standardized tests, objective tests suited to local student populations and courses, rating and ranking procedures, paper and pencil tests, observations, and anecdotal records. The teacher will also determine when the measurement is to be made, whether at the close of the term, several times during the term, prior to and at the close of a unit of learning, or at some other moment.

Grading in physical education, perhaps as in other subjects, has not been uniform. Several questions illustrate the different bases. Should the grade be based on achievement in skills alone? Should the grade be based on achievement in skill relative to ability potential? Should the grade include judgments of attendance, cleanliness, completeness of costume, regularity of showering, and attitude? Should grades be based on effort, or on effort and achievement? Should a student be given a grade of "A" if he puts forth all his effort, although his final achievement is relatively low? Is improvement a basis for grading? Is improvement relative to potential achievement a basis for grading?

If one uses any of the following suggested factors as a basis for grading are there still further questions to be raised?

FACTOR MEASURED	REFERENCE POINT
Improvement	Related to equal amounts of gain for all people who start at a similar point?
Improvement	In terms of known top limits of achievement, with grade values varying according to the distance toward the top which the individual has achieved? (Curve of improvement)

FACTOR MEASURED	REFERENCE POINT
Improvement	In simple, gross amount?
Achievement	Related to individual's own potential?
Achievement	Related to achievements of all others similar to him?
Achievement	Related to effort?
Achievement	Related to achievements of all others?
Effort	Related to effort of others?

It is difficult to answer these questions about the factors which have been used for grading purposes. Thorndike and Hagen suggest that the answers can be given only "in the light of a decision as to the functions which the grade is to serve," and they list four functions which they believe a grade performs:

1. To help guide the student and his parents with respect to educational plans.
2. To help a school decide upon a pupil's readiness to enter certain selective programs or courses, e.g., a college preparatory program or a special mathematics or science course.
3. To help higher educational levels to appraise an applicant's acceptability for the program they present.
4. To help a potential employer to decide upon the suitability of the student for certain jobs that depend upon academic skills.[20]

The administrator and physical education teacher should not think that these functions are remote from those which grades in physical education may perform. If educational plans include personal development, social maturity, and the ability to utilize one's person effectively in work, then physical education grading is pertinent. If the school provides for advanced programs and courses in physical education for selected students, grading serves an important function here. Where development of the individual's total capacity for enduring and vigorous work is valued, where evidence of education in physical skills is needed for admission to specialized programs, and where there is interest in the individual's general maturity, the grade in physical education can be a useful indicator.

[20] Thorndike and Hagen, *op. cit.*, p. 475.

Employers are often concerned with the applicant's ability to work with other people, in addition to any specialized or technical education which he has had. Also, some jobs require the skills learned in physical education. Grading in physical education is of value in these areas, too.

Grading practices which have been recommended for use in physical education courses are not uniform. One writer believes that the grade should represent the degree of proficiency which a pupil achieves in the objectives of the course as established by the teacher. Another holds that grades should be of two classes, general and specific, and that grades in physical activity courses should be based on the individual's achievement in relation to his potential maximum performance. One writer would give each student a grade based on his achievement relative to others, and a second grade based on his achievement relative to his own potential.

Another view is based partly upon the procedures used to report the progress of the young child through his early years of schooling. The single grade may be considered inadequate as a measure of pupil growth, learning, and total development. For those who hold this view, the evaluating instruments are rating scales and check lists, and the evaluation is made through a report on the items included in these instruments. The evaluations made by these means have the distinct advantage of being reported in terms of the traits measured. Their disadvantage is their cumbersome and relatively unreliable measuring procedures.

Beyond the elementary school, grades are given to represent the student's achievement in a particular subject. If grades are to be used for the purposes listed earlier, they must give teachers, students, parents, and others a clear and reasonably uniform meaning concerning the accomplishment of the student in the subject. Usually, however, unless one knows the content of a particular course of study, he will have difficulty in making a precise, or even a close, interpretation of the meaning of a grade. Knowing the content will be only partially helpful, because the value given to each part which is graded must also be known. Whenever a grade includes items which are not directly related to the central content of a subject, its interpretation becomes almost impossible. The teacher, therefore, should try to make the grade a "pure and uncontaminated measure of competence in the field."[21] Acceptance of this criterion raises problems of choice in a subject which has multiple goals. In fact, in any teaching situation there are significant factors other than those represented by the primary subject matter. It is important to record judgments made about these factors for whatever use they can serve, but these judgments should not be concealed within the grade for physical education. Such factors as completeness of costume, condition of the locker, attendance, effort, and attitude may be important and should be noted, but they should be detached from the record of learning through class instruction and practice. Perhaps the factor of attitude is significant; if it can be measured as objectively as other units, it is conceivable that it can be included in the grade for the course.

Grading often becomes a means of rewarding good behavior and punishing bad behavior. If physical education is to maintain its status as an educational subject, factors such as discipline should not affect the grade. Regulations concerning student conduct may be applied to remove the student from class or the institution, or to penalize him in some other way, but the grade should not be prejudiced by the ratings on these unacceptable behaviors. Discipline may be administered in a manner which affects a student's success in a course, but it should not be confused with a grade as a measure of competence unless it is interpreted broadly to mean intellectual control over skills and responsible behavior. Even in this situation, disciplinary behavior should be part of the course content if it is to be graded.

If a single grade is to be recorded, it should be based on a single factor if possible, or if this is not possible, on as few factors as can be meaningfully related to give the best available estimate of competence in the area of instruction. If the objectives of instruction are clearly defined and generally known, and if the levels of achievement in each one which warrant any assigned grade are also defined and known, the use of a single grade to represent achievement in more than one ability may not be too misleading.

In one system of grading the following factors were included: attendance, decathlon or rhythms, hygiene inspections, tests on rules and strategy, physical fitness test, posture tests, skill-citizenship

[21] *Ibid.*

estimate, stunts test, towel and lock fees. Each item was weighted by a numerical value and by frequency of measurement. In this system grades of A and E (on a five-step scale) can be interpreted generally as being relatively competent or incompetent in all items. Grades of B, C, and D are not so readily interpreted. The C grade can mean almost anything within the list of items for which measures are secured. One may ask whether the course represented by the grading system is one subject of instruction or several. One may ask also whether or not it is necessary to record everything in the final grade. Perhaps some very significant learnings can be acquired without being graded, or at least without being included in the final grade.

Cowell and Hazelton prefer that evaluation of student participation in physical education instructional experiences include measures of achievement in a variety of goals. To assign a single letter grade to represent the sum of achievements in these goals would pose a problem of interpretation not readily solved. The list of evaluating criteria for aquatics in the seventh and eighth grades indicates the degree of difficulty inherent in the situation.

1. Do they understand the importance of safety around the water?
2. To what extent do they use community swimming facilities?
3. Can they execute artificial respiration correctly?
4. How many "sinkers," beginners, intermediates, advanced, and junior life savers compared to the first of the year?
5. Time trials, form ratings, participation in intramural meets?[22]

Reports of grading practices in colleges and universities indicate that the single letter grade is used and frequently is based upon a combination of factors which include the following: attendance, physical fitness score, rated skill performance, improvement in skill, attitude, knowledge of rules and strategy, and personal health practices. If one follows the admonition that the single grade should represent as pure and uncontaminated a measure as possible of the competence in the field, he is vulnerable to criticism if his grading is based on a variety of factors, such as those listed in this paragraph or those given as evaluation criteria by Cowell and Hazelton. Furthermore, the student may rightfully be uncertain, if not con-

[22] Charles C. Cowell and Helen W. Hazelton, *Curriculum Designs in Physical Education,* Prentice-Hall, Inc., 1955, pp. 306.

fused, as to what the course in physical education aims to achieve. Is it also possible that the teacher may weight unduly those factors which are least relevant to the major purposes of instruction?

USING THE SINGLE GRADE

If one wishes to use the single letter or symbol grade how does he assign it? The teacher approaches the end of the term with several scores, or grades, or marks recorded for the student during the course of the term. How does he arrive at a grade of A or B or F for any one student? What shall be the distribution of grades in each category for the class? According to Thorndike and Hagen two fundamental facts must be faced:

1. The composite score representing our pooled appraisal of competence is a *relative* appraisal only, not an absolute one. It permits a comparison of one individual with another and a judgment of more or less. It does *not* permit a judgment of absolute amount or of level of excellence by an absolute standard. The score shows relative performance only in the group for which common evidence is available. By intuitive judgment or by collateral evidence, we may have some impression of how this group relates to other groups. Inevitably, such judgment entered into the tasks we set for the group or the standards by which we appraised performance. But this reference to other groups or broader standards is fuzzy and undependable at best.

2. The meaning we give to numbers, letters, words, or other symbols as standards of excellence is a matter of *completely arbitrary convention.* It is utterly futile to argue whether 10 per cent or 25 per cent of a student group *should* receive A's, as if there was some eternal verity that determined this. Each teaching group must define what the symbols they use are to mean. Furthermore, in view of the relativity of our appraisals, in the last analysis the only definition that can be defended is a definition expressed as *a range of percentiles in a defined group.* Thus, A might be defined as "the top 10 per cent of a representative group of freshmen at W college," or as "the top 25 per cent of the group of M.A. candidates." There are no right or wrong definitions; there are only more and less socially useful and expedient definitions.[23]

With respect to the second item, students often ask whether or not the instructor "grades on the curve." The practice of making a

[23] Thorndike and Hagen, *op. cit.*, pp. 482–483.

frequency distribution of class grades and arbitrarily assigning the grades according to the percentage of a "normal population" who might be expected to achieve a certain position on the distribution is not as common as it was several years ago, but it still is followed by a number of teachers. The decision as to what percent of a class should be given A's or F's is not statistical. It is a practical administrative decision. The assignment of a grade to a predetermined percentage of the students must take into account the purposes of the institution, the meaning of the grade in terms of those purposes, and the type of students accepted by the institution. When this information is at hand, it may then be possible to state that a certain percentage of students should receive a grade of A, a certain percentage a grade of F, and so on.

If grades are to be assigned rationally and consistently, it is suggested that procedures be developed in reference to the following three rules:

1. Explicitly recognize the arbitrary social judgment that is implied in defining grading categories and make that judgment for our school and college on the basis of full understanding and rational analysis of the implications of our decision.
2. Establish general adherence to the definition among the individual faculty members of the institution.
3. Devise techniques to assist the instructor in adapting and applying the definition to each specific class.[24]

GRADE DIFFERENCES BETWEEN COURSES

One of the problems which an institution faces in interpreting the grades given in various courses is the lack of uniformity of meaning for the same grade as it is assigned in different subject areas. One hears the comment that "a grade of A in course X is equivalent to a grade of C in course Y." If the grading practices are carefully defined and administered, this discrepancy will not exist. A grading symbol should be defined explicitly for an institution. It should be agreed that a grade of A means that the individual who receives that grade is in the highest 10 percent (or whatever percentage is agreed upon) of students in this area of study within the institution.

[24] *Ibid.*, p. 483.

If selected courses are to be graded by different standards, the basis for assigning grades in these cases also should be clearly set forth. Making the general meanings of grades and the exceptions to them explicit is the first step toward achieving uniformity of meaning.

If physical education classes involve instruction—and they should to justify a place in the school or college curriculum—grading practices should be as carefully chosen and as skillfully applied as it is possible for the professional teacher to do. Having clearly stated objectives and professionally selected and prepared course content, and using the best in teaching methods and procedures of evaluation, including the assigning of grades, are the minimum essentials of educational practice which an educational institution expects from its constituent departments. If the administrator of physical education insists that there are differences between the purposes of his subject and those of classroom subjects, such differences may be accepted, but the organization and conduct of the program of physical education must apply the best educational practices to its special purposes. If exceptions are to be made, they should be clearly stated and their reasons given.

Grading systems are handed down from one generation of teachers to the next, and rarely does anyone cast a critical glance at the practices. Elementary teachers and administrators seem to have given more thoughtful attention to revising their grading procedures than have the persons at any other level of the educational system. On college and university staffs, where the science of teaching receives the least attention of all in teacher preparation, grading procedures are traditional, immutable, and subject to all the criticisms which apply to a single symbol grading system. Staffs and faculties would find grading more meaningful to all concerned if they would analyze the basis for grading in each subject and the meaning, i.e., the interpretation, of each grade.

The previous discussion has dealt with the use of a single symbol as a means of indicating pupil and student achievement in physical education. For some grade levels and for certain objectives a single symbol may be inadequate or entirely unsatisfactory. Where some other form of reporting upon pupil achievement is used, the general principles concerning the application of evaluation procedures and their interpretation should be followed. There is always need for uniformity of interpretation according to some standard. Simply changing the form of reporting a grade does not obviate the requirement for uniform interpretation. If symbols are to be used as single indicators of student achievement, they should be handled in a competent and consistent fashion.

For the functions that it serves most appropriately, a grade should represent as pure a measure of competence in a field as can be prepared. It should have consistent meaning from instructor to instructor. To achieve such comparable appraisal of competence, the following steps are necessary:

1. Define the knowledges and skills that constitute competence in a field and decide what weight should be given to each.
2. Decide what types of evidence will be accepted as evidence of this competence, determine what effective weight should be given to each component, and handle the weighting of raw scores so that the desired weighting is in fact achieved.
3. Reach a negotiated agreement on the statistical meaning of the grading symbols in terms of percentiles of a defined group or groups.
4. Work out procedures for adapting the definition to small or atypical class groups.[25]

Where there is only one teacher of physical education in the schools, the responsibility for devising the grading scheme will be his. All that has been written in this text concerning the basic principles of preparing grades and grading practices applies to the small school as well as to the large institution. In either situation it is the individual who is being evaluated on his work and progress in the educational programs, and it does not matter that in one institution there are only a few hundred students with one teacher, while in the other there may be a dozen or more groups of this size, each with a different teacher.

The teacher in the small school also has the problem of defining meaning of the grades he uses, as well as selecting the procedures by which he identifies the items to be graded. It is important for him to know the school policy concerning grading and what grading practices are used in other subject areas. Perhaps it is most important to inform other teachers as to the meaning of the grades in physical education.

Public school administrators give attention to the maturity levels

[25] *Ibid.*, p. 489.

of pupils when they are ready to move from one school level to another, e.g., from elementary to junior high school. The physical education teacher's appraisal of observable maturity factors should become a part of the total appraisal of the child. The grade in physical education may include a judgment of these factors. If the grade is a single one, it may not correctly indicate the maturity of the child, since other items are also part of the grade. In this situation separate ratings, reports, or grades should be developed to express the teacher's judgment on the matter.

Application of reasonable and consistent policies in the development of a grading scheme will enable students and pupils to understand more fully the relationship of their day-to-day participation to the achievement of stated objectives, and will provide the school administration and staff in other areas with a clear understanding of these matters.

The following is an example of the kind of evaluation procedures which may be followed by the teacher in a small school. In the first place, if he is in a secondary school, his classes will probably include students from all grades. A curriculum including progressive stages of learning requires some classification of students according to their standing in the major objectives of the program. The teacher can use a simple classification index supplemented by a record of student's past activities. If physical fitness standards are among his objectives, he can use the tests developed by the AAHPER and assign grades to the scores earned on the tests. The scores, or accompanying grades, can then be described in terms of the measures upon which they were based. If the teacher chooses, he can give these tests at the beginning of a term of instruction and practice, at intervals throughout the term, and at the close of the term. For purposes of over-all evaluation the results achieved by his pupils can be compared with norms for the state or the nation at large. Results of the physical fitness testing are of interest to the entire school and to the community.

Measures of achievement in the skills and knowledge of physical activities in which the student has received instruction can be made by means of rating procedures and isolated skills tests. Where the emphasis is upon achievement of individual items in a total game or sport, the isolated skills type of tests can be used, e.g., pitching a softball at a target, basketball dribbling and shooting, hitting a tennis ball against a backboard, soccer maze dribbling, serving a volleyball into marked zones, and so on.

Written knowledge tests taken from standard texts or carefully developed by the teacher can be administered along with skill achievement tests. Questions concerning the historical background of the activity, its cultural relationships today, significant rules and regulations governing play, ethics of play, and criteria for selection of suitable equipment can be included in such a test. Such subjects as training and conditioning for play in the activity, observing safety measures, and strategy of team play (for team games) can provide additional questions for a written test.

Finally, the teacher may apply a measure of personal development and of social maturity according to the goals which the department has set up for achievement in these qualities. The measuring devices can be rating scales, paper and pencil tests (e.g., a social distance test), or an observational record made according to a predetermined plan.

The summary evaluation should represent a mark, grade, or report for each achievement, with a comment concerning expected achievement, or with a standard to which the individual's achievements can be compared. If the teacher uses a single grade to report the student's various achievements, he should note the limitations imposed and should present explanatory material which will assist others to interpret the grade correctly.

EXCUSES

The influence of student attendance upon grading practices troubles many teachers, because its effect is not uniform from student to student and its value is not equal for all subjects. Since public schools generally benefit financially when the student is present, they require careful reporting of attendance and of absences. A high school student who is absent must present a written statement explaining his absence upon his return to school. Colleges tend to adopt the procedure of requiring excuses without the compulsion which attaches to the public school practice. Physical education, because of its unique requirement of active participation, places special emphasis upon the student being in attendance; thus attendance is apt to be one of the bases upon which a grade is formulated. The following discussion attempts to put the matter of class attendance into perspective in relation to the purposes of physical education.

If one considers the tenets of good mental health, he will recognize that there is no such thing as a good excuse. Various explanations may be given to explain individual behavior under known conditions, but these are not excuses.

The difficulty with the excuse is that both students and teachers tend to consider it as a form of acceptable exemption from the requirements of a course. The student may feel that he is not obligated to meet the full objectives of the course. The teacher may give special consideration to the student when evaluating his performance in the course. Neither attitude is appropriate to the educational treatment of the problem created by the student who is absent from class.

In subjects other than physical education, student absences affect the course grade to the extent that the student does or does not complete the course work or perform it satisfactorily. Course requirements are not modified to suit variations in the amount of time and effort which the individual chooses to put into the course. On the other hand, a student can concentrate his effort in the majority of school subjects and learn in a shorter time that which a class as a group takes a longer time to cover. A student who has been absent because of illness may, upon his full recovery and return to school, regain his class standing by doing the extra study demanded. Although there is no way for the student to recover the complete experience of the class during his absence, in terms of achievement in subject matter as measured by written work and examinations, he can meet the requirements of the course. If he does not, he is not excused from his failure to achieve.

Attendance as it affects achievement in physical education can be treated in a like manner. If the course objectives require participation in the class period, then students who are absent are going to have difficulty meeting them unless they work harder and spend extra time on their study. If one of the objectives is a stated standard of physical fitness which can be achieved only by regular participation in physical activity, it will be difficult, if not impossible, for the student who is absent for a large part of the term to meet the objective. An excuse cannot repair this deficiency.

Perhaps physical education teachers are reluctant to do what amounts to penalizing the pupil or student who is absent because of illness. A person usually cannot take part in physical activity when he is ill. The point has no special significance for physical education, however, because the individual cannot take part in other school activities when he is ill. As a rule, if the individual is allowed to remain in school, or is able to attend classes in college, he is able to take part in all parts of the school or college program.

The principle of adapting the curriculum to meet marked individual differences is not violated by dealing with student absences in the manner described above. The objectives of physical education are broad enough to allow for setting specific individual requirements suited to the capacity of the student. Once the specific goals have been established, he is expected to work to achieve them.

It is important to realize that student absences are not simply events to be entered in a record book. In any school or college where students are expected to attend all their classes regularly, the student who is absent has some problem in meeting his obligations. The teacher should talk with each student who has an absence record to learn the cause for his behavior and try to help solve whatever problem may be uncovered. Explanations for absences are helpful only to the extent that they provide a basis for improving the educational growth of the student. Teachers working with younger children will seek information from other teachers, the school nurse or physician, the attendance officer, and the parents about children who are absent frequently.

Each term several individuals will have to make radical changes in their plans because of an injury, an operation, prolonged illness, or extended medical treatment. How shall the teacher deal with these individuals? Answers to the following questions may serve as guides. First, will the individual be able to achieve the objectives of the course after he returns to class? Second, have new, special objectives to be achieved through physical education been created by his condition? Third, is the student unlikely to return to activity for an extended period, necessitating his removal from the course for the semester or term? Fourth, is the nature of his condition such that he should not participate in physical activities during the rest of his school career?

Each instance where a person cannot meet the demands of a full program of physical education must be treated individually, and his placement in physical education instructional classes should be decided according to his ability to benefit educationally from participation. The problem of absences from physical education in schools is complicated by the fact that a pupil's parents may easily obtain a statement from a physician purporting to excuse the student for his absences. If the teacher will observe the procedures already described for dealing with pupils who are absent, the problem should be solved. The principle that decisions concerning the educational standing of the individual are wholly the responsibility of the school and completely within its jurisdiction gives the administrator and the teacher the authority to apply these procedures.

The problem of absences from college and university classes should not be difficult to solve. Each institution has its own medical personnel who judge the fitness of the individual to engage in physical activity. The college physician and the teacher or administrator of physical education can work together closely in this area of joint responsibility. Students who are in residence at an institution are usually under the full jurisdiction of the institution with respect to all matters affecting their standing in the institution.

A professionally conceived, organized, and administered program of physical education, which is known as such in the institution and the community, can be conducted with full understanding and support. It is important, therefore, that the administrator make known his program.

Since World War II there has been an increase in the number of community colleges and new junior colleges serving local residents. Also, established institutions are receiving more students who live within commuting distance of a college and who can, by living at home, afford to go to college. If the institution has been primarily a residential college, the policies governing health supervision of its students will apply to all students, with the possible exception that infirmary care will not be given to the commuting student. If the institution has no students in residence, it will need to apply procedures described earlier for dealing with absences in the elementary and secondary schools. As a rule, however, this type of institution has its own medical personnel who exercise full jurisdiction over the college student as far as health matters are concerned.

The term *excuse* as used in this discussion applies only to the absence from class and the attempts to deal with it constructively. Requests for extended exemption from participating in a course will be considered under waivers and exemptions from physical education as a required subject.

MAKING UP CLASS WORK

Administrators may ask whether students should be allowed to make up work in physical education. If such work can be accomplished so that the goals of the course are met, students should be permitted to do such work. It is most important to realize, however, that the writers are concerned with an integrated program and not with a collection of unrelated actions on the part of the student. Some teachers are not really interested in how a student meets a standard as long as he meets it. Their argument is that only the final result counts. In this instance the final result is usually a score on a test, a measure of proficiency, or a position on a ranking or rating. Education, however, is concerned with the process as well as the measured results of learning. Continued education depends as much upon the process as upon the accumulated facts.

To determine the validity of a student's request to make up work in which he is deficient because of absence, the teacher will consider the reasons for absence as they reflect student behavior and the possibility that the student can achieve the goals of the course by doing the required work on a make-up basis.

Make-up work in physical education frequently has been done in unacceptable ways. For example, if make-ups are allowed, it is a common practice to require students who have been absent to spend time during the last two weeks of the term in physical activity. The amount of time is to equal the total absences. Occasionally, the student must put in twice as much time as he has been absent. These periods of activity are not part of regular classes. Although the institution may control the number of class periods which a student can make up in one day, it is possible under some circumstances for the student to make up a half term of work within a week and keep up his current attendance in his class, too! Practices of this sort foster an attitude that physical education is little more than busy work and that the physical education requirement sinks to the level of the "sitting" requirement occasionally found in academic courses.

The plain fact is that any course in which a student may be a nonparticipant for a sizable portion of the term and then, by concentrated application during the last few weeks, achieve a satisfactory standing in the course does not justify the time given to it. Perhaps the objectives are not suited to the abilities and interests of the group; or, the plan for the course may have been carelessly drawn, so that it is not clear to the students. The objectives themselves may be limited to those designed to keep students busy. Whatever the cause may be, a term course which can be completed satisfactorily within a relatively small portion of the term demands a careful review and possible revision.

The problem of make-ups for willful absences occurs almost entirely in colleges and universities where students may choose to attend class or not. The problem of absence because of illness is the same at all grade school and college levels, and is one which causes the administrator concern as he endeavors to conduct his program fairly for all students. Formulation of educationally sound policies will provide the solution for the problems and will give status to the program itself.

EXERCISE AS A PENALTY

One final comment concerns the teacher and the administrator who use some phase of physical education as a punishment for students who are absent or late to class, or who are to be penalized for some other reason. One teacher required students who forgot their gymnasium costumes to run forty laps on the indoor track. The boy who forgot his uniform frequently was in better physical condition than those who took part in the class activities, but he had no liking for track. Another teacher made students who were late to class do push-ups for five minutes. Obviously, they look upon push-ups, and ultimately exercise, as a form of punishment. Physical education activities should never be used for punishment. The greater punishment is to deny the student the privilege of taking part in the activities of the program.

EVALUATION OF THE TOTAL PROGRAM

Earlier in this text it was stated that any educational program must yield the greatest possible accomplishment in pupil and student learning if it is to retain a place in the school curriculum. The administrator, being fully aware of this fact, will judge his total program according to professionally accepted criteria of educational accomplishment.

Although a physical education department may embody several distinct but related programs, the worth of the total endeavor is measured by the degree to which it achieves its goals. The matter of evaluation according to objectives has been discussed at length in other sections of this text and will not be repeated here.

In order to assist teachers and administrators to check their total situation with respect to professionally accepted practice in both education and physical education, several evaluative devices have been developed. In a way these devices become platforms for action, because they describe situations which are not exactly like the ones found in many schools, hence create needs or wants to be fulfilled. Also, these devices provide the means for surveying practices in a local system or institution so that the administrator may gain support for his plans to improve his own program, and so that the community or the college administration may judge the quality of their programs according to criteria accepted by the profession.

LaPorte, in his capacity as Chairman of the Curriculum Committee of the College Physical Education Association for more than twenty-five years, felt the need for a form of rating to be used in judging the strengths and weaknesses of school programs. Under his direction, score cards were devised to be used in the rating of physical education programs in elementary and secondary schools. The score cards developed by LaPorte have had considerable use. Like curricula, they need regular review and revision if they are to continue to represent the best practices in a field. If this review is neglected, such a device could actually hold back progress.

In a conference held in 1954 on college physical education, criteria were drawn up to indicate the significant aspects of instructional programs for college men and women. The criteria are grouped under Program, Administration, Evaluation, and Methods of Teaching. Although the statements are broad in their implications, nevertheless they are definite to the degree that they can serve as evaluative criteria.[26]

The State Education Department of the University of the State of New York issues a form of rating scale entitled a *Check List for Physical Education*[27] which is designed to assist schools and interested community groups in identifying the strengths and weaknesses of their physical education programs and to plan steps for their improvement. Other criteria for evaluating physical education programs have been proposed by Jackson,[28] Cowell and Hazelton,[29] Daniels,[30] and Meyers.[31] The administrator will find these devices of valuable assistance in stimulating him to continue to seek improvement in his own program. It is satisfying to know in which respects his program meets or surpasses the criteria on a rating scheme, but it is of equal value to know what lies undone or where revision is needed.

For an over-all view of program adequacy the following tests, or criteria, may be applied:

Physical education, as is the case with any school program designed for the interests of our society, must meet at least five tests of fitness.

1. It must have a socially realistic content, a series of learning experiences

[26] American Association for Health, Physical Education and Recreation, *Physical Education for College Men and Women,* rev. ed., Washington Conference on Physical Education for College Men and Women, 1959.

[27] State Education Department, Division of Health, Physical Education, and Recreation, *A Check List for Physical Education,* University of the State of New York.

[28] Chester O. Jackson, "How Does Your Physical Education Program Rate?" *Journal of the American Association for Health, Physical Education, and Recreation,* June 1954, pp. 20–21.

[29] Charles C. Cowell and Helen W. Hazelton, *Curriculum Designs in Physical Education,* Prentice-Hall, 1955.

[30] Arthur S. Daniels, *Evaluative Criteria for Physical Education: A Self-Appraisal Check List for Ohio Secondary Schools,* Columbus, The Ohio State University, 1954.

[31] Carlton R. Meyers, "Suggested Criteria for the Selection of Program Content," *The Physical Educator,* December, 1952, pp. 103, 104.

growing out of community life and directed toward its improvement.
2. It must be democratic in its human relations, doing all that is possible to see that people treat people in terms of personal worth and growth potentials.
3. It must make use of the most productive teaching-learning methods.
4. It must continually appraise the effectiveness of its work and planning.
5. It must change as the times change, keeping itself adjustive to new needs and conditions.[32]

BIBLIOGRAPHY

"A Physical Education Program for Today's Youth," *Journal of the American Association for Health, Physical Education and Recreation,* May, 1951.

A report from the National Conference for the Mobilization of Health, Physical Education and Recreation includes recommendations for physical fitness standards and for program content. The conference was called because of the Korean War.

Bucher, Charles A., "Fit for College," *Journal of Health, Physical Education, Recreation,* May-June, 1959, p. 12.

Suggestions are given for the use of the College Physical Education Association's report entitled, "Fit for College."

"Elementary School Physical Education," A Report, *Journal of Health, Physical Education, Recreation,* February, 1960.

A report of the National Conference on Fitness of Children of Elementary School Age, held in Washington, D.C., on November 29-December 3, 1959.

Hein, Fred V., and Donald A. Dukelow, "The Second National Conference on Physicians and Schools," *Journal of the American Association for Health, Physical Education, and Recreation,* September, 1950, p. 20.

Contains the principal conclusions of the conference.

Hein, Fred V., and Donald A. Dukelow, "School Health Today," *Journal of the American Association for Health, Physical Education, and Recreation,* January, 1952, p. 16.

A brief commentary on the Third National Conference on Physicians and Schools. One conclusion: "It stressed that physicians, communities, and school administrators must recognize the importance of the

[32] Florence Greenhoe Robbins, *The Sociology of Play, Recreation, and Leisure Time,* William C. Brown Co., 1955, p. 75.

teacher's role in health appraisal if conditions in some schools are to be improved."

Hunsicker, Paul, "AAHPER Physical Fitness Test Battery," *Journal of Health, Physical Education, Recreation,* September, 1958, p. 24.

A summary report is given of the results of the national testing of a sample of 8500 school children on the seven items intended to measure aspects of physical fitness.

Joint Committee of the American Medical Association and the American Association for Health, Physical Education, and Recreation, "Exercise for Fitness," *Journal of Health, Physical Education, Recreation,* April, 1958, p. 40.

An excellent statement of the relationship of exercise to total fitness, to individual capacities, to sex, age, and physical condition. This is a revision of a statement prepared by a joint committee.

Kelly, Ellen, "Excuse the Pupil or Adapt the Program?" *Journal of Health, Physical Education, Recreation,* December, 1955.

LaPorte, Wm. Ralph, *Health and Physical Education Score Card No. II,* The University of Southern California Press, 1938.

"Physicians and Schools, Report of Section III: The Physician and Physical Education," *Journal of Health and Physical Education,* April, 1948, pp. 257, 304.

Recommendations are made about the excuse problem in physical education.

Scott, Harry Alexander, *Competitive Sports in Schools and Colleges,* Harper & Brothers, 1951.

Solley, William H., and C. Frazier Damron, "Skill Development–Essential Objective," *Journal of Health, Physical Education, Recreation,* May-June, 1959.

The authors' thesis is that "accomplishment of goals in physical education is dependent on the emphasis placed on skill development."

Weiss, Raymond A., and Marjorie Phillips, *Administration of Tests in Physical Education,* The C. V. Mosby Company, 1954.

The manual describes a number of tests serving several purposes in the teaching of physical education, and does so in a uniform manner in order to assist the teacher in making more effective use of tests.

Chapter 9

THE EXCEPTIONAL STUDENT

IN THEORY all education should be individualized. Educational writing long has emphasized the necessity of building curricula which are adaptable to the needs and capacities of the individual. Although theory has been followed by practice in a small number of instances, school curricula today commonly are designed for the larger segment of the total school population. The special needs of the exceptional child and youth are not provided for adequately in either the school or college curriculum. What is true of the traditional classroom subjects is true of physical education.

The goal of universal education is one of our democratic necessities; its accomplishment is near but not yet fully realized. In the earlier days of public education those most likely to go to school and to finish were the more educable members of the population. The early colleges did not aim to provide broad higher education for large numbers of the people. Their curriculum could be more fixed without missing completely the needs of individual members of the institution.

The schools were concerned originally with verbal learning or, as some say, with the education of the mind. They were unprepared to deal with individuals who were physically subnormal or abnormal. Furthermore, the schools did not intend to include education of physical abilities as part of their curricula.

In this century the concept that educational practice should take into account the individual and his differences, as well as his similarities to others, has developed a concern for the child or youth who is markedly different from his fellows. Recognition of the importance of child health and of the school's responsibility for providing a healthful environment, as well as for giving children and their parents health guidance, started a movement in the middle of the nineteenth century which has resulted in nationwide school health programs. Individual differences receive direct attention when individual health is under scrutiny. States have enacted laws authorizing the subsidizing of education for selected classes of severely handicapped individuals. The number of individuals and agencies who are striving to help ill and handicapped children to better health and adjustment to their environment are numerous. Being handicapped no longer need mean relegation to a category of useless invalidism.

It seems that suddenly some persons outside the field of education have discovered that there are gifted individuals, too, whose needs for a greater challenge and more work have not been met. Professional educators have been acquainted with this group for a long time. Terman and his associates have studied the gifted child for more than thirty years. Schools operating under a budget system which requires each teacher to teach thirty or thirty-five periods per week, and to have classes of not less than twenty-five pupils—usually more—can do only so much for the gifted individual. In spite of these limitations, teachers have given what time they could to the unusually able student. The problem today is to make regular provision for as many of the gifted as can be identified in order that they, too, may not be hampered by limited educational programs.

The previous discussion was in terms of the total school, but all of it applies to physical education as a subject in the school. The remaining discussion in this chapter attempts to answer some of the questions raised by teachers and administrators who may wish to give attention to the exceptional individuals in their programs.

If for the moment one accepts the idea that all education should be individualized, but that the accomplishment of this purpose is still in the future, for which persons should special adaptation of program be made immediately?

The term *exceptional* has been applied to those for whom special educational programs should be provided. For classification purposes this term has replaced the word *handicapped,* which formerly described the entire group of children and youth requiring special education. The exceptional individuals are described as "those who deviate from what is supposed to be average in physical, mental, emotional, or social characteristics to such an extent that they require special educational services in order to develop to their maximum capacity."[1]

Three groups will be identified for whom special physical education provisions may need to be made. There are handicapped children and adults at all grade levels, and there are those who are gifted in abilities and understandings important in physical education. A third group, found principally in the colleges, but to some extent in public schools, consists of adults who are older than the customary student group. The third group is not an exclusive class, because occasionally some of its members will also belong in one of the first two categories. The older age group is becoming increasingly larger in the colleges and universities and requires special consideration in its physical education.

Among the handicapped there will be those with physical conditions which limit their ability to take part in physical education. It is easy to recognize orthopedic impairment, visual impairment, deafness, heart defects, and marked underweight as conditions affecting the individual's ability to engage in muscular activity. Other conditions of either permanent or temporary nature are limiting in their effect as well. In addition to the physical disabilities there are mental, emotional, and social abnormalities for which special arrangements may be made in the physical education program.

The gifted group is not easily defined, because little effort has been made to identify them for purposes of education. Empirically, the selective process which takes place when a coach has team tryouts at the beginning of a season and retains those who show the most promise finds the more gifted individual in a particular sport. It should be noted, however, that the boy or girl who performs best

[1] "The Education of Exceptional Children," *Forty-Ninth Yearbook,* Part II, National Society for the Study of Education, The University of Chicago Press, 1950, p. 3.

in a tryout may not be gifted but only older or more experienced at the time. The point is, though, that physical education, if it is to satisfy the needs of the individual with a greater capacity for learning, and if it is to utilize its own professional and physical resources wisely and economically, is obligated to find the gifted individual and to provide special programs for him.

IDENTIFICATION OF THE EXCEPTIONAL INDIVIDUAL

The exceptional individual must be identified, and the basis for his exception described, before appropriate educational measures can be taken. The conditions upon which exceptions are based are numerous and varied, and there are many means for finding them.

Obviously, for the third group (those who are older), the initial selective factor is chronological age. Because members of this group may also belong in one of the other two groups, they should be examined and tested by means used to identify other exceptional traits. The diagnostic procedures for this group should be suited to the age of the individual.

Because all children, youth, and adults should be given a physical examination before they enter upon vigorous physical activity, the examination itself serves as the means for finding individuals with physical defects which limit their physical activity. Upon the basis of findings made during the entrance and later physical examinations, students can be referred to the department of physical education for special education. Recommendations of the examiner concerning adaptations in the physical education program become part of the record of the exceptional student.

Tests of intelligence and of personal and social adjustment also yield bases for selecting exceptional individuals. If physical education can assist in the education of these persons through special adaptations of its program, such modifications should be made. Information about individuals who are exceptional because of intelligence, personality, or social behavior should be noted on the record of the student and made available to his teachers. Levels of disability should be established in order that the act of making and transmitting records does not consume so much time that the utility of the record is lost. Test score levels, qualities of behavior, and degrees of emotional behavior will be set forth as guides for the selection of exceptional individuals.

Selecting the gifted individual in physical education poses a problem. Tests of motor educability have been devised and tried over a period of years. Their use is not widespread. Perhaps expanding the use of the currently available tests will give a beginning basis for finding the child or youth who has the innate capacity to learn motor skills rapidly.

Achievement tests may be used to select those who have reached objectives in physical education earlier than most of their peers. In an earlier section of this text, examples were given in which the student met the physical education requirements on the basis of successful performance in achievement tests. Because this type of achievement is strictly motor in nature, it does not measure the individual's learnings in other areas of social and personal adjustment which are considered important in physical education, and it cannot be a completely valid measure of accomplished objectives. On the other hand, an individual who is advanced in motor achievement may also be tested for his achievements in other areas. If he is advanced, the least that the physical education department can do is to provide him with opportunities for further learning which will challenge his interests and abilities.

Diagnostic tests usually are given at stated times, such as at the entrance to an institution or at the beginning of a term of study. With children and youth, who are changing as they grow, it is helpful to supplement the test findings with other measures which can be made more frequently during the school year. One of the most useful and valuable sources of additional information is the teacher, who sees the child daily in work situations and under a variety of circumstances. The expert teacher is able to detect changes in the child's health status, alterations in his behavior, and difficulties he may have in performing class work. Severe illness and accidental injury to the individual are known to the teacher. Information, as well as judgments, which the teacher has about the child should be made available promptly to other members of the school staff who should know of it. Specific items may be placed on the pupil's record. Wherever this kind of information is secured and is used by teachers, the exceptional individual may be kept working to near capacity.

Where valid and reliable tests which measure individual abilities and achievements are not available, the judgments of qualified personnel should be sought insofar as this method of measurement is practical. In a way this resembles the day-to-day observations of the teacher. As a measuring procedure the method of observation could be described and the periods of observation specified.

An institution may use a diagnostic procedure primarily to discover the exceptional individual. The testing which has been suggested here can be applied to all individuals, and the test results may have meaning for the unexceptional student as well as for the exceptional. Physical examinations are given to all children and youth. Motor ability and achievement tests can be administered to all individuals in a school or college. The exceptional person is identified by his position on the test results in relation to established criteria.

One should not be led into thinking that the identification and classification of the exceptional child and youth are easy, routine procedures. Although individuals may be grouped roughly into categories, the test and examination results for an individual are highly personal and represent only a part of his total personality. Interpretation of these results is critical if effective programs of special education are to be developed. Clearly the attitude of the physical education administrator who deals with exceptional individuals is that there are categories of exceptions which for practical purposes roughly define the educational problem and supply the broader administrative guides upon which to begin his work. However, when he meets with the individual who has been identified as exceptional, he can make no routine decisions according to established categories, but must decide only upon the basis of the individual who is before him. That many individuals may receive similar programs of special physical education means only that the available resources are limited and must accommodate many people. The way in which they are used, however, is subject to wide variation, and so is the manner in which the exceptional individual himself utilizes them.

OPPORTUNITIES FOR SPECIAL EDUCATION THROUGH PHYSICAL EDUCATION

"It must always be remembered that the education of exceptional children has basic concepts and goals in common with the education of all children,"[2] and presumably uses the means of education which are open to all children. The objectives of education for exceptional individuals must be the same as for all others in the schools. "They do not differ from the general objectives of education for all children. Exceptional children, like others, must become well-adjusted members of the family and the community, must participate in the activities of the work-a-day world, and must assume responsibilities in keeping with their capacities as citizens in a democracy."[3]

One may continue this generalization by saying that the objectives of physical education also apply to the education of the exceptional individual. In physical education, as in other phases of education, some types of condition may require a special goal. Where therapy, remedial work, and retraining are necessary before the individual can become educable to the limits of his capacity, objectives to be achieved through one or more of these means may be set first or concurrently with other educational objectives.

The wide range of resources in physical education supplies the means for meeting individual needs in organic vigor, motor skills, personality improvement, and social adequacy for all individuals who are able to take part to any extent in any phase of the program. The physically handicapped individual can learn activities suited to his abilities which he may enjoy himself or in which he may take part with others who are not handicapped. He learns to use his abilities rather than live under the limitations of his handicap. He finds that he can belong to groups of nonhandicapped individuals and can work and play with them without requiring protection or undue attention. He gains in strength, agility, and endurance, all of which are valuable assets in his everyday life. In some instances these qualities may save his life.

[2] *Ibid.*
[3] *Ibid.*

The gifted student finds opportunities for greater development of skills and organic endurance. Because of his exceptional physical ability, he may also find frequent opportunities for leadership through the physical education activities. Under proper guidance he matures personally and socially, perhaps to a greater degree for his age than those who are not gifted. He may delve deeper into the learnings in one area or one activity. If all objectives are taken into consideration, his total healthful development should be exceptional.

The older individual may learn new activities which are useful in his recreational hours. If he has need for social learnings, he may acquire these, too. His personality factors also may be modified through his experiences in physical education. If he is in classes with younger students, as may be the case in college, he and his classmates gain in mutual respect and understanding. Perhaps of signal importance to the older person is the renewal of physical vigor and an appreciation of its value to him in his work as well as his play. Maintenance of this vigor may become a continuing practice with him.

PROGRAM OF PHYSICAL EDUCATION FOR THE EXCEPTIONAL INDIVIDUAL

An outline of important matters to be considered in preparing a program of physical education for the exceptional person will be given in this discussion.

The first step, and the fundamental one, is the administration of suitable procedures for selecting those persons who require or can benefit from special educational programs. These procedures may be termed diagnostic and should include appropriate tests, examinations, interviews, ratings, combined judgments, and data from cumulative records.

The second step, also significant, is the assignment of the individual to a program of special education. Because special education is individualized education, the assignment must be individual. Following the testing and diagnosis based on the test results, a teacher will confer with each selected individual. The conference may offer further information about the person's background and his physical education experiences. Insight into his attitude about himself and his participation in physical education may be gained. The individual should state the goals he expects to achieve through education, especially through physical education. In the latter area the teacher may need to point out the opportunities which are open to the student.

Special education programs must be meaningful to the individual in terms of his needs and goals, purposeful for the individual and the institution in terms of broad educational objectives, and effective in the utilization of time and energies of both student and teacher. Comment on these points has been made earlier in the text, but one may repeat that just keeping students busy, without knowing what their business is supposed to accomplish beyond meeting a time requirement in a course, has no place in a professionally conceived and administered educational program.

All that has been said in the preceding paragraphs applies equally to all classes of exceptional persons in educational institutions. Information pertinent to specific groups will be presented in the following discussion. The procedure for selecting the exceptional students within a school or college, and for assigning them to physical education courses will be described first.

The physical examination is a basic test for all students which should be given prior to entry into any program of educational activities. The examination of children and youth in the public schools is usually done by a private family physician. A record of the examination findings is sent to the school, where it may be reviewed by the physician and the nurse. Whether the school employs a physician for full-time service or utilizes one as his services are required, there should be a school physician. If there is none, the school nurse, if there is one, and the physical education teacher will review the physical examination reports. The family physician should state any limitations which should be observed in planning the participation of the individual in any school programs. On the basis of this examination, the individual may be classified as exceptional or unexceptional. Actually, terms such as *restricted* and *limited* may be used for the exceptional student.

Let us deal for the moment with the student who is physically limited in his ability to participate in a full program of physical education. The physical examination record and the recommendations of the examining physician will be reviewed by the school physician. He may accept the findings of the family physician, he may call the student in for a reexamination and a further check on the conditions reported, or he may confer with the examining physician for further information and clarification of his report. After this review, a report of pertinent information from the physical examination and the recommendations for physical education activity should be given to the physical education teacher.

The physical education teacher should interview each student to gain further information concerning activity history, possible special exercise which may be considered remedial, and the interests of the student in physical education. Upon the basis of the physical examination report and the interview with the student, the teacher can select the program which the student is to follow. In some instances the teacher may give further tests to determine the needs and abilities of the student. For example, in the case of a student with residual flaccid paralysis the teacher may make simple tests of muscle function and latitude of joint movements in order to determine more accurately the student's best assignment in physical education.

Those exceptional students who are assigned to a class activity may be checked further concerning their standing in the skills of the activity. For example, in a swimming class for handicapped boys, after each student had indicated his goal in the activity, he was given an opportunity to demonstrate his knowledge of swimming by performing whatever he could of various events in the water. With this information at hand the instructor planned with each student the steps to be taken to reach his goal and developed an instructional plan to help students learn the skills needed to achieve their goals.

Students who require special kinds of activity, such as strength-developing for certain muscle groups, can be given programs of regular directed exercise which they can follow individually as part of a group working in a gymnasium, or they can follow their programs at regular times other than those of organized classes. In the latter instance, a regular schedule is to be agreed upon and the student is to be checked at least weekly on his observance of the schedule. Special programs are designed primarily to enable the student to reach a level of strength and ability to take part in other activities. In order to achieve this purpose, the teacher must make regular tests of progress and reassign the individual when he demonstrates ability and readiness to enter another activity. The student may, of course, elect to continue with his special program on his own time and also enter another class activity.

Public schools are not likely to allow students to work outside of class unless they are under direct supervision. Also, youngsters in the lower grades require supervision and must be assigned to class groups. The teacher can plan individual programs to be carried out during the class period and within the confines of the class area. Assignment to a special class is the usual practice in the grades through high school.

Students may be periodically reexamined by their own or the school physician. The physical education teacher can help by noting any changes in the condition of the individual which warrant the attention of a physician.

If other tests are used to select those who are exceptional, many of the same steps will be used. It is assumed that the student will be given a physical examination before he is scheduled for tests involving physical activity.

That large body of students who are classed as unexceptional will be placed in the regular instructional program of physical education. Whether or not further classification of students is to take place before they are assigned to instructional programs will depend upon the attitude of the school and the department of physical education staff toward the matter of homogeneous grouping. The number of persons available to handle the testing required and the special classes which will develop within the situation are other determining factors. In the small school with only one teacher, the variety in the program is limited by his own time as well as by the number of students in the school. Furthermore, the number of exceptional students will also be small, unless it is a school especially for exceptional children.

If there is no further classification testing prior to the student's assignment to class, the teacher may need to do further diagnostic testing at the beginning of the course in order to suit his own teaching to the students' needs, and also to sharpen the students' ideas as to their own needs. Tests of activity skills, i.e., achievement tests, can be given, tests of general motor ability may be used to determine the individual's capacity for achievement, and tests of physical fitness may be given. Each of these yields information which cannot be combined to produce a generalized score. On the other hand, the program of instruction can be planned to recognize the standing of students in these tests and to provide means for improving their abilities in those areas which the tests purport to measure. This kind of program can be carried on in a school of any size, because it is under the immediate control of the teacher.

There is a limit to the variety of needs which can be met satisfactorily within any single class. It follows, therefore, that an attempt should be made to form classes of students who are able to progress somewhat uniformly under instruction which they can all follow. Students who do meet these requirements should be placed in groups where they have a chance for achievement.

A college department of physical education may find, as one did, that many students entering from a metropolitan area have neither the background nor the physical capacity to benefit from participation in college physical education courses. The department developed a sports skills test and arranged to administer it to all entering students, men and women alike, before they enrolled in physical education. Those students who were deficient in sports skills were assigned to a special course designed to concentrate their efforts upon developing sufficient skills to enable them to enter regular courses in physical education. That program met the purposes for which it was established.

THE HANDICAPPED INDIVIDUAL

Three classes of handicapping conditions are commonly listed. They are: physical handicaps including orthopedic defects, organ deficiencies, such as heart defect, defects of the sense organs, and defects arising from acute or chronic diseases; mental deviations which impair the ability to learn; and emotional or social maladjustments which affect the person's ability to meet everyday requirements and to work and play satisfactorily with others.

The teacher of physical education may work with handicapped individuals from all three groups. It is more likely that the usual diagnostic procedures will select those with physical handicaps for special work in physical education. For these individuals the first aim is to overcome the condition, that is, to correct it. Usually, the primary corrective measures are taken outside the school or college. Often, however, continuing or follow-up corrective measures can and should be part of the physical education program. If correction of a handicap is possible, and if there are resources in physical education which can assist with the correction, the first goal of the individual and of the institution should be to overcome the defect. In accepting the goal of correcting a handicap, the teacher of physical education must be sensitive to the total educational needs of the individual, so that the limited type of activity which may characterize corrective measures does not become the student's only physical education activity if he is also able to participate in other suitable activities which yield additional important and necessary values. The number of physically handicapped who can hope for correction through special exercise programs in schools and colleges will be relatively small.

The larger number of handicapped students will be able to improve their general physical condition through participation in activities in which they do not risk further injury or aggravation of their handicaps. The aim of this group is to utilize their capacities for taking part in activities which help them to reach their goals and which lead them toward the goals of physical education and of the institution. They will be able to achieve the benefits of the total physical education program.

The resources for a program of special physical education are the total resources of physical education. Because of the great number of handicapping conditions, some of which vary greatly in degree of the same condition, there is practically no resource of physical education which cannot be used by these individuals. The key is to select those resources suited to the individual and his needs.

The term *adapted physical education* has been applied to programs of sports and games modified to suit the needs of the handicapped individual. For purposes of physical development, of gaining basic skills leading to the acquisition of the total skills of an activity, and of improving mental attitudes and emotional stability, the modification of sports and game activities is necessary and valuable. One goal of education is for the individual to achieve satisfying human relationships. Physical education will offer him this kind of relationship when he is active with heterogeneous groups of persons, most of whom are not physically or otherwise seriously handicapped. The ultimate goal of the handicapped individual in physical education is to be able to enjoy satisfying relationships with others in sports, games, dance, and other physical activities. If the modification of an activity is so great that the nonhandicapped student finds no interest in performing it, the basis for participation by both handicapped and nonhandicapped does not exist. It is important, therefore, in the special education of the handicapped that adapted activities be taken for what they are, namely, suitable modifications of more complete activities. Ultimately, the handicapped individual seeks to make the adjustment which permits him to engage in an activity with a nonhandicapped person or persons. One of the functions of special physical education is to find that activity or another in which the handicapped individual can participate at least to a degree, with nonhandicapped persons. Knowing what he can safely do is as important for the handicapped persons as knowing what he cannot do.

The handicapped person should be given the opportunity to try his skills with the nonhandicapped in order to learn the limits of his ability and to gather the emotional strength necessary if he is to place himself in situations of comparison with others. An important associated outcome accompanies this kind of experience. The handicapped individual learns to face the reactions of nonhandicapped persons and to acknowledge his limitations to himself without apology. The nonhandicapped individual also learns to accept the handicapped for what he can do and to appreciate his achievement. He also learns to be at ease in the presence of an obviously handicapped person, neither overly sensitive about the difficulities nor sentimentally immature in his manner.

Unless the handicapped individual is to live in an institution, or to remain under constant custodial care, he must learn how to live in a society where he is in a minority, one which is organized and operated as though no one is handicapped. In physical activities one's limitations are glaringly disclosed. The physical education teacher is in the most favored position to help the handicapped individual make the best possible adjustment to his total environment, not only to the physical education situation.

Wherever physical education is required by the school or college for graduation, every student enrolled in the institution is expected to fulfill the requirement. This policy applies generally to all required subjects. Because the ability of an individual to take part in a physical education program seldom is a prerequisite to his admission to a school or college, whereas ability to take part in the other parts of the curriculum is required, the physical education department is faced with a unique problem when severely handicapped students enroll in the institution. Just as students possessing reading deficiencies, lower learning ability, and other limiting characteristics are placed in remedial classes and special sections where rate of progress is slower, or in special curricula, so, too, the handicapped students must be placed in courses or programs which utilize their capacities and, if possible, help them to remedy their condition and to improve their adaptability to their environment.

If a student is found to be limited in his physical abilities but able to take part in physical activity, he should then enter physical education courses suited to his abilities, and he should be expected to meet fully the obligations of the course. If the number of these students is very small, they may be placed in courses in which they can perform a major portion of the activities but be restricted in others. In this situation these students should be expected to achieve within the limits of their abilities the objectives of those portions of the course in which they do take part. An understanding and knowledge of the remainder may also be required.

If it is determined that the student cannot benefit educationally from participation in a program adapted to his abilities, he should be exempt from the requirements of the department. Rarely will an individual who is able to attend school be unable to take part with benefit in the physical education program. For some types of handicapping conditions, however, a school may not have facilities which permit a suitable program, or may not have enough personnel for the extra work which these special programs entail.

The administrator may feel that everyone who attends school

should take part in physical education, regardless of his ability to benefit from the program. As a result, an individual who is unable to take an active part in any phase of the program may be given office work to do, or he may handle towels and equipment, or perform some other tasks of clerical or custodial nature. Some teachers require the individual to write a paper on a topic chosen from a prepared list. All of these attempts to provide a basis for assigning credit or grades in physical education generally come under the heading of busy work, because none of them leads the student to fulfill the purposes of the physical education program. There is so much for every student to learn that his time should not be wasted by the school itself. Rather, the school should bend every effort toward helping the individual to acquire attitudes and skills which will make his learning purposeful, meaningful, and efficient.

THE GIFTED INDIVIDUAL

The term gifted may lead to misunderstanding as it is applied to physical education. In this text the term connotes those who are above the average individual in their ability or capacity to learn and to perform motor skills. Such a capacity is not a single factor, but is made up of a number of items. Basically one's coordinations, reaction time, insight into the nature of the total performance, and muscular and organic capacities contribute to his total motor ability. Attempts to measure the educability of the individual, as the psychologist attempts to measure the intelligence, utilize motor skills which are not performances of usual activities, or skills which are performed for test purposes in special and unusual ways.

In selecting the gifted individual the teacher must distinguish between accumulated experience, which results in better than average performances, and the basic ability to learn and to achieve in a superior fashion in motor skills.

Education of the gifted is not as clearly conceived as that of the normal or that of the handicapped. The gifted have not received special attention, perhaps for the reason that they are not obviously in need of special consideration. If programs are to meet individual needs, and if education is to provide opportunity for the most effective use of each student's abilities, more concern must be evidenced for these abler persons.

"Democratic education is founded on the ideal of equality of opportunity. Too often equality of opportunity has meant identical opportunity. Opportunity to be equal must be measured in terms of individual abilities and capacities to the end that all will be challenged to utilize their powers to the fullest."[4] One may ask whether or not our opportunities in physical education have not been identical rather than equal. In a physical education program of rich variety the gifted may find the opportunity for superior development, although no specific plan exists in the department to encourage such progress.

The more demanding needs of the gifted may be met through physical education programs which provide opportunity for greater physical development, richer learnings in the many activities, and a broader experience. The gifted may be served also by making it possible for them to achieve the goals of physical education at an earlier age and more quickly than the average student. Providing greater opportunities for development and learning seems to be the answer for the younger groups. More rapid attainment of goals may be better suited to the college and adult groups. For these latter ages advanced programs also should be available which will challenge the abilities of the gifted who may have met institutional and departmental goals in physical education more rapidly than the usual student.

Resources for the physical education of the gifted are found, for example, in (a) higher achievement levels established for them, (b) advanced courses in chosen activities, such as dance, swimming, fencing, and skiing, (c) participation on interscholastic and intercollegiate athletic teams, (d) seeking membership on an Olympic team, (e) participation in special programs in which the performance level is that of the expert, (f) becoming a squad leader, an assistant to the teacher, or a group leader in a community organization.

The screening and selecting procedure has already been discussed briefly in this chapter. The devices or means used to select the gifted

[4] Merle R. Sumption, Dorothy Norris, and Lewis M. Terman, "Special Education for the Gifted Child," *Forty-Ninth Yearbook,* Part II, National Society for the Study of Education, The University of Chicago Press, 1950, p. 261.

should be related to the goals set for this group, that is, the test items and their scores should be meaningful in terms of the ends sought.

Finally, the individual program should be based on both the suggestions growing out of the selection procedures and the individual's own purposes as they may be disclosed in a conference with him.

THE ADULT

For purposes of this discussion the term *adult* means persons who are several years older than the typical college student at graduation. Although it is somewhat difficult to set age boundaries for this group, one may think of them as being in their late twenties and older. Today college and university populations will have in their undergraduate student bodies many who are in their thirties and older. The larger universities are more likely to have these older students in numbers. The smaller colleges are finding them among their applicants, too.

The pressure for more education, and especially for the baccalaureate degree, is raising the value of higher education for the adult. A change in the family-rearing patterns in this country is releasing women from household and family duties to seek employment outside the home. Adults who may have left college before completing their work for a degree are returning to earn the degree for their own personal fulfillment. For these and other reasons, adults are enrolling in numbers in the undergraduate programs of colleges and universities.

It has been common college practice in the past to exempt adults from all physical education requirements. There is no justification for this policy now, and probably there was none in the past. When there were very few adults in an undergraduate student body, the department may have felt obliged to extend them special treatment. The policy may have been based upon the erroneous belief that adults would endanger their health if they participated in physical activities. Perhaps it was thought that physical education was play, unsuited to the adult level. It seems likely that many college programs were designed for youthful ages only, and were actually not suited to the age and interests of the adult. A few college departments may not have wished to be bothered with the adult.

There has been a change in attitude concerning the adult and college physical education. Oberteuffer states that "far too little attention is paid to the physical activities of older people. It has been said that older people cannot learn a new activity. We have seen that that is not true. Some say the older person will endanger his heart or his life or his something or other if he plays tennis or goes skating after fifty. This is sheer nonsense. Given an undamaged heart to start with and decent regard for the hygiene of the activity the great majority of people can remain pleasurably active without fatigue or strain well into old age."[5]

While the dictum "do not exercise after forty" held the attention of the country and even of medical men prior to World War II, the concern of physical education and medical personnel today is to encourage people of all ages to engage in suitable, stimulating exercise. Studies of the effects of exercise upon adults demonstrate that exercise is not harmful to the adult when it is practiced in accordance with the condition and capacity of the individual. Instead of risking harm, the adult who participates regularly in suitably selected exercise gains in total vigor and may increase his resistance to the development of a condition leading to arterial and heart disease. The argument that adults should not take part in physical education because vigorous physical activity is likely to harm them is not supported by objective study and the evidence which it produces.

Physical education offers the adult more than exercise, as important as this is to his well-being. A shorter work week, longer vacations with pay, greater mobility by means of automobiles, and the construction of more outdoor recreational facilities have changed adult attitude toward recreation. The number who take part in active recreation grows each year. Skiing, which until a few years ago was hardly available to any but a few hardy individuals living in areas where skiing often was a necessary skill, is now enjoyed all across the country wherever suitable snow conditions are found. A machine for making snow is even used in some resort areas to make skiing possible during the winter season whenever the snowfall is inadequate. To enjoy these recreational opportunities the adult

[5] Delbert Oberteuffer, *Physical Education,* rev. ed., Harper & Brothers, 1956, p. 302.

must have both the skills and the physical well-being. Furthermore, there is a body of knowledge going along with these activities which the adult should possess if he is to enjoy his participation thoroughly. He needs a continuing program of physical education, just as he may need a continuing program of education in other areas of knowledge, such as political affairs, philosophy, and literature.

The physical education program for the adult should be based on the principles and practices of an effective program for all ages. The goals, that is, the major goals of physical education, are the guiding statements for the organization and conduct of the program. The principle that individuals differ, and that these differences are to be taken into account when one plans a program, applies to the adult group as well as to other groups. Within the purposes of physical education those which the adult seeks will be emphasized and others which are more appropriate for younger ages will be given less emphasis. Adult programs take into consideration age, experiences, previous learnings in physical education, physical condition, and interests, as well as the needs which all adults may have. The resources to be used and the methods of using them will also be suited to the age group.

The program recommendations for adults apply equally to men and women. Both sexes need the benefits attending regular participation in physical activities which are organically stimulating, personally satisfying, and socially sound.

When one writes about special education, or about adapting programs for special groups, he knows that the application of already tested and proven educational theories to the organization of a curriculum and the teaching of individuals through a curriculum means that all education, in a sense, is special education, for it should suit the needs, interests, and capacities of each individual, and should aim for the fullest development of an individual within the scope of a democracy. The separation of certain groups for special treatment cannot mean, therefore, that all others are ignored as individuals and treated as a homogeneous mass. The interpretation must be that the fundamental pattern of program planning, organization, and conduct yields in reality a program which fits the best concepts of educational practice. The discussion of special educational programs means simply that there are individuals with unusual needs which make their education a bit more difficult. These persons must be brought to the attention of the teacher and the administrator so that appropriate programs can be developed for them. If education in a democracy means equality of opportunity, then the differences, which are more numerous than the similarities, must be recognized if identity is not to be substituted for equality. All individuals in a grade or age group do not have equality when all the programs are identical.

INTERDEPARTMENTAL RELATIONSHIPS WITH REGARD TO SPECIAL PROGRAMS

Relationships with other offices and departments of the school and college are identical in both regular and special educational programs. The important factor is the maintenance of full communication between departments and offices in matters pertaining to the educational guidance of any individual student.

Information which the medical office may have about a student which bears upon his participation in physical education should be transmitted promptly to the physical education office. For equally good reasons information which a teacher of physical education has about a student which may be helpful to the medical, or counseling office should be sent on promptly. The method of exchanging information may be by letter, by telephone call, by personal conference, or by regular sessions in which assembled information is discussed; decisions are made with respect to actions to be taken affecting students.

Occasionally the division of responsibilities between the physical education teacher and the medical office is not well defined, nor really understood. The relationship between the administrator and the teacher of physical education and the medical personnel within an institution is that between two specialized professional persons working together in the interest of the best education of each student. The physician judges the capacity of the student to participate in the physical education program, and the teacher of physical education follows the recommendations of the physician with respect to kind and amount of exercise which students can take and carries out special remedial measures recommended by the physician where possible.

Administrative Policies Applying to Programs for the Exceptional Individual

In general, administrative policies of the department apply equally to all students. The administrator may not see how this is possible where the exceptional student is involved. In this aspect of the program, in which one may encounter difficulty in applying the policies, the following discussion may be helpful.

Evaluating and Grading the Exceptional Student

If an individual is enrolled in a course or program which normally awards academic credit, and for which grades are given, he is to receive whatever measures and rewards go with his achievement, whether he is exceptional or not. The procedures for grading have been discussed in a previous section. A problem does arise when the exceptional student is handicapped and may be thought not able to perform as well as a nonhandicapped student. The teacher can handle this matter without difficulty if he recognizes that evaluation is in terms of the goals which the institution and the department have established for this particular individual. Confusion may arise if a letter grade is used and is applied to a general subject area, such as physical education. The teacher rightly has difficulty explaining that a student in a regular class, a student who is in an advanced section of a course, and a handicapped student all may receive a grade of A in their respective courses. Only by defining the meaning of the grading can this inconsistency be resolved. The policy is to treat the exceptional student the same as others in the matter of evaluation and grading.

Credit

The exceptional student should receive credit for the satisfactory completion of subjects for which credit normally is given. The basis for credit should be consistent with the institutional basis for awarding credit. In order to be eligible for credit the educational program upon which the individual works during a term, must meet the grade level of the institution in terms of content, methods, and results. Because students are not admitted to higher institutions on the basis of their achievements in physical education, many of them may enter a college or university with physical education learnings of an elementary or junior high school level. In a sense these students are exceptional, but no more so than the student with a deficiency in mathematics or English. The exceptional student may be even further retarded than the others because he has not had opportunities to learn physical education skills and related subject matter. His program, however, should be at the grade level of the institution if he is to receive credit. Otherwise, he may be expected, even required, to take part in study and practice, in remedial work, and extra activities without credit, in order to be able to participate in courses for which credit is given. This particular problem may not be a serious one in grade levels below college, but still should be considered by the administrator. Even in the lower grades students with deficiencies are not promoted. The policy is to award credit to the exceptional student who performs work satisfactorily at the grade level of the institution.

RECORDS

A record of each school or college student is maintained in some administrative office of the institution. In addition, other records, such as a medical examination record, are kept in special offices. It is common practice for the physical education department to maintain records for the students who are enrolled in their courses. It is essential that the department prepare and maintain a record for the exceptional student.

Such a record will contain the results of examinations and tests and their interpretation, the content of interviews or conferences, the course registration, grades, and instructors' remarks, and comments from any source which have bearing upon the student's educational progress. The record is only as valuable as its use makes it. This means that instructors not only must keep records, but they must refer to them regularly.

In those instances in which the individual is under close supervision on a very restricted program, it is most important that a record be maintained and that entries concerning student's progress, changes in assignment, and recommendations of the teacher be kept up to date. The policy is to maintain a current record for each exceptional student, and to use the record in guiding the student to his fullest possible educational achievement.

Admittedly record-keeping takes time. If the use of records is acknowledged as an important part of the teacher's preparation for instruction and evaluation of outcomes, the time factor may be included in the teaching load. Also, if the value of the record for the student and the teacher is more effective use of the time and resources of both, time given to making and maintaining records may result in a saving in the long run. One does not argue for adding to the already burdened public school teacher who must make what seems to be endless reports. The argument is for an aid to instruction, rather than something which may have only statistical or historical uses.

REGULAR OR SPECIAL CLASSES FOR THE EXCEPTIONAL STUDENT

Should the exceptional student be assigned to a special class? Should he be allowed to take part in a regular class, i.e., one which meets the needs of the majority of students? Should other arrangements be made for his learning activities? When special education was thought to be only for those with handicaps, the tendency was to segregate the handicapped students from the others in their class work. This policy has been replaced by one which places the exceptional, including the handicapped, student in class situations or in learning situations where he can progress to the best of his ability toward the goals of the institution.

If one approaches program planning for the exceptional student as an individual matter, it is a relatively easy task to work out with the student a suitable physical education program. When this approach is used, one finds that some students will require individual work which has to be prescribed for them, others will need special classes in activities which they can perform and in which they will be associated with others. Perhaps the larger number among the handicapped will need this kind of learning arrangement. Another group will be able to enter classes in selected activities with the larger group of students not classed as exceptional. In these classes the exceptional student is expected to meet all the demands and requirements of the course unless some minor modifications have been allowed. Some students may be referred to special programs and activities outside the usual class pattern. Among this group may be found the gifted, who may enter demonstration groups and leader groups, and who may carry on projects beyond those ordinarily provided by the institution itself. In any event, there are several ways in which the program for the exceptional student can be planned and conducted in order to utilize his abilities completely and to fulfill his major purpose in attending an educational institution, namely, to acquire the knowledge, skills, and attitudes which the institution, and ultimately society, deem desirable.

CONSISTENCY OF PRACTICE

The school and college are educational institutions, first and principally. Programs for the exceptional student must look to the education of the individual, not to his treatment or therapy. If the individual presents himself for admission to an educational institution but is unable to engage satisfactorily in its program because of conditions over which he, or his family, has some control, he should be expected to prepare himself by whatever means are required to enter educational programs rather than therapeutic ones. Because the school is the only agency in the community which sees every youngster, through its own health program the school finds those individuals who need therapy or other corrective treatment. The school, too, is interested in the health of all children, as well as in their educational growth, and does what it can to encourage the improvement in conditions affecting health. The school itself is not a treatment agency, although it may often be tempted to enter this field when it observes the reluctance with which many adults assume even their minimum responsibilities in families and communities.

Maintaining an educational program for the exceptional individual also means the avoidance of busy work. If an individual can attend a school or college, there is almost no reason to believe that he cannot take part with profit to himself in some acceptable form of physical education instruction and practice. Furthermore, if the individual is already advanced in his physical education, other new and valuable opportunities must be offered to challenge him and justify his continued participation. There will be some individuals, however, for whom the returns hardly warrant the effort which they have to make to take part in any kind of physical education class of an active nature. If a subject is required, as physical education usually is, the teacher must not feel that his standing is in jeopardy if not every student enrolls in the courses. The teacher and administrator must study carefully their own goals as well as those of the individuals, before deciding that these persons must enter into physical education.

Finally, the administrator must maintain a meaningful relationship between the policies of the institution in assigning units, or credits, and the nature of the special education programs. Such a relationship must have considerable elasticity in order to accommodate the fact that individuals are not all alike. There are outer boundaries, and these suggest the limits within which special education is to work.

Chapter 10

EDUCATIONAL ASPECTS OF SAFETY

An area of great concern to school administration is that of safety or the prevention of accidents. The cost of lost time and care, to say nothing of the tragedy of suffering and even death, is so awesome that schools feel a direct responsibility. This responsibility includes the presentation of knowledge, the development of attitudes, and the practice of desirable skills for the purpose of inducing proper behavior. The complexities of living are so numerous and so great that the home is unable to cope with all the problems of safety which children encounter. Therefore, the school must accept a major role in teaching its students accident prevention.

When we think of our schools, we generally respect the safety which prevails. However, to think that students do not encounter safety hazards is unrealistic. The very nature of youth is venturesome, and this trait is not necessarily supported by sound judgment. The superior judgment which comes from experience is not present in young people, and consequently they often err.

The school, therefore, takes every possible precaution to protect its pupils against harm and at the same time provide them with knowledge pertaining to danger and safety. The establishment of proper attitudes toward safety is an important objective of every comprehensive educational program. The school also insists that behavior conducive to safety must be observed by all students and staff members.

THE SCOPE OF SAFETY AND PROTECTION

In spite of vigilance for the safety of all, there will be an occasional accident. This text will point out the responsibilities, both moral and legal, which the school has regarding the safety of its pupils. In addition, the safeguards which the school must provide in order to prevent accidents and injuries, are also discussed.

The scope and responsibilities for safety go beyond the activities in the physical education program or the academic classes designed to include units of safety. Safety is schoolwide and resolves itself into an individual and group attitude toward safe methods for doing things. It is through individual and group consciousness that accidents can be prevented, and in this aspect everyone has a responsibility. Therefore, this text goes beyond the realm of safety instruction, attitudes, and behavior of the physical education classes and points out other areas in the total school curriculum where safety is of utmost importance. It would be ridiculous to observe safety measures only in the gymnasium and playground and disregard them in other areas of school living.

School personnel are often confronted with difficult problems when they try to carry on certain kinds of approved activities for their students for which little or no provision has been made. These problems are presented, and a rational approach is offered. The importance of the total fitness of pupils in physical education is discussed, and some practical suggestions are offered. The chapter concludes with a description of protective insurance which is currently typical and in which there appears to be a growing interest. Insurance is not the answer for better safety programs, but it does ameliorate problems resulting from accidents or injuries.

Legal Responsibilities Relative to Safety

The legal responsibility connected with teaching is an area which has received little and sometimes no attention in the preparation of teachers. However, there has been an increasing number of court cases implicating a teacher or administrator when an injury to a child has occurred. The teacher may become involved in litigation upon the slightest whim of an irate parent. This does not mean that there is or ever will be judgment for financial liability, but the loss of time, the anxiety caused by facing court proceedings, and the financial costs for legal counsel and defense can be most annoying, if not disastrous. In order to offset the latter, many school personnel have availed themselves of personal liability insurance covering their needs, but even this does not completely mitigate the worry connected with being brought to trial.

Liability is based upon negligence, and this is ordinarily interpreted as failure to act as a reasonably prudent and careful person in the particular circumstances. Negligence occurs when a person fails to recognize and perform his duty to others. The teacher is considered *in loco parentis* to the student, and this relationship has many implications as well as extensive complications. It is so important that no teacher can ever take the responsibilities of his position lightly. To have the responsibility of a parent to a child has implications which sometimes cause one to shudder, yet there is little to fear if a teacher recognizes and accepts the conditions for which he is accountable.

A teacher who is reasonably prudent and careful will anticipate the danger involved in an activity and take the necessary precautions to avoid an accident. If he fails to anticipate or report hazardous conditions, or carries on an activity in spite of hazardous conditions, this may result in an unfavorable court decision if an accident and subsequent lawsuit takes place. The precautions must be those which would be held to be in accord with the behavior of an adult, not that of a child, who is ordinarily far more venturesome.

It is interesting to note that a common principle of law is that the school board or school district is not, in the absence of a statute, subject to liability for injuries suffered by pupils. The school board performs as a governmental agency in carrying out the functions of the state. The state is immune from liability, and this immunity is transferred to the school board. Robert L. Drury cites this quite adequately in his *Ohio School Guide*[1]:

[1] Robert L. Drury, *Ohio School Guide,* The W. H. Anderson Co., 1954, p. 199.

In accord with the general rule in this country, a board of education, in the absence of a statute imposing liability, is not liable for injuries to pupils of public schools, suffered in connection with their attendance at such schools, even if the negligence of its employees is the direct and proximate cause of such injuries. A board is not liable for injuries to pupils arising from the dangerous condition or improper construction of buildings, failure to repair, dangerous condition of school grounds, unsuitable, or dangerous or defective appliances, unsafe transportation, or the negligent acts of officers, servants or agents.

Common law exempts the board of education from liability, but such immunity does not apply to the teacher. He may be held liable for negligence. It has happened that in cases which have been filed jointly against the board of education and the teacher, as an employee of the board, the board was held immune and the teacher liable. Since school boards are immune, the tendency to file suit against the teacher would appear more attractive to anyone seeking redress. It behooves the teacher, therefore, to conduct his classes and maintain such concern for the safety of each student that negligence cannot be interpreted as part of his conduct.

In the eyes of the law it is permissible for the board of education to take full cognizance for the safety of pupils and make provisions for their protection. Drury states:

A board of education may, in its discretion, employ persons for the purpose of promoting safety of children when crossing the streets in front of school buildings, in going to and from school or to and from playgrounds. . . . A board may approve the claim as a moral one, and pay medical bills and other reasonable damages. Other opinions hold payment on a moral obligation may not be made unless by act of legislature.[2]

Although school officials, including teachers, are always liable for their own negligence, they have the legal defense of interpreting the cause of the accident as an act of God if the elements were uncontrollable, claiming that participation in certain activities necessitated the assumption of risks by the child and its parent or guardian, or pleading contributing negligence when the child performed unreasonably, imprudently, or carelessly. A multitude of circumstances would be considered in any case where a teacher became a litigant in a suit to recover damages under personal liabil-

[2] *Ibid.*

ity. It is not necessarily a condition to be feared, but something of which a teacher should be fully aware and vitally concerned.

SAFETY ASPECTS IN THE TOTAL SCHOOL ENVIRONMENT

The acceptance of environment as a contributing force in shaping the lives of youth is universal. The degree or import of environmental influence is a point upon which there is a divergence of opinion. It is not the intent of this text to debate the importance of environment in the school, but certain elements within the environment will be presented and discussed. Environment is considered as those conditions or influences which the student encounters during his school day. It is almost needless to say that a school should offer a wholesome environment in order that the most effective educational program can be presented. The American Association of School Administrators states this in its national publication: "The school plant should not only protect children from harm, but should provide a healthful environment that will be a positive influence toward the best possible physical and emotional development for living, growing children and youth."[3]

One can scarcely approach the wide variety of conditions and responsibilities which are a part of environmental safety and isolate only that part which is directly associated with physical education. Red lines may be used to define areas of particular danger or hazard, but they do not define areas of responsibility. To develop the notion that students observe safety regulations and maintain safety behavior while under the supervision of the physical education teacher and toss away this learning under other circumstances would be unwise. If the physical education teacher is to be concerned with the learning of the total child, then he must be concerned with the safety of the total child. Therefore, this text concerns itself with safety beyond the gymnasium and playground.

LOCATION. If a new school is being built, certainly profound thought must be given to its neighborhood environment. Schools must be located where children live, but areas within the same neighborhood offer surprising contrasts in environmental conditions.

[3] American Association of School Administrators, *American School Buildings*, Twenty-Seventh Yearbook, National Education Association, 1949, p. 85.

It is often astonishing what a difference a shift of a few blocks will make in neighborhood surroundings. When there is only one logical location, the board of education can often use its preemptive powers to eliminate undesirable elements which happen to be nearby.

Often it becomes necessary to police the area around a school until desirable conditions are secured. If it is an area in which there is considerable loafing, those who are not wanted will soon find a different place to loiter. Students are entitled to have their school and its surroundings free from molesting influences. Surely the area around a school is no place to permit loitering either during the day or at night. Children and older youth often need school and police protection from those who might victimize them. Loafers do not wish to be disturbed, and an active campaign to keep them moving, even picking them up for questioning, will usually discourage them to the point where they will stay away from the vicinity of schools. It might be added that if former students tend to loaf in the vicinity of the school, it is often best to work with them as individuals in attempting to solve the problem. In almost all instances cooperation can be secured if the proper approach is made.

Boards of education need to be alert to the physical appearance of a school building. It is not always possible to erect a new building, but surely children are entitled to have their buildings kept in a state of good repair. Under no circumstances should unsafe or dangerous physical conditions be permitted to exist. However, as previously cited in the *Ohio School Guide,* a board of education is not legally liable if it does permit such conditions. Nevertheless, if conditions covered in the law do exist, community groups will be quick to react and demand corrective measures.

The general appearance of the building and its surroundings should be the concern of those who administer the school program. The collected dirt and grime of decades do not add to the valuable traditions of the school. They can detract immeasurably, not only from the appearance, but also from the wholesome attitude which students should have for their school. Writings and drawings on the building should be removed immediately. If walls are kept clean, there will be far less desire to deface them. The cost of steam washing and sanding is not prohibitive, and those responsible for the maintenance of buildings will find this to be an economical approach to the total program.

GROUNDS. If the grounds are surrounded by fences or walls, these should be constantly checked for damage and kept in good repair. Sidewalks and steps should not be allowed to deteriorate so that they become hazardous. They should be cleaned and well drained to contribute to sanitation, safety, and sightliness. If grass, flowers, and shrubs can be planted and properly cared for, they will add immeasurably to the general attitude and behavior of the students.

PASSAGEWAYS AND EXITS. The state laws usually cover the conditions which must be observed in stairwells and passageways. These are not places where things may be stored or temporarily deposited. The hazards associated with the presence of materials left on stair landings and in halls are so great that this should never be tolerated. Stairs and halls should be well lighted and kept clean. Exit signs must be correctly located and properly lighted. The doors opening from exits must have panic bars and must be always in good working order. An administrator cannot be too strict in enforcing these safety measures. In case of building evacuation, there must also be unobstructed areas leading away from the building. No compromise may be permitted in providing for the safe and rapid evacuation of the students and staff of the entire school.

CLASSROOMS. In the classrooms, where the major portion of the formal teaching takes place, excellent maintenance should be in evidence. The desks and floor should be clean, the windows should function for proper ventilation, and the shades should be in good working order, but also those in charge must use the facilities efficiently. Good administration necessitates a knowledge of the most effective room usage. Students cannot perform at their best in a room which is either too cold or too warm. Neither should they be subjected to air contaminated with unpleasant odors. Light conditions change with weather conditions, and an alert administration requires that proper action be taken. The location of a room in a building, the seasons of the year, the proximity of the playground, the presence of street traffic are all factors which must be recognized by those in charge. To ignore these conditions by not attempting to correct or improve them for the best interests of the pupils is negligence. It is easy to become so involved with classroom procedures that the temperature, amount of light, and the condition of the air are overlooked. It is much easier to come from outside the room and detect undesirable conditions than to be aware of them when teaching in the room. Therefore, it behooves the teacher in charge to be constantly alert to the conditions under his cognizance or control.

There should be a minimum of disturbance to the effective carrying out of the day's objectives in the classroom, gymnasium, playground, or pool. Good administration demands that classes start from organization, not from chaos. The time when certain procedures must begin is at the opening of the class period. These procedures should be known and followed by all the students, and the teacher should demand their cooperation. The student who is willing and does follow the dictates of good organization is entitled to class conditions which are most conductive to good learning. The good administrator sees to it that these conditions are in operation.

SAFETY ASPECTS IN ORGANIZATION AND FACILITIES

The first safeguard is the careful and thorough organization of pre- and post-activity time in a regular physical education period. This means the time which is set aside for dressing for the activity and the time set aside for showers and preparation for return to other classes. Unless the use of this time is well understood and observed, some serious difficulties can develop. When students enter a dressing room for the regular daily routine, there often is a tendency to digress from normal safe practices and indulge in what is commonly called horseplay. This can be far more hazardous than even the most arduous type of organized sports. The best way to control this tendency is to establish complete understanding the first time that the students report for class instruction. It may be necessary to take serious steps in handling offenders, but the teacher or administrator who cannot control this part of the daily lesson period will quite likely have difficulties in other phases. There should be no compromise in the enforcement of rules for safety and good conduct. Valuable lessons can be learned by proper control; it need not require an accident or injury to prove the point. Another phase which must be closely checked during this period is the tendency for some to loiter in their preparation before or after the activity. It seems natural to some to take it easy and relax when they enter the locker room. This can result in getting a lesson started late, or in the student being late for the next period assignment. Sensible but rigid enforcement of rules will reduce these problems to a minimum.

It should be accepted that the physical education department needs facilities to carry out its program to the same extent that other departments needs facilities. It would be highly unreasonable to expect a science department to meet its teaching obligations without the use of a laboratory. By the same token, it is essential that physical education facilities be provided which meet the needs of the program. These facilities consist of an adequate shower and locker room and adequate indoor and outdoor space. Sufficient time must be provided for students and teachers in order to meet the needs. Essential facilities also must include a planned course of study which will result in a realistic progression toward the desired objectives. Students should be assigned according to their ability and need. In order to do this it is necessary to have substantial records which include those qualities upon which grouping will be based.

LOCKER ROOMS. The locker room should be well lighted and ventilated. It must be adequate in size to accommodate the largest classes with locker storage and dressing space. Students should be provided with full-length lockers for their school clothing so that it is not crumpled or soiled when placed in the locker. Smaller or half lockers may be used for storage of activity equipment. These lockers must be of sufficient size and properly ventilated so that the equipment will dry between periods of use.

Lockers should be set upon concrete islands six to eight inches higher than the floor. These islands may be finished with smooth concrete or faced with tile. The space between locker rows should be wide enough for free passage and dressing. Benches should be anchored so they will not topple when in use. Some schools have found it advantageous to build the locker base or island approximately two feet wider than the lockers and twelve to fifteen inches high. This provides sitting room and removes the necessity of a bench in the middle of the aisle.

All artificial lighting fixtures should be controlled from a point remote from the shower end of the room, so that the hazards of electrical contact are removed. It is essential to place the lights so that they shine upon the area between the lockers. This enables the participants to see combination locks and eliminates the hazard of benches or loose equipment in dark or shadowed places.

SHOWER ROOMS. The shower room must have vaporproof lighting fixtures controlled from a remote switch. The shower heads should be at shoulder height of the tallest student and the water flow should be controlled by the individual shower. However, the mixing chamber for hot and cold water should be under the control of the teacher, so that there is no chance of scalding water being sent into the shower. Students too often are tempted to tamper with this equipment, and serious injury can result. The floors should be nonslip and nonabsorptive, constructed from concrete, terrazzo, quarry, or ceramic tile. They should slope toward the drains at a pitch sufficient for drainage, but not steep enough to add to the hazard of slipping.

ACTIVITY AREAS. Inside play areas must be free of all dangerous obstructions. Hot water or steam pipes should be so installed as to be out of reach of participants. Windows should be glazed with wire glass or covered with protective screens. Drinking fountains, radiators, pipes, and similar objects must be recessed. Never should building supports, guy wires, or low beams become obstructions in a play area. Serious accidents are certain when conditions like these are permitted. Walls or backboard supports which are close to end lines must have heavy mat protection. Bleachers and benches should be at a minimum of six feet from the end lines and three feet from the side lines. Floors should be free from uneven joints, projections, or depressed areas.

A few generalizations will govern outdoor play areas. The grounds must be smooth and free from obstructions. The space should be large enough to accommodate the types of activities which will be included in the physical education program. If the space is limited, the teacher may have to choose between playing with modified rules or eliminating the activity. The safety of the participant is of utmost importance. Adjacent streets, buildings, walks, and power lines may govern the types of permissible activities on a play area. All rules designed to protect the participant must be taught and strictly observed.

CHECK ROOM. Although it is not essential for the safety of individuals, a facility which should be provided for all participants in physical education is a place to check valuables prior to dressing for an activity. In a general dressing room open to all members of a class, and to an occasional transient, there is too much opportunity for the loss of valuable articles. In spite of rigid rules for the protection of valuable material in lockers, some carelessness may result in a loss. Insistence upon the use of the checking privilege will bring gratifying results in the reduction or perhaps even in the total elimination of lost possessions.

SWIMMING POOL. Some hazards are peculiar to the swimming pool, but there are problems which are basically the same as in other areas. Those in charge must rigidly enforce the rules of good conduct in and around the pool. Running, pushing, wrestling, ducking, or other similar acts must be forbidden and violators punished severely. All rules concerning conduct in and around the pool must be thoroughly learned and respected. Beginners should start at the shallow end and learn to swim before entering the deep section. No one should be permitted to dive from the sides of the pool adjacent to the diving board, when it is in use. There should be only one diver on the board at any one time, and the board must be used only for its intended purpose. Swimmers are required to stay out of the center lanes when the board is being used. There should be several skilled swimmers in or around the pool whenever it is in use. Solo swimming or unauthorized use of the pool should never be permitted.

When the pool is not in use, the passageways leading to it should be securely barred. The pool and surrounding area should be well lighted and the deck maintained clean and free from obstacles. All pools should have the depth clearly marked, and in some instances the deep areas should be indicated with buoys. The ceiling over the diving boards must be of sufficient height to permit safe take-offs. The water should be maintained clear, at standard depth, and within the required bacterial count. The latter is usually regulated by laws of the local board of health and inspected by a member of that department. It has been found that bromine does not irritate the eyes and mucous membrances and does not cloud the water, yet it does restrict bacterial growth so as to meet the requirements of the board of health.

Although the cold plunge is relished by some, the majority recommend that the temperature in a general usage pool be kept at 78 to 80 degrees Fahrenheit. A pool used by smaller children should be several degrees warmer, while one used for competitive swimming may be preferred several degrees colder. The room temperature should be slightly above the water temperature. The pool should be free from all obstruction, with the walls and bottom smooth and clear. The best set of rules and safety precautions are valueless, however, unless they are strictly observed.

SAFETY ASPECTS IN THE USE OF EQUIPMENT

The price which one pays for equipment is not always indicative of its quality, but rarely can good equipment be found at bargain prices. Administrators should be prepared to evaluate the quality of equipment and make their purchases accordingly. It might be added here that good equipment is entitled to good care if it is to serve its purpose and justify the expenditure. Where rugged usage is expected, it is only short of criminal neglect to provide equipment which does not give adequate protection. If a boy is expected to play football, he must be provided with equipment of the quality necessary to do the job. A student cannot be permitted to use parallel bars, mats, ropes, balls, and bats which are of substandard quality.

After good equipment is secured, its proper and safe usage must be demanded. Violations of safety rules and regulations should never be permitted. Rings and ropes should be tested before they are used. Periodically there should be a thorough inspection of such details as the catches, turnbuckles, guywires, and crossbars on the high or horizontal bar, the supports on a ladder, the anchors and pulleys or rings and ropes, as well as the ropes. With the use of electrical equipment in tape and record players, another potential hazard is introduced. Teachers must be certain that equipment is free from shorts and that outlets and cords are safe. There is an added hazard when this type of equipment is used for instruction near the pool, and the teacher must be extremely careful lest an accident occur. The teacher must always be certain that the equipment which is being used corresponds to the ability of the user and that it is being used for the purpose for which it was intended. Every teacher of physical education knows that there are dangers peculiar to certain activities because of the variation in abilities and physical development of the participants. Good administration will eliminate the chances of injury which may be created by this situation. Participants are entitled to the opportunity to compete with others of similar development, skill, and experience. Occasionally the more daring students will attempt to do things for which they have not been properly prepared. Daring may often exceed knowledge and skill, and accidents may result. The skillful teacher progresses with his groups from the least to the more difficult activities. This insures the progressive improvement of skills so that there is safeness when the more exacting performances are executed. Good equipment, proper instruction, and enforcement of sound safety rules will all but eliminate accidents.

RECOGNITION OF HAZARDS. The teacher must be particularly sensitive to the hazards peculiar to each type of equipment. The trampoline presents the dangers involved in not bouncing properly or landing on the supports or entirely off the equipment. Proper instruction and strict observation of safety rules are essential. A sharply hit foul ball or thrown bat are inherent dangers in indoor softball or baseball. Safety rules must be taught concerning the proper use of the bat and the location of the batting team members. Parallel, high, and horizontal bars, rings, ladders, and horses have their particular hazards. Teachers are cautioned never to permit students to use the equipment until they have been taught the essential skills along with safety aspects. Then strict observance of these learnings must be maintained.

The physical education teacher should keep alert to the findings of research in safety. Many rules have been changed and new ones introduced to protect the participant in sports. Some activities have been materially altered or even eliminated because of the injurious effects revealed by research. Boxing, which was a part of many physical education programs from junior high school through college, has been very nearly eliminated as an activity. It is unnecessary to point out that the settlement of youthful altercations through the use of the gloves has dubious value. The outcome may be convincing, even disastrous, but still offer little toward the solution of the original problem.

Rule changes have brought about the use of the protective helmet by all batters in baseball, the helmet face bars and hard surface padding in football. There is a demand by some to enforce the use of fitted mouthpieces when there is a chance of injury to the teeth.

The physical education teacher should be no less alert than the football coach who checks every piece of protective equipment which his players wear. The fit in equipment is as important as its quality. The finest cantilever shoulder pad may be of little value if it does not fit its wearer. Likewise, the best planned program in physical education may annul its value if the equipment is not suited to the purpose or is improperly used.

Football and wrestling coaches emphasize safety when they use exercises designed to strengthen those body areas in which injuries most frequently occur. A participant who is adequately conditioned and who is taught how to execute properly the maneuvers which are needed in football and wrestling is rarely injured. Injury generally results from lack of condition, inadequate equipment, improper instruction, or failure to carry out an assignment correctly. However, injuries may occur because of the matching of unequal opponents, imprudent acts, unsportsmanlike conduct, or tiring of the participant. Provision for emergency care for the injured is an essential part of every safety program.

SAFETY IN SUPPLIES

The supplies needed in physical education are limited in number, but not in quality. First-aid supplies should be those items essential for the immediate handling of emergencies. Substandard materials should never be purchased. It will be well to remember that the first-aid room in a gymnasium is not a drugstore, a doctor's office, or a hospital. The teacher or administrator is not permitted to issue drugs, but he must use prudent judgment in handling emergencies.

Training supplies should be restricted to those items which have stood the test of time or which have been sufficiently recommended by competent medical authority. Extensive harm can come from training supplies which are spurious in quality or improperly used. These materials must be of standard quality, used only for the purpose for which they were intended.

Other supplies such as cleaning and disinfecting materials are usually under the control of the custodial department. There should be close working relationships with the custodian, so that the best results are obtained. The job of being a good custodian is not easy. It requires the fullest cooperation of those in charge of physical activities. Cleanliness and safety are of prime importance, and these can be secured through proper administration. The custodian is just as proud of his job as the teacher, the coach, or the administrator. He is entitled to fair treatment and will respond by satisfactorily keeping the facilities clean and in good repair. Every safety precaution must be observed in the storage, handling, and use of first-aid and cleaning supplies. Adhesive and germicides are frequently irritating to the skin. Some removing agents are highly inflammable and cleaning materials may be quite caustic. These matters require the closest cooperation and understanding among all who have a part in the handling and use of supplies.

SAFETY ASPECTS IN THE TRANSPORTATION OF STUDENTS

As schools have accepted more responsibilities and have extended the curriculum to include a larger number of activities, the needs for transportation have increased greatly. One definition of curriculum is all of the activities or experiences which a student encounters while under school supervision. This, then, goes beyond the normal school day and includes night and weekend activities. Not all these activities will be held at the student's own school, and as a result the problems of transportation develop. It is generally thought that as long as the activity is held at the school, it is the student's responsibility to be present. Even under these circumstances, the responsible teacher often arranges for transportation to the home.

Events occur during the school day which necessitate the transportation of students to another location. This could include a great variety of field trips, the appearance of a choral group at a service club luncheon, taking students to a luncheon honoring scholarship, or transporting athletes to the local newspaper office or radio station. In addition, other groups might be called to install a new chapter of Quill and Scroll at another school, to attend a county- or city-wide Arbor Day Program, or participate in athletic events. Transportation is secured through the use of school buses, public transportation, chartered buses, parents' automobiles, the students' own cars, or the automobiles of teachers. In any event, the teacher usually assumes a moral obligation for the safety of all students involved. Most schools require a written statement from parents before they will permit a student to leave school on a sponsored trip. It is stated by most authorities that although written permission from parents is highly desirable, it has little or no bearing upon legal responsibilities.

LIABILITY. If trips are made in vehicles classified as public conveyances or carriers, the legal responsibilities are assumed by the carrier. If transportation is made in school-owned and -operated buses, the school board usually is not liable as a party, and the driver is liable only for negligence. However, he still may become involved in a lawsuit if there is an accident. If students are transported by other students, parents, or teachers, the nature and extent of the drivers' liability will depend upon the laws of the state in which they operate. In case of accident, all could be subject to legal suits. The circumstances would determine the extent of civil and criminal liability. Liability from negligence cannot be avoided.

The normal activities of students often require transportation away from school. The participation in the activity will be known to and approved by the board of education and the administrators of the school, but too often the responsibilities for transportation are overlooked. The teacher occasionally, if not always, finds himself engaged in a task necessitating transportation and resolves it by taking students in his own car and securing other teachers to do likewise. If activities requiring travel are important enough for transportation, this travel should be provided through officially recognized means. It is unfair for the teacher to have the responsibility for a program and not be furnished the wherewithal to carry it out. If transportation cannot be supplied, the board of education or superintendent should so state and curtail or abolish the program. When the hour is late or the distance great, students should never be allowed or required to find their own ways home. Transportation may safely be provided a thousand times, but one tragedy could mar it all. If there is a school function in which students are participating, their transportation should be provided. When the hour is late, they must be returned to their homes. Accepted means of transportation within the community will most often suffice, but it requires only one accident to arouse the most placid community to the dangers involved in anything less than the most carefully planned program.

SAFETY AND FITNESS

Teachers of physical education must be concerned with the total fitness of their students. Likewise, they must not overlook the essential safety measures required in attaining or maintaining this status. Fitness is the goal sought from the time when students first report to the physical education class. Inasmuch as total fitness implies physical, emotional, mental, and social well-being, these conditions influence the selection of activities and the method by which they are taught.

The laws of most states provide for the teacher to evaluate the physical aspects of students. Physical education teachers are trained to observe normal physical conditions and reactions and to detect deviations from the normal. Experienced teachers usually become quite adept at discovering variations in the physical, emotional, mental, and social behavior of their students. Through their preparation to administer tests, evaluate results, administer first aid, work with doctors and nurses, keep case histories, and deal with the everyday problems of students, teachers extend their knowledge and skills to encompass the many behavior patterns of youth. They therefore learn that fitness is inseparable from the quality of performance and the degree of participation in physical activities.

Fitness is definitely related to the vigor of participation and the pleasure secured by youth in the physical education program. Teachers know that attendance, cooperation, punctuality, sociability, morale, and many other characteristics are tied in closely with fitness. Those aspects which are significant in appraising physical fitness include: growth record, carriage or posture, condition of skin, eyes, and ears, including vision and hearing, condition of mouth, including teeth and breath, and the development of the hands, arms, feet, legs, and general body. The latter should include muscular tonicity, bone and joint formation, and ease and grace of movement.

Physical fitness necessitates the efficient functioning of all body systems. It also describes an organism which can perform at capacity over reasonable periods of time without greatly depreciating in effectiveness. With relaxation and rest the physically fit person recovers quickly from the effects of fatigue. The optimum in physical fitness is achieved when the body can operate skillfully and effectually with a minimum of fatigue.

Since students do not enter classes at the beginning of a term with equal degrees of fitness, the alert teacher determines the degree and progresses from that point. To direct or permit students to participate in activities beyond their capacity may retard or stifle progress toward total fitness. Safety is of utmost importance not only to prevent physical injury but to prevent injury to the emotional, mental, and social aspects of fitness. Physical education activities must be graded and so arranged that all students can participate with enjoyment and receive the accrued benefits of activity. Progression toward the optimum development of each student is a worthy goal for the physical education program.

Fitness has many components, intellectual and emotional as well as physical, according to a joint committee statement from the American Medical Association and the American Association for Health, Physical Education and Recreation.[4] Fitness depends upon good health, exercise, adequate nutrition, rest and relaxation, suitable work, and avoidance of excesses. The statement goes on to emphasize that exercise is desirable, but not harmful exhaustion. Dr. Thomas Shaffer[5] writes that the nonmedical person interprets physical fitness as physical perfection, maximum strength and suppleness, and vast endurance. More realistic understanding implies an individual's optimum ability to perform the tasks which are necessary to realize his own potential.

[4] "Exercise and Fitness," *Journal,* American Medical Association, April 5, 1958, pp. 1744–1746.

[5] Thomas E. Shaffer, "Health Services for School Age Children," *Journal,* American Medical Association, April 5, 1958, pp. 1698–1700.

Some students are accident prone and suffer physical injury in the most peculiar ways. Safety experts in industry have known for some time that certain employees produce the accident record. Physical education teachers should know their students well enough to detect the traits which lead to injury. Some students are careless and reckless, seeming to disdain all safety rules and regulations. Others suffer injury because of a variety of psychological factors. Coaches know well that some athletes will nurse a mild injury until the close of the season, while others refuse to recognize the most painful conditions. Often participants are injured in activities for which they were not adequately prepared, either physically or emotionally. An important part of the teaching program is to prevent this type of injury.

When it is found that a student cannot or does not engage in physical activities with beneficial outcomes, there should be an investigation as to the reason. This may call for a more complete health examination, including a thorough study of the growth and development pattern. Surely students should not continue to take part in activities which produce negative physical, emotional, mental, and social results. Fitness cannot be achieved in this manner. The axiom that there is an activity for everyone and everyone for an activity is correct, but it cannot be understood to mean that everyone can be tailored to profit from every activity. The goal of total fitness can be attained only in a progression of well-chosen activities taught with regard to safety precautions.

SAFETY ASPECTS REFLECTED IN INSURANCE AND ORGANIZATION

With the trend toward a more complete insurance coverage for employees in business and industry, and a greater public interest in various forms of insurance, there has been an increase in the amount of accident insurance involving students. In some instances the state athletic associations have supported a particular form of insurance designed to cover injuries to participants in athletic contests. Accident protection plans have been extended to cover all students in almost all circumstances. Students are often covered by the insurance plan of their parents, which may be carried privately or under a group plan in business or industry. Some may carry special coverage.

INSURANCE PLANS. These plans usually include medical and hospital expense coverage in cases of accidental injury. Often there are special benefits which allow for specific additional amounts when there is a loss of a member of the body such as a hand, foot, or an eye. The usual costs which are covered by the student plan are doctor and surgeon fees, hospital care, anesthesia, X-rays, medications and dressings, laboratory tests, ambulatory service, use of operating room, and nursing fees.

To represent what appear to be common regulations concerning the protection of a student against accidental injuries, the following is selected from the Student Accident Protection Plan of the Michigan Life Insurance Company. According to this, protection applies to mishaps occurring:

1. While attending the regular school—including the lunch hour.
2. While traveling to and from school as a pedestrian, a passenger in a school bus or common carrier, or while operating a non-motor driven vehicle.
3. While practicing or participating in any school sponsored athletic event except high school football, grades 9-12, and while traveling to and from such an event in any vehicle selected and operated under the supervision of the school, during the regular school term.
4. While attending or participating in any school sponsored and supervised activity, including religious services, and while traveling to or from such activity in any vehicle selected and operated by the school.[6]

There are certain items which are not covered and for which benefits are not granted. Under the plan described these include hernia, eyeglasses, sickness or disease, bacterial infections except pyogenic ones due to accidental cut or wound, treatment rendered by a school doctor or by a person employed by the school to render such treatment, injury received as a spectator other than those occurring during the regular school term at authorized activities sponsored by the school, injuries received while participating in a fight or riot, and blisters. Injuries occurring in football played in the ninth to twelfth grades are not covered.

[6] Student Accident Insurance Policy. Michigan Life Insurance Company, Royal Oak, Michigan.

When a school system adopts a basic insurance plan, it may then subscribe to an optional high school football coverage plan. This allows for additional special benefits in the areas included in the basic plan. Premium rates are established for both deductible and nondeductible types of policies. Other exceptions, limitations, and general provisions are included in the body of the policy.

REPORTING ACCIDENTS. Almost all school systems require the prompt reporting of accidents which occur to students and employees. Some require a report whether or not the accident took place during school time or in an activity under school jurisdiction. School employees are usually covered under workmen's compensation, and accidents occurring while under school jurisdiction must be reported. Reports include personal information about the victim, time and place, nature of the injury, description of the accident, and the procedure followed in handling and reporting the accident.

TEACHER'S RESPONSIBILITY. The two broad categories which cover the responsibilities of school personnel for the proper protection and procedure for caring for a student are classified under moral and legal. It is likely that most teachers know their moral responsibilities. Many, however, are not fully aware of their legal responsibilities. School authorities should provide protective measures and effective procedures for greater student safety. This is both a moral and a legal responsibility. Protective equipment and policies should cover the cafeteria, classrooms and corridors, gymnasium and other play or recreation areas, laboratories, shops, and transportation on all trips.

An outstanding safety record does not just happen. Safety must be taught and lived. It is not enough to have essays, posters, discussions, and warnings about safety. The proper attitude toward hazardous conditions and situations must become a part of each student. Students must become conscious of safety for themselves and for others. Little can be said when a few exercise safety precautions, only to be injured by the negligence of others. All must behave according to the best patterns of safety.

Some of the factors which contribute to dangerous conditions and frequently cause accidents are lack of firm and well-informed leadership, unequal competition, activities advanced beyond the skill to perform, fatigue, overcrowded classes, and improper or faulty equipment. However, if all of these factors were eliminated, there still could be accidents. Constant attention to proper behavior must be foremost with every teacher. There can never be a compromise with the safety, health, or possibly the life of a student. Either there is conformity with the safety rules and regulations, or the penalties which are provided must be enforced.

In spite of genuine efforts on the parts of teachers, administrators, and other school personnel, students may become injured or fall ill. At these times carefully planned policies and effective procedures pay their largest dividends. When a life is at stake, an error or a delay may result in fatality. Teachers must know and apply the accepted procedures in first aid. Medically competent help should be secured when so indicated and parents should be notified. When parents are called about the welfare of their children, it must be done tactfully and the information must be accurate. The advice and permission of the parent must be secured with regard to handling the child. If hospitalization is required, the parent should indicate what hospital and which physician. The method by which the child is to be transported must also be arranged. The parent may want to come for the child or indicate responsible public transportation. Under no circumstances should an ill or injured child be sent home unaccompanied.

All teachers should have knowledge of the common symptoms of illness and be able to observe when students in their classes appear to deviate from the normal. The appearance of the eyes is often a revealing source of information for both the general and the immediate condition of health. The color and texture of the skin and appearance of the mouth, nose, and ears may aid in determining an abnormal health condition. Unusual pain may often indicate serious consequences. It is definitely advantageous for the school to have access to the immediate services of a nurse and the facilities of a first-aid room. This is where students who show symptoms should be cleared. This is also the place where malingerers can be detected and proper disposition made of their cases.

The gymnasium and athletic field often present conditions at variance with those in the classroom. There should be a definite arrangement for medical attention for cases in this area. Certain types of injuries are incurred in athletic practices and games. To believe that there will be no injuries is naive; to plan carefully to prevent them is realistic. The teacher or coach in charge must have extensive knowledge concerning the handling and care of an injured player. Well-organized athletic departments have definite procedures for the treatment of injuries. The injured student should not be left to the care of a student manager, even though these boys often show surprising efficiency at their jobs. An injured student morally and legally requires the attention and attendance of the teacher in charge. No teacher can afford to give less than complete supervision to all that takes place in the handling of an injury, from the time it occurs until it is properly taken over by parent or qualified medical personnel. It is essential that the son or daughter of another be treated with the same attention that the teacher would give his own.

Chapter 11

FACILITIES AND MATERIALS

THE FACILITIES designed for physical education are the classrooms and laboratories for its instructional and practice endeavors. The equipment and supplies are the instructional materials used by teachers and students in their learning activities. Both the facilities and the equipment and supplies must be adequate to meet the requirements of the program, and must be suited to the purposes which the program serves. These are the primary considerations which the educational institution must have in mind as it utilizes its current facilities and plans to develop new ones.

Educational facilities are used for secondary purposes also, and wherever such purposes exist and can be served by the school or college, the design, construction, and use of its facilities should aim toward accommodating these secondary purposes.

The responsibility of the administrator and his staff is to plan for the fullest possible use of the available facilities within the limits of the means for satisfactory supervision and of the funds and service personnel to maintain them in first class condition for their educational uses by the school or college.

When new facilities are to be built, the administrator and his staff are responsible for the initial statement of specifications and the suggestions for general layout and design. If the administrator has a long-range plan for the development of facilities, the more general aspects of his planning for an immediate project will have been done. There will remain the job of reviewing the plan in the light of the present situation and in terms of the money which is available for building. Any plans for the future should be reviewed periodically, because the changes which take place over a period of time in institutions alter their facility requirements.

The program of physical education includes a wide range of activities, each requiring its own type of facility, or at least its own type of area. Although programs of physical education at each grade grouping, such as elementary or high school, may be similar in content and in their needs for facilities, there are important differences between schools. Facilities should be designed to meet the program needs of the local institution. The first consideration, therefore, is the program. The steps to be followed in planning for new facilities will be discussed later in this chapter and should be studied carefully.

Information concerning planning, design, and construction features of facilities for physical education, health education, and recreation is plentiful and is increasing in amount each year. Prior to World War II texts on administration in physical education were the principal sources for this information. The College Physical Education Association had a committee on Construction and Material Equipment which published a brochure in the early twenties on standards for gymnasium construction. This brochure stood as the only document in the field dealing specifically with gymnasium construction until 1946, when publications based on the work of the National Conference on Facilities for Athletics, Recreation, Physical and Health Education appeared. Since then several publications have included information on physical education facilities and have given details of construction as well as the more general characteristics of buildings, special rooms, and outdoor areas. The administrator who is preparing to plan a new facility will wish to study the more detailed materials found in these publications.

From the standpoint of administration, the aim of this chapter is to present basic criteria which should guide planning, and which should aid the administrator in judging the adequacy of his own facilities. Consideration will be given to equipment and supplies. Furthermore, the management of the facilities and supply usage will be discussed. The basic guides to establishing management policies will be of principal concern. Finally, selected items which are of special importance to the physical education administrator will be dealt with individually.

FACILITIES

A grouping of physical education facilities gives one a basis for planning. Such grouping also helps in viewing the adequacy of one's present facilities. Finally, management practices can be related to the kind of facility. The following grouping indicates the variety of units found in physical education facilities. Although the list probably is not complete, it does set forth the major units usually provided for physical education programs in educational institutions.

I. Administrative units
   - Central administrative offices
   - Staff offices
   - Medical suite, or medical station in gymnasium
   - Auxiliary services rooms, e.g., duplicating, projection rooms
   - Conference rooms
   - Ticket sales rooms

II. Instructional and recreational areas
   - Gymnasiums
   - Special activity rooms, e.g., dance, corrective, boxing rooms
   - Swimming pools
   - Classrooms
   - Playing fields (including stadia)
   - Outdoor courts, e.g., tennis, basketball, shuffleboard courts
   - Other outdoor areas, e.g., a track, archery ranges, lawn bowling green, outdoor education area

III. Service units
   - Student and staff lounges
   - Locker and dressing rooms
   - Shower and toweling rooms
   - Toilet rooms
   - Equipment drying rooms
   - Public checkrooms

Supply issue rooms
Supply and equipment storage rooms
Training rooms
Basket storage rooms or areas
Maintenance and custodial staff rooms
Laundry area
Pool filtration and circulation equipment area

The first group of basic criteria includes those items which encourage one to give a broad consideration to the plan for physical education facilities and their use. The criteria in this group and those which follow are stated briefly. If additional explanatory discussion is needed, it will follow the statement of criterion to which it is related.

ANTICIPATED USE OF FACILITIES

Facilities should be planned for:

1. Joint use by both boys and girls, men and women wherever this is practicable.

In coeducational institutions there is no reason why facilities should be duplicated when they can be used by both sexes. Occasionally, and especially at college and university levels, the organization of the instructional staff into two separate departments is the only reason for duplicating facilities. Although an institution is large enough to justify the building of separate units, insofar as possible within these units the facilities should be usable by both sexes.

2. Multiple use within limits of the principal function of the facility.

The construction of facilities which can be used for only one activity by a small group of participants and for a limited period of time is extremely costly. The increasing cost of facilities forces institutions to plan for their multiple use, if they are to have the facilities at all. The term *multiple use* means intelligent and appropriate use. Facilities are designed to accommodate certain kinds of activities. To permit them to be used for inappropriate activities is to make them unusable for any. A gymnasium is often the only large open area in an institution. In colleges the registrar wishes to use it for registration two or three times a year; the president wishes to hold commencement and other public ceremonies there; a community group may wish to hold a conference in the room; student groups wish to hold dances, and so on. In public schools a similar list of diverse requests could be compiled. A gymnasium floor can withstand a good deal of wear, but its major function is to provide a safe and pleasing surface for the games and sports normally played on it, and it can be permanently impaired by unrestricted multiple uses.

One hopes that combinations of the gymnasium with other facilities are not as common today as at one time. If a unit, such as an auditorium-stage-gymnasium, or an auditorium-gymnasium is contemplated, the following comments are pertinent. The auditorium-stage-gymnasium is unsuitable from any standpoint. Almost without exception it is too small for the institution. There is no way by which it can be altered to increase its size. Transmission of sound to the auditorium, which may be in use at the time physical education classes are in session, cannot be adequately controlled. There is the hazard of a player running off the stage accidentally. There is only one side from which spectators can view gymnasium activities.

Combination auditorium-gymnasiums are found in a number of schools, especially in elementary and junior high schools. It is possible, of course, to set up chairs on the gymnasium floor and to convert it into an auditorium. Beyond this change the gymnasium, if it is constructed correctly, presents no other characteristics of an auditorium. The fixtures, ceiling height, lighting, and window arrangement must be suited to the gymnasium, not to the auditorium function. A more serious drawback is the fact that the conversion process takes time and labor. What often occurs is that the physical education classes preceding and following an assembly program become the custodial crews to set up and take down the chairs. What justification exists for this on an educational basis has never been identified. Furthermore, the labor of moving chairs consumes a sizable portion of the physical education class period.

Auditorium functions also may suffer. If there is need for an area for band or glee club practice, the auditorium usually serves.

If the room is used for a gymnasium also, either the music practices do not occur, or the physical education program must step aside for these practices.

One other example of questionable multiple use may be given. Field areas generally can be used for a variety of activities. The infield of a varsity baseball diamond, however, should be used only for baseball, and this does not include softball. The exception could be in the institution which can afford to replace worn and damaged areas in the turf with new sod each year. The raised pitcher's mound would have to be leveled, if other activities were to be played on the area, and then rebuilt each spring. Unless funds and personnel are really available for this type of renovation and maintenance, this particular outdoor area should be reserved for baseball. If such a facility is properly located, it need not interfere with the multiple use of adjacent (outfield) areas.

3. Local geographical and climatic conditions, so that opportunities are available for participation in both indoor and outdoor activities throughout the year.

The gymnasium has become the principal symbol of physical education facilities, even in areas where outdoor activities may be carried on during a large part of the year. In metropolitan areas there is often failure to provide adequate outdoor space for physical education. This deficiency is accompanied by a tendency to emphasize indoor facilities which are still not adequate in spite of the emphasis. One may note that Thomas D. Wood spoke of gymnasiums as facilities for use "when the weather is too bad for outdoor work." His view was that physical education is a program which should be conducted out of doors as much as possible.

4. Possible future expansion as enrollments increase and the proportion of the total number of students participating in physical education becomes larger.

The administrator facing the problem of planning for future growth has two solutions. In one plan, he may request that facilities to be constructed now incorporate the units and areas which will accommodate an estimated growth to take place over a stated span of years. If the present enrollment in his institution is 2000 students, he may plan a facility in which a program for 4000 students may be accommodated. The higher figure may indicate the anticipated enrollment within a ten-year period. One institution with an enrollment of 4000 students today is planning facilities for a student body of 20,000 within ten years.

The alternate solution is to plan facilities to meet the current and near future needs, and to design them so that additional units may be built as the student body increases in size. Additions would be constructed at five-year intervals, or at whatever period has been tentatively agreed upon. In following this procedure the administrator must be sure that (1) the current facility is a complete one which can be fully used and (2) the funds for additions will be available when they are needed. The uncertainty of this latter item causes many an administrator to secure the whole job at the beginning. In public institutions the demand for capital funds is so great today that those who get major facilities this year may not expect to return to the tax source for additional ones, or for additions to the present ones, for a long time. Full and accurate knowledge of the policy and practice of the governing body in this matter is essential before the administrator can make a decision as to the magnitude of the facility he should plan.

5. Community use when it does not interfere with the intended educational uses by the school or college, when there are *ample funds* for maintenance, repair, and supervision, and when such community use is necessary. Likewise community facilities should be open to the schools and colleges when their presence does not interfere with planned community activities.

A community in a congested area may look hopefully upon the possibility of using the athletic fields of a nearby college. They are not in use every hour, seldom on the weekends, and the summer programs may be very light. Why should not the community be allowed to conduct community recreation programs and various types of athletic league activities on these fields when they are not in use by the college? The answer lies not in the fact that college fields are nearby and not in constant use, but in the availability of outdoor athletic areas in the community and the extent to which the community is able and willing to provide adequate supervision and has funds for maintenance and renovation. It is a fact that athletic fields cannot be used continuously and be maintained in suitable condition for the best player safety and performance.

Indoor facilities may be more readily used if the requirements of supervision and maintenance are met. Again it is extremely important to make sure that community use does not impair the facility, interfere with the time on which the school or college depends for its own program usage, or divert funds from school and college appropriations which are needed by these institutions for the proper conduct of their own programs.

6. Health service facilities in or near the gymnasium, and athletic fields to provide emergency care and other prescribed services maintained by the institution.
7. Flexibility, so that modifications within the facilities can be made without changing the overall construction.

The degree to which one plans facilities for flexibility is limited. After all, if one cannot be reasonably confident that his plans for facilities will suit the institution's program needs for some years in the future, he should not permit them to serve as a basis for construction design. One cannot plan buildings or permanent outdoor facilities with reservations which may be taken up within a few years. On the other hand, the criterion of flexibility means that unusual programs requiring unusual facilities are likely to be uneconomical and inflexible, and, because they usually are untried, they may be of short life. If a specialized facility is constructed, it should be arranged to permit subsequent alteration without requiring major construction changes. Discussion of this criterion can be complete and meaningful only in the context of a specific situation. Its general implications should be understood by the administrator.

8. Ease of movement of users from one facility to another, where functions are related. Gymnasiums, swimming pools, and other activity areas should be within easy reach of the locker, shower and dressing rooms, toilet facilities, and other service areas. Indoor dressing facilities should be readily accessible from outdoor areas without necessitating student traffic through other portions of the building.

It seems clear that facilities should be grouped and arranged on the basis of functional relationships. Preconceived ideas of building or field arrangements should be laid aside in favor of a functional study of the program and the needs for facilities. Careful planning of the movement of traffic within facilities is often neglected. If a facility is to be used by the public as well as by the students of an institution, the control of public movement within the building is most easily achieved by planning for it before the facility is built.

The remaining criteria bear more directly upon the details of facilities which are of significance both in planning for new ones and in judging the adequacy of ones already in use. There are four groups of criteria, dealing with the details of (1) size and number, (2) location, (3) safety, and (4) economy.

SIZE AND NUMBER

1. All facilities should be of sufficient number for class instruction in activities under actual game conditions.

Not only should there be enough teaching stations to accommodate the program, but the size of the facilities should permit laboratory experience under game conditions. Standard court and field dimensions should be followed in the planning of new facilities.

2. "Units should be sufficient in kind and number to provide opportunities for peak load participation in informally organized activities, intramural sports and intercollegiate (interscholastic) athletics."[1]
3. "Every effort should be made to provide the maximum amount of space for participation in activities by limiting administrative and service units to spaces essential to meet the criteria of efficiency, comfort and sanitation."[2]
4. An important dimension of activity rooms is the ceiling height. Multipurpose rooms are more economical to construct if the activities planned for them all require about the same ceiling height.
5. The outdoor areas should be sufficient in size and variety to accommodate the typical sports, games, and other activities

[1] *College Facilities for Physical Education, Health Education and Recreation,* College Physical Education Association, 1947, p. 2.

[2] *Ibid.,* p. 3.

of the physical education, athletic, and recreational programs associated with the institution.

An essential need of children and youth is vigorous out-of-door activity. A major deficiency in educational facility planning is the omission of adequate outdoor space adjacent to the school building. In large metropolitan areas schools may be built with no outside play space. When the schools were constructed, there may have been available open land about them. The lack of foresight, and perhaps outright ignorance on the part of the school planners, resulted in failure to acquire adequate land for playfields around the new buildings.

The importance of land area adequate to meet the present and future needs of an institution, whether a public school or a college, is too often acknowledged after there is no land available for the institution to acquire. Foresight exercised in long-range planning can see the logic of acquiring the land which the institution will need for years to come. Scott states that "where additional land is required for the building program, an effort should be made to determine probable institutional requirements for a period of fifty to a hundred years. Since land deficiencies are one of the most serious limiting factors in the development of college facilities, the greatest possible acreage should be acquired whenever it is available. Where the development of a college is concerned, time serves to make land shortages more acute and the price too exorbitant for most institutions to bear."[3]

The following standards indicate the minimum land space for play areas which should be provided for each level of school. The standards are recommended by the National Facilities Conference.[4]

Elementary schools—For urban areas, ten acres or more, depending upon the population.

For rural areas five acres or more for single schools, and ten for consolidated schools.

Junior high school—twenty-five acres for a school-community center.

Senior high school—forty acres or more, for a school-community center.

[3] Harry A. Scott and R. B. Westkaemper, *From Program to Facilities in Physical Education,* Harper & Brothers, 1958, p. 17.

[4] National Facilities Conference, *A Guide for Planning Facilities for Athletics, Recreation, Physical and Health Education,* The Athletic Institute, 1947, pp. 7–9.

Outdoor areas for colleges and universities are not defined as precisely as those for the lower school grades. Hughes states:

Every college and university, regardless of size, should attempt to provide such minimum outdoor facilities as the following:

1. Separate playing fields for men and women, within easy walking distances of the dormitories.
2. Several playing fields, in addition to varsity facilities, suitable for such activities as touch football, field hockey, soccer, and speedball in the fall, and baseball, softball, soccer, and lacrosse in the spring.
3. Multiple-paved area for court games, skating, and other activities requiring a hard surface.
4. Football gridiron and practice field for men.
5. Baseball diamond.
6. Quarter-mile cinder track with a 100-yard straightway.
7. Tennis courts (at least one for every fifty students).
8. Archery range.

Other facilities which are highly desirable are: camping facilities, golf course, one-wall handball courts, dancing area, horseback riding facilities, and hiking trails.[5]

According to the National Facilities Conference, many communities over the country have acquired 40 to 100 acres and more for high school sites. A list compiled for the conference in 1946 showed only one high school site under 40 acres, whereas there were 11 within the range of 80 to 99 acres.[6]

As communities grow in response to population increases, the importance of securing ahead of time the necessary acreage for the schools as well as the playing fields becomes greater. Real estate developers work to secure all the land possible in a growing area. Only where the community requires developers to set aside adequate tracts for school purposes can the school itself be assured of needed areas for play fields and recreational uses. Although the physical education administrator has no authority in the matter of site acquisitions, he should exercise the responsibility of setting forth the needs of the school to those who are going to select sites for new developments. He also should make every effort to correct past errors in the matter of inadequate site acquisition.

[5] William L. Hughes and Esther French, *The Administration of Physical Education,* A. S. Barnes and Co., 1954, p. 298.

[6] National Facilities Conference, *op. cit.,* pp. 5–11.

Colleges and universities face similar problems in the matter of land acquisitions and site development. All too frequently in this day of rapidly increasing enrollments and demands for new buildings a confined campus devours its open land for buildings and, occasionally and indefensibly, for automobile parking. Again the physical education administrator must anticipate the changes which are likely and prepare his argument, setting forth his needs (which really are the needs of the students, who have no one to speak for them) for outdoor areas as part of the instructional and recreational facilities of the institution.

LOCATION

1. Facilities should be accessible to those who are to use them most frequently.

This statement makes a point so obvious that one may wonder why it is mentioned at all. In public schools the gymnasium and other indoor facilities are usually incorporated within the total structural plan of the school. In colleges and universities the buildings are usually units in themselves. As units they should be located near the major classroom buildings and dormitories.

2. Facilities should be located away from industrial buildings, hospitals, and any unusually noisy or hazardous installation. Likewise, the play areas should be located and constructed so as to minimize the interference by the physical education activity with other school and college activities.

Noise from outside the teaching area increases the difficulty of instruction and introduces an element of tension in the total situation. Facilities which are close to airfield runways, to railroads, or to noisy industrial operations are used less effectively than those which are more favorably located with respect to the noise factor.

The level of activity in the physical education class should not be controlled by the needs of other nearby classes. Noises from outdoor activities are not likely to disturb indoor classes unless the outdoor activity is almost against the building. Indoor construction of heating conduits or air conditioning units which places classrooms on the same conduit as the gymnasium or other exercise area is undesirable, since these conduits are excellent channels for conducting the noise from one area to another. One must insist that such construction be avoided, for it cannot be assumed that all architects are aware of the problem. One can find the mistake being made today in new construction.

3. Facilities should be arranged so that effective supervision is possible with a minimum of effort and cost. This applies to the general arrangement for the major units, as well as the internal arrangement for each unit.

In small installations it is possible to locate the departmental office adjacent to the gymnasium. Direct supervision is possible from the office through a window looking out into the gymnasium area. The location of the office could be such that it overlooks the outdoor areas also, thus giving direct observation of both indoor and outdoor facilities.

In schools or institutions which possess several facilities, the location of the office in a position to give direct observation of all units is impossible. Supervision becomes a matter of having personnel present at the facilities whenever necessary. In this situation the location of offices should be as convenient to all facilities as possible. An institution may decentralize its instructors' offices by placing them in a location from which each facility, at least each indoor facility, can be observed. It would seem that staff unity might be impaired by this arrangement of offices and become a more serious problem than the more difficult matter of maintaining supervision of facilities from a centralized office area.

Supervision means the involvement of people. Since people can move about, in the assignment of space other factors are of more importance than the location of an office solely for purposes of direct supervision. For example, in colleges equipment and supply issue rooms are usually located within or adjacent to the dressing rooms. Supervision of the locker room is possible from the supply issue room.

Swimming facilities, on the other hand, require constant supervision when they are in use. An office located next to the pool with a large window opening onto the pool area permits direct observation and supervision by the instructor in the office. When swimmers are in the pool the supervisor must be within the pool room area if there is to be maximum protection against accident.

4. Buildings (gymnasiums and fieldhouses) should be located in attractive surroundings and should themselves be pleasing in design.

The design of gymnasiums should be functional rather than traditional. Functional design should produce a structure which is pleasing to the eye. In general the design should blend with the architecture of other buildings in the institution, although new buildings erected on a campus or in a community where the predominant architecture is very old, and lacking in functional qualities, should depart from the traditional pattern. It should be possible for an architect to plan a building whose design will be modern and functional, but still blend in with the older architecture of the area.

5. Fields for intercollegiate practice and competition should be located so as to provide a minimum of interference with the required or elective programs.

Where fields are subject to multiple use this criterion is met without difficulty. It may be more correct to state that the scheduling of field area usage should result in a minimum of interference with the instructional program.

6. The facility should be located so as to make the effective exclusion of unauthorized persons from all activity areas as certain as possible.
7. Facilities which are to be open to spectators should be accessible to the public with a minimum of traveling on or through other facilities areas, and with no intrusion upon playing areas.

The last two criteria relate to the control of use, and of traffic on and within the facilities. An administrator and his staff who are planning for new facilities will find that time devoted to making a careful analysis of traffic flow in the buildings and on the outdoor areas will pay enormous dividends in terms of easier supervision and lowered maintenance costs when the facilities are finally put to use. School buildings which are used frequently by the public are planned to admit the public only to those areas which they are to use. Gymnasiums should incorporate the features necessary to exercise this control. Outdoor areas in heavily populated neighborhoods must be fenced if their use is to be controlled. Certainly any facility which may be hazardous when used carelessly should be securely enclosed.

On the other hand, it is important to make public access easy to those areas which are to be used, and to avoid having the public pass over or through areas which they are not to use.

8. "Orientation of the building should provide the maximum amount of natural light without permitting the direct rays of the sun to shine in the eyes of the players during active games."[7]

Similarly, outdoor areas should be laid out according to the direction of the sun's rays during the hours of greatest use. Orientation charts can be found in the book on college facilities.

9. Facilities should be located so as to permit possible future expansion.

There are two reasons for attending to this criterion. One is that school and college enrollments are rising and are expected to continue to rise for some years to come. Another is that an increasingly large proportion of the students uses the facilities of physical education. It was pointed out earlier that the administrator may arrange for the areas necessary to meet the predicted growth of the institution when he is planning for new facilities. If this kind of construction is not possible, by all means the administrator must define the future needs of the institution and specify the location of currently planned facilities so as to permit additions or augmentation through the acquisition and development of adjacent areas.

SAFETY

1. "Facilities should be planned and constructed to provide for the safety of participants and staff members, and for the maximum sanitation of the plant."[8]

[7] *College Facilities for Physical Education, Health Education and Recreation, op. cit.*, p. 14.
[8] *Ibid.*, p. 3.

2. Especial attention should be given to such features as lighting, floor and wall surfaces, location of fixtures, and use of glass with the purpose of designing for safe construction.

ECONOMY

1. All facilities should be constructed at the lowest cost compatible with (a) highest quality of construction for the uses to which the facility will be put, and (b) greatest ease of maintenance at a low cost.

Several factors other than the cost of labor and materials enter into the cost of facilities. An important factor in school building construction is the code of state requirements and, where one exists, of the city. Building codes are notoriously behind times; often they represent the built-in desires of labor unions and of manufacturers, too, who hope to benefit from public construction projects. Code provisions, which may be reasonable for certain types of buildings, may be almost meaningless for other types. One cannot overlook the importance of safety features, such as the number of exits and size of stairways in public buildings, and those which improve fire protection. On the other hand, when lighter construction would be suitable and durable, the building requirements may call for structures of almost bastillelike proportions which increase costs without increasing usefulness.

The design of an architect anxious to enhance his reputation by creating a plan of unusual character may at first viewing appeal to those for whom the building is intended. When the costs are reviewed in terms of the facilities acquired, however, the design may prove to be in the luxury class and threaten to absorb funds which could be used for additional facilities or for other new projects.

Creating a facility to serve a highly specialized and unique program will prove costly, if the program is short-lived and if the facility cannot be readily modified for other uses.

Labor costs are so high today that the architect and the builder must seek construction methods which will utilize the least labor. In general, the result of such planning will provide as good a building as if more labor had been used. Of greater concern, however, is the quality of materials used. Although there is no single policy which can be followed with respect to the selection of materials, one can point out that the use of cheaper materials does not mean automatically that the construction will be less costly, or that the building, in the long run, will be less costly. Conversely, using the most expensive materials may not result in a better constructed nor more durable building. The significant task is to select those materials which fulfill the uses to which they are to be put in an entirely satisfactory manner, which are durable as may be required, and which will serve with a minimum of repair, replacement, or servicing. Furthermore, labor costs are about the same whether the workman is handling cheap or expensive materials. In some instances, labor costs actually are less when more expensive materials are used.

Butler states that "Maintenance costs often bear a direct relation to construction costs; a small addition to the latter through the use of better materials may result in a considerable saving in maintenance."[9] Again the factor of labor costs enters in, not as a single expense but as one which will continue during the life of the facility. The decisions affecting materials costs relative to maintenance costs are based on technical and somewhat complex factors. The administrator who is concerned with the development of new facilities should be aware of these relationships.

2. Advantage should be taken of newer types of construction, which may lessen construction costs.

The better architects will be familiar with materials and design development tending to reduce construction costs without lowering the quality of the final unit. A building or other facility is a creation. An architect who indicates only that he will follow, i.e., in a sense imitate, what has been standard practice should be shunned.

3. The estimated useful life of the facility may be one factor in determining the permanence of construction.

School and college buildings are built to last and last. An estimated minimum life of fifty years attaches to the specifications upon which the planning is made. In some ways a long building life is essential if communities and states are going to be able to afford to build them at all. There are areas in the country today which are turning to lighter and less permanent construction for some facili-

[9] George D. Butler, *Recreation Areas,* A. S. Barnes and Co., 1947, p. 7.

ties. Rapid population growth now requires greatly expanded facilities. Before the life of a permanent type of structure has been terminated, the population may shrink. In several communities adaptable and less costly units have been constructed which can be demolished when their usefulness is ended. Let it be said with emphasis that only the best professional and technical personnel, pooling their resources, can decide what is the appropriate type of construction for any specific area.

4. Auxiliary uses, such as fall-out shelters and the like, may also influence building construction.

It may be pointed out that these auxiliary functions may be provided, if the community desires, if the building construction is not altered in a manner to limit its educational usefulness, and if funds needed for school or college educational facilities construction are not diverted to these auxiliary units.

SELECTED ITEMS CONCERNING FACILITIES

This discussion of facilities could terminate with the listing of basic criteria to be followed in planning new facilities and in judging the adequacy and suitability of those already in use. Any person who has planned a facility for his institution knows too well that every detail is important. For the physical educator who is approaching the task of stating important specifications for his facilities, there are "selected items" to which special attention may be given briefly. The following list is short. The items chosen are those which too often are assumed to be correctly planned in new facilities and prove not to be.

FLOOR SURFACES. Obviously, floors should be suited to the principal activities to be carried on in an area. Experience has demonstrated conclusively that no one type of floor surface can be used for all activities and maintained in the best condition to serve the principal activities to be played on it. A hardwood (maple) floor more nearly satisfies the requirement of an all-purpose floor surface, but it cannot be maintained satisfactorily under all kinds of use.

In a major facility which will incorporate several activity areas, the administrator should plan for the accommodation of activities requiring one kind of floor surface in one area, and those requiring another kind in another area. He should be definite in stating those activities or events which cannot be accommodated in each area.

Administrators who are not in the field of physical education are prone to see a gymnasium floor area as a large, unobstructed space which can be used for every conceivable kind of event, from the athletic activities for which it was primarily planned, to registration (in colleges), commencement, conferences and conventions, inaugurations, community meetings, and anniversary banquets. Only where a gymnasium floor surface is fully protected by a covering made of suitable fabric should it ever be used for anything but the physical education activities.

Floor surfaces of vinyl or other composition tile are more suited to general use, but are not safe to use for activities involving rapid movement, sudden stopping, and sudden changing of direction. Also, because this kind of surface usually is laid on a felt base directly over a cement slab, it is not as resilient as the wooden floor.

All flooring materials should be protected from moisture underneath them. The base upon which the floors are laid should be dry, and should remain that way. In the past, to place a gymnasium floor immediately above the swimming pool room was to invite certain damage to the flooring. Today, in buildings whose floors are constructed of concrete poured in a solid slab, it is possible to incorporate a permanent moisture barrier in such a floor base, thus eliminating the danger of damage to floors laid above a pool area. The administrator must make certain that this type of construction is incorporated in new facilities wherever it is required.

Surfaces for running and jumping should be resilient if the players are to avoid rapid fatigue, and in some instances actual incapacitation. One will choose a surface that insures resilience and will see that the surface materials are set on a base with cushioning construction or that cushioning materials are laid over the base before the final floor surface is put down.

Physical education activities take place on both indoor and outdoor playing surfaces. The administrator should specify fully the requirements which the construction must fulfill, and he should not compromise with these specifications.

PERMANENT AUDIENCE SEATING. Whether an institution seeks

large public audiences at its athletic events or not is determined by institutional policy. Except for a few large universities, indoor sports events are conducted in the gymnasium which also serves as a teaching area for the physical education program. To serve the dual purpose as an area for teaching and a location for public events, the facilities for seating the audience should not utilize teaching space when no audience is present.

The argument, therefore, is against permanent types of seating construction for indoor events in all situations in which the gymnasium is used principally by the physical education classes. Space allocated to permanent seats is dead space as far as the instructional program is concerned, no matter what kind of space is provided underneath it.

Permanent seating construction is permissible in outdoor areas where there is ample room for the class program. Where outdoor areas are used extensively by groups, such as varsity teams, a building which will provide dressing, shower, and uniform storage facilities may be combined with construction of permanent seats. It should be recognized that this is not the least costly way to construct a building, but, given the necessity of building permanent seating facilities, the space and areas under the seating structure can be utilized. Scott states that "under-stadium development that meets the functional standard of use is economically advisable only if the cost of construction is less than it would be at other available sites."[10]

STORAGE ROOMS. A common complaint of people who occupy older facilities, and of several who have moved into new ones, is that adequate provision was not made for storage. Since space for storage costs about the same as space for classrooms and other teaching areas, the tendency is to use only odd-shaped areas or space left over in a corner or off a hallway for storage rooms. One can see a parallel between residence dwelling construction and school construction in that the older homes seldom had enough closet space built into them. Today it is essential to have adequate and conveniently placed storage space if the facilities are to be fully usable.

Equipment, such as net standards, nets, mats, and apparatus should be kept in storage rooms adjacent to the exercise areas in

[10] Scott and Westkaemper, *op. cit.,* p. 419.

which they are to be used. Instructional supplies, such as balls, racquets, boxing gloves, and similar items, should be kept in closets adjacent to the class areas.

Other storage needs, such as those for office records, for reserve instructional supplies, for seasonal equipment when it is not in use, and for gymnasium and team uniforms, should be provided as needed and in the most suitable locations. Maintenance of control over supplies and equipment, as well as the better care of these items, is possible only when adequate and proper storage space is available.

After a building is completed it is almost impossible to add storage space, unless that space is taken from areas which were designed for other uses. The period for thoughtful planning of storage needs is at the moment when one is setting forth his total space needs.

FOLDING DOOR PARTITIONS. A large indoor area may be divided to provide separate rooms, each visually and acoustically isolated from the others. In general the best types of folding doors now available are entirely satisfactory in operation and in fulfilling the function of separating the areas effectively. The type of folding partition which moves on an overhead track and is not borne by the floor is superior to one which runs on a track laid in the floor. Expansion and contraction of the wooden floor during changes in weather and seasons can force the track out of line and cause increased maintenance problems in keeping the doors operating.

The surfaces of the doors should be strong enough to withstand the impact of balls striking them and should even serve as a surface against which students may practice skills, such as serving in volleyball, passing in basketball, and serving in badminton.

In the planning stage the area to be divided should be studied carefully with respect to the location of playing courts. These courts should be arranged so that they are fully usable for teaching and playing purposes when the partition is in place. Simpler suspension devices for backboards may be installed, too, if it is possible to place the partition so that it does not bisect the exhibition basketball court lengthwise.

ACOUSTICAL PROPERTIES. One of the most difficult problems in building construction is that of achieving suitable acoustical properties in the teaching areas. There is less effort and strain for the teacher working in a room with good acoustical properties. For the students in the same situation, there is easier participation in the instruction and less strain because of the absence of interfering noise.

The administrator can point out the significance of having good acoustics in the teaching areas. Beyond that he must leave the design and materials selection to the architect and the engineer.

The swimming pool room presents special problems because of the high humidity which is always present. The walls, floors, and ceiling surfaces are likely to be covered with nonabsorbent hard materials which provide reflecting surfaces for sound. If it is possible to introduce sound absorbing materials into the construction of the walls and ceilings, this should be done. Correctly planned and installed heating and ventilating systems may prevent excessive condensation on these surfaces and make possible the use of sound-absorbing materials.

The important point is that the design for facilities should incorporate the features which keep noise levels at the lowest possible point, especially in teaching and office areas.

PUBLIC ADDRESS SYSTEMS; TELEVISION PICK-UP. Whenever audiences gather to view athletic events or other public affairs held in a gymnasium building, it is desirable to have a public address system in operation. It will be wise to plan for the installation of the system as part of the building construction. Outlets for microphones and amplifiers can be provided and the loudspeakers can be installed. Conduits for the transmission lines can be installed at slight extra cost during the construction of the building. Because there seems to be no way now by which the acoustical character of any completed public room can be predicted accurately, after the building is completed the speaker systems may require adjustment to achieve an acceptable performance.

If athletic events and other programs are to be televised from any of the areas within the gymnasium building, it is important that plans for the building include the bringing of adequate power to the areas and the installation of necessary conduit to carry lines from the camera to control and transmission equipment. Although television cameras are somewhat portable, platforms should be built upon which to place them in the larger areas.

Events which are to be televised must take place in areas with high illumination. Scott states that "twenty-five foot candles of light at playing surface will suffice for taking motion pictures at sound-film speed, provided the camera lens has an appropriate aperture. Activities can be televised in black and white, but for most satisfactory production, a minimum of 50-foot candles of light is recommended. For color television, a minimum of 75-foot candles is recommended."[11] One plan for lighting an exhibition area is to provide adequate lighting for the playing of the games, and for instruction and practice purposes during classes and intramurals, and to provide supplementary lighting units which can increase the intensity of light in the area for exhibition and television.

Television installations are less costly now than they were originally. Aside from the use of this medium to carry events to larger audiences, television may be employed effectively to supervise large areas in a building. Fixed cameras of a relatively inexpensive type can be located so as to look out upon an exercise area. The monitoring set can be placed in the office, where personnel is on duty at all times. By checking the pictures transmitted by each camera at regular intervals, large areas can be supervised, in the sense that the presence of persons on them is known, the kind of activity going on is known, and the presence of persons not properly costumed is detected. It is also possible, of course, to have the monitoring set operate continuously, or to have a small set for each camera, and to have all sets operating continuously. If television equipment is to serve in this way, the necessary conduits to carry the cables should be installed at the time the building is constructed.

SHOWERS FOR GIRLS. New gymnasium construction for girls and women should plan showers of the open type for women as well as for men. The trend for a long time has been toward this type of shower arrangement for girls, and there should be no reversing of the trend. It will be necessary to provide a few individual booth showers along with the open ones, but the number should be kept small. The often complex dressing booth and shower unit which

[11] *Ibid.*, p. 464.

was installed in the girls' shower facility was costly, unsanitary, and practically impossible to protect against the deterioration caused by water. There are no sound reasons today for continuing to use this kind of unit.

Hair driers must be provided in sufficient numbers to serve the largest number of girls regularly using the shower and dressing facilities at one time.

TEAM LOCKER-DRESSING ROOMS. In those grade levels which permit regular programs of interscholastic athletics, as well as in colleges, the question arises during the planning of new facilities as to the necessity of providing separate locker and dressing rooms for athletic teams. It has been argued that one of the purposes of physical education is to improve the social maturity of the participants, and that making it possible for contestants to share dressing facilities before the game, as well as afterward, provides an excellent means of educating for social maturity. Also, housing its own athletic teams in the central locker-dressing-showering facilities used by other students in the institution minimizes the special privilege feeling which may develop among athletic participants. There is argument in favor of this position.

If all attitudes directing player and coach behavior prior to, during, and following an athletic event were attuned to the idea of seeking social maturity among the several possible outcomes, the use of a common dressing room would be commendable. Because no such attitudinal condition is general within the realm of athletics, it seems more expedient to provide separate dressing and locker rooms for the home teams and the visiting teams.

If it is planned to have all athletic squad members use the central dressing unit, special units will have to be provided for certain teams because of their uniforms and playing equipment. Football equipment cannot be stored satisfactorily in the usual type of dressing locker. Some recommend that football uniforms be placed on special hangers on open racks. Lockers of the usual type are unsuitable. Uniforms worn by players in other sports may also require special dressing and storage units. To provide separate rooms where these special units can be placed may be as economical as trying to arrange for them in a larger central unit.

Although Scott and Westkaemper hold that the use of a central locker-dressing-shower facility by all students who engage in any phase of the physical education activity program is educationally sound, they state that "the particular requirements of the program of competitive athletics . . . are such that specially designed dressing quarters are desirable. In addition to meeting the requirements of care and storage of athletic team equipment, the team dressing rooms enhance morale factors and ensure "privacy for pre-game and between-halves relaxation and briefing."[12]

The aim is to provide a facility which meets the requirements of care and storage of athletic equipment, which maintains the maximum of integration of the athletic facilities and program with the total physical education program, and which can be constructed economically. The principle that the facilities are to serve the program should be followed. Program comes first. Facilities are one of the means by which the program can be carried on. Whether separate dressing facilities are to be provided for teams will be decided in the light of the goals, organization, and conduct of the program of physical education in the institution.

PLAYFIELDS. The planning, construction, and maintenance of playfields are subjects which require separate and detailed treatment. For the administrator who is looking forward to the development of outdoor areas, two statements are offered. The first is obvious, namely to secure the latest and most authoritative information concerning the design and construction of the outdoor areas. The second, with reference to playfields (which means a turf area), is to plan for more field area than will be used regularly throughout the year. The reason for this is that turf areas cannot be maintained under constant and intense use. Butler states that turf "can rarely be maintained, however, on a small intensively used area, especially if open for play the year round. . . . Occasional periods of rest are necessary to keep turf in good condition."[13] He states further that "rest periods must be provided if the area receives intensive use, and game areas should be shifted from time to time or from season to season, wherever possible, to distribute the wear on the turf."[14]

[12] *Ibid.*, pp. 286, 287.
[13] Butler, *op. cit.*, p. 9.
[14] *Ibid.*, p. 10.

Unless the policy of *resting* a field area is followed, the alternatives are (1) to give up the hope of maintaining a turf field by ordinary means, or (2) to plan on expensive maintenance by placing sod on worn areas each season. Sodding of denuded areas may not be fully satisfactory unless the new covering is given time to take hold in order to provide a firm surface.

AVOIDING ERRORS IN CONSTRUCTION

To secure the facilities which one desires means planning ahead, and too much stress cannot be laid upon this step. One who plans intends to secure facilities in which there are no unwanted features. To the extent that planning has been unhurried, careful, and thoughtful, the resulting facilities will be relatively free of construction errors. For whatever help they may give, several common errors of construction are described. These are taken from the text on college facilities.

One of the factors most discouraging to the professional worker in his attempt to improve and extend programs of health, physical education, and recreation is the tragic prevalence of errors in the construction of facilities. In fact, such errors of omission and commission are so widely spread that there are few facilities in existence today which meet all desirable known standards. Due to such things as (1) the absence or ignorance of desirable standards, (2) the failure of designers and program specialists to pool their knowledge, (3) a policy of false economy and (4) the tendency to imitate, grievous mistakes have been made and repeated. The result has been the construction of monstrosities that have persisted for generations.

Common errors in gymnasium construction include: slippery or splintery floors, low ceilings, inadequate lighting, leaking skylights, permanent or portable bleachers which occupy valuable playing areas, insufficient storage and office space, no sound-proofing, a routing of traffic which requires students wearing street shoes to walk across main gymnasium floors to reach dressing rooms or other facilities, and supporting columns which obstruct the view of spectators and form dangerous hazards to players in activity areas.

Lockers and showers are frequently placed in small, dark, basement areas which are difficult to keep sanitary. Floors in these units may be dangerously slippery.

> One of the most glaring errors of omission is failure to provide sufficient outdoor facilities for the general student body. Fields may be too far from dormitories or the center of the campus to permit regular use. Valuable play space may be confiscated for college buildings. . . . Running tracks have been built without the services of a surveyor to insure official width and distance, and jumping pits, insufficient in number, have been constructed with unprotected side walls. Few institutions provide sufficient tennis courts for even one physical education class of 40 students.[15]

That other errors of construction occur, any teacher of physical education can attest. One large and relatively modern gymnasium had a special locker, shower and toilet facilities for the handicapped students in the university. The showers were placed in a common area with the toilet facilities. Although the showers were built with floor drains, water from the showers would splash onto the floor of the larger area. There was no floor drain in this area to carry away the water nor to permit the washing and flushing of the floor itself.

One need not dwell at length on errors, for the list could be extended almost endlessly. Common errors should be avoided. Thinking and rethinking about the proposed needs, and a most thorough and careful review of specifications and plans as they are developed by the architect, will bring to light other features which are to be corrected before the facility is constructed. Constant supervision of the construction will prevent expedient alterations which the builder may wish to make, most often to save money, and which to him seem to cause no basic change in the structure itself. An example of this latter occurred in a new building containing radio studios. A steam line was to be laid underground, according to the specifications. For some reason the contractor's men forgot to put the line down before the foundation floor of cement was poured. Rather than go through the costly process of placing the line where it was supposed to be, the contractor suspended it from the ceiling of the radio studios. Because the pipe ran through two studios, it became a sound conductor from one studio to the other. Furthermore, the changes in steam pressure during various hours of the day produce noises within the pipe itself. All the cost of soundproofing the studios was wasted. Also, the studios themselves are relatively worthless for the purpose they were to serve unless the line is

[15] *College Facilities, op. cit.,* pp. 5–6.

changed. To change the line is costly, and the cost must be borne by the institution. Planning is not enough. Expert and continuous supervision is necessary during the construction period and final inspection.

PLANNING NEW FACILITIES

There are several reasons for an institution to seek new facilities: the student enrollment has increased to the point where present facilities are entirely inadequate to provide the space and other means with which to conduct educational programs; a plan for expansion of student enrollment poses the need for added facilities; changes in educational programs require additional facilities; current facilities have reached the period when their useful life for educational purposes is past and they must be replaced; and current facilities have not been adequate for the programs which the institution is conducting, although under handicaps. These factors can apply to a public school system as well as to a college or university. Although an institution which has a long-range plan for the development of its facilities will have taken these factors into account, they are, nevertheless, the causes for new facility development.

Because new facilities for any particular phase of the educational program are constructed to serve for many years, when the administrator of physical education has the opportunity to plan them, his proposals should be based on the projection of a thorough educational program already in operation. His thinking should explore completely the realm of possible achievement.

It may seem that the importance of careful, thorough, and competent planning is stressed too greatly. If this kind of work is not done, the new facilities may be unsuited in part to the needs of the institution and may not meet the requirements of the physical education program. Planning is the responsibility of the administrator. This means that his is the task of seeing that competent planning is done, that all the factors bearing upon the nature of the plans are brought into consideration, and that persons who can contribute to such planning are called upon to take part.

The administrator and his staff are the principals in the planning organization. Their function is to state the kind of program which the facilities are to serve, and to describe the specifications in suitable detail. Obviously building design, engineering features, and construction specifications are not usually within the province of the professional physical education staff. These features, however, will be determined by the architect and his engineers according to the general specifications which the administrator and his staff present to the architect.

The institution, whether a school or a college, will have a committee whose concern is the building program for the entire institution. In large school systems there may be a professional staff whose sole responsibility is to develop plans for the capital expansion of the system. The physical education administrator and his staff will work closely with whatever group has this responsibility. An institution's building committee may have a long-range plan into which the development of facilities for physical education are to fit.

STEPS IN PLANNING FOR NEW FACILITIES

A series of steps for planning is suggested in the following discussion. Before proceeding to a brief consideration of these steps, the administrator will wish to know what his planning is to achieve. Two purposes are to be served. The first is to present a plan for facilities which anticipates the need of the physical education program at present and in the foreseeable future. The second is to state the requirements in a manner which the architect can use to prepare a design to accomplish the plan. Here are steps to follow to achieve the above results.

STATEMENT OF NEEDS. A statement of needs is a detailed description and listing of all rooms, special areas, service facilities, offices, swimming pools, and any other areas to be incorporated in the building. In other words, every feature of use within a building is to be described. Corridors and stairways generally need not be specified, although one can allow a percentage of the total area for such features. If there are to be unique problems in handling traffic within a building, these should be specified.

The statement of needs should be detailed to the point of suggesting room dimensions. One purpose for this is to tell the architect what is intended with respect to the sizes of the various areas. Another is to get a rough idea of the cost of the structure. Building costs are estimated on a cubic foot basis, or upon a square foot basis. Describing the areas to be provided permits one to arrive at estimate of total cubic feet or square feet. In computing an estimated cost, an allowance must be included for corridors and stairs. Also, an extra ten or fifteen percent of the total should be allowed for errors in estimating. Let it be clear that this estimate is of the grossest kind and should not bind either the institution or the architect.

STATEMENT OF SPECIAL CONSTRUCTION FEATURES. If there are minimum ceiling heights for certain rooms, if the light intensity in an area must be of unusual degree, if a certain arrangement of facilities for proper supervision is required, prepare a separate statement of these needs. Specify types of flooring for various areas. In other words, give the architect information about construction features of a gymnasium which are to be included in his plans. Occasionally, the administrator may make a model of a unit which has special features to be called to the attention of the architect.

PRESENTATION OF STATEMENTS OF NEEDS TO THE ARCHITECT. The statement should be a carefully prepared compilation of the materials developed in the first two steps. Usually the architect will wish to study these materials prior to a meeting with the administrator or the building committee. At this meeting the architect will discuss the statement of needs and will present a plan for working with the administrator and the committee. After this meeting he may set his staff to preparing a design for the building.

EMPLOYMENT OR USE OF CONSULTANTS. The point of view taken in this section is that the administrator and his staff should prepare the statement of their needs for facilities. The use of outside consultants has limited value. Consultants may be employed under the following circumstances:

1. The program of physical education is considered inadequate for the needs of the institution, and the inadequacy is due in part, at least, to the physical education personnel themselves. In this situation an evaluation of the entire department by an outside consultant may be necessary before the institution prepares specific plans. The best evaluation procedures involve both the department staff and the visiting consultants.

2. The administrator and his staff desire more expert assistance in developing a statement of need. After the departmental group has prepared its statement, a consultant may meet with them and review their work. This kind of consultation is carried on informally by administrators as plans develop for facilities. A more formal arrangement may be required where the staff is small, or where their familiarity with new facility design is limited.

3. The local staff has limited knowledge concerning the desirable features of special units, such as swimming pools, tennis courts, and field areas. Because of the particular construction of these facilities, the administrator may seek expert assistance to prepare his specifications.

4. Some types of physical education equipment require built-in fixtures. Consultants can be helpful in this area by stating in detail the special construction features to be incorporated in the building.

5. The architect usually will present a set of preliminary plans which indicate general design and layout. An expert may review these plans with the departmental staff in order to question points which the staff would overlook.

PRESENTATION BY ARCHITECT OF PRELIMINARY PLANS. After the architect has studied the statement prepared by the physical education administrator, he will make a preliminary design for the facility. In designing a building based on a statement of needs, the architect has a problem to solve. He must incorporate all the space requirements in the building, meet the criterion of ease of movement within the building, meet the requirements of local building codes, and produce a plan for a building of pleasing design which has no unassigned space within it. His initial design will attempt to encompass the major features of the building, including its external appearance.

The administrator, his staff, and the building committee of the institution should study these preliminary plans very carefully, because they form the basis for the later and final ones. At this point, too, the administrator may seek the services of a consultant (see item 5 above).

APPROVAL OF PRELIMINARY DESIGN AND LAYOUT. If the preliminary plans presented by the architect are acceptable, they may be approved by the administrator and the officials of the institution. The architect will now begin to draw the plans and list the specifications for constructing the facility. When this stage is reached, neither the departmental staff nor the institution should anticipate major changes. All decisions concerning the features to be incorporated in the facility should have been made.

Change in the plans is not entirely impossible, even after the architect is well along in the development of his plans. Changes requested which cause the architect to redesign a part of the facility, however, impose additional work upon him, cost additional fees, and delay in the progress of his work. One cannot say with absolute confidence that these are the requirements; nothing has been overlooked. On the other hand, the time comes when he must approximate that statement in order to allow the work to proceed. At that point, as a general policy, changes should be ruled out.

PRESENTATION OF FINAL DRAWINGS AND SPECIFICATIONS. The administrator and the building committee may review these. It is of utmost importance that an architect and an engineer representing the institution review these plans and specifications in detail in order to check the degree to which the final presentation meets the statement of needs and the plans which were approved initially. Construction and engineering details must be checked. The specifications of materials to be used in the construction of the facility have to be checked and approved. This step is essential; no economy is served by minimizing or eliminating it. It is not a step which can be served by nonprofessional personnel.

APPROVAL OF PLANS AND SPECIFICATIONS BY THE GOVERNING BOARD OF THE INSTITUTION, OR BY THE BOARD OF EDUCATION. When the design, construction drawings, and specifications have been approved by the architect and the engineer serving the institution, the governing board may be asked to approve them. Upon receiving their approval, and upon the allocation of funds for construction, the steps leading to building the facility follow.

Stress has been placed upon the involvement of several persons in the planning. In an educational institution there is no reason to lay aside this principle at any time. Departmental personnel should be competent for the job. However, they may not be fully competent, they may be selfish with respect to their demands, and they may not concern themselves with the place of their work in the program of the total institution.

Buildings appeal to individuals, too, as concrete evidence of accomplishment. Some persons look upon planning a building as if it were to be a monument to themselves. They are most reluctant to let anyone else have a part in planning lest some of this monumental character be lost. Insistence upon a planning procedure involving a number of persons who have educational responsibilities in the institution will obviate the errors which one individual is bound to introduce into his plans.

CONSTRUCTION OF FACILITIES

After the plans for new facilities have been approved by the governing board or the board of education, the next steps are taken by the administrative unit whose job it is to secure the builder, commonly called the contractor. The administrator of physical education has little or no responsibility for these steps. He may be interested, however, in the procedure commonly followed in the construction of facilities for publicly supported institutions. The following sets forth briefly the major steps.

SECURING THE BUILDER (CONTRACTOR). The general practice is to advertise the project for the attention of contractors. Those who are interested may secure copies of the drawings for the building (or other facility) and the specifications, including the terms of the contract. Those contractors who are interested will submit sealed bids by a specified date. At the announced time the bids will be publicly opened and read, and the lowest bidder will be indicated.

The board or other administrative unit will investigate the standing and responsibility of the lowest bidder in order to determine that he is qualified. If he is judged to be responsible and competent, he may be certified as the successful bidder. Contracts are then drawn up and signed by both the contractor and an officer of the governing board.

It may be noted that the lowest bidder is not always the successful bidder. There must be acceptable and available evidence that the contractor has the competence to construct the facility. If a contractor has never erected a large building before, and is now bidding on a multimillion-dollar structure, there is good reason to question the accuracy of his bid. In spite of the possibility of applying penalties for jobs which are not completed, the contracting institution generally suffers if it employs a contractor who cannot complete his work because he underestimated the cost of the job. It is also necessary for the builder actually to know how to do the job and to be able to employ an adequate crew of workmen for the construction. The low bidder must satisfy the board that he is entitled to the award on these bases, in addition to his low price.

CONSTRUCTION AND SUPERVISION. When the contract has been awarded, a beginning date is specified and the contractor may begin his operation at that time or later. Usually a definite date is specified for completion, and it is to the advantage of the builder to get underway promptly.

During the building of the facility, either an employee of the architect who designed it or an employee of the institution represents the institution as supervising architect or engineer. It is his responsibility to see that the facility is constructed according to the design and the specifications. He will prevent short cuts which the contractor may seek to take; and he will see that the materials used meet the specifications. The job of supervision is a critical one if the facility is to be constructed according to plan.

The supervising engineer also makes decisions with respect to alterations which may be required as the construction proceeds. The money spent for the salary of an able supervising engineer is money that is saved several times over in the avoidance of careless workmanship and in securing the kind of building or facility for which the institution is paying.

INITIAL ACCEPTANCE. When the builder has completed the facility to the best of his knowledge, it will be accepted and put into use by the institution. Because there is usually a provision for requiring the builder to correct errors or unsatisfactory conditions found in the building during a period of time after it is put into use, the institution and its supervising engineer will prepare a list of items to be taken care of by the builder. When he has completed work requested on such lists, and when the building has been in use for a stated period of time (for example, one year), the institution may give final approval to the building and release the contractor from further responsibility. Because a period of time is allowed for determining how the facility functions in service, it is important that all who use it report features which are unsatisfactory in order that the administrator may transmit information about them to the supervising engineer or other institutional officer for action. The administrator also will have to follow up on the matters which he presents.

ALTERATION OF FACILITY AFTER PLANS AND SPECIFICATIONS HAVE BEEN APPROVED. It is not uncommon for the contractor to propose changes in the specifications after the contract has been granted. The fact that he knew what he was bidding on and that his signing the contract was an agreement to build according to specifications will have little influence if he can convince the institution that a substitute item is just as good, even though it costs less. No alterations by the builder should be allowed without specific written approval (change order) by the institution. Also, the contract should specify that savings made by changes reduce the sum of the contract by an equal amount.

The administrator and his staff should avoid requesting changes unless the result will be a definite improvement worth the extra money. Changes cost more than the construction planned as part of the building. The builder may also make a considerable profit through the changes. When a department requests many changes, there is good reason to suspect that the planning was careless and perhaps the planners were not competent.

SUPPLIES AND EQUIPMENT

The teacher of physical education uses supplies and equipment in his teaching. Occasionally he may have to go through the motions without the benefit of materials, but such practice has very limited value. Many activities cannot be limited, hence, they cannot be practiced without equipment and supplies. Planning, selection, purchase, and verification of materials received are necessary steps in securing and maintaining adequate resources for use by the instructors. Policies to be followed by the administrator are suggested for each step.

The term *equipment* has been used to mean both supplies and equipment. Because institutional business practices tend to differentiate between equipment and supplies in the matter of allocating funds, assigning budget codes, and defining maintenance procedures, the distinction based upon the following definitions will be continued in this discussion. Supplies are considered as those items which have a relatively short life. They may wear out in one period of use, or they may last through several seasons or years of use. Generally a period of three to five years is taken as the maximum life of items defined as supplies. The term *consumable supplies* is used by some institutions for this class of material. Equipment, on the other hand, is that item, or group of items which has a relatively long period of life. If an item will last more than five or six years, some say ten years, it may be classed as an item of equipment. The definition of supplies is relatively easy to follow because these are items which are consumed, i.e., worn out, within a relatively short period of time. Equipment items may be more difficult to define, because their lifetime may normally be ten years or longer, but the actual treatment to which an item is subjected may cause its life to be very short. A record player, for example, may have a normal life of eight to ten years under conditions of correct operation and reasonable maintenance. If it is used incorrectly, or abused, or used intensively for long periods of time, it may last no longer than a supply item, such as a badminton or tennis racket. The point here is that the administrator may be expected to differentiate between these two items for budget and purchase purposes.

PLANNING. The quantity and kind of supplies and equipment to be ordered are determined by the subject matter of the program. The nature of the subject matter, i.e., the activities, the variety, and scope are considered. Other factors, which in part have already influenced the situation through being considered in planning the program are the age of the students, their sex, the number of participants (students in classes), and the frequency with which each person or each class is to receive instruction. Aspects of the program, such as intramural athletics, recreational activities, and intercollegiate athletics augment the needs for supplies and equipment. Polices dealing with the quantity of supplies to be allowed a class will be decided by the administrator in consultation with the teachers. The number of items provided to a class should aim to make possible the most effective use of the student's time for learning.

Equipment purchases are made less frequently than are purchases of supplies and generally in smaller quantities. Such items as heavy apparatus, basketball backboards, mats, and net standards are purchased when new buildings are opened and will last for years under regular heavy use. Planning for the purchase of these items, therefore, is really a part of planning for new facilities. It will be important for the administrator to note that a piece of apparatus or a mat is wearing out and to plan for replacements so as to distribute these costs over several budget years. Such planning means scheduling purchases for replacement of equipment items in order to avoid a critical year when everything seems to need replacement at the same time.

SELECTION. Three criteria should be observed in setting policy to govern the selection of supplies and equipment. The first one is the amount of money available. The second is the requirements or specifications which the item must meet. These may be durability in use, suitability for use by the student (e.g., a mat that is thick enough, a badminton racket that is rigid enough), and suitability for storage from one season to another. The third one is availability of the item from year to year in order that certain supplies may be replenished.

In this context the act of selecting is that of determining what items and specifications will be placed upon a bid request or a purchase order. The process of selection can be improved in several ways. The teachers in different institutions can discuss their own experiences with supply items. A department can test items in its own program. One basis for selection is the performance record of the item during a known period of use. Reference can be made to available texts which describe the qualities of fabrics, materials, and construction features of a long list of supplies and equipment. From these sources of information the administrator can determine the features which the supplies should have for service in his program. Reputable dealers who know their products and who are able to judge new products which come to them also can be most helpful in the matter of selection.

PURCHASE. The policy should be to plan to make purchases at regular times. Usually school and college fiscal practice imposes a demand for regularity in this matter. Unless a budget request, when granted, becomes an order to buy, the purchasing of supplies and equipment depends upon requisitions submitted by the administrator. If his routine administration is well organized, he will present his requisitions at regular times, and well ahead of the date when the materials will be needed.

If supplies are purchased on bids, it may be advantageous to buy annually. The amount of the order is larger, and the number of items is greater, hence the bidder may be more interested in securing the order and will offer lower prices on the items. Some items, however, should not be purchased a year ahead because they deteriorate in storage. Also, items which endure storage without deterioration should be purchased ahead only if there is secure storage. Even small losses increase the unit cost to a point which makes annual purchasing uneconomical.

Purchasing should be made on the basis of specifications which have been carefully drawn. Whether buying is on the basis of bids or orders given directly to a vendor selected by the department, specifications should be prepared.

Finally, departmental purchases of supplies and equipment are aimed at bringing their total stock, including their inventory of materials on hand, to the level required to meet their program needs. Inventory records, therefore, are important to aid in planning and to supply information concerning the consumption of supplies.

Purchasing of supplies and equipment is a business transaction and should be conducted on a businesslike basis. This means an objective treatment of selection and purchase. Vernier states that "public schools systems as governmental units are increasingly required to follow the practice of objective buying to consolidate quantities, simplify requirements, establish quality standards, and reduce costs."[16] Objective buying means to buy the products, not special dealer favors.

In smaller communities there may be pressure from a local dealer to do all purchasing through him, even though he may not be able to offer specified supplies at the lowest prices. On this point Vernier makes an interesting observation. "Specifications are written so as to invite competition from reliable dealers. This tends to build

[16] Elmon L. Vernier and Malcolm B. Tebbs, Jr., "Be Specific!" *Journal of Health, Physical Education, Recreation,* December, 1958, p. 9.

good public relations as well as to establish economy of purchase."[17]

VERIFICATION AND PAYMENT. Supplies which have been ordered should be checked promptly upon their arrival at the institution. A delivery statement usually accompanies an order. An institution may provide a copy of the order against which the received supplies may be checked. Materials received are checked against the original order for adherence to quantity and to specifications. When the shipment has been checked and found to be correct, the invoice should be approved, certified for payment, and forwarded to the business office. Often the prompt payment of bills earns a small discount, which over a year can be sizable.

If items are received which are not acceptable, the administrator should notify the vendor promptly and arrange for an exchange or a return of the items for credit. A statement to the business office should be made at the same time, listing the items deducted from the bill.

MANAGEMENT OF FACILITIES, EQUIPMENT AND SUPPLIES

Management is the administrative operation of a unit, program, facility, or other item which is subject to control. The purpose of management in this phase of physical education departmental operations is to achieve the maximum utilization of these items, with the minimum of maintenance and administrative costs, and to conserve and enhance the usefulness of facilities and equipment. According to this definition the minimum costs are not absolute values, but values relative to the other parts of the definition.

FACILITIES: USE. Physical education facilities will be used by the institution to serve the space needs of a variety of activities, both instructional and otherwise. In addition, there will be requests from groups outside the institution for occasional use of these facilities. Who establishes the policy governing the assigment of the physical education facilities?

Because facilities are part of its capital assets, the governing board of the institution actually establishes policy. The actions of this board may be specific, such as banning the use of facilities to indi-

[17] *Ibid.*

viduals or groups listed officially as subversive, or the policy may be broad, indicating only that the facilities are to be used for educational and worthy community functions which conserve the facilities for institutional use. Defining the specific application of the policy in this latter instance is the responsibility of the institutional administrator.

Where specialized facilities are involved, policies governing their use should be established with the advice and recommendation of the departmental administrator. He may wish his own staff to take part in policy formulation. It is vitally important for the institution's administrator to share this policy development with the departmental administrator in physical education. Among institutional administrators, college presidents, deans of administration, school superintendents, and principals there is singular lack of understanding concerning the kinds of uses to which physical education facilities should be put. These people need the counsel of the physical education administrator.

In the utilization of facilities for its own programs, the departmental administrator should arrange a full schedule. It is said that classrooms are not used to full capacity and that laboratories may be used for only one quarter of the time. Full scheduling rarely means total use at every available hour. There must be capacity for peak loads which do occur, but which are not typical. As highways are built to carry the load of weekend and rush-hour automobile traffic, but are used below capacity during a greater part of the week, so educational facilities are provided to carry unusually heavy loads at certain times. If an educational facility is always in maximum use it is inadequate, because (1) there is no longer opportunity to meet anticipated heavier demands, and (2) there is a loss of flexibility in program scheduling. In this instance, the facility determines the program instead of serving it.

When members of the public seek to use the school or college physical education facilities, definite plans must be made to accommodate the approved requests for use. The public should be informed as to the facilities, or the special areas of a facility, which it may use. Will college tennis courts be available for public use? Can members of the community use the swimming pool? Is the main gymnasium available for housing a high school graduation ceremony? Colleges frequently open their facilities to children of faculty members and to alumni. Public schools, especially if there is a cooperative arrangement with the recreation board, open their recreational facilities to general public use. Special events, such as sectional athletic meets or statewide athletic competitions, are held on college facilities.

Where facilities are made available, the periods of the day when they may be used should be stated; age limitations placed upon the users should be made known. Unless the event is of great significance both institutionally and publicly, and unless there is no way to avoid it, no event should be scheduled to interfere with the normal instructional program. In this matter physical education teachers and administrators are likely to be the worst offenders. Because they are the ones who set the values of their work, their readiness to cancel classes, to change activities, or to alter in any way the conduct of their scheduled courses suggests to others that the teaching is not important. There is no other subject in the school or college curriculum whose teachers would permit the amount of interference with their instructional classes which occurs in some physical education programs.

Scheduling the use of facilities resembles planning a budget. If all the demands for the use of facilities are known at the time of (or before) the opening of the school or college term, all events can be treated equitably, and the instructional program, if it must alter its schedule temporarily, can be planned to take this fact into account.

Because an institution must pay for several services when the public uses its facilities, it may decide to charge the public for such use. Charges may be determined according to the services rendered by the institution, in which instance the charges will vary with extent and kind of use. Rates of charges may be established which are the same for a certain facility, regardless of the extent of use. Whatever these may be, prior notice of the charges should be made to the public.

One often hears the remark that the schools belong to the people. No one will contest the statement as long as it is interpreted broadly. An individual community member may place a literal interpretation of possession upon this phrase and insist that the group he represents is entitled to use the school facilities almost at its pleasure. Obviously, there are many facilities, such as parks, highways, transit facilities, and government buildings, which belong to the people but which are never open to individual or group use at the will of the group. The school is not expected to be an exception to this established practice.

An institution which permits public groups to use its facilities will require responsible supervision while the group is in attendance. Usually a representative of the institution will be present, even though a member of the employing group will do the actual supervision. If physical education facilities are to be used, it is essential that a member of the department staff be on hand during the time that the outside group is using the facilities. Custodial personnel will almost always be required and also can aid in supervising the facilities.

When public groups use the facilities, they should be informed about the regulations governing their event at the time arrangements are made for such use. One item often overlooked is the costume which participants wear. If the department has a uniform (costume) supply plan, it may arrange to provide all the necessary costumes. If there is a charge for this, the group should know and, of course, agree to pay it. If it does not have such a plan, it should be sure that participants are suitably dressed for the activities in which they are to engage.

Whether the institution or an outside group is using the facilities, the institution should be fully aware of its liability for the safety and welfare of the participants. Planning for each event, regular inspection of facilities, prompt reporting of hazardous conditions and their correction, provision of adequate supervision, and informing participants concerning safe procedures all minimize the chance of accidental injury and almost eliminate the chance of liability for injury if it occurs. In physical education activities minor injuries occasionally happen. Except for events in which injury is likely to occur occasionally in spite of all efforts to prevent it, no serious injuries should result from acts of the institution itself.

The subjects of safety and liability have been discussed in Chapter 6.

FACILITIES: MAINTENANCE. The management of the custodial, maintenance, and repair functions of an institution is the job of one individual, who may have the title of superintendent of plants and grounds or custodial engineer. This individual is one of the chief administrative personnel in the institution.

Policies governing maintenance and custodial functions are recommended by the superintendent of plant and grounds and authorized by the administrator of the institution. The precise line of administrative authority will be determined locally. For example, in a community with a single high school, the principal may determine building, custodial, and maintenance policies. In a large community one administrator may be responsible for these services in all the schools. Policy in this community would be determined at a level above the individual school principal, although he would exercise jurisdiction over the administration of policy in his own school. In a college or university the maintenance and custodial services are managed by a service division of the institution under the direction of an administrator. Policy will be formulated by this individual, and, if approved by the administration of the institution, will be administered by him.

The administrators of departments which use special facilities requiring more than the usual care and maintenance should share with the person in charge of maintenance the setting of policies and practices governing the servicing of their facilities. For instance, the gymnasium floor requires specialized care, and procedures for assuring that it will receive this care should be established. When public use of physical education facilities is permitted, policies should be set concerning the number of custodial persons on duty at the time and their remuneration, if the work is overtime, their authority with respect to the public, the work to be done in preparation for such use, and work to be performed after the event in order to prepare facilities again for institutional use.

There is very limited discussion in physical education literature of the importance of maintenance services, although the continued usability of facilities is dependent upon the quality and adequacy of these services. It is important, therefore, that the physical education administrator act to bring about the adoption of policies which will secure the necessary custodial and maintenance services. Important administrative functions are indicated in the following material.

Adequate maintenance is dependent upon the adequacy of the custodial and maintenance staff. Although the physical education administrator may not employ this staff, he can indicate to the maintenance superintendent the needs for personnel, and he can also report on inadequacy in custodial services resulting from having too few persons on the staff.

By regular inspection of facilities the administrator can observe their condition and can report regularly to the maintenance superintendent those items which need attention. Regular inspection and reporting contribute to the efficiency of the maintenance department in keeping up with its own work. By detecting minor conditions and having them corrected, the administrator avoids the liability of a major breakdown or an upheaval in the working practices of the custodial and maintenance staff.

Both outdoor and indoor facilities will require renovation, occasional rebuilding or replacement of excessively worn parts, and repairs where unusual damage or wear occurs. If sizable sums of money are to be spent for a job, the annual budget should carry an item to cover the expenditures. For other items a periodic request made to the superintendent of plant and grounds, or the head of the maintenance department, will state the services which are needed. The administrator of physical education should prepare a schedule on which are listed the maintenance and renovation jobs that are regularly required throughout the year. Repairs which have not been made also should be placed on this schedule. Such a schedule may be based on services which are required periodically, such as the conditioning of the track and the baseball infield each spring. To present a complete statement of maintenance needs requires periodic inspections of all facilities and equipment.

The administrator will perform this duty efficiently if he has a prepared list of items, such as is given below, to be checked regularly.

1. Indoor areas
   a. Main gymnasium and similar types of exercise rooms
      Lighting—all lights working; windows clean

Walls—note breaks or other damage; observe condition of paint

Windows—note cracked and broken panes; test operation of windows

Floor—note condition of finish, worn spots, damage to finish, stained and dirty areas; look for broken boards and for protruding nails; note curling and heaving of boards, and raised edges of tiles (vinyl or asphalt); note court markings for completeness; test anchoring of floor plates

Movable bleachers—test for ease and correctness of operation; note completeness of units with respect to railings; test steps for security

b. Shower room—note the following:

Shower heads on and operating

Shower drains functioning fully

Shower control handles on and tight

Evidence of leaking valves

Condition of floor; no broken tiles; grouting in good condition

Soap dispensers, if any, operating and securely fastened

Walls clean, free of mildew or discoloration

c. Toweling room—note the following:

Fastening of towel bars

Floors—clean, unbroken surfaces

Walls—clean, free of mildew, or discoloration

d. Storage areas—note the following:

Light and dryness

Security of room

Adequacy of shelving to permit orderly storage of materials

Cleanliness of area

e. Swimming pool—note the following:

Adequacy of lighting

Condition of water (should be checked daily)

Bottom of pool, free of settled dirt

Scum gutters clean and drains operating correctly

f. Diving boards: complete and safe; matting or other covering securely fastened; supports and fulcrums secure and in good working order; deck tile clean and unbroken; no obstacles or items of equipment lying around on the deck

Locks on entrances to pool in working order

g. Lavatories and toilets—note the following:

All should be in working order

Room clean and free of odors

Hand driers, or paper towel dispensers in working order; and towels available

Soap dispensers, if any, in working order, and securely fastened

2. Outdoor facilities
   a. All grass fields—note the following
      Bare areas needing seeding, or sodding
      Boundaries clearly marked
      Fences and gates intact
      Gate locks in working order
   b. Baseball diamond—note the following:
      Infield smooth
      Skinned area firm, smooth, free of weeds and rocks
      Pitcher's mound intact, rubber securely anchored
      Outfield free of obstacles, and depressions
      Backstop intact
      Benches and bleachers in safe condition
      Fencing intact
   c. Outdoor water hydrants and drinking fountains in operating condition
   d. Track—note the following:
      Free of stones and large cinders
      Surface hard and smooth
      Curbing intact
      Field event areas in proper and safe condition
      Equipment for maintenance prior to and during meets on hand and in working condition
   e. Tennis courts—note the following:
      Surface in correct condition for play
      Net posts at correct locations
      Nets in good condition and at correct heights
      Boundary lines clearly visible and complete
      Fencing intact
      Gate locks in working order

The above examples show clearly that inspecting the facilities and equipment is a major task. One will note also that all items are not inspected with equal frequency. Some facilities, such as outdoor fields and courts in a northern climate, need only seasonal inspection. On the other hand, the swimming pool (indoors), gymnasiums, and shower and dressing facilities could be inspected weekly.

In a small institution with few facilities the administrator will probably do the inspections himself. In a large institution a custodial foreman on the departmental staff may do most of the inspecting. In this case the administrator should inspect all the facilities at stated times to maintain his own familiarity with their condition and to note their adequacy to meet the demands which are placed upon them. Because he prepares budget requests, he must have a clear understanding of the extent and condition of these facilities and equipment.

Each teacher is responsible for the safety of his students. He is obligated to inspect equipment before he uses it, and to report on unsafe equipment and damaged facilities. Reports of this kind from teachers and from maintenance personnel are the basis for the requests for repairs and replacements which are not anticipated specifically when the budget request is being prepared.

In an efficiently organized educational institution the division of plant and grounds or the building superintendent will take care of routine and seasonal inspection and maintenance of all facilities including special ones. The departmental administrator will be relieved of a large share of this work. The important point in this section is, however, that regular inspections must be made, facility and equipment maintenance, renovation and rebuilding must be scheduled, and financial planning must include, in addition to funds to carry these items, an allowance for the incidental repairs which cannot be specifically anticipated.

SUPPLIES: UTILIZATION. Supplies are purchased according to the planned requirements of instruction and administration. It is expected that these materials will be used within the limits of the plan. Because needs for supplies are expressed at the time budget requests are prepared, the reader is referred to the chapter on budgets for a review of the steps to be followed in planning.

SUPPLIES: MANAGEMENT. In order to have the supplies available for instructional and administrative use when they are needed, the administrator must do the following:

1. Make timely and adequate purchases.
2. Maintain the necessary reserve of supplies in secure and proper storage facilities.
3. Arrange for the repair and reconditioning of selected worn or damaged items.
4. Keep an inventory of supplies on hand.
5. Prepare and follow a schedule for replacement of items as they are worn out.

The matter of purchasing has already been discussed. The quantities which are ordered should meet the immediate needs and also provide, wherever it is feasible, a reserve to be held in storage until it is needed.

Storage of new supplies should be secure. Access to this storage room should be limited to the person who is responsible for the supplies. In a small department this may be the administrator; in a large department the control of supplies may fall to one person. The importance of this kind of control cannot be overemphasized. There is an all-too-prevalent attitude that these items are plentiful, that they do not belong to an individual, so no one person will be harmed if a baseball, a set of arrows, or a half dozen golf balls is removed for personal use. Both teachers and nonteaching members of the institution's staff are apt to help themselves to supplies which are not carefully managed.

In one institution the reserve quantities of supplies were kept in a storeroom which was locked, but to which all members of the departmental staff and several members of the custodial staff had keys. Two actions were depleting the reserves. Teachers who were careless in managing the supplies assigned to them for instructional purposes found it convenient to replace their losses by going to the storeroom. Other persons, who were not identified, were also helping themselves to badminton rackets and birds, tennis balls, baseballs, and other items which could be used at home or at the beach. The person in charge of the supplies finally had a special cage constructed within the storeroom in which all new supplies were placed. Only this person and the administrator had keys to the lock on this cage. Loss of new supplies stopped immediately. Teachers who had accepted little responsibility for the care of supplies assigned to them now had to take care of their supplies or find themselves with insufficient materials with which to conduct their classes. Others who had been acquiring items for personal use no longer had access to the storeroom.

If the administrator will set up the steps by which a periodic inventory can be made, he will have an accurate means of planning his budget and his purchases and of controlling the use of supplies. Also, he will be able to estimate the repair and reconditioning needs each year.

Business firms try to maintain a running inventory, which is a record of stock on hand at the end of each business day or other chosen period. This kind of information is not required by a department of physical education. On the other hand, semiannual, annual, or seasonal information is required and should be secured. The inventory is a record of supplies on hand. A careful inventory will encourage the department to discard items which are no longer serviceable and those which are unsafe to use, thus assuring that supplies on hand are usable and safe. Furthermore, storage space will not be wasted by placing in it items which can no longer be used.

There are firms which specialize in the cleaning and reconditioning of game and sports equipment. The bulk of their work is the care of uniforms, shoes, and special protective items used by interscholastic and intercollegiate athletic teams. These firms also will store the articles until the next season. Because of the high cost of these types of athletic supplies, the reconditioning service may save the department money. If the supplies used principally in physical education instructional classes can be reconditioned at a saving to the institution over the purchase of new items, the service should be used. It should be pointed out that in order to determine whether it is cheaper to buy new supplies or to recondition used ones, the administrator will need to know a unit cost in terms of periods of use.

In a completely integrated department there may be a tendency to use the same item for intercollegiate athletics, intramural athletics, class instruction, and recreation. Although a single policy cannot be set forth to cover all uses, one can state generally that separate complements should be prepared for each major phase of the program. In fact, a basketball which is fully satisfactory for class instruction may not be "official" under the rules for intercollegiate play. The policy should be to purchase new supplies for each of the major divisions of the program.

GYMNASIUM COSTUME SUPPLY AND STORAGE

A matter of special consideration when new facilities are planned, or as older ones face additions and remodeling, is that of the organization, equipment, and management of the locker-dressing rooms. Because the kind of gymnasium costumes which the students are to wear and their storage are an integral part of any plan for the arrangement of locker-dressing facilities, attention will be given in this section to the costume as the principal determining factor in the matter.

The importance of this approach will be recognized by anyone who has observed physical education classes in which the students are variously costumed—some in an appropriate uniform, others in half a uniform plus street clothes, a few in old clothes from home, and several in the clothes worn to school or college—and by anyone who has been able to locate the gymnasium building and its locker rooms by the strong "locker room odor" diffusing from its source in the dressing lockers containing soiled clothing through all hallways, stairwells, and adjacent rooms. Scott and Westkaemper write, "Since the very beginning of instruction in physical education in schools and colleges, students have been taught the necessity of practicing personal and community hygiene. Yet, paradoxically, many schools and colleges fail to practice what they teach. Prominent among the areas in which practice often fails to meet acceptable health and aesthetic standards is the physical education locker-dressing facilities."[18] The policies governing both the kind of costume to be worn in physical education and its care are a part of the body of policies concerned with the outcomes of instruction, the health supervision of the students, and the management of student use of the facilities.

The following criteria should be met by any plan for costume supply and storage:

1. A complete uniform for every student each time he is in class.
2. A clean uniform regularly, and upon demand when the student is unusually active.
3. An appropriate costume for the activity.
4. Control of persons permitted to use the facilities.
5. Minimum space for storage between periods of activity.

The only system which meets fully all the criteria is one in which the uniform is supplied by the institution and is stored in baskets or tote boxes. Modifications of this plan may provide several of the

[18] Scott and Westkaemper, *op. cit.*, p. 263.

desirable features, but will not achieve the full value of the basket storage and uniform supply plan.

Scott states that "in order to create a climate conducive to favorable health and educational experiences, students in schools and colleges must dress in appropriate costumes while participating in physical education activities. These costumes must be clean, attractive in appearance, and sufficiently durable to withstand hard usage and frequent washings with soap and water. In addition, they must provide freedom of movement and encourage, rather than restrict, vigorous participation in the activities of the program."[19]

There are four aspects to a uniform supply and basket storage system: (1) purchase of the gymnasium uniform (costume) by the institution, and supplying a uniform to each student who takes part in any phase of the physical education program; (2) laundering the uniforms; (3) central storage of uniforms in wire baskets when they are not being used by the students; and (4) provision of full-length, unassigned dressing lockers in which students store their street clothing while taking part in physical education.

Planning for items 3 and 4 is done as follows. The total number of costume storage receptacles (wire baskets) should equal the total number of students engaging in all phases of the physical education program. Where all students are likely to take part in some activity at one time or another, the number of storage receptacles should equal the total enrollment of the institution. If one is looking ahead, he may include in his plans room for expansion as the enrollment of the institution increases.

Because the full-length dressing lockers are unassigned and are used by students only during the time that they are costumed for physical activity, the total number of these lockers should equal the anticipated peak load of participants plus a percentage, for example 10 percent, to allow for unusual periods. Again the administrator may plan to allow room for expansion, or he may actually provide the larger number of lockers at the time the facility is being constructed. According to Scott and Westkaemper, the ratio of costume storage receptacles to full-length dressing lockers is usually from five to seven baskets to one dressing locker.

[19] *Ibid.*, p. 263.

If an institution of two thousand students provides a basket for each one, the maximum number of dressing lockers required will be four hundred. Actually, the number probably will be less when the data on anticipated peak load is assembled.

In addition to all the values inherent in the uniform supply system, is the one of economical use of space. For example: 2000 baskets, each 15 inches long, 10 inches wide at the top, 9 inches wide at the bottom, and 9 inches deep, can be stored in racks with ample spacing around them for movement and for service counters in a room of approximately 850 square feet. If 400 full-length dressing lockers are provided, an area of approximately 2440 square feet would be required to house them with ample aisle and traffic space around them. The total area for basket storage and dressing would be approximately 3290 square feet. If, on the other hand, the institution decided to provide a half-length locker for each of its students, an area of approximately 6100 square feet would be required. Twice this area would be needed to house the same number of full-length lockers. The area required for the baskets and full-length lockers for 2000 students is only 54 percent of the area required for 2000 half-length lockers, and 27 percent of that required for 2000 full-length lockers.[20]

Planning to purchase gymnasium costumes involves first determining the costume which will be supplied. In college the usual costume for men includes a T-shirt, trunks, supporter, and socks. In cool and cold climates a warm-up shirt and sweat pants may be added. Costumes for women may be blouse, shorts, underpants, and socks, or a tunic, pants, and socks. Warm-up shirts and sweat pants may be supplied to the women also. Other costume items which may be supplied are swimming suits for men and for women, and leotards. Towels are supplied in all plans. Shoes are not supplied.

Once the type of costume has been selected, the next step is to decide upon the frequency of laundering and the rate of replacement. If students are taking physical education daily and are re-

[20] Computations are based on a plan for a basket storage room given by Scott and Westkaemper (*op. cit.*, p. 261), and on the allowance of 6.1 square feet of dressing room area for each student when a full-length locker with the dimensions of 12 inches in width, 15 inches in depth, and 60 inches in height is used.

ceiving clean clothes each day, the number of uniforms which the department must have on hand will be equal to the number of students using the facilities each day, plus one uniform per student in reserve from which clean clothes are provided, plus one uniform per student for each day that clothes are at the laundry. If the department has 24-hour laundry service, about 3 to 3½ uniforms per student will be adequate. If laundry service requires two days, the department will require 4 to 4½ uniforms per student. This is the stock which the department must have on hand at the beginning of a year.

Because the life of one or two articles of the costume will be less than one year, a replacement stock for these items should be on hand at the beginning of the year. Replacement schedules should be prepared for all items of the costumes. Periodically these should be compared with the actual experience. The length of life of the various items of a costume depends upon the original quality of the article, the kind of use it is given, the kind of laundering process used, and the frequency of use. The following figures indicating the wear life of articles of costume are based on experience in colleges where the participants are in physical education classes at least three periods per week.

Item		*Expected Life*
Towel		5 - 6 years
Men:	trunks	5 - 6 years
	T-shirt	3 "
	supporter	5 - 6 "
	socks	4 months
Men and Women:	warm-up shirt	5 years
	sweat pants	5 "
	swim suits	5 "
Women:	shirt (blouse)	6 "
	shorts	6 "
	underpants	5 - 6 "
	tunic	6 "
	pants	5 - 6 "
	socks	6 months

The final aspect of the system for which the administrator will plan is that of laundering the costumes. If the college or the school system operates its own laundry, the cost of this service will be a fraction of the charges made by a commercial laundry. The costs can be secured from the manager of the school laundry and can be used to compute the cost per student and the total annual costs for providing clean uniforms to all participants in physical education activities. In 1939 Messersmith estimated that the total annual cost per student per year for maintaining the uniform (replacement) and for laundry would not exceed $1.50. If costs have increased 400 percent since then, the annual cost will be $6.00, or 60 cents per month during the school year for the use of a uniform and for its laundering. This is a negligible charge for the valuable service provided by the uniform supply system. It should be noted that Messersmith's figures included paying commercial laundry rates.[21]

If a basket system is used, it will be necessary to make a small number of full-length lockers available for storage purposes to members of athletic teams whose game uniforms require special storage equipment. Facilities and equipment to meet the local needs can be developed by the administrator and provided by the institution. Because athletic squads often are assigned separate locker and dressing rooms, no difficult problem is presented. The operation of a uniform supply system makes it possible for teams to use appropriate items from this system and to have them laundered regularly. If the institution operates its own laundry, all athletic team uniforms which can be washed can be kept clean throughout the season.

An attendant must be employed in any institution which installs a uniform supply system. It is not possible to control the large stock of materials, prepare clothing for laundering, receive it from the laundry, and maintain the necessary daily records without the services of at least one full-time attendant.

Only the complete uniform supply system has been described. This type of system is found in a number of colleges and some high schools. It is suitable for operation in any situation in which the participants change into a costume at the school. There are

[21] Lloyd L. Messersmith, "Physical Education Uniform and Laundry Costs," *Journal of Health and Physical Education,* September, 1959, Vol. X, No. 7, p. 404.

modifications which may suit the circumstances in some institutions. One adaptation is to take advantage of the space-saving features of the basket storage system without supplying the costumes. Students supply their own gymnasium costumes and store them in the baskets between classes. Insistence by the teachers upon clean clothing and upon the student maintaining a complete, specified uniform helps to avoid undesirable aspects of the system of student-owned uniforms. The reader is referred to Scott and Westkaemper for further discussion of the uniform storage systems.

The avoidance of situations and circumstances which may lead to accidental injury is a constant concern of the administration and the teachers in schools and colleges. The subject of safety has been brought into the discussion of construction features of new facilities, and of the inspection of equipment, supplies, and facilities. Other procedures for maintaining the safe condition and use of these institutional properties is discussed in the chapter on protecting the students.

As part of the management function, the administrator should have prepared a manual of procedures for teachers, custodians, groundkeepers, and students. The manual can describe safe procedures to be followed by all in using facilities, equipment, and supplies. Constant alertness on the part of each responsible person is demanded if accidental injury is to be avoided.

The discussion of this chapter is aimed at having the physical education department secure the best possible facilities for its institution and to manage them effectively. "The final test of all facilities lies in the extent to which they make possible the greatest degree of participation in the activities which go to make up the . . . program of physical education and recreation."[22]

Let this be the ultimate, as well as the first criterion.

[22] *College Facilities, op. cit.*, p. 1.

Chapter 12

OFFICE ORGANIZATION

THE OFFICE is the center of administrative activity, and serves as a work and study room, a conference room, a negotiating room, an information center, a service center, a room for records, a reception room, and often a symbol of status. It is the coordinating center for the various functions, services, and programs carried on by the unit or department. Efficient performance of the office functions means that the work is accomplished on schedule and that the labor required to perform the functions is at or near the minimum. In a large department an efficient office operation relieves the administrator of most routine tasks and permits him to give his energies and time to those matters of curriculum, public relations, facility planning, securing and supervising faculty personnel, and others which are his principal responsibilities. In a small department there is still need to organize routine office work so that it is performed efficiently.

In the schools central offices perform most clerical functions and maintain the school records for students. Development of extensive guidance services in schools has created two centers for keeping student records. Official reports and records are maintained in the office of the principal, whereas personal information, including results of tests administered for purposes of securing measures of aptitudes and abilities, is kept on the student's record in the guidance counselor's office. Efficient office practices are relevant to the central school offices as well as to the office of a department. Whatever office functions may be required of a departmental chairman in a school can be related to the discussion in this chapter.

The following discussion concerns the planning, organizing, and operation of an office for a department of physical education. Since departments vary in size, complexity of function, and extent of responsibilities, not all the matters to which consideration is given here will apply to all departments. Also, not all matters of importance to the operation of an office in a department will be touched upon in this discussion. Administrative organization is individual and local, and the procedures adopted should suit its own needs. It should be added that the office under present consideration is that of the departmental administrator.

PLAN AND ORGANIZATION

Office Work

An office is set up to carry out certain functions. What are the jobs which a departmental office may be expected to perform? One may list usual, or regular jobs most likely to be performed by persons in the departmental office.

1. Maintaining records of various functions, activities, and services, and of student performance in courses and activities.
2. Preparing purchase orders, receiving and inspecting equipment and supplies, and certifying their receipt.
3. Meeting the public: by telephone, in person.
4. Writing letters.
5. Preparing reports.
6. Typing: course outlines, committee reports, course examinations, letters, copy for printed items, such as bulletins, fliers, announcements.
7. Making appointments for various kinds of meetings.
8. Filing.
9. Preparing news stories.
10. Conferring with students.
11. Duplicating materials, such as course examinations, programs for public events.

12. Distributing tickets for athletic events.
13. Assembling information for use by administrator.

The above list is not a summary of duties of the administrator, or of his staff, but is a list of tasks whose performance is centered in an office. Who does them is dependent upon who is available to do them. The administrator has other duties whose performance will determine many of the office functions. One may say that these exist only to the extent that an administrator or other staff member has need of them in carrying out his own responsibilities.

PERSONNEL

The personnel required to staff an office is determined by the amount and kind of work to be done. An office may have secretaries, typists, a receptionist, file clerks, a bookkeeper, a telephone operator, and other more specialized personnel. More often a department office has one secretary who must serve in all the above capacities to the best of her ability.

Usually the first member of an office staff to be employed is a secretary, a person who can do stenographic work. A great deal has been written about the importance of the secretary to the success of an administrator, and one can attest to the correctness of this evaluation. De Young states: "So important to the schools and colleges is the office personnel that many an executive would rather accept the resignation of two teachers than that of one clerk or secretary."[1] Voltmer and Esslinger suggest the role of the secretary as the following: "An important asset which many administrators overlook in planning their work is a capable secretary. By working with an intelligent secretary and learning to delegate to her all the responsibility which she is capable of assuming and by leaving in her hands many time-consuming routine matters, the administrator will find that he has much more time for creative work and will thereby be of much greater value to his profession."[2] She is a key person in gaining and maintaining the good will of those who come into contact with the department. Hughes and

[1] Chris A. De Young, *Introduction to American Public Education,* 3d ed., McGraw-Hill Book Company, Inc., 1955, p. 392.

[2] Edward F. Voltmer and Arthur A. Esslinger, *The Organization and Administration of Physical Education,* 3d ed., Appleton-Century-Crofts, Inc., 1958, p. 478.

French emphasize her responsibilities: "Teachers and administrators in educational institutions also should realize the importance of good will and the role of the secretary in developing and maintaining it. Her contacts with students, faculty, fellow employees, parents, and public are going on for better or for worse every hour of every day. The good secretary knows that the department's 'public' is everyone with whom she has dealings. She knows that these people, as human beings, appreciate and have a right to expect courtesy, thoughtfulness, tact, and general good taste in conduct."[3] There seems to be no question concerning the important place held by the secretary in an organization.

A person who can meet the qualifications suggested by the writers referred to must have the technical skills required to perform the job and the personal qualities which suit her to the roles described. The secretary to the administrator should have a real concern for the efficiency of the office, she should know that her work is important, she should have imagination and ideas about improving the office operation. Certainly she should be loyal to her administrator. If she cannot fulfill this last qualification she should seek employment elsewhere.

If the office is large and several people are employed in it, they should have the qualifications demanded for efficient performance of the jobs to which they are assigned. In large cities these persons may be chosen from civil service lists. Civil service candidates will have met minimum technical requirements. The administrator will interview prospective employees in order to judge better those qualities which are not readily measured by the usual civil service test. In smaller communities individuals will be employed from available sources. Where there is no civil service, there is always the possibility that someone in the community or in the school will have a friend or a relative who needs a job or who prefers to work in the environment of an educational institution. In order to avoid being burdened with employees who cannot fulfill the demands of the job, the administrator and the institution should establish job standards which candidates must meet to be considered employable. Clerical and stenographic employees should be

[3] William L. Hughes and Esther French, *The Administration of Physical Education,* A. S. Barnes and Co., 1954, p. 329.

selected upon the same basis as other professional staff members. Their education, specialized training, experience, character, and personality should be considered, and the best candidate for a particular job should be chosen.

The work of an office may vary in amount according to the season of the year. There may be periods during which two or three times the usual work has to be performed. To meet these peak demands the administrator may employ temporary personnel on a full-time or part-time basis. Insofar as possible he will seek individuals with qualifications equal to those of his regular staff. During the non-peak periods the office can be operated by the regular, full-time personnel, who may be thought of as the core staff. These are the persons who give integrity and smoothness to the office operations.

DIVISION OF LABOR

Effective office operation depends upon the thoroughness with which the work is analyzed and described. The nature of the major jobs should be described in some detail and the steps set forth which one follows to accomplish them. Job description gives new personnel the maximum opportunity to inquire about aspects of the work which they do not understand, and enables them to acquire proficiency in performing the task within a minimum time. Jobs which are performed periodically can be approached each time with more facility if the steps required to do the job have been recorded. The kind of job description referred to in this discussion pertains to functions, duties, and tasks to be performed by office personnel, and does not mean the description of a position for which a person may be employed.

Analysis of office functions, like curriculum revision study, should be made periodically. In a department which is growing in size, new administrative duties may be added, and the actual bulk of work may increase as well. To meet the need for getting work done the administrator may seek what seems to be the obvious solution, namely the employment of additional office personnel. Because educational institutions rarely have funds for the employment of even an adequate number of personnel, it is essential that office functions be studied periodically and that reorganization of work functions be accomplished wherever possible in order to maintain an efficient unit. Such periodic studies may result in the introduction of machine operation for the performance of some functions, contracting with outside groups for special jobs, and revision of procedures formerly followed.

Although in the one-secretary office all the jobs are performed by one person, with some part-time student help assisting occasionally, job analysis continues to be important, perhaps even more so than in an office with several employees.

Finally, when the office functions are analyzed, the administrator will face the reality that he cannot continue to add new tasks to the load being carried by his office people and expect them to be performed properly, if at all.

SUGGESTIONS FOR OFFICE OPERATION

WORK SCHEDULES

The matter of planning work has been discussed in the section above. The administrator, or his secretary, if he has a large office, can prepare work schedules based upon the analysis of the work load. These may be of several types.

In an office which prepares a large amount of typed material for a number of people, a work sheet should be kept which lists the item, the date that it was received, the date that it is due, and the date of completion. Departmental offices which prepare examinations, course outlines, syllabi, and other types of course materials will find it necessary to maintain this type of work schedule.

A special project may be planned which will require the temporary reassignment of office responsibilities. In this circumstance a new schedule of office responsibilities and a schedule of work assignments on the special project will be required.

A calendar (which is a form of schedule), should be prepared for the entire office operation, listing the major jobs to be performed during the year, the date upon which each job is to be completed, and a suggested date for starting it. Preparation of budgets, requisitions for annual or semiannual purchases, athletic schedules, materials to be submitted for printing, and other jobs of similar nature may be listed on this calendar.

During the summer, when members of the office staff normally take their vacations, a schedule of vacation allowances indicates which members are to maintain the work of the office. In a large organization the summer months may be busy ones from the standpoint of preparation for the next academic year. It will be important to schedule personnel vacations so that the work of the office will be performed adequately and satisfactorily throughout the summer period.

SUPERVISION

Perhaps it is unnecessary to suggest that supervision in the sense of reviewing work performance, job accomplishment, and suitable personnel utilization is an essential part of effective office management. In a small office supervision is likely to be inherent in the frequency of communication between the administrator and his secretary. In a large office, however, this kind of communication does not exist. Other procedures of supervision must be adopted.

Immediate responsibility for office management should be delegated by the administrator to a competent person in the office. This individual can then select the methods for judging employee performance and assuring that the work of the organization is accomplished. All that has been written earlier concerning job descriptions, assignment of duties, and making of schedules is involved in the supervision of an office and its employees.

In addition to these actions, the supervisor should hold employee meetings (a form of staff meeting), periodically in order to review office procedures and to secure from employees their reactions to assignments and their suggestions for changing and for improving the work procedures. At such meetings instructions for new procedures can be reviewed in order to make them clear.

If materials are typed for duplication, an occasional spot check upon the quality of the work will give the supervisor an idea as to the suitability of the form of the work and its accuracy. In general, typed materials which are to be duplicated should be proofread. The employee may decide whether a simple rereading of her own work is all that is needed, or whether reading as another check against the copy is necessary.

If employees may earn tenure in their positions, it is important that the organization have standards of job performance by which it can rate the employee's work before tenure is considered. Such rating procedures may also be used periodically as a means of improving the job performance of both tenure and nontenure employees.

Supervision is essential to the efficient operation of any unit in which there are several employees. This applies to instructional as well as noninstructional workers.

RECORD FORMS

Record forms must be prepared according to local needs, if they are to function best. Today, the tendency toward using machines for handling records leads to a standardization of forms. Insofar as a record can be handled most effectively by machine, it is desirable to adapt the office and departmental function to the required record form. In saying this, one assumes that the purpose for which the department keeps the record will be served fully by the utilization of the machine-processed record.

The following listing suggests records which may be kept by a department.

Personnel:
- Student cumulative record
  - Performance in classes (grades)
  - Nonclass activities
  - Anecdotal items
- Student cumulative health record (may be part of the over-all student cumulative record; in general, however, this is a separate form)
- Employee records (nonteaching)
  - Date of appointment
  - Term of employment
  - Salary
  - Other pertinent items
- Teacher records
  - Date of appointment

Term of employment
Tenure, leaves
Change in status (promotion)
Work schedule
Special assignments
Other pertinent information
Accident report and record
Materials and Supplies:
Inventory
Requisitions
Bid sheets
Purchase orders
Payment vouchers
Replacement schedule
Uniform supply system records
Laundry service record
Instruction Records:
Test forms (for recording scores)
Attendance reports
Grade reports
Notices to students
Special permission forms

Departments which are responsible for interscholastic and intercollegiate athletics will require a number of forms suited to the recording of matters pertaining to supplies, equipment, budget, and finances. Among the records which have been listed above are several which will be used in the management of the intercollegiate athletic program as well. Any other phase of the department's program which has its own special administrative needs should develop and use records which will facilitate the operation of the program.

Any record form should be easy to use and to file. Standardization of size helps in the filing procedure only because it makes possible the utilization of a minimum number of different filing or storage units. If records are to be processed by machine, obviously the form which the machine can handle will determine the form of the record. It should be pointed out that a good deal of planning is required before machine operation actually saves time and labor. The entire process of record preparation and processing should be studied carefully in order that the best procedure for the particular office is chosen.

Before a record form becomes final, it should be dittoed or mimeographed and used during a trial period. The suitability of the form as well as its actual usefulness can be judged in this trial period. If it performs a necessary function, it can then be prepared for multilithing or for printing. The quantity of any item prepared in this way should be sufficient to carry through one year, but not more than two years, under ordinary circumstances. Changes in administrative practices during the year may make a record form obsolete. To have a large quantity on hand is both wasteful and bothersome. Furthermore, suggested minor changes in record forms can be incorporated in the reprinting within a reasonable time when this is done on an annual basis.

FILING

People who make records usually prefer to hold them for a period of time. Storing records so that they are useful to the administrator and his staff is one of the office practices which receives insufficient attention. If the administrator hopes to make efficient use of the records, which are prepared almost daily, he must utilize a filing procedure which will accomplish this. Systematic handling and keeping of records is filing.

Entire volumes are devoted to the matter of keeping records. Only a few points which seem to be particularly relevant will be touched upon here. Suggestions given here can be very helpful to the typical departmental office unit. One who desires to organize or to reorganize a sizable office unit should consult texts in the field.

Retained records serve definite purposes. "Simplified plans and procedures will enable an organization to have records maintained for future use in terms of (1) quick reference in further dealings with the same (individual) or correspondent, (2) guidance in the processing or handling of similar cases so that uniform procedures will result, and (3) a historical record of the policies and actions of the organization."[4]

[4] Margaret K. Odell, and E. P. Strong, *Records Management and Filing Operations,* McGraw-Hill Book Company, Inc., 1947, p. 5.

If records are to serve any of these purposes satisfactorily the method of filing them must insure easy access to needed records at any time. Whether the administrator is starting a new office, or he feels the need to improve the handling of records in his present office, he will do himself and his organization a service by taking the time to study his records, his own needs, and the indexing and filing procedures. Then he can put into operation that system which suits his type of office and which he can maintain successfully with his own staff.

Not only is it important to have a system of record filing which permits the full use of the records, but it is equally important to have a system which stores records in a minimum amount of space. To achieve this latter objective, the system must provide for the regular disposal of unneeded records and for the more economical storage of records which must be retained indefinitely but which are not in immediate use. Space and equipment are costly and should be used for current functions rather than for dead storage. Departments with closets full of old records need to review their filing and storing procedures.

Indexing and filing can be covered by two general classifications: name and subject. Records may be filed according to the name of the person, organization, or other identity, or according to the subject, such as travel, contracts, personnel, and other items. It is possible also to combine these two so that the major classification would be the name, and the subclassification the subject. Thus, Dean Jones—personnel, Dean Jones—curriculum, could be two titles for index tabs indicating filing of correspondence with the dean of the institution according to the subject with which the correspondence deals.

According to Odell and Strong there are only two methods or arrangements for indexing and filing: (1) alphabetic and (2) numeric. Each of these methods is subject to application in several forms.

1. *Alphabetic* (alphabetic by surnames, company names, location names, geographic location, or topics)
2. *Alphabetic-numeric* (coding by surnames, company names, location names, or topics)
3. *Group-name alphabetic* (grouping by family names, regardless of spelling)

4. *Code group name* (grouping by surnames, regardless of spelling)

and

1. *Serial numeric* (consecutive)
2. *Numeric coding*
3. *Decimal numeric*
4. *Duplex numeric* (numeric numbers and letters, and numbers and symbols)
5. *Terminal-digit numeric*[5]

When the appropriate system has been selected, and if the office staff is of a size to permit it, one person should be made responsible for the files. An indexing system should be worked out by the administrator in cooperation with his office supervisor. The person responsible for filing will follow this index and any supplementary instructions concerning handling materials already in the files and those to be filed. In a small office where the secretary is the entire staff, the same procedures can be followed, except that she will also be responsible for the files.

With a system of indexing and filing in operation, it is likely that the number of items filed under one listing will almost automatically be limited. The following quotation will serve as a guide to one who wishes further information on this point: "It is fairly widely considered that an individual folder should be made when 5 to 10 papers have accumulated for a correspondent; that papers in a miscellaneous folder are filed alphabetically and that from 30 to 50 papers constitute the maximum number for a miscellaneous folder; that when an individual folder contains more than 50 papers, a second individual folder should be prepared."[6]

One of the problems in every office is disposing of inactive records. How long should records be kept? On this matter the individual institution will have to make its own decisions. General regulations may be set forth by the governmental control, by the school superintendent, or by the management of the institution concerning those items which are to be retained. When there are policies in force concerning the retention of materials, the administrator or his secretary can mark each item as to its disposal

[5] *Ibid,* pp. 8–9.

[6] John J. W. Neuner and B. R. Haynes, *Office Management and Practices,* 2d ed., South-Western Publishing Company, 1947, p. 188.

date. The files can be checked periodically and items taken out should be destroyed.

Also periodically, items to be retained can be removed to inactive storage. The filing of these items should follow the same scheme that is used for handling the active items. Materials stored in this manner also may have disposal dates. If they do, the filing should show the date so that the materials can be easily located, and destroyed without requiring someone to make a complete search through all stored materials.

While there are many possible faulty practices to be found in record handling, many of these pertain to large organizations. Those which seem most relevant to the departmental office operation are the following:

Unfinished-business files. Suspense or pending files (not confidential) are often improperly kept in desk drawers or office files by secretaries and executives. (Records which are not centrally filed cannot be located easily.)

Indexing records by names of individuals rather than by names of the governing unit. Wherever possible, records should be indexed by the name of the firm, department, activity, or title of the position rather than by the name of the individual, officer or employee. Officers and employees may leave an organization but the functions within the organization remain, which makes it imperative that definite rules be used for correctly indexing and filing all records.

Records not filed properly. Active records may be taken out of their proper places and placed in the front of the drawer for "ready accessibility." Records may be mis-filed.

Memory files. No cross references are made. The person filing trusts his memory to locate records filed under the correct topic but requested under another topic. Correct indexing and cross-referencing will insure finding the records when personnel changes.

Free access to files. All records removed from files should be charged to the person using them according to an established policy. In general, free access to the files should not be permitted.

Bulky folders. For quick finding, a main subject having an excessive number of papers should be subdivided by phases of the subject.

Policy not established for the retention or disposal of records. There is often no appraisal of records or schedule for their retention or disposal. This schedule is essential before a system can be established for current records.[7]

[7] Odell and Strong, *op. cit.*, pp. 9–10.

Records which are to be kept for long periods of time but which have little or no use beyond their historical function can be placed on microfilm at very little cost. A complete four-drawer letter file of records can be stored on microfilm which will occupy less than 192 cu. in., or a space about 12 in. x 4 in. If one wishes to refer to the record, he will need a reader, but such a machine can be rented at a nominal cost. Libraries use microfilm for storing daily newspapers and for other printed material and are likely to have one or more readers available.

CENTRALIZED OFFICE SERVICES

As an institution increases in size, and usually in services, the duplication of certain services is too costly to be continued. A plan for centralized services, which can encompass many of the functions commonly performed by individual office staffs, is then instituted. To place all duplicating work, such as mimeographing and multilithing, in one office makes for greater efficiency. The operators are trained and the machines are in use more hours of the day. Actual work output will be greater in quantity and better in quality.

Centers for stenographic work occasionally are established. A member of a departmental staff who wishes to dictate materials to be typed, or who has copies of course materials or examinations to be prepared for duplicating can call upon the services offered by the stenographic center. If the person wishes to dictate letters he may have to go to the stenographic office. It is possible, of course, to do machine dictation which can then be transcribed by a typist in the center. Educational institutions do not regularly supply staff members with dictation equipment, although a departmental office could have such equipment for use by all of its staff members.

Other management functions, such as purchasing and accounting, with which a department of physical education may be involved, can be carried on more satisfactorily through a centralized office which serves the entire institution. This statement is based upon the assumption that these central offices are staffed with competent people who make every effort to fulfill their functions in the interests of the departments and the institution.

Because of the diversity in size and organization of educational institutions, it is not advisable to try to further the idea of centralized office services. The most important point of this discussion is that the administrator must study his own office practices and institute those which are going to get his work completed most efficiently and expeditiously at a minimum cost. If centralization of a service is indicated and the institution is prepared to open such a service, the departmental administrator should cooperate fully in its establishment and operation.

There are services in a departmental office which cannot be transferred to a centralized office. The departmental administrator should have personnel in his own office to prepare and maintain departmental records; assemble information for him to use as a basis for reports and budget requests; to institute purchase orders; to answer inquiries, and perform other necessary services.

Office Location and Arrangement

The simple act of planning office arrangements in academic buildings can improve the efficiency of office services. One receptionist can serve a number of departments as well as one. Typists also can serve a number of departments as well as one. Locating departmental offices so that these services are equally available to several departmental office groups should result in better utilization of office personnel.

A department of physical education is likely to be housed in a separate building or a separate wing of a building. Two criteria are to be observed in locating the departmental office. First, it should be accessible to students, public, and members of the instructional staff without such accessibility interfering with classes or other activities of the department. Second, it should be located so that supervision of the playing areas is possible. Supervision may be interpreted to mean actual viewing of the areas from the office, or being in a position to reach all playing areas easily for periodic checking. In a building with one gymnasium and one locker room adjacent to it, the office can be located so as to view the playing areas and, if desired, the locker room. In a large gymnasium building with several exercise areas at different levels of the building, such viewing from one office is practically impossible. If constant surveillance is required, the installation of closed circuit television cameras in each area, with all cameras being connected to a monitoring set in the office, can provide excellent viewing of the areas at all times.

GENERAL COMMENTS

Because the office is a working center in which people spend a good deal of their lives, and because it is also the door through which students, members of the public, colleagues from other institutions, and colleagues from one's own institution enter into acquaintance with the department, an atmosphere of friendliness, warmth, and efficiency should prevail. Efficiency in this sense means that the outsider's impression is that the office gets its work done.

Offices can be the best public relations centers which the institution has, or they can be the means of alienating the interest and support of persons from the outside. Departments of physical education are regularly involved in nonclass programs which bring them into close relationship with members of the public. The office personnel are the people most often dealing with the public. The department office characterized by a manner which is considerate, informed, friendly, and efficient enhances all of these relationships. Furthermore, such an office surely can perform its own duties better than one which presents the opposite qualities.

Good housekeeping in an office makes for a good appearance and improves the opportunity for efficient work. Good housekeeping minimizes the number of movements that a person has to make to perform a single function. The "looking for that letter which I had in my hand yesterday" kind of performance is eliminated. There is room to work unhampered by piles of papers, circulars, books, and other materials. In general, tasks are completed rather than laid aside temporarily.

Smoking usually is not permitted in public school buildings. In colleges, however, the regulations governing this practice are local. While personal opinions may vary on this matter, it is suggested that smoking not be permitted in the offices of a department of physical education. Reference is being made here particularly to clerical and secretarial staffs. There is no evidence to support a feeling that the worker who smokes at his desk is more efficient than the nonsmoker, and there is reason to believe that the smoker is less efficient. Smoking takes time, whether it affects the person in any other way or not.

Of more importance is the fact that physical education represents some relationship to better general health practices. Because the population with which the members of this department deal are almost entirely younger people, there is some obligation to maintain an atmosphere in the department and in its offices which gives no approval to smoking.

One recognizes that adults cannot be required to live according to standards set for children and youth. On the other hand, those who are working with children and youth cannot detach their own behavior from their principal job, namely that of educating the school and college students. Members of physical education departments are particularly obligated because of their influence upon the younger people with whom they work. This position, with its attendant responsibilities, cannot be dismissed lightly.

The discussion of smoking belongs in the consideration of the office, because it is most often in the offices that teachers, administrators, and the clerical staff smoke during the day. The confirmed smoker may rebel against the point of view expressed above, but he cannot ignore the importance of his conduct before his students.

Loyalty to the organization is a primary requirement for members of an office staff. The confidence which members have in each other, and which the administrator has in his staff, exists only because there is an underlying loyalty to the organization and its people. If a person finds that he cannot accept this requirement, he should remove himself from the staff, because his usefulness is lost and his potential for harming the operation of the office is sizable. Furthermore, he adds to his own personal problems when he remains in a situation for which he feels no loyalty.

Loyalty is a quality of value to all employees in an organization, whatever positions they hold. Implications of the discussion so far suggest that only the office staff should be loyal. This is half the picture. The administrator must be loyal to his office staff in the sense of having confidence in them and of supporting them in their work. Members of the instructional staff also must manifest the same spirit.

The department office is an important part of the administrative organization. From the standpoint of the administrator, the office, its personnel, its tone, and its operation determine the effectiveness of the administration and actually decide the degree to which the administrator can fulfill his own duties.

Chapter 13

THE STAFF

It is axiomatic that the quality essential to effective education is competent and imaginative teaching. In recent years, many persons not professionally associated with education have deplored the shortage of qualified teachers. The profession of education itself for a long time has been earnestly striving for improvement in teaching and has made notable progress. The key to good teaching is, of course, good teachers; in other words, they are the individuals who are fundamentally capable and interested and who are prepared through formal education and experience to teach effectively.

Teachers working together in a subject matter field in an institution comprise either a staff, a departmental faculty, or an area faculty. Because this text deals with matters of an administrative nature, the principal concerns of this chapter will be the securing and maintaining of a departmental staff, directing its work in the department, and giving professional stimulation to its individual members and educational leadership to the staff as a unit. A uniformly effective teaching staff is superior to an occasional outstanding teacher within a generally weak staff.

Chandler and Petty have indicated the importance of a staff in the following statement: "A competent staff with a sound educational philosophy, working with virile and dynamic leadership, is an element in the school administrative process for which there is no satisfactory substitute."[1]

PROFESSIONAL QUALIFICATIONS FOR TEACHERS

Staffs and faculties are composed of individuals. Who among those prepared for teaching have the qualifications of the good teacher? Efforts to establish the measurable qualities of a successful teacher have not borne particularly useful results, although one may conclude that there is agreement as to general qualifications which the teacher should possess. Bixler[2] reported in 1939 that nearly five hundred studies had been made in the previous three decades in an attempt to secure more adequate knowledge of the factors that condition success in teaching, but that only slight progress had been made. The investigations have continued, but the goal of securing a device for the more accurate measurement of teaching success is yet to be achieved.

Although precision is lacking in the specification of needed qualities for successful teaching, there are statements which describe the more desirable personal traits of persons who may be acceptable as teachers and successful in their teaching.

A. S. Barr[3] lists the following qualities of successful teachers: resourcefulness, intelligence, emotional stability, considerateness, buoyancy, objectivity, drive, dominance, attractiveness, refinement, cooperativeness, and reliability. He also lists three other categories of qualities, namely, knowledges, attitudes, and skills. In each of these he places items which should be part of the preparation and professional development of the comprehensively educated teacher.

Another description of the good teacher appeared in a well-known weekly magazine. "The good teacher must be a person with a profound love of a subject, born of the fullness of familiarity. He must have an excellent operational understanding of basic educational principles, not the mere word-shadows of professional jargon.

[1] B. J. Chandler and Paul V. Petty, *Personnel Management in School Administration,* World Book Company, 1955, p. vii.

[2] Roy W. Bixler, *Institution-Faculty Relations in the College of Integrity,* Teachers College, Columbia University, 1939, p. 24.

[3] A. S. Barr, "Characteristics of Successful Teachers," *Phi Delta Kappan,* March, 1958, pp. 282–284.

The teacher must have a love of people in general, and of children in particular, must have the ability to awaken and to maintain the interest of students and to direct those interests toward successful experiences. Above all, the teacher must be able to foster wonder."[4]

Hughes and French speak of the necessity of the teacher being a mature adult, "a well-integrated person who feels secure and adequate and is emotionally and socially mature." Among evidences of maturity and good adjustment, they include "concern for the freedom and growth of others, rather than an attempt to keep them dependent upon the teacher; responsibility and self-direction; broad avocational interests; placement of the welfare of boys and girls first in all relationships; liking for persons in general and finding of more good than bad in associates."[5]

Whatever technical qualifications teachers may be expected to have, above all they should be persons with a primary interest in the development and ultimate success of others, an interest in and concern for the general welfare of people, an ability to understand others and get along with them, and the skill and knowledge to attack their problems with objective and considered steps leading to socially accepted solutions.

It may seem that this is the kind of person sought by any profession, the type who should be representative of all mature adults. One cannot argue with this feeling. In the profession of education, however, one can state emphatically that members of a teaching staff should possess these characteristics. A staff, which is a kind of social unit, functions best when its members are mature in attitudes and behavior, and when they are primarily interested in matters outside themselves.

Even with all the excellent personal qualities set forth above, a person still will not be an effective teacher unless he is fully versed in his field. Because of the breadth of knowledge in the realm of teaching, one can only say that the teacher must have command of his own field, "a profound love of subject, born of the fullness of familiarity," if he is to serve with success in his profession. Fur-

[4] Frank G. Jennings, "Most Dangerous Profession," *The Saturday Review*, March 8, 1958, p. 22.

[5] William L. Hughes and Esther French, *The Administration of Physical Education*, A. S. Barnes and Co., 1954, p. 36.

thermore, if the previous statement restricts the meaning of *subject* to subject matter, the teacher also must possess the knowledge and skills required to conduct learning situations, that is, to teach.

There has been much ado about methods versus subject matter, with the implication that all prospective teachers devote most of their time to the study of methods. If this were true, teaching generally would be more effective. The good teacher needs both subject matter and methods for teaching his subject. At the college level, where teachers are usually employed without any previous training in the science of teaching, the growing pressure for improving the effectiveness of teaching will lead to a consideration of methods, too.

To insure a minimum level of preparation for teaching in the schools, state governments have established state regulatory bodies with the authority to establish and administer requirements for the certification of teachers. Certification is based upon general and technical education, with the requirements in the latter being stated quantitatively as well as qualitatively, i.e., in terms of the specific courses.

The student preparing to teach can obtain information about certification from his advisor or from the department of education in his institution. Successful completion of a curriculum in teacher education should qualify the student for certification as a teacher in his state.

The state does not grant certificates or require certification for college teachers. It is possible, therefore, to employ anyone to teach in college, regardless of educational and personal qualifications. Practically, however, colleges have set their own requirements for those employed to teach, and accrediting associations use the yardstick of graduate study and graduate degrees to judge the quality of an institution's teaching staff. The colleges are more likely to seek people with competence in subject matter than they are to seek expertness in teaching. Perhaps, in view of the difficulty of securing objective evidence of teaching competence, it is easier to choose persons on the basis of their demonstrated knowledge in a subject field.

In college physical education the administrator who deals with intercollegiate athletics as part of his program will need to make clear statements of qualifications for membership on his staff if he is to secure fully prepared teachers rather than highly trained sports specialists. The status of intercollegiate athletics in the larger universities and colleges today is such that to consider the application of sound educational practices to their administration at any point is a questionable use of time and energy. In the smaller institutions which have well coordinated, or integrated, programs of physical education, including intercollegiate athletics, educational qualifications should be required of all persons employed in any teaching position on the staff.

There is no reason, of course, why the college teachers of physical education should not meet the same requirements for appointment to an institution's faculty as do teachers of any other subject. There should be no second-class members on a college faculty. Certainly physical education personnel should not seek to set up such a class of membership.

Each time that a school or college department appoints a teacher of physical education, it should secure the best person available for the position to be filled. Only in this way can competent staffs be developed and maintained. It is recognized that the best persons are not always available because of any one of several factors, such as salary, location, teaching load, and others; nevertheless, the institution is obligated to try to secure these highly qualified people. A competent staff means stimulating and skillful teaching by people who know what they are doing and why they are doing it.

SELECTION AND EMPLOYMENT OF STAFF

Teacher selection is the base upon which a competent staff is built. It is generally held that the selection of teaching personnel is the single most important responsibility of the departmental and school administrator. To secure the best available person for a position on one's staff requires the administrator to follow regular procedures in the selection of new personnel. Recognized and acceptable procedures are described in the following pages.

The first step is to define the job which is to be filled. Accurate descriptions of the duties of the position which is vacant naturally lead to a clearer specification of the qualifications which the successful candidate should have. Furthermore, careful job descriptions direct the search for candidates and, if the vacancy is widely known, may attract those applicants who possess the required qualifications.

Unless any interested person is qualified to apply, the description of the position normally is accompanied by a statement of major qualifications required of applicants for the position. The following list suggests items which may be included in a job description. Jobs, however, are usually totalities in themselves, hence must be described as a whole and not according to a generalized list.

1. Name and location of the institution. Pertinent information which will help to identify the general character of the institution.
2. Position to be filled.
3. Salary and rank; or salary range and available ranks if persons with varying levels of qualifications are to be accepted as candidates.
4. Major responsibilities of the position: subject, grade (if in the schools), teaching load, auxiliary responsibilities, length of academic year.
5. Working condition, i.e., facilities, equipment, research opportunities, especially where any of these factors is unusual.
6. Academic and professional qualification of the applicant: graduate degrees required, certificate required, professional preparation, and teaching experience.
7. The significant purposes of the institution which each teacher is expected to help achieve.
8. Information about the community and the living conditions within the areas adjacent to the institution.

The preceding list attempts to cover all educational levels through the undergraduate college. To repeat, the administrator and the institution will describe the *particular* job for which a candidate is being sought. Such a description may include more or less than appears in the above list.

The physical education administrator may be faced with applications from persons with high specialization in one skill area. Unless the job demands this qualification alone, the administrator should evaluate it in terms of the overall requirements of the job. In teaching, specialized skill is useful to the extent that the person visualizes the educational values to be achieved through such skill. This statement may be strictly gratuitous in view of previous discussions within this text. It is important, however, to keep one's eye on the total job, which in physical education is more than high competence in skill performance.

The second step in selection of staff is to secure several candidates who meet the stated qualifications in order that one may have a choice to make. Where does one find applicants for a position?

Candidates for a position may be divided into two groups, namely, those whom the institution seeks by any one of several means, and those who apply directly to the institution without invitation, the self-nominated candidates. The number of this latter group who may seek employment depends upon the reputation of the institution, its salary scale, its location, and other factors, some of which may be important to one individual but not another. Candidates who apply in a fashion which indicates that they are really interested in working in a particular school system or institution should receive consideration to the extent that the administration will review whatever credentials the individual supplies with his application. There are persons who apply for positions in a wholesale fashion. These individuals mimeograph or ditto their personal vita and send them to an officer of the institution. Institutions treat these briefly and do not often give them consideration. Whether this is warranted practice is not clear, but the feeling is that the person applying in this manner is scattering his applications widely on the chance that one school or college will give him consideration.

When a department or a school system has one or more positions to be filled, it follows some kind of procedure to secure applicants who may become candidates for the job or jobs. The steps followed may be carefully planned in order that the largest number of qualified applicants will be secured, or they may be haphazard and nothing more than a telephone call to a friend, a placement bureau, an agency, or a college or university department of physical education.

Today it is probable that school systems within a state depend upon their own colleges and universities for their teachers. These institutions which prepare teachers also wish to place their graduates, so they actively seek information about available jobs in the schools of their state. Colleges and universities who are seeking staff members also may look to graduate departments in universities near them for prospective candidates. The professional ties among members of a profession may lead one institution to seek direct recommendations from another. Institutions of higher learning also try to induce well-known members of faculties of other colleges and universities to join their own faculties. This latter action is one that needs to be carried out carefully, so that ethical considerations are observed.

Although it seems likely on the basis of empirical observation that a systematic searching for applicants is not a characteristic procedure, it is a superior method by which faculties and staffs of excellence can be assembled within school systems and institutions of higher learning.

With respect to the selection of college teachers, a report[6] made a number of years ago listed outstanding weaknesses in recruiting practices, as follows:

1. They take into account too small a number of applicants.
2. They proceed on incomplete knowledge of the candidate.
3. They pay too little attention to personal qualities of the candidate.
4. They employ no definite standards of qualification.
5. They do not discriminate between ordinary persons and persons of exceptional ability.
6. They overlook persons of talent in small institutions.
7. They do not systematically promote scholarship.
8. They are based on inadequate and narrow theories of education.
9. They increase the exercise of autocratic power in the hands of a few.

Since this report was written, the method for selecting candidates has probably improved at the college level. The truth is, though, that a number of these practices persist to hinder the development of the best possible staff in an institution. The serious weakness still is in the search for candidates. This weakness may result from the institution making insufficient inquiries for candidates, or from limiting its inquiries to graduates of a certain institution, or from inquiring only of professional acquaintances, or from the operation of any other irrelevant bias. Item (9) in the above list may be more potent in determining selection practices than any staff or administrator would admit. Like the hidden emotions which prompt seemingly acceptable but unexplained behavior, this factor can operate subtly.

[6] *Report of the Committee on College and University Teaching,* American Association of University Professors, 1933, p. 19.

Public school systems, because of the larger number of new employees engaged each year, may be more systematic in their search for candidates. A recent study of teacher personnel practices revealed the sources of teachers for schools in cities of varying sizes. Of the 1027 cities reporting, 66 percent secured names of candidates from college and university placement bureaus, 19 percent from self-nominated applicants, and only one percent from state teachers associations.

Chandler and Petty summarize the data presented in this study in the following:

> In the large cities publication of announcements of positions to be filled accounts for the location of 45% of the applicants, but in the smaller towns this source accounts for less than one half of one per cent of the applications. The large cities depend upon published announcements, college placement bureaus, and direct recruitment on campuses for about 9 out of 10 of their prospective teachers, while the smaller towns depend primarily upon college and university placement offices and voluntary applications.[7]

To secure the best candidates for a position an institution must let it be known that a position is open and must give a careful description of the qualifications required of persons wishing to apply. The institution, whether it is a school system or a college, may have to review more applications and face a more difficult task in making its selection, but it should gain by having a better group of candidates from which to choose.

Ideally a school or college should give extensive publicity to its available positions and seek candidates from a wide geographic area. In practice, limitations are imposed by candidates themselves. Moving long distances is troublesome and costly. Leaving a situation where one has made friends and a place for himself in the community is not easy. Perhaps he prefers to stay near his relatives. The person may prefer the climate and other natural advantages where he lives. Except for the more responsible and higher salaried positions, it may be difficult to secure candidates from afar. The effort, however, should be made.

Larger cities which do announce their vacancies publicly are not likely to reach persons outside their geographic area. Although this

[7] B. J. Chandler and Paul V. Petty, *op. cit.*, p. 129.

is giving public notice about job vacancies, the result may be to attract only those from the limited number of candidates within the city itself. The goal of securing the best candidate may be only partially realized.

One factor of considerable importance is that of employing persons who come from the same teacher preparation program, or from the same locality, or in the case of a college, from the college itself. This kind of situation is termed *inbreeding* and is one that should be avoided. Bixler argues against inbreeding for the college:

> Those who have been trained in a given institution understand its philosophy and aims, have already made certain adjustments to students, members of the faculty, administrative officers, and the community in which the college resides; but this is only partial integration. The world outside is changing, and the college needs to change also to maintain its adqustment to movements of thought and social trends. It is doubtful that the loading up of a faculty with its own graduates is the best way to adjust to change.[8]

A professionally active and competent staff, intellectually alert and responsive to demands for change, can best be maintained when a sizable percentage of its members originally come from another community or state, and when they have had teaching experience in other institutions.

It should not be necessary to remark upon the undesirability and questionable ethic of employing friends, relatives, or relatives of friends, unless these persons, on the basis of cold, objective appraisal are superior to all other candidates. Schools and colleges have worked for a long time to free themselves from the pressures, especially those of a political nature, which have been used in the past to gain employment for a friend, regardless of his qualifications for the job. For a school system or a college administrator to follow a practice today which is in essence worse than yielding to political pressures of old, is unsupportable. Neither excellent staffs nor high staff morale can be developed and maintained under such circumstances.

Procedures for staff selection, therefore, should involve a wide

[8] Bixler, *op. cit.,* p. 24.

search, with information about the available positions being given appropriate general distribution. Sources approached should be selected without irrelevant bias.

The third step is the actual selection of the person for the position. How is the selection finally made?

In public schools it is generally agreed that the teachers should be selected by the superintendent. In small school districts the superintendent may make all the selections personally. In larger districts and in city systems the superintendent determines the appointments to be made, usually with the advice of assistant or associate administrative officers, and accepts recommendations from whatever unit in the system is given the authority to assist in the selection of personnel. In the larger districts the several school principals may interview, select, and recommend candidates for appointment. In a city such as New York, a Board of Examiners selects the candidates eligible for appointment and places their names upon a list from which they are drawn as vacancies arise. The school principal has a limited choice among the persons on a list. Teacher selection practices must be in accord with the laws and regulations of the state and with the policies set forth by the local board of education.

Selection of personnel for departments of instruction in colleges and universities is a process which may be initiated either at the highest administrative level, or at the basic instructional unit level, namely the department. In either event, the final section is the responsibility of the president. In small institutions the selection procedures may be informal and intimate, with the president participating over several steps in the procedure. In large colleges and universities the deans work with the departments in the preliminary stages, before the recommendations finally go to the president from the deans. The president makes his recommendations to his board.

In colleges and universities, departmental staffs may take part in all the stages of selection of new personnel except those reserved for the authority of the dean and the president. College staffs may participate informally in the selection of new teachers. Meeting candidates at luncheon or dinner or taking part in the description of the institution and the department are ways of interviewing prospective teachers. The procedure may be formalized in institutions in which candidates must be interviewed by a departmental committee which has been elected by the membership of the department, and must be recommended by committee vote for appointment. In this kind of organization the departmental administrator is a member of the committee, with no more power to choose than any other committee member. Because such committees can only recommend appointment to a higher authority, such as a dean or the president, actions taken which are not in the best interests of the institution are subject to review and modification.

Although it is recognized that the superintendent of schools makes the final recommendations to the board of education for the appointment of new teachers, the growth in size and complexity of many school systems makes the job of selecting new teachers one to be shared with other school personnel. Previous mention was made of the role of the school principal in teacher selection. Chandler and Petty cite an instance in which the teachers working with the principal assisted in the selection of new teachers. They state that "experience and study in educational administration have shown that effective selection requires staff participation. From an organizational and professional standpoint the teaching and administrative staff is qualified to assist or participate with the superintendent in the exercise of the authority and responsibility for the selection of new team members."[9]

Three facts should be kept in mind with regard to the appointment of new teachers to a staff.

1. The final authority for appointment rests with the body responsible for the institution under the laws of the state. Because this is so, this body and its delegated administrative representative have the final decisions on new personnel.

2. All stages in the selection of new personnel, from the initial contact to the one of official appointment, are in the nature of recommendations without finality.

3. Schools and colleges wishing to secure well qualified persons who can become full working members of existing staffs will utilize the knowledge and opinions of teachers and administrators in the preliminary stages of teacher selection and will give full consideration to their recommendations for new appointments.

[9] Chandler and Petty, *op. cit.*, p. 119.

DEVELOPING AND MAINTAINING STAFF MORALE

In all forms of organization created to perform a job the ability of the members of the organization to work together is of utmost importance. The quality of a group bound together in a common enterprise which causes them to work together harmoniously day in and day out, to focus on the purposes being sought, to lose their individual selves to a considerable degree in the work, and to feel as a cohesive group is that intangible but real element of morale. The developing and maintaining of this quality may be the responsibility of each member of a staff, but it is definitely a major responsibility of the administrator. Weak administrators may have staffs with high morale because they have on their staffs persons who have given leadership in developing this factor. In essence, however, it is the administrator who can bring morale to its highest point and maintain it.

The morale of a staff is affected by a number of factors. For discussion purposes these have been grouped under nine topic headings. Matters of working conditions, of staff management, as well as matters of personal relationships are included.

Before entering upon the discussion of the several areas, let it be said that basically the function of all suggestions concerning morale is to make it possible for each member of a staff to find a measure of personal fulfillment in working for common goals. Man may work because of necessity. Men who do not need financial return for their work, nevertheless must work for personal fulfillment. Sears states that "morale built in terms of common professional purposes and cooperative effort in behalf of the interests of the children and the community is indispensable; and this, regardless of how important it may be, also, for teachers to work together in terms of their own interests."[10] The job and its purposes are important. They give meaning to the task and the structure within which the individual works. The individual is important, too. Although the job is not altered to fit each individual on a staff, each person must find a means of adding to the job something of himself to make the situa-

[10] Jesse B. Sears, *The Nature of the Administrative Process,* McGraw-Hill Book Company, Inc., 1950, p. 305.

tion meaningful to him. Consideration is given to this point of view in the following material.

DEFINE THE RESPONSIBILITIES

An administrator who is seeking new personnel will certainly describe the nature of the job for which a person is to be employed. Areas of responsibility with respect to the total program of the department should be set forth. Is the person to teach classes only? Does he have nonclass duties? Are there others for whom he is immediately responsible in a supervisory capacity? Outlining as clearly as possible the areas of responsibility helps to set the purposes of the position and to locate it within the functions of the total staff. Lack of clarity in this matter leads only to aggravation, which in turn creates other problems of morale.

The teacher's relationship with others who are doing similar work can be pleasant, stimulating, and productive if the personal responsibilities are described as clearly as possible. If two teachers work together in one large class, who plans for the class instruction for the term, for each class period? How is teaching within the class divided or shared? If the individual has coaching duties as part of his job, to whom is he responsible? If he is coaching a freshman or junior varsity team, does he teach the materials and skills which the coach of the varsity team chooses? In specialized areas of instruction, e.g., dance, swimming, health teaching, is there a member of the staff who directs the planning and general conduct of the teaching? Is one expected to take part on departmental committees and on all-college committees? What duties and powers do such committees have? The previous questions suggest several of the situations in which more than one person is involved, and in which some person is likely to have authority as well as responsibility for the operation of the activity. The administrator will indicate as clearly as he can how the new teacher should work in these and other similar situations.

Teachers very often have working relationships with nonteaching personnel in the institution. Physical education teachers will frequently find that the effective conduct of their jobs depends upon the work of noninstructional personnel. Among the groups with whom the teacher will work are administrators of the institution and of other departments, medical doctors and nurses, custodial workers, financial officers, supply room attendants, clerks and other office personnel. Whether the teacher deals directly with any of these people or reaches them through the chairman of his department is a matter of importance to the smooth functioning of the total organization. The administrator can help both the teacher and himself by indicating the appropriate relationships of the teacher with these persons. If secretarial assistance is available in the department office, the administrator must indicate whether a particular secretary is assigned to the teacher, how much of her time is available to the teacher, and the kind of work which he may have done. An administrator may find that there are institutional administrative officers who do not wish to take up departmental matters with anyone but the chairman of the department.

If the teacher is to have a working relationship with community groups or agencies, he will need direction.

The administrator cannot describe every detail of the teacher's responsibilities, nor can he define the nature of interpersonal relationships for every situation and circumstance. The capable teacher must know many of these matters himself. If the teacher does have the knowledge of his major responsibilities and of the lines of authority within the department and institution, he will be better able to define his own job and will know how to utilize more effectively the supporting resources of the institution.

A manual or handbook which describes the aims of the school or college, the regulations governing the operation of the schools, the offices of administration with their attendant powers and duties, the institutional responsibilities of teachers, statements on other managerial matters, and a general presentation of philosophy with respect to the purposes of the organization and the expectations held for those belonging to it, helps greatly to acclimate new teachers. A manual of this type can also be prepared for departmental purposes and can give more detail concerning the work of teachers in one subject matter area.

ACCORD EACH INDIVIDUAL RESPECT

"Each individual person wishes to be important and to feel that his importance is recognized. Each wishes to be accepted by the group with which he works as one who meets the standards of conduct which it approves. Each wishes to be recognized as 'belonging.' Each, in short, seeks to associate himself with the many influences which impinge upon him, in such a way that his personality becomes more nearly integrated. Only then can he find the personal satisfactions which produce 'morale.' "[11] An individual's conception of himself with respect to the job which he is doing and the institution in which he is working is as important to his morale as any other factor. One cannot completely ignore other factors in a job situation, because many of them are of critical importance. None, though, seems to possess the quality for developing morale which arises from the individual's interpretation of the acceptability and standing of both himself and his work. Chandler and Petty state: "For many years efforts to 'recruit' teachers have been unsuccessful. Experience has proved that the faith in *security* as *the* motivating factor is ill-founded. Higher salaries, ironclad tenure, retirement benefits, and automatic salary schedules—these *may* help; but standing alone they are inadequate." They quote from a 1925 publication entitled the *Mainsprings of Men.* " 'It is impossible, therefore, to judge the effect of either wage or other conditions of work apart from the relationships the work permits with other persons. What every worker knows is this: that sooner or later the final joy of his work is settled, not by him nor by his employer, but by the social standing awarded him by his fellow citizens.' "[12]

An administrator and his staff show this respect in every way possible. From the standpoint of administration it is shown in several ways.

1. Assignment of the individual to teaching and other duties for which he is fitted. Avoid making assignments for which the person is not adequately prepared, at least until he has had time to secure the needed preparation.
2. Assignment of individuals to teaching, and other duties, in which they find opportunity for personal and professional growth.
3. Involve staff members in the total work of the department to the

[11] Willard B. Spalding, "Organizing the Personnel of a Democratic School System," *Forty-Fifth Yearbook,* Part II, National Society for the Study of Education, University of Chicago Press, 1946, p. 81.

[12] Chandler and Petty, *op. cit.,* p. 89.

extent that they can make contributions and to the degree that they have some responsibility for the outcomes.

4. Within the staff, develop participation in cooperative methods for planning, for problem-solving, for evaluation of departmental activities, for research, and for improvement of interpersonal relationships.

5. Recognize individual achievement. Recognize achievement of individuals as a staff.

6. Establish regulations governing the job which indicate the importance of each individual's work to the department and to the institution.

There are many small ways in which the administrator and teachers show their respect for each other daily. Those who have a sense of respect for individuals behave in a courteous, congenial manner in dealing with their colleagues. They believe in the worth of the individual. In democratic educational institutions this kind of behavior is to be expected.

PROVIDE LEADERSHIP FOR GROWTH

From the viewpoint of schools and colleges, teachers as a group must continue to grow professionally. The individual also is deeply interested in professional growth, because of his desire for advancement in his profession and in his school. In the first instance the institution is thinking about teaching competence and scholarly achievements. In the second instance the individual is concerned with his professional standing, greater responsibilities in his or another institution, and higher salaries.

An administrator has special responsibility for new members on his staff. In the first weeks of their work he must be readily available to them for discussion of questions about their work. He will have described the departmental programs, interlocking responsibilities, institutional policies, and regulations. After the teachers have been at work, these items assume new meanings and may well benefit from a review and further elaboration.

If the new teacher is also beginning his first year or two of teaching, both the administrator and staff members will observe and help him with planning, teaching procedures, resources, special aids, student relationships, and other matters with which he may have had little experience. The administrator will wish to encourage the young teacher to continue with his scholarly activities. One person should pursue graduate study; another should plan to carry on research; still another may be writing for publications. There also will be opportunity for the young teacher to assume a share in the regular study of the departmental curriculum, which should be an activity involving the entire staff.

Older staff members should be proceeding under their own momentum and in response to their own motivations. When the circumstances under which a staff may have to work are such that the motivation for productive scholarship of any kind is lacking, a careful study of the causes should be made. Staff members can participate in such a study if the problem of becoming active in scholarly endeavors is sufficiently clear to motivate them. The role of defining the problem belongs to the administrator. Is the staff coming under scrutiny of the institution because of its failure to grow in scholarship? Are advancements being held up because of deficiencies in this area? Is it difficult to attract qualified people to the staff because the atmosphere for scholarship seems to be lacking? Are staff members finding themselves out of touch with their fields because they do not continue to study in their special areas? Recognition of one or more of these items may stimulate the older staff members who have become professionally and scholarly inactive.

According to Spalding, "the administrator does not motivate persons. He can only introduce incentives into the immediate environment of the employees. As these incentives appear to be desirable, the lack or need of them produces those imbalances, tensions, differences in potential, and changes in the chemistry of the body which are characteristic of true motivation and which result in subsequent action."[13] The administrator can assist in the motivation of his staff by changing the conditions which hamper scholarly activities. Adjusting the teaching loads, providing clerical assistance, obtaining funds for special equipment needed for research, assisting in the arrangements for exchange teaching, securing funds to help pay travel expenses of teachers to professional meetings all represent ways in which an administrator can change the situation and encourage staff interest in productive scholarship.

If teachers who have been at their jobs for several years can reach a point where teaching loses excitement for the teacher and interest

[13] Spalding, *op. cit.*, p. 78.

for the students, where imagination is dulled, and where routine, repetitive performance is the rule, how much more quickly can a department, whose program is dependent upon several persons, set its work into such a monotonous pattern that change of any kind is resisted. Into such a situation, which may be likened to a creeping paralysis, an alert administrator can introduce steps which will cause a staff to seek ways to improve its daily work. Curriculum study can be initiated, measuring results can be planned, and appraisal of goals and the general guiding philosophy may come about because of an aroused responsibility for doing a thoroughly professional job. Teaching methods may become the concern of the entire staff, whose members will welcome the visits and appraisal of their colleagues. Supervision, which has been the duty of one or a few persons, now becomes a project in better teaching.

Teachers working together on problems of common concern under the leadership of a competent administrator develop a team spirit. In this atmosphere each person is essential to the functioning of the group, and each is interested first in the welfare of the group rather than in his own personal status. As a member of the team he grows with them, enjoys their successes, and shares in their failures, but above all he works with others for the common good.

One form of reward for professional growth is promotion. In both public schools and colleges today, a certain amount of advancement is possible according to the graduate work completed. Beyond that, promotion in rank in colleges and in level of position in schools below the college level may be based on a number of factors. In colleges the scholarly contribution of the teacher to his field of specialization offers a universal basis for recognition. The forms of scholarship will not be discussed here, because institutions are likely to indicate those forms which are important to them. Excellence in teaching is equal to scholarly activity, but is somewhat more difficult to appraise objectively. Nevertheless, the importance of good teaching should not be minimized among the factors considered for promotion. At the levels below college it is likely that the achievement of outstanding quality in teaching will stand higher than either research or writing when teachers are being considered for advancement.

The administrator plays an important role in promotional procedures. He holds the greatest amount of information about his own staff members. He has intimate knowledge concerning their personal characteristics with respect to working on a particular job with others. He is able to secure judgments of a committee which may be authorized to make recommendations concerning promotions. Also, he has the personnel organization of the entire department in mind and can estimate the effects of promotions upon the morale of the staff.

To those who are his superiors the departmental administrator represents the best single source of information about the members of his departmental staff. If the administrator is known to have the welfare of the entire institution in mind, his superiors can depend upon him for carefully considered judgments growing out of his study of the needs of his department and those of the institution at large. To his superiors, also, the departmental administrator presents his needs with as much force as the circumstances warrant.

MAKE STAFF PARTICIPATION THE POLICY AND PRACTICE

An important factor in the morale of a worker is that he understands and accepts the purpose of his work, and that he feels he has a part in planning and carrying out the job. In a complex job, such as that of teaching or of administering an educational program, the participation of those working in various aspects of planning, organization, and evaluation is essential to the development of high staff morale.

Mackenzie writes as follows: "If administration is truly a service for furthering progress toward educational goals, all those concerned with and affected by administrative procedures should participate in appropriate aspects of the program. There is no other way that administration can be fully informed as to goals and needs."[14] Education as an organized function is carried on by individuals who are an integral part of the total process. Each one has a personal stake in the planned nature of the process as well as in the results which it achieves. Instruction, learning, and the evaluation of achievements are the central and principal functions of an educational unit.

[14] Gordon N. Mackenzie, "Developing and Administering the Curriculum and Pupil Services," *Forty-Fifth Yearbook,* Part II, National Society for the Study of Education, University of Chicago Press, 1946, p. 22.

Administration is concerned with harmonizing the various forces which give energy to education, so that the principal functions can be carried on with the greatest effectiveness. On the one hand, therefore, the administrator needs the benefit of the knowledge and experience of teachers in determining matters of policy, in planning for curriculum development, new and expanded facilities, and improved equipment, and in evaluating and selecting supplies essential for effective teaching. On the other hand, he is responsible for improving staff performance, stimulating an interest in curriculum revision, encouraging staff members to accept changes—in short, for developing in the staff an attitude leading to a continuous study of their jobs.

With this kind of attitude a staff can maintain a program which recognizes the needs and demands of a changing society. The staff members themselves will seek to keep up to date in the knowledge in their fields and in improved methods of teaching. The importance of this last point is emphasized in criticisms of high school science course content. One university dean stated that "the content in physics, chemistry and other sciences (in secondary schools) reflects concepts so out of line with current theory as to produce unscientific, if not anti-scientific biases."[15]

One may ask, "How much course content in physical education is based on concepts long since outdated?"

Staff growth depends upon the willingness of the staff to continue to learn. The administrator can facilitate learning on the part of his staff by bringing up problem situations in such a way that the members are motivated to seek solutions aimed at reaching desired goals. Ultimately, members of a professionally growing staff will themselves set forth problems for solution by their colleagues. Thus, impetus for continued growth will have been developed.

Where a staff participates in developing recommendations for policy and in planning for other activities within the department, institution, or system, the administrator must be sensitive to the fact that each person views the group activity in relation to his own interests and standing. An essential part of the background against which group study and planning are conducted is understood when

[15] Francis S. Chase, quoted in "Education in Review," *The New York Times*, November 22, 1959.

the administrator and his staff are cognizant of these individual concerns. Because the professional teacher has a deep personal interest in his job, he is rightly concerned with matters affecting it. His own feelings as a member of the organization will be influenced by his participation in planning for those actions which affect his own job.

A brief discussion of this factor of staff participation in preparing recommendations of policy and in other aspects of the departmental operation will be inadequate, however, if it leads to a conclusion that the staff participates in deciding upon all administrative matters. There are a number of areas of responsibility in which the staff has little or no jurisdiction, and wherein the administrator acts according to regulations or as he chooses, in light of his considered judgment.

Not every staff member will respond to the kind of group activity discussed previously. Furthermore, a teacher or other employee who is acting or recommending actions contrary to institutional policy cannot be allowed to influence departmental policy and administrative practice. Morale can also be destroyed by useless debate.

The administrator represents the focus of institutional authority with respect to its regulations and policies. His ability to carry these out in a way which is correct and which enhances staff growth improves morale.

PROVIDE FOR READY COMMUNICATION

An atmosphere in which members of a staff within a department or an institution find easy communication with each other and with the administrator contributes to the maintenance of a high morale. A feeling of freedom to talk with others on matters of common concern, or on personal problems which may be only remotely related to the job, grows out of a situation in which members are accustomed to participating in the planning, conduct, and evaluation of the departmental programs. Because morale is an individual condition and not the average of a total group feeling, the person who thinks of himself as a full member of a staff and is able to discuss equally with others and with the administrator matters which concern him and perhaps the department derives more satisfaction from his work and feels more wholly a part of it. This is a factor in maintaining high morale.

The administrator who works with his staff keeps them informed on matters of importance to all. In his position he is likely to learn of new proposals, possible changes in institutional policy or practice, and of other actions and plans which may affect the individual teachers. He may not be at liberty to discuss all information which comes to his attention from his own administrative superior, but on items which concern the individual staff members he must supply them with information.

The establishment of procedures for ready communication between the administrator and his staff is important if grievances are to be handled fairly and expeditiously. A grievance may arise when there is conflict between the teacher and the administration, or between teacher and teacher. The administrator may have a grievance because of actions of a teacher, or because of the actions of organizations with which a teacher may be associated. Grievances which are not resolved contribute to the disintegration of morale. Obviously there are varying degrees of seriousness; one may find that some grievances are chronic, but their causes are accepted because the possibility of removing them is remote. This type of grievance probably has little, if any, effect upon morale.

Authorities in the field of educational administration are not in full agreement as to the procedures to be followed in settling grievances. Spalding strongly urges methods patterned after those followed in industry. He would have teachers develop strong organizations whose membership would not be open to administrators. Formal procedures for presenting and settling grievances would be established and followed. Spalding states: "Those grievances which arise wherever large numbers of persons are employed can be dealt with best under the provisions of an agreement arrived at through collective bargaining. If this does not exist, and it usually does not, then some plan of organization should be set up for the redress of just grievances. This is absolutely necessary if relationships are to improve and harmony is to be restored."[16] As a part of improved communication aiming at reducing conflict, Spalding holds that the conditions of employment, which become an agreement between the

[16] Spalding, *op cit.*, p. 71.

teacher and the board, should be set forth clearly and as fully as is needed to define the teacher's rights, duties, and responsibilities.

Bixler takes a somewhat different view of organizations whose principal aim is to protect the teachers. After discussing the development of administration as a higher paid, higher status position, one which dominates all aspects of the school operation, he states: "Unfortunately the industrial pattern has been carried over into education. As previously noted, in the early stages of development it was natural for administration to look to industrial organization for a pattern, and when teachers began to sense the need of organizing, it was natural for them to adopt the pattern of labor organizations. Now, the teachers who belong to the unions think of themselves as workers and of administration as management. It is as wrong, from the point of view of integrity in education, as anything could be."[17]

It is likely that in every department and every institution situations will arise in which there is conflict between persons. These conflicts, which affect the morale of individuals, may be between teachers and other teachers, between teachers and administrators, or between one administrator and another. The term *grievance* is used commonly in industry to describe a variety of conflicts which develop between employee and employer; its use suggests that one who has been wronged seeks redress for the wrong. In an educational enterprise where teachers and administrators usually have similar backgrounds, serve the same commonly held goals of the school and college, and actually work as partners in achieving the purposes of education, this definition of grievance is not appropriate.

In recent years a growing emphasis upon democratic administration precludes the rigid separation of teaching from administration. The teacher working under such strict division loses some of his potential services to administration, and the administrator loses the breadth of knowledge and experience which the teachers may lend to the development of plans and policies. If one agrees with the following statement, he will not support the idea of employee organizations for the protection of teachers. "The employees of public school systems are individuals who have been selected to become members of a cooperative enterprise, the purpose of which is to provide instruction and to improve the quality of living in the community.

[17] Bixler, *op. cit.*, p. 55.

Wholehearted, loyal, and enthusiastic support of a school system by the school personnel will be increased by their participation in formulating and executing the policies of the educational system."[18]

It may be assumed that teachers working in a department or institution which follows the practices of democratic administration are able to find the means within such an administrative framework to work out the conflicts which do arise. It would be naive to assume that all administrators have the same concerns as the teachers for the improvement of the teachers' working conditions. If one thinks of the public, and the boards also, as administering the schools and colleges, he realizes that some publics are not really interested in improving the teaching job if it means increased costs to the community, or to the governing body of the institution. It follows, therefore, that teachers should not forego their requests for improvement in their own working conditions simply because they are participating in a democratically oriented administration.

The importance of easy communication between members of teaching staffs and between staffs and administration is underscored when one studies the procedures suggested for handling conflict situations. Whether the methods established are on the order of collective bargaining, or are built into the cooperative type of administration-staff organization, communication must be readily carried on, and the channels of communication must be understood. This is essential to maintaining high staff morale.

WORKING CONDITIONS

Each of the items discussed so far has been concerned with some facet of the job and may be considered as a condition of the work. Spalding[19] lists thirty-two items which he believes should be covered in a basic agreement between an employer and an employee; each of these items is a condition of work. A selection of items of particular significance for staff morale is considered in the following material.

SALARY. The individual's morale is raised if his salary meets certain criteria. In the first place, it must be adequate at least to meet the needs of a teacher and his family for a reasonably satisfactory

[18] *The American School Superintendency,* Thirtieth Yearbook, American Association of School Administrators, 1952, p. 164.

[19] Spalding, *op. cit.,* p. 70.

living standard. In the second place, it should recognize the high qualifications which his position requires and pay him accordingly. Third, it should be in line with other occupations requiring similar training and qualifications, and holding similar expectations for responsible conduct of the work. Fourth, the salary paid to an individual should be commensurate with his experience and professional achievements.

Studies of factors affecting individual morale agree that the salary which an individual receives is not necessarily the principal morale factor. In other words, there are other attributes of a position which are at least as important as the money which one earns. It can be stated emphatically, however, that salaries paid to teachers are important morale factors with respect to the criteria listed above. The departmental administrator, who must select new teachers, is limited by the salary schedule of the school system or college in which he works. He can, however, secure the best salary arrangements possible according to his schedule and the qualifications of the new appointee.

The administrator will seek increases in salaries of those teachers who have been with the institution for one or more years. School systems usually have a schedule of increases which teachers earn through teaching service. Colleges and universities also frequently have schedules of salary increments for each of the instructional ranks, which teachers also earn through service.

With the increasing cost of education, and with the need to attract qualified teachers, some administrators are reviving the idea that salary increases should be based on merit rather than on years of service alone. Because there is no rating procedure which is not open to misuse, teachers' organizations are opposed to the introduction of merit schemes to determine which teachers shall receive salary increases.

It is necessary to reward merit, and a special salary increase is one way to do this. In a realistic manner merit is rewarded whenever outstanding teachers receive offers of employment at higher salaries at other institutions. The administrator will seek to secure whatever benefits he can for those teachers who deserve special consideration and will strive to maintain equitable salary treatment for all members of his staff.

PROMOTION. In colleges and universities teachers who continue to increase in stature as teachers and scholars can be rewarded by promotion to higher instructional ranks. Each institution usually states the criteria for judging the eligibility of a person for promotion. The departmental administrator must forward his recommendations for promotion when the institution calls for them. In exercising his educational leadership he will stimulate and encourage his staff members to achieve eligibility for promotion. As one of his tasks in keeping his staff informed, he will discuss with the members the institution's requirements for promotion to the various ranks, indicating as best he can the attitude of those who make the final decisions on promotion.

In departments where few or no promotions take place over a period of time, morale may be low. In such a situation, too, the administrator should review his own efforts in this area as well as consider what kind of staff he has. If he has people who do not present records which merit recommendation for promotion, perhaps changes in the staff are indicated. If the administrator himself has been remiss in fulfilling his role as leader and guide for members of his staff, he should alter his ways. Administrators also may be replaced!

Promotion normally means an increase in salary. Institutions which offer promotions with no possibility of improvement in salary are playing upon the teacher's desire for status instead of making the promotion both a gain in status and salary. Promotion to higher ranks costs institutions nothing unless there is an additional financial commitment.

FACILITIES. Teachers prefer to work in facilities which are suited to the job and which are well maintained. Responsibility for keeping facilities clean, in good repair, and in condition for use by all teachers is shared by both the teachers and the administrator. Teachers, who are the users of the facilities, should use them correctly, leave them in good condition, and report damage or wear which needs to be repaired. The administrator is responsible for general supervision, for securing adequate custodial care, and for ordering the repair of damaged and worn parts.

TEACHING LOAD. The debate over the advantages and disadvantages of large or small classes for effective teaching may never be settled to the satisfaction of either side. One point which is clear, though, is that the teacher's effectiveness is related to his total teaching load, of which the size of classes is one factor. The teacher whose load allows him adequate time for preparation, for grading student papers and examinations, for meeting with students on individual problems, and for carrying on some scholarly activity of his own feels that he is doing his job well and is not exhausted by it. The problem is to find the basis for determining a reasonable teaching load.

A teacher's load may appear to be defined by the number of classes which he teaches. In some colleges and universities this definition is correct. In schools and in many other colleges and universities, however, the size of the class load is only one item in the total load. Physical education teachers may find that they have to spend almost as much time on nonclass duties as they do on class teaching, in addition to whatever preparation is required of them in their teaching.

This discussion is not intended to present the arguments for lighter teaching loads and for elimination of many of the nonteaching chores which teachers are required to perform. The aim is to urge administrators to assign teaching loads in the expectation that teachers will perform satisfactorily their principal function (namely, to instruct the pupils and students) and to define carefully and fully the load the job entails. It is easy to dissipate teachers' energies by casually adding one small task after another. In industry nothing of this sort can be done unless the individual is given extra pay, often at overtime rates. There is no reason to expect teachers to accept additional tasks and responsibilities which were not included in the original definition of the job, unless added remuneration accompanies the performance of the tasks. Furthermore, the teacher should have the privilege of declining to do the extra work.

The practice of paying extra amounts for certain additional activities (school band, dramatics, athletic coaching, school publications) is not unusual. There is serious question as to the wisdom of continuing the practice. Some feel that extra pay for extra duties converts a professional position, in which it is expected that there will be flexible working arrangements, into a time-clock job. This point of view can be supported within reasonable bounds, and these bounds are the definition of the position which the teacher was employed to fill.

A stronger argument against the extra pay for extra duties is found in the reason for limiting the teaching load. If it is held that teachers cannot do effective work when their load exceeds a certain number of class hours and total students, it can only be concluded that added duties, whether paid for or not, must lower the efficiency of the teacher. Such an effect can lessen the professional aspect of the teacher's work as much as the attitude that teaching is a time-clock job. The ideal situation is to employ enough qualified persons to carry on all the activities of the school, equalize their load, and eliminate the practice of giving extra pay for extra work.

Teachers of physical education often are expected to carry a larger class hour load than teachers of other subjects. Insofar as there is less outside preparation and other work associated with the teaching of the course, such a differentiation may be justified. This kind of evaluation should be applied to all subjects, however, in order that others which resemble physical education in their content and in the classroom demands can receive similar treatment.

Administrators who wish a guide to establish teaching loads and class sizes may find the following helpful. In public schools the maximum class hour assignment for a teacher should not exceed thirty classes in activities per week. This assignment should include the time required by extra duties, such as supervision of recreational activities, faculty sponsoring of a club, coaching of interscholastic teams, conducting intramural activities, and any other regularly scheduled duty. Teaching hours in excess of the thirty should be paid for on a prorated basis, or the teacher should have the option of declining the extra work. If any of the assigned teaching hours involve subjects requiring additional preparation and the reading and grading of students' papers and examinations, the total load should be reduced according to the ratio of total load of activity classes to total load of so-called academic classes.

When planning the teaching schedules, the administrator will recognize that the basic load is the number of class hours per week. When other duties which are not normally called class teaching are included in the teacher's schedule, it is necessary to equate them with the class hour. The procedure for doing this will be decided by the administrator in his own institution. Activities which do not require previous, regular preparation, and which do not demand the kind of intense performance characteristic of class teaching, will not receive an hour of schedule credit for each hour spent on the activity.

For some activities which can require many hours of time each week the administrator will have to decide how much time is needed to achieve the goals of the activity. Coaching an athletic team may require three hours daily as well as the time for playing the games. Also, the coach may wish to begin practices unusually early and to play a long season. In some instances the length of a season and the number of games which a team can play are controlled by league or conference regulations. In others, there are no such controls. The administrator must consider the number of students on an athletic squad and the proportionate instructional cost when evaluating the activity in relation to the teaching time to be allowed for the coaching. This kind of evaluation will be required for each nonclass duty.

Ultimately, classroom teaching must face a similar evaluation. The task will be most difficult because of the long-standing tradition concerning the sanctity of the classroom activity. The pressure from the community for more productivity in education, and the insistent demands from teachers for higher salaries along with a reduction in teaching loads, will force consideration of present procedures in education with respect to course and class organization, methods of teaching, evaluation, and the use of auxiliary aids.

The physical education administrator now should face realistically the way in which his staff resources are being utilized in order not to waste them in any phase of his program. Teachers of activity classes in colleges and universities may have a teaching load equivalent to that of teachers in other subjects or slightly higher. Voltmer and Esslinger state that the "activity class work should be computed on the basis of one and a third hours for each academic class hour."[20] With the trend toward making the maximum class load twelve hours per week, the teacher of activities would be expected to teach sixteen hours per week. It should be pointed out

[20] Edward F. Voltmer and Arthur A. Esslinger, *The Organization and Administration of Physical Education,* 3d ed., Appleton-Century-Crofts, Inc., 1958, p. 131.

that an academic class load of twelve hours per week usually assumes that additional duties will be carried on by the teacher. These include meeting with students outside of class, some committee work, advising the major students in one's department, and participating in departmental and institutional staff meetings. Similar demands are made of the teachers of activity classes.

CLASS SIZE. Class size is related to the activity of the class and to the purposes which the teacher has for the class. Class size also, too often unfortunately, may be determined by the facilities available. For a situation in which the teacher plans to instruct students regularly throughout the term, a maximum of thirty-five students should be suitable. It is obvious that some activities cannot be taught satisfactorily with as many as thirty-five students. The figure of thirty-five serves only as a guide to the upper limit.

In suggesting either maximum teaching loads or maximum class size, it is recognized that the authors may be treading into the area of fixed ideas on the administration of all programs. Neither of these matters is fixed for all schools and colleges. Each institution decides what it wishes to accomplish through its educational program. If baby-sitting is one of its goals, then teachers can handle a much larger number of individuals in a class than is indicated here. If the development of excellence in performance leading to possible specialization is a goal, then the instructional classes may have to be smaller. If goals generally accepted by the nation's schools are being sought, then the remarks concerning the load assigned to the teacher, including the size of his classes, are relevant.

LEAVES. Regulations permitting teachers to take leaves of absence for specified reasons are valuable in maintaining individual morale. Colleges and universities provide for sick leave, leave for special study, and leave for travel and for health purposes. Leaves for special study may come under the heading of sabbatical leaves, or they may be specially granted to an individual who has received a study grant or fellowship. Provisions for sick leave with pay removes the burden of worry concerning his income from the teacher and his family during the period of illness. Sick leave provisions are a part of public school personnel regulations and practice.

While some public schools have granted special leaves and sabbatical leaves, it has not been common practice. Recently, however, school administrators have indicated a mounting interest in allowing the teacher to take time for additional study, for exchange teaching, and for travel. Where sabbatical leave provisions are in force, school boards pay part, or all, of the salary during the period of the leave.

The responsibility of the administrator in the matter of leaves is to assist in arranging for them and, in the case of special leaves, to prepare a recommendation stating that the leave has been considered and is approved by the department. In the event of extended sick leaves, the administrator arranges for a substitute to carry on the work of the absent teacher. In the schools the principal actually secures the substitute teachers.

TENURE. Tenure provisions are aimed at protecting the teacher against unwarranted dismissal. Tenure normally is granted only after the teacher has served in a school, college, or university for a period from one to three or five years. The decision to recommend that a teacher be reappointed with tenure should be based on reasonably extensive information as to the teacher's competence, his personality, his promise for continued growth and service, and the continuing need of the department or the institution for his services, especially if his competence is highly specialized. This kind of prediction is done with considerable reservation, at best. It behooves the administrator to learn as much as he can over the entire probationary period about the candidate who will soon be considered for a tenure appointment. Once a teacher has been appointed with tenure, the department and the institution have a lifetime member unless the person himself chooses to resign, or unless changes in needs for staff require a reduction in the number of teachers employed. Some administrators consider the actions centering around the tenure decision to be among the most important which the departmental and the institutional administrators engage in with respect to personnel.

The morale of teachers who are on tenure is maintained because they are reasonably secure in their positions, and because the act of recommending tenure is a kind of recognition given by the department and the institution to the teacher. The probationary teacher can be helped to do his best work if he is taken in as a fully participating member of the staff, if he is assisted in orienting himself to the department and the institution, if his work is observed by the administrator and suggestions given for improvement, and if his standing with respect to the department's expectations is made known to him from time to time.

It should be noted that administrators are restudying current laws and policies governing teacher tenure. The finality of a tenure appointment under existing laws occasionally places an institution in the position of being unable to relieve itself of an incompetent, troublesome, and uncooperative teacher. Probably tenure laws were not intended to produce this result. Change in this area will be extremely difficult to accomplish, but some modification of current practices is needed.

REWARD FOR MERIT

Recognition of the good work which individuals perform is necessary to their morale, and has been referred to frequently in this chapter. Feeling that he is doing a worthwhile job is essential to one's mental well-being. To have others share the feeling and express their approval raises one's morale.

During the rapid business and industrial growth which occurred following World War II, teachers lost status because of relatively poor salaries and lowered morale. The effect of this condition on the schools and colleges has been acknowledged, and a change in the attitude of the community toward teachers is taking place. The change ultimately will place teachers in a position of recognition which is superior to any which they have held before. The teachers and administrators can accelerate this movement by being more sure of their own profession and by giving recognition to effective work within the profession.

One of the means which some schools and colleges use to reward outstanding teaching is to give pay increases which may be termed *merit raises*. In a previous section of this chapter it was pointed out that schools and colleges customarily have salary schedules which permit the granting of salary increments for service and for educational preparation. In systems which use a merit pay increase as a reward for effective teaching and other service, the increments for educational preparation and service may be limited in number, with additional raises to be awarded on the basis of merit. The administrator may be interested in arguments for and against the use of merit scales. In a study made by the New York State Education Department the following views were listed. Those favoring merit scales gave their views:

1. The possibility of higher salaries will attract capable young people into teaching.
2. Merit pay will act as an incentive to practicing teachers to undertake self-improvement.
3. It is possible to develop fair and equitable measures of the quality of teaching to determine which teachers deserve merit pay.

Those opposing merit scales offered the following reasons:

1. It is impossible to make fair and accurate measurements of all that goes into good teaching.
2. Any system of rating teachers that did not have the confidence of the entire staff would destroy staff morale.
3. Under an established system of quality measurement, teachers would strive to fit the pattern and "please the administration." This would have a stultifying effect on originality and on good teaching generally.
4. There are other, more efficient ways—such as in-service training programs—to improve the over-all quality of instruction.[21]

The New York State study showed that about 20 percent of the districts surveyed reported some merit provisions, but most of them were not firmly committed to the idea. Only eighteen districts had an established plan for granting merit increments, which included definite criteria of merit and a formal procedure to evaluate the quality of service.

A strong stand in favor of merit pay scales is taken by Chandler and Petty. The following paragraph deals with the criticism that it is not possible to measure all that goes into good teaching:

> The rationalization that no satisfactory measure of teaching quality is available needs to be carefully re-examined by members of the teaching profession. Merit pay scales are commonplace in business, industry, and civil service. The fact that the free enterprise economic system prevails in the United States and the mounting pressure to pay for quality in educa-

[21] Leonard Buder, "Merit Scale for Teachers Studied," *The New York Times*, August 24, 1958.

tion would seem to point clearly to two alternatives for the teaching profession. One alternative the profession must choose. Workable merit scales must be developed and adopted, or reasons for continuation of the preparation-experience schedule must be provided. It is likely that the former is the wiser choice. People of a nation who are capable of developing atomic energy, miracle drugs, and faster-than-sound airplanes are likely to grow impatient with the plea that "it should be done but no satisfactory devices have yet been invented."[22]

The current texts on educational administration support the view that the best administration occurs when staffs work together to solve their problems. One may conclude that the problem of merit pay could also be dealt with by staffs on a cooperative basis. Some doubt lingers, however, as to the influence of the rating procedures upon the cooperative spirit of a staff. Perhaps it is no greater than that which occurs in a college where recommendations for promotion are initiated by a committee of the departmental staff, which committee evaluates the work of all staff members and selects those who are to be recommended for promotion.

The administrator will find two possibilities in the discussion of the recognition of merit. One is to give appropriate recognition to each individual, and occasionally to the staff as a group, for meritorious work. There are several forms of recognition other than pay increases which are rewards for individual merit. Awards in recognition of outstanding teaching are given by students, alumni, and occasionally by institutional administrations. Individuals may be commended in a staff meeting by their colleagues or their chairman. A report of the person's outstanding work may be prepared by the chairman and transmitted to the school or college head and the staff of an institution. Assigning an individual to a committee chairmanship may be a form of recognition. Invitations to present papers, and to participate otherwise in the activities of professional organizations are recognition of noteworthy accomplishment. The second is to establish reliable and valid means for regularly evaluating individual teacher performance and to record the results of these evaluations. If merit pay raises are to be a part of the school system, they can be accepted only if the basis for granting them is considered fair by the teachers.

[22] Chandler and Petty, *op. cit.*, p. 249.

STAFF MEETINGS

It is obvious that staff participation in policy consideration requires the members to meet together. Departmental staff meetings should be held regularly throughout the school year. The number and frequency depend upon the work which the staff has to do and the time which the teachers can be expected to give to this function. In colleges and universities it is assumed that time for meetings is a part of the assigned teaching load. In public schools provision of time should be made so that teachers can attend regular staff meetings. The morale of a staff is maintained better when staff meetings are held at regularly scheduled times.

Simply holding a meeting is no guarantee that morale will be bolstered or that the work of the department will be improved. A staff meeting is an important activity which must be conducted according to a plan and must be planned for. Productive staff meetings can result if these suggestions are followed.

1. Announce the schedule for staff meetings for a semester or a year ahead. The schedule may be altered to meet unforseen factors.
2. Prepare an agenda for each meeting to be sent to members several days ahead of the meeting date. Staff members should submit to the administrator any items which they wish to have included on the agenda. The administrator should insist that the meeting devote its time to matters placed on the agenda and, except in cases of urgency, that new items may not be introduced during the meetings.
3. If there are reports or other prepared materials to be discussed during the meeting, these should be distributed with the agenda in order that the staff members will have time to study them before the meeting. The meeting time should not be used for reading and study of new materials.
4. Conduct the meeting according to recognized rules of procedure. Strict formality may be eased in small staff groups. In large group meetings it will be difficult to accomplish the business of the meeting unless rules of procedure are enforced.
5. Do not waste time. If rules of procedure are followed, there should be little, if any, time lost. Probably the greatest timewaster is the administrator who does not plan his meeting. A second timewaster is the staff member who wishes to talk about anything but the business at hand. Staff members who are interested in serious matters do not feel kindly toward either.

6. Formal actions taken by a staff should be followed by the steps required to implement such actions, if implementation is specified. Failure to implement staff recommendations makes the staff meeting relatively meaningless. When recommendations for subsequent action are made, it is the duty of the administrator to carry out the recommendations, or to appoint the responsible individual or committee. Occasionally the staff may elect a committee. This should be done only in matters in which the staff has authority to carry out its recommendations and is in the position to accept responsibility for its actions.

7. Distribute copies of the minutes of each meeting to members of the staff promptly following the meeting.

8. In general, allow no other activities to be offered as substitutes for attending staff meetings. If the meeting is worth holding, it is important that each staff member be present.

Committees are useful units in a department and an institution. They can give intensive consideration to a matter with more ease than a larger body. Committees should be kept as small as the assignment permits, but large enough to hold the number of people required to do an effective job. In the departmental staff organization committees can study a problem, do a large amount of preliminary work, and report to the staff. They may be operating units also, in that they plan and conduct phases of a departmental program. In a sense this kind of a committee is a smaller edition of the staff, with authority to plan and carry out its delegated functions. To do this, specific tasks will be assigned to individual members of the committee, with the committee chairman serving in the role of administrator. Normally, committees function with more informality than the larger staff.

A sample agenda for a staff meeting may include the following categories of items:

1. Reading and approval of minutes of previous meeting
2. Announcements and communications, usually by the chairman
3. Committee reports
4. Old business
5. New business

Staff morale is strengthened by the holding of regular staff meetings which are planned and conducted as an integral part of the department's program. The administrator is responsible for the quality of the meeting.

INTERPERSONAL RELATIONSHIPS

People must work together. An organization cannot function effectively if its members are at odds or do not choose to work with each other. When personnel officers are asked to list the qualities which they seek in candidates for employment in their businesses and industries, they place ability to work with others at the top of the list. Without this trait the excellent technical capacities which a person may have will find little outlet for service in an organization. One recognizes that there are circumstances where provision must be made for the difficult personality, but by and large organizations can go only so far in making such provisions.

People can work together. Morale of the individual members is best when they can and do work together in the common enterprise to which they are bound. It is not expected that a staff will be in complete harmony at all times. In fact, it is said that a normal amount of complaint indicates a healthy situation. Perhaps the word *complaint* does not describe correctly the kind of critical activity of an individual who is not satisfied with the situation as it is, and who wishes to improve it. If the people on a staff have similar professional backgrounds, a commonly accepted goal, a feeling of belonging to the venture, and an opportunity to gain increasing competence in the job, they can work together and probably will.

However, there will be occasional conflict in a staff, differences of opinion, personal hurts, differences in achievements and rewards. Any of these may create interpersonal difficulties which affect the morale of a staff member. How are these resolved in the interest of high individual and group morale?

In the first place, the administrator is involved at some time in every matter that affects the work of the department. He has a part, therefore, in resolving interpersonal differences. He must expect some conflict and be prepared to meet conflict situations. It is not possible to describe methods to be used to solve every individual difficulty which may arise. The following suggestions are in the nature of general principles.

1. One way to avoid the kind of personality conflicts which are petty and annoying is to select as staff members only those people who are emotionally mature and stable individuals. If the reader

will refer to the earlier section in which the qualifications for a teacher were listed, he will find that emphasis is placed upon these qualities. The administrator knows that the judgment of personality cannot be reliable until one has known and worked with a person for some period of time. On the other hand, with the information about a candidate which is available and with one or more interviews with the candidate, the administrator can detect evidences of those personality traits which suggest immaturity and instability.

2. Observance of the factors contributing to morale already described previously in this section will assist in creating satisfying interpersonal relationships on a staff, and provide the means for airing and resolving many of the conflicts which do arise. Where morale is high, interpersonal relationships also are likely to be satisfactory.

3. Physical arrangements can be utilized to make for easy interpersonal communication and for congenial relationships. One factor to which the administrator should give attention is the arrangement and allocation of office space. The teacher's office is his workshop on campus, his conference room, and his place to relax for a few minutes when he feels the need for it. Office arrangements which permit some staff members to remove themselves from frequent contact with others are conducive to clique formation and to isolationism. There are good reasons for having a large office in which the staff members have desk and file space. Small rooms adjacent to the office may then serve as private conference and study rooms. There are equally strong arguments for having smaller offices to which one or two persons may be assigned. Whichever method is used, the offices should allow ready communication and meeting between staff members and should never become the strongholds of personalities who live behind closed doors and who admit only others of their clique.

4. An administrator is a lonely individual. He cannot have alliances. Because he often is expected to make decisions which affect individuals, and must render fair and just decisions to the extent of his ability, he cannot be committed or bound by previous understanding to any member of his staff. Intimate friendships may be rare. An administrator, however, is not a cold, insensitive person. On the contrary, because he must always be concerned with the

human factors, he must be in a position to see all of them and not only those which concern persons in whom he may have a personal interest. Staff morale can be destroyed rapidly if it is found that the administrator treats some members more favorably than others.

5. Finally, the administrator should establish an attitude toward staff relationships which does not allow for or tolerate the petty activities which may undermine staff morale. Each reader will know of situations in which one or two persons who really should not be on a staff, but are protected by tenure laws, take more departmental, administrative, and often institutional time simply to handle their petty and unnecessary actions than is required to do all the remainder of the departmental task. Usually there are means by which such persons can be dealt with. The best procedure, however, is to create an atmosphere within the staff in which such petty affairs are emphatically disapproved. The tone of personal relationships can be set by the administrator.

It has been pointed out that staff morale, which is an expression of the high individual morale of all its members, is essential to successful departmental and institutional functioning. Nine factors of importance to the development and maintenance of morale have been discussed in this section. The administrator can utilize the suggestions as he is able to identify the circumstances and the time in his own institution when these factors are to be applied. Adaptation of ideas may be helpful to the extent that they are integrated into the organizational and administerial patterns of the department and the institution.

THE TEACHER'S RESPONSIBILITY AS A MEMBER OF A PROFESSION

The professional status of a staff is determined by the qualifications of its members in relation to those of the entire staff or faculty, and by the achievements of its members in fields commonly recognized as belonging to the realm of the educator. One of the more important fields in which the teacher may achieve is that of scholarship. Richness in teaching depends upon scholarly activity. Teaching itself is a scholarly occupation. Scholarship in this context means, in broad terms, the constant search for knowledge which increases one's understandings of the universe or of any part of it. It is a search for truth. Scholarly activity, therefore, is concerned with seeking fundamental knowledge, regardless of its usefulness.

Neither the time nor the resources are available to all teachers in their regular search for new knowledge. Scholarliness, however, can be shown in other ways which approach the search for new knowledge. Study which extends and increases the teacher's understanding of man, of society, of the forces active in the world, and of the place and worth of his own subject area in his society lends stature to the professional teacher. Study which produces useful results in terms of enriched curricula, improved teaching methods, and better evaluation procedures must take into account the society and the individuals, if its outcomes are to be pertinent to the purposes of the school. Scholarship is evidenced by an attitude of considered study as one seeks a solution to a problem. It symbolizes a universal interest, rather than a narrow one.

The scholar is deeply interested in a field in which he studies intensively, but he also is sensitive to the continuity of human experience and the relationship of his own studies within the totality of all activity. To fulfill the expectations which his profession holds for him, the teacher must also be a scholar.

The teacher who has no interest in scholarly activity slowly but surely loses ground in the movement of his own profession. He may have been well qualified and able when he started as a teacher, but his failure to maintain the kind of study which originally qualified him leaves him farther back in the profession of his choice. The end result, which is earnestly to be avoided, may be the person who looks at his job as so many hours of work to be completed each day. Enthusiasm is gone, initiative has vanished, and even interest in the job itself is really lost, except for the fact that it is a way of earning a living.

The importance of scholarly activity to all teachers of physical education is voiced by Scott:

> As an integral phase of the instructional program, physical education takes its place alongside of the other traditional educational disciplines. Personnel in this field must, therefore, accept the same responsibilities as representatives of other areas of the educational program. One such

responsibility concerns the area of productive scholarship. Research, contributions to literature, and other forms of scholarly productivity are components of the teaching profession, particularly at the college level. If, therefore, scholarly activities are expected of faculty members in other areas of education, then there should be no exception to personnel in the field of physical education. Representatives of this field should be held responsible for demonstrating the same kind and degree of scholarship as other members of the faculty.

While present practice may exempt personnel primarily engaged in sports instruction, the not-too-distant future will witness many colleges holding the football coach, and others similarly engaged, to the same standards as apply to other faculty members. Physical educators in general are coming to realize, as practitioners in other professions have already learned, that there is no terminal point in the education of a professional person. The acquisition of a college degree, the attainment of a teaching or administrative position, or maturation through age or experience does not relieve the person of the ever-pressing need for continuous professional development. Teaching calls for constant study and self-improvement. In this respect there is nothing inherent in the field of physical education that makes it different from any other area of education.[23]

The administrator of a physical education department may feel that individual staff members should engage in scholarly activity without his urging or guidance. He will find, however, that some will need the stimulation which he can give in order to get started. He may also find that there are some members who are not interested in additional work for which there does not seem to be an immediate monetary return. In the latter case, the department may establish policies concerning reappointment and promotion which take cognizance of scholarship as one of the grounds for favorable action. In any event, the administrator will need to place an appropriate value upon scholarship as an attribute of members of his staff.

The teacher himself, in the final analysis, has the responsibility for his own scholarly activity. He must be dedicated to the search for knowledge if he is to give of his time and energies for scholarly pursuits. If he is to maintain his position as a qualified teacher and as a member of a profession, he must be a scholar.

[23] Harry A. Scott, "Report of a Sub-Committee on Professional Status," *Proceedings,* College Physical Education Association, 1957, pp. 246–247.

STAFF STATUS WITHIN THE INSTITUTION

Administrators and teachers of physical education are concerned that their subject and their positions be accorded status equal to that of other subjects. It is right that they should be so concerned. Any subject accepted in the curriculum of the school or college is presumed initially, at least, to belong there because of its importance in the education of children and youth, and those who are to administer and teach the subject are expected to meet the professional standards applied to all personnel. Because physical education primarily uses activities as its resources rather than printed texts, it is difficult for many nonphysical education teachers to visualize the educational aspects of this subject. They can be helped to see the place of physical education in the school and college programs by teachers of physical education who in their teaching and participation in other educational activities of the institution demonstrated their professional competence and scholarliness.

Physical education has as much to offer to the effective education of children and youth as any other subject in the curriculum. Furthermore, it is possible today for the physical education student to receive professional preparation that is at least equal to that given teachers of other subjects. There is every reason for the people in this field to stand with members of other subject areas in a position of equal consideration and status.

The physical education personnel can achieve the status they desire by their work and their conduct in the institution. In the first place, they should assume that they are a part of the staff of the institution or the school system. This means that they should take part in staff meetings and other functions, serve on committees, make suggestions for the general welfare, and generally participate in all educational activities of the institution. Although physical education has unique aspects, the rules and regulations of the institution governing the conduct and administration of the instructional program should apply fully to physical education.

Members of a physical education staff may fall into the practice of wearing gymnasium class costumes as regular dress all day long. They appear in lunchrooms, in committee meetings, and even in staff meetings in their gymnasium or sport garb. There is no question as to which person is the physical education teacher. Such a practice is not likely to make a favorable impression upon colleagues in other departments. While dress may seem to be a relatively unimportant matter, in the realm of status it is very important.

Although it seems an unnecessary statement, physical education teachers must speak and write correctly and with relative ease. There is nothing appealing or effective about careless and colloquial speech, either in teaching, coaching a team, or in conversing with others. If one wishes to lose status quickly, he can find no better way to do it than to speak incorrectly before a faculty. His status as a person may not be greatly affected, but his standing as a member of learned groups in teaching loses ground rapidly.

Participation in the activities of professional organizations benefits the individual participant and the organization as a whole. Being associated with these organizations is one of the marks of a professional man.

Among the liberal subjects, physical education is as old as any in the curriculum. To keep physical education as a subject in liberal education, the administrator and his staff must conduct a program of the highest quality. Perhaps this is the most important factor in maintaining a desired status in the institution.

"The esteem accorded members of a profession by society is determined primarily by two factors. The first of these is the standards of admission to the profession, and the second is the quality of service rendered by members of the profession."[24]

BIBLIOGRAPHY

Brace, David K., "A Code of Ethics for A Dynamic Profession," *Journal of Health, Physical Education, Recreation,* January, 1960.

A progress report of the AAHPER Committee on Professional Ethics. A list of unethical incidents is given, based on reports of a questionnaire study.

Committee on Professional Ethics, "Suggested Code of Ethics for Teachers of Physical Education," *Journal of Health, Physical Education, and Recreation,* June, 1950.

[24] Chandler and Petty, *op. cit.,* p. 83.

Haas, Werner, "The Physical Educator's Education," *Journal of Health, Physical Education, Recreation,* April, 1959.

Emphasizes the need for a broad education for teachers of physical education, and indicates possible benefits from such an education.

Laird, Donald A., and Eleanor C. Laird, *The New Psychology for Leadership,* McGraw-Hill Book Company, Inc., 1956.

Sets forth new ideas on "bossing." The book reports research in group dynamics, and is rich in ideas on group productivity and maintaining group morale.

Scott, Harry A., "The Function of the Director of Physical Education in Colleges," *Journal of Health and Physical Education,* January, 1933.

Attention is given to the breadth of responsibilities of the chairman of a department, and to the necessity for continued scholarly endeavor if he is to meet the expectations of the teaching profession.

Yeager, William, "The Service Load of Faculty Members in Education," *Educational Research Bulletin,* February 8, 1956.

A rather complete discussion is given of the bases for computing teaching loads.

Chapter 14

PUBLICITY AND PUBLIC RELATIONS

PUBLICITY may be a process or it may be a result. It is a process when the various media available to a school system are utilized to carry a story to the many segments of society which the school serves. It is a result when these segments receive the story, when the information is made known, and a point of view is established. Schools are given extensive publicity through the common news media, because the public is vitally interested. When their activities have news value, the common news media are generous with time and space. There are times when little news or publicity comes from the schools, while at other times they appear in the headlines.

Not all the information which comes from the schools is designed to be news, nor does it always produce a desirable impact. Activities often produce unanticipated publicity, and unfavorable public relations result. Publicity frequently develops from most unusual incidents, which go far beyond their real importance in establishing public relations or a public point of view. Inasmuch as the public is made up of many publics, it is occasionally quite difficult to predict the reactions which publicized events will engender. Nevertheless, it is essential that a school use every medium at its command to keep people informed about the activities which take place under its jurisdiction.

It is the purpose of this chapter to present the need for publicity and public relations and show examples of how they may be carried on. Publicity and staff relations within the school are of major importance to the success of the physical education department. Many practical suggestions will be made to the physical education teacher who desires to develop prestige for his department within the school. Publicity and public relations within the community are discussed, and many of the problems which are encountered are presented. Opportunities for desirable and sound publicity and public relations are suggested to the physical education teacher. The chapter concludes with practical suggestions for the use of media within the community through which publicity and public relations may be secured.

THE NEED FOR PUBLICITY AND PUBLIC RELATIONS

Since a major objective of publicity is to create desirable public relations, schools which are alert to their responsibilities should provide for the type of publicity which will present a true picture. It is through the creation and maintenance of good public relations that schools receive the support necessary to carry on the work of the community. Many communities have rejected needed and valuable projects because of poor school and community relations. Other communities have been known to support every request from their schools because as a result of sound public relations the community believed in its schools. In order to secure the latter relationship, it is axiomatic that the school should tell a clear and timely story to the public it represents.

The school cannot overlook the slightest detail in establishing or maintaining good public relations. Public relations start in the classroom with the contacts which the teacher makes with the student, the parent, and the public. This relationship may never gain the stature of publicity, but it may be the grist which is ground around the bridge table, during the coffee break, or over the back fence. It goes to make up the contents of the conversation in which every parent indulges when he speaks about his children. There is really no choice for a teacher or a school as to whether either desires to engage in public relations; the issue is the kind of public relations and the nature of the impact which the actions make upon the children, parents, and the public.

Today, when there are some parents who know only that their children are enrolled in school, the job of desirable public relations ofttimes becomes more difficult as it becomes more essential. Some parents are close to their children and schools, while others scarcely know the name of the teacher. For the latter, it may be quite an ordeal to discuss the subject areas, activities, and events associated with their progeny. Some parents will support the teacher and the school over and against the word of the child. Others immediately spring to the attack, however wild the story that their offspring may concoct. It is essential that the schools who wish for good public relations keep the parents informed about the activities and events in the school life of the student.

The classroom teacher, because he has direct access to a number of students and their parents, is the best means for beginning good public relations. The teacher must be interested in the child and the teaching profession. When this interest is instilled in the child and thence to the parent, a good public relationship has begun. The physical education teacher must be able and willing to show that his work is essential to the total education. This is best done through a program of activities vital to the developmental needs of the students and the translation of this program into effective action. How this is accomplished will be presented in the sections which follow.

PUBLIC RELATIONS WITHIN THE SCHOOL

Public relations begins at home. Unless those who are involved in physical education establish themselves as genuine members of the school staff, there is often a tendency to underrate their contribution to the objectives of education. It is quite easy for the teacher of physical education to come in the back door, put on the uniform of his profession, and spend the entire day in his own section of the building and grounds. Days and even weeks can go by when he may not be seen by other members of the staff. This type of self-imposed isolation is one of the greatest deterrents to good public relations within the school.

Physical education teachers must be active members of the school staff. They must belong to and participate in all staff activities. They must be available when help is needed by other teachers. They should be staff leaders when events occur in which they can make a real contribution. The physical education teachers should take a leading role in preparing for faculty picnics, organizing and directing faculty recreation, arranging and promoting social activities, and aiding other faculty members when their talents are needed. They can help the dramatic coach with makeup, costuming, or maintenance of discipline. They can help the English teachers by using correct English themselves and insisting that English be spoken correctly in their classes. They can contribute to guidance and counselling by helping those students who depart from accepted conduct. They can exercise a powerful and effective influence over students to form proper respect for school regulations and rules. They can support the music department by directing those boys and girls who have musical talent to participate in instrumental or vocal music.

The physical education teacher should be seen in the library, selecting and perusing good books. A mere handshaking acquaintance with good literature is not enough. There should be a sincere and deep appreciation of the writings of those authors who are accepted by literary authorities. It is perfectly natural to read the sports page, but that is only one part of the newspaper. The physical education teacher who appreciates good music is well on his way to sound staff public relations. What an asset for the physical education teacher to be qualified to judge debate and deliver a speech which is commended by the teacher of forensics for its quality! It is valuable for the physical education teacher to take his turn at writing for the school paper. A genuine appreciation of art provides the teacher with another interest which he can share with other members of the faculty.

Physical education teachers do themselves and their department immeasurable good when they appear punctually at staff meetings, well-dressed and well-groomed. A staff meeting is no place for T-shirts or warmups. They also gain prestige with their fellow staff members when it is shown that they really teach and secure the objectives of general education through their activities in physical education.

The physical education teacher should never overlook the public relations potential within his own area of teaching responsibilities. There are no better press agents than a group of students who are enthusiastic about their experiences in physical education. They tell other students, other teachers, and their parents. Their attitudes and behavior reflect their appreciation and enthusiasm for well taught, interesting activities. Much of the student's enthusiasm is generated by the enthusiasm of the teacher. How well classes are organized, what knowledge and skills are learned, how much fun there is in participating—these are some of the factors which form the basis for a strong public relations, both in and outside the school.

The teacher of physical education should use the best teaching methods to motivate interest and obtain desired results in his classes. The effective use of charts, diagrams, illustrations and pictures displayed on the bulletin boards, in addition to a complete and accurately kept record book, are highly useful in motivating physical education. Students will be aided in their learning if appropriate illustrations and pictures are skillfully used. They develop a sincere interest in records and may remember years later that they had fifteen straight free throws, put the shot 41 feet, 2¾ inches, and repeatedly teamed up with Joe Thomas to win the wheelbarrow or sack race. A teacher is often unaware of the events which have a lasting effect upon the students. One is often startled when years later a grown man brings to his attention something which was said or done in one of his classes. The importance of these events should not be overlooked; use them so that the finest of public relations will result.

Never permit students to feel that it is unimportant whether or not they dress for class. Never permit them to feel that this is just another period in which roll was taken and a ball was tossed out. Each period is too short to teach everything that needs to be taught, and one can never be entirely satisfied with the results. When the class periods are only play periods without a plan for instruction, little good is derived and learning which takes place is incidental and too often accidental. Many class periods are sacrificed to provide temporary pleasure for the students and relief for the teacher. Too often the teacher permits student aids to referee while he pursues an easy chore in his office or visits in some other part of the building. When this practice is repeated over and over, the students develop an indifferent attitude toward the benefits of the physical education program. Fellow teachers soon learn the quality of work being performed in the gymnasium and evaluate it accordingly. The community eventually becomes acquainted with the nature of the activities in the gym classes and refuses to place much value on this phase of the total educational program.

At times when all phases of the educational program are under critical evaluation, it behooves every teacher to do a superb job so that the nature and extent of his contribution can be fully appreciated. A physical education program which provides only exercise and fun cannot justify itself in today's curriculum, which has many pressures for allocated time. It does not require the services of trained professional personnel to carry on this type of program. Almost any agreeable adult can do it, and students often are quite adept to perform in this capacity. When this type of situation is encountered, it is easily understandable why the American public begins to question the value of the play period in school.

In order to provide the best basis for top public relations within the school, the physical education program should be able to meet the most exacting demands of critical staff members. This program then must be fully and properly interpreted. Frequent exhibitions can contribute immeasurably to a better understanding of what is being done in the gymnasium, pool, or playground. When these opportunities are provided, the accomplishments or achievements can be seen and the goals can be explained. An understanding and sympathetic administrative staff and student body will be gained. The school's athletic program is put on display each weekend, the marching band must display its skill at football games and in community parades, the dramatics department presents two or three productions annually, the vocal music department offers its spring musicale, the school newspaper comes from the printer, and the yearbook is delivered. All these are judged by the informed and the uninformed alike. They are evaluated upon the basis of the impression which they make on the one who judges. Sometimes the judgments are fair, sometimes they are unfair. The teacher and the students who work to make their productions high in quality are rewarded by the satisfaction which their efforts bring. The fact that their efforts are being presented publicly will usually bring out the finest performance. These are a few, and too often the only, ways in which departmental contributions to the total educational program are seen and judged.

Therefore, it is vitally important for the physical education teacher to present to the school and the community the results of his teaching. Let staff members and others know what is going on in the gymnasium. These programs can be presented before the staff and students during their regular assembly period, either in the gymnasium or in the auditorium. A well-prepared exhibition in physical education needs very little to be added in order to secure the approval of all those who see it. One which is poorly prepared cannot be aided by additions. Any exhibition should be an honest interpretation of the activities which are part of the regular program.

Adequate publicity must be given within the school. The most minute details should not be overlooked when the physical education department brings its program before the school. This is essential, because other departments are frequently aware of their own contributions but are oblivious to the contributions of others. In addition, it is a prestige factor when the physical education department displays its activities with the precision and dispatch which indicate planning for the achievement of goals.

PUBLIC RELATIONS WITHIN THE COMMUNITY

The community at large is a substantially different body of people from the school population so far as public relations are concerned. The community usually will be less understanding and less sympathetic to the benefits of the physical education program. It is relatively easy to reach some people, but others will be contacted only with great difficulty, if at all. Some members of society have never participated in physical activities and have no desire to support them as part of the school program. Some have rather jaundiced memories of their own experiences in physical education and see no connection between what they remember and what they consider to be the real purposes of public education. Others, who are influenced by the hallowed contributions of the three R's, accept nothing in the curriculum which does not apply directly to this concept of education. There are always a few people in a community who are opposed to public schools per se and some even to youth. To establish good public relations with this type is a herculean task, if not totally impossible.

It is fortunate that most people in a community are favorable to public schools and are willing to have the board of education, and the professional educators which it employs, determine what shall constitute the curriculum. Some of the people have children in school or have had their children educated in the same schools. Some are seeing their grandchildren go through the progression, which closely resembles lingering memories of their own experiences. Every community has some people who will support schools and youth in all worthwhile enterprise. In some instances their public education may be very limited, but they will do everything possible to make their community a better place in which to live. Probably every community has a large segment of its citizenry who are neither strongly opposed to nor strongly in favor of the schools on certain issues. Others may be swayed by meager evidence to support or oppose the schools on any issue.

These are the citizens who constitute the public with which sound relations must be established. These people must be given a regular presentation and interpretation of the achievements, accomplishments, problems, purposes, proposed goals, and objectives of the school's program. The physical education department must contribute its fair share to the whole program and carry almost the full load for its own section. This will not be easy, when emphasis is being directed toward the academic obligation of the schools.

The distressing reports concerning the physical condition of our young men who entered the armed services in the first and second world wars created fertile conditions in which physical education received widespread public and professional support. This support diminished as other phases of the curriculum gained more prominence. The emphasis on the various facets of public education ebbs and flows as the public dictates. The curriculum is made up of its present elements because the public has required it. Laws are passed to include or eliminate certain parts of the curriculum. Since nothing is static, that which seems highly important today may be removed from the requirements tomorrow. It is necessary, therefore, for everyone who knows of the contribution which physical education can make toward educating the student to do his job in the finest manner possible. However, this alone is not sufficient. Although an excellent job will speak for itself, there are times when the intensity and timbre of its voice is lost in the multitude of appeals for a place in the school day. The physical education teacher must continually bring to the attention of those who determine the course of education the contributions made by his program.

Students are the best salesmen for the physical education department, for they have direct access to their parents, neighbors, and friends. Staff members, including the administrative staff, are perhaps next in importance in supporting favorable impressions for the physical education program. Others need to be shown or told through every available medium. The alert physical education teacher will make periodic reports to his supervisors. These may include a presentation of activities with an explanation of purposes and results. They may include a brochure which describes comprehensively the contribution of physical education to the total education of the student. Physical education exhibitions of class activities are a potent means of interesting the people of a community in the products of education. This also supplies the press, radio, and television with materials which can be distributed, described, and commented upon. An excellent exhibition will provide for better understanding and increased support. Demonstrations before various citizen groups will carry the message and secure the objectives which are sought through good public relations. Playdays, sports festivals, and other events which provide activity for all who wish to participate, should pave the way for many additional, well-informed and enthused citizens within the community.

When planning for a program to develop community interest, the teacher must be aware of the potential of including all grades. The following program, which was presented on a citywide basis, was received with tremendous interest and a generous acclaim.

PHYSICAL EDUCATION REVIEW
Memorial Field House

STORY PLAY—SINGING GAMES
Second and third grade boys and girls

TUMBLING
Fourth through eighth grades
boys and girls

PYRAMIDS
Sixth, seventh and eighth grades
boys and girls

FOLK DANCES
Fourth and fifth grades
boys and girls

COMBATIVES
Seventh and eighth grade boys

DRILL
Seventh and eighth grade girls

ORGANIZED GAMES
Fifth through eighth grade boys

RELAYS
Fourth, fifth, and sixth grade boys and girls

SQUARE DANCING
Sixth, seventh, and eighth grade boys and girls

Students from each of the elementary schools take pleasure in presenting this program.

More than 1200 children participated in this review and several thousand parents came to see it. The activities which were presented were selected from the regular activities being taught in the physical education program. The students were chosen from the various schools and there was genuine enthusiasm in taking part. The entire program within the schools was stimulated because of the interest developed in preparing for the review. Those children who participated were genuinely happy. The adults who attended caught the enthusiasm with a better understanding of the magnitude and scope of the physical education program. They left with a full knowledge that physical education involved more than the flexion and extension of muscles in setting up exercises and included more than the athletic contest on Friday night. Here was a program in which every child in the community could participate. Here was a program which was graded to meet various skills and maturity levels. Here was a program in which children entered with enthusiasm and in turn motivated enthusiasm in their parents and friends.

The same type of program was also presented by the students on the secondary level. More than four hundred were selected to participate. Activities were chosen from their regular program and improved a bit for their exhibition or review. It is not difficult to develop enthusiasm when the students know that the product of their labors is going to be presented before an audience of parents and friends. Some extra preparation may be essential in order to get certain activities ready for presentation but much more is accomplished in the same amount of time when there is enthusiasm for doing a good job.

The activities which were chosen to be presented in the review were: A mass exercise drill for both boys and girls, folk dances in native costumes, relays which incorporated speed and skill, tumbling, stunts and pyramids, modern dance with lead-up exercises, apparatus for both boys and girls and costumed square dancing.

When a program of this type is presented, it is necessary to keep it moving and to have people informed. It is therefore essential to have a printed program in the hands of all who attend. In addition, it is necessary to describe and interpret, via the public address system, the activities in which the students are taking part. It does not necessarily follow that because a vast number of students took part that either participant or spectator will leave the affair with a greater appreciation of the physical education program. The contrary could be the outcome if a mediocre performance is presented. Hard work precedes the presentation of every activity. Every facet in preparation for an event of this size must be meticulously detailed. Problems must be anticipated, but the generous acclaim for a job well done is sufficient remuneration. This type of program projection will reach many people who cannot be approached through the regular service program operating within the gymnasium.

The physical education department may publish and distribute a brochure or booklet which describes the philosophy, procedures, activities, and objectives of the program. Such a brochure can suggest the importance of the physical education program in the total school curriculum, and can describe salient features of the program to give the reader a clear picture of the actual class activities and procedures and some of the anticipated outcomes.

Valuable contacts with other staff members, parents, and the community may be made through printed folders which include the materials suggested above. In schools which use grade card inserts to describe the facets of the total educational program, the physical education department should provide information about its program as the occasion permits. A well-illustrated and clearly written leaflet which accompanies the grade card provides a most valuable introduction into the home. This may be one of the few opportunities which the physical education department has to present its story to some people. It should be good, and it can be effective.

Too few communities have seized upon the excellent example which the city of Flint, Michigan, has provided in its community school. This program is built upon the concept that public schools are supported by all the people, therefore they should serve all the people. It is the product of cooperation between the Mott Foundation and the Flint Board of Education.

The community school director takes over after the regular classroom activities have finished at 3:30 P.M., and coordinates the programs until closing time and all day on Saturday. He is hired by the board of education to supervise and coordinate youth and adult work. He teaches in the regular school program in the afternoons. All schools participate; in each school the principal is the chief administrator and the community school director is responsible to him. The director is paid by the board of education and supplemented by the Mott Foundation.

The Flint community school program grew out of a fundamental philosophy of the Mott Foundation that it does not invest its financial resources in the buildings but in the individual. This is done by expanding and improving family recreation and educational services and opportunities for the entire community. The Mott Foundation program attempts to fill in where other resources are inadequate or nonexistent. The implementation of this philosophy has resulted in numerous community activities. The community school is only one.

The challenge to physical education comes in the variety of activities which are offered or may be added if a need is indicated, and in the type of person required to direct the program. Most of the directors have physical education backgrounds and preparation. It is this type of person who reflects the qualifications essential for the job. Thousands of people are enrolled and hundreds of courses are offered. The success has been so great that Flint has become the mecca for those who wish to see a fine example of the community school in operation.

MEDIA FOR PUBLICITY AND PUBLIC RELATIONS

In securing publicity and maintaining public relations the schools need to use the media of press, radio, and television, which reach every facet of the public. To have anything short of complete and mutual cooperation between the school and these media is foolhardy. These outlets for news and information are essential to sound community life. The fundamental part of their job is to report the news, but in order to report it, they must have it at a time when it is still news. Nothing is more irritating or of less value to the press and radio than to receive material after its news value has been depleted. Since they deal in news, they must receive material before it has received full treatment in the homes of all readers and listeners.

When the schools have news, and this is usually most of the time, the public news media must be supplied with the information in good time and in proper order. These media work on close time and space schedules and they need to know in advance when a story of real import is to break. The information must be organized so that the more important items will receive their proper space. News reporters and writers are not experts in all types of information which they receive, and they are willing almost without exception to give importance to the items which justifiably are entitled to it. News and special feature writers and reporters are usually quite capable of picking out the news items which will draw most attention from their reading and listening public. It is highly desirable to present all the facts to the press and radio and expect them to be held in confidence when that is essential. The school public relations personnel will have little value if they deal in partial or incomplete stories, biased or shaded statements, or indulge in personal axe-grinding. The press and radio are dedicated to public service, but that means all of the public and not only to the schools. In many communities the public schools are in a very favorable position with the press and radio and they receive the fullest cooperation and support from these media. There is, therefore, a pleasant climate for the acceptance of school news. Some press, radio, and television agencies assign personnel specifically to cover the school news, including sports events, open house, special assemblies, dramatic presentations, musicales, and board of education meetings. With a mutual understanding of needs, procedures, and problems, the schools and news media can work together to give better service to the total community.

The physical education teacher who seeks to get material before the public must know the policy of the schools in handling news. It is possible that someone is assigned to handle all material which is given to the public. In other systems, the individual is permitted to release information to the public news media. If direct release is permitted, the physical education teacher needs to know the personnel with whom he works in each of the news media. He needs to acquaint himself with the procedure he is to follow in furnishing the news. He needs to be cognizant of news deadlines in the various media. He needs to be explicitly honest. Even when he tries to be most understanding, he must remember that news media are in competition with each other. It is an exceptional person who can always release news to the satisfaction of all media, but reporters and writers are forgiving and understanding. A physical education teacher should not expect everything which is prepared to be newsworthy. He cannot expect everything to be given a prominent place on the page or in the program. This is a decision to be made by the press, radio, and television staff. Some papers and stations feature school news on special pages or over special programs. The rules are then more definite and the teacher with information for the public can plan with this in mind. When pictures are involved, the press usually prefers their own composition and photographs. They know what they want and they can visualize how arrangements will appear on the printed page. Pictures are costly and are used only when needed to illustrate and enhance the story. If the press does wish to take pictures, it is advisable for the physical education teacher to have his personnel or illustrative material ready when the photographer arrives.

Another way in which the work of the physical education department can be presented is through the Superintendent's Annual Report. These reports vary considerably in content and length, but if they are comprehensive, there is usually space for department coverage. Occasionally the reports are of such nature that all departments have an opportunity to prepare their portion. There are times when the report is very limited and does not provide for department information. To limit a report in physical education to participation statistics has little, if any, value.

There are occasions when schools find outside bulletin boards to be an effective way to reach the public. This is especially true for athletic schedules, but it can be important for other school events, including physical education activities. Boards of this type must be located in a prominent place, preferably in front of the school. The board must be highly presentable, attractive in appearance, and well lighted. The contents must always be properly presented.

Schools often find that local merchants are willing to accept school displays in their places of business. These may range from table and counter cards to full window displays. When physical education teachers seek media of this type to present their story, they need to do so with thoughtful planning and the utmost care. There must be complete understanding of the problems of the merchant and the fullest cooperation. If he is willing to permit the use of his place of business for display purposes, the teacher should know what can be permitted and the length of time allowed. One should not be disappointed if he is occasionally unsuccessful in securing display space.

Some schools have found moving or slide pictures to be highly effective in presenting their story. Lectures with slides or movies are in great demand in every community. This often proves to be a most desirable way to publicize and create sound public relations. When these programs are presented before civic, parent, religious, or fraternal groups, it is often very valuable to have students participate actively. Their point of view and presentation usually stimulate additional interest on the part of the adult audience.

Public relations is a continuing process. The job is never finished. It often happens that desirable public relations can be turned into undesirable public relations by a few unfortunate incidents. The best way to prevent this from happening is to keep the public constantly aware of the events occurring in the school. General news releases, department releases, feature stories, human interest stories, direct contact with public groups, reports, brochures, displays, exhibitions, and programs are media which must be properly and continuously used. Behind all these must be a sound program of activities which contribute to and enhance the total educational program.

Chapter 15

EXPANDING RESPONSIBILITIES OF PHYSICAL EDUCATION

The range of physical education is influenced, and often determined, by the vision of those who direct the activities and teach the students. To some, the extent of physical education lies within the scope of varsity athletics. To others, it is the process of building muscle in the gymnasium. There are those who will claim that physical education is the keystone for all education, while others visualize little beyond the increase in heartbeat and the production of perspiration. To those with imagination and vision the responsibilities of physical education are ever-extending. The responsibilities encompass areas which were previously overlooked, unclaimed, or considered to be of minor significance.

This chapter discusses these areas of expanding responsibilities. The area of community recreation is discussed, and the role of various community agencies is submitted. Communities differ so greatly in their needs and organization that only a few of the most common can be used here. Camping and outdoor education has grown quite rapidly in recent years, and in some places schools find themselves in the center of this growth. Outdoor education has taken on some very significant facets, and here again schools can offer valuable leadership. Youth agencies and organizations are a vital part of our present-day society, and these are included because of their contribution to the education of youth and their close relationship to the school. The chapter concludes with the expanding responsibilities which the department may recognize in the areas of music, arts, and crafts.

THE SCOPE OF RESPONSIBILITIES

The nature and extent of the responsibilities of public schools have undergone a substantial change since the first schools were established in the United States. Considerable impetus has been added to both nature and extent in the last two decades. Many activities which were once the avowed prerogatives of the home have now gone to the schools by default or design. Large segments of society have neglected the responsibility for the direction of their children, and community agencies have stepped into this void. The public school has found that it is providing more and more for the development of the children who are enrolled.

With this additional role of the school, the physical education department has found that there are many and varied opportunities in which it can contribute. Any ambitious program will encompass all areas where valuable contributions can be made. As programs are extended and expanded, enlarged or more extensive use of facilities is required, personnel are increased in numbers and abilities, and broadened community relations are developed. The alert physical education department recognizes these opportunities for their challenges as well as for their added problems.

The physical education teacher who has ability, imagination, and the desire to accomplish is an indispensable asset to his school and community. He will strive for extended areas in which he can make contributions. In so doing, many individuals and organizations will be brought into some phase of the total program. Thus, the scope of responsibilities become greater and greater. They include the recreation, social activities, outdoor education, and even survival living in these times of great international dangers.

RESPONSIBILITIES FOR RECREATION

Recreation is generally thought of as embracing those activities and interests in which a person engages voluntarily and which he enjoys during his leisure time. We are concerned only with those activities and interests which are beneficial and not harmful to the individual or society. Recreation can vary from quiet, relaxing types of activities to those which demand the most vigorous physical output. Recreation can include those aspects which have mental, social, or physical implications and benefits. It can contribute to the development of skills, knowledge, and appreciation and provide an outlet for emotions, energy, and tensions. Participation in recreational activities can provide for greater depth and breadth for the enrichment of living.

The program in recreation can provide opportunities for men, women, boys, and girls. It does not require one to be tall or short, stout or slim, young or old, rich or poor. Appropriate activities can be found for all who wish to participate. The All-American athlete and the victim of a crippling disease can find enjoyment in recreational activities. The bounds which encompass the programs for recreation are almost limitless.

Even as the scope of recreational activities and types of participants are all-embracing, the sponsors are likewise countless. Community recreation programs are supported by governmental or public agencies and an extensive list of voluntary agencies. The public agencies may be the federal, state, or local governments, agencies of these governments, or the public schools. The federal government controls and operates numerous park systems with their great varieties of recreational activities and opportunities. The state government provides parks, historic museums, and a substantial number of other projects which contribute opportunities for recreation. The local government provides many facilities, activities, and services for the instigation, promotion, and provision of public recreation. The park and recreation departments of the city government are the agencies which most frequently provide extensively for the needs of the community which they represent. Both may receive their financial support from publicly voted taxes. Both may be administered and controlled by paid employees, voluntary citizen boards or committees, or combinations of each. Any of these methods of administration can operate to the greatest good for the greatest number if the objectives are right and there is efficiency and harmony in operation for the attainment of those objectives.

The schools often play a major part in the recreation of the community. It is not unusual to have the board of education members serve as members of the park or recreation boards. Frequently the board of education is the sponsoring authority in requesting tax levies for the support of public recreation. School buildings are often the recreation centers for the after-school activities administered by members of the city recreation department. Frequently schools may use park and recreation facilities for school activities. This exchange may include personnel, services, and materials. One of the finest types of cooperation and coordination to be found is when a park department, a recreation department, and the schools work closely together for the benefit of all. Facilities are exchanged and used for mutual benefit, and the personnel cooperate for the efficient functioning of all concerned. To go even a step farther, the Community School operated in the city of Flint, Michigan, is an example of what can really be done when people wish to combine their efforts.

COMMUNITY AGENCIES IN RECREATION

Every community can offer examples of outstanding contributions by voluntary agencies toward the total recreation program. Almost all religious organizations have activities which provide for the needs of their group. Many of their activities are of an educational-recreational nature. They are designed for their moral and religious content as well as for the fellowship gained by participation in religion-sponsored recreation. Some of their activities are linked to the religious calendar, while others are dependent upon the season. It is not uncommon for a religious group to own and operate a camp with a full program in recreation. Almost all groups design or adapt indoor facilities to include recreation. These facilities may be a building with a swimming pool, gymnasium, parlors, auditorium, and stage with all the equipment needed for a full program. They may include only a basement area or an added room to meet limited needs. The activities which may be found in the recreation program of a religious group could include: dancing, singing, bowling, picnicking, hiking, softball, dartball, basketball, sewing, camping, vacation school, reading circles, service societies, lectures, movies, and many types of social affairs. Many groups sponsor Cub Scout and Boy Scout, Explorer Scout and Girl Scout troops. Some groups include only members of their own faith, while others extend their programs to all who wish to participate. Throughout the nation there are many fine examples of recreation programs operated by religious groups and other community agencies.

Fraternal and civic organizations support a great variety of recreational activities. Some provide for their own membership and their families, while others carry on extensive communitywide programs. In some communities service groups such as the American Legion have taken the initiative and, with public support, provide for the recreation of the community. Their post quarters are extended to the public for indoor activities, and the playgrounds and recreation parks are managed for outdoor affairs. Fraternal organizations such as the Loyal Order of Moose, Fraternal Order of Eagles, or the Benevolent Protective Order of Elks will contribute toward or provide the facilities for the community recreation. Civic organizations such as Kiwanis, Rotary, Lions, and the Junior Chamber of Commerce often provide for the support of recreation. Frequently their efforts are directed toward the youth programs, but they may include many others. The American Automobile Association sponsors many valuable recreational activities largely for youth groups in their safety patrol units. It is not uncommon to find any one of these groups contributing funds, facilities, materials, and personnel to support the recreation program which is maintained by another community agency. For example, the members of Kiwanis may take the responsibility for the construction of a cabin at a YMCA camp, the Lions Club may set aside financial support for campers, and the Rotary might transport groups to and from the camp. The Junior Chamber of Commerce may take as a project the construction of a Mother Goose Land, while the members of other civic groups will contribute time and material to aid in the job. The examples of cooperation in community recreation are multitudinous in quantity and variety.

The School and Recreation

School personnel often serve, and school facilities are often provided for the recreational program in a community. It is not uncommon for the school's director of physical education, director of athletics, or one of the sports coaches to serve as the director of the community recreational program. Frequently members of the teaching staff serve as playground directors or teachers for various segments of the total program, such as art, crafts, reading, swimming, drama, music, or even gardening.

It seems only natural that the school personnel are used in the capacities cited. It is readily conceded that all learning does not take place in the classroom, but effective learning takes place under qualified teaching. Certainly the teacher who is prepared in the areas included in recreation has the leadership and understanding essential to secure the best results. The school and its personnel are basic to the existence and development of every community. They serve all the people who wish to be served and should provide the focal point for this service. They can vary with the needs and demands of the community which they represent and serve. The school and its staff are responsible for most of the formal education in the community, and this responsibility can easily be interpreted to include those attitudes, appreciations, interests, knowledges, and skills which are inherent in recreational activities. Many of these qualities have been founded and cultivated in the basic educational program of the school.

With the ever-increasing realization that recreation provides for a basic human need in a society which is rapidly extending its leisure time, the schools may be called upon to provide facilities and personnel to take care of this need. Leisure is the time when there is freedom of choice, and the choices may have a great influence upon the direction which a nation may take. What people do in their leisure time may eventually mean the difference between national destruction or survival. The importance which is attached to leisure implicates the schools as a responsible agent in determining the direction which recreation shall take. Schools are then called upon to provide for the implementation. The worthy use of leisure time is one of the cardinal principles of secondary education. Many of these activities which are provided in school find direct continuity in the recreational program of the community. To see that this is done should not be a casual outcome of education; there should be a positive design toward this end. The activities taught in physical education, art, dramatics, and music should include many with recreation potential. Many clubs such as aquatic, art, aviation, chess, graphic arts, library, radio, and rifle have immediate and carry-over values in recreation.

There are times when the salaries of the school personnel are paid by the school board, sometimes by the city, and occasionally from funds solicited through public contribution. The laws within the various states may or may not permit these arrangements, and the particular wishes of the community may be the determining factor as to how the organization functions. In the state of Ohio, boards of education may provide or approve, subject to the approval of parents, activities for children during the summer vacation period which will promote health, civic and vocational competence, and industry. Boards may cooperate with other public officials in recreational activities. The law states that the boards of education may cooperate with county commissioners, boards or other public officials having custody and management of public parks, libraries, museums, other buildings, and grounds of whatever kind. This cooperation may provide for educational, social, civic, and recreational activities. The law further provides that school grounds and schoolhouses shall be made available as social centers for the entertainment and education of people, including the adult and the youthful population.

Thus it would seem that any community which so desires has readymade organizations and facilities for the operation of a comprehensive recreational program. To have less than complete cooperation between interested and responsible agencies within the community is sheer folly. Cooperation and coordination should enable every community to avoid unnecessary duplication and should result in the combining of efforts toward the most useful program for all. Many communities have learned that it is too costly to close facilities such as school buildings and then construct other centers for activities which could have been held in the unavailable building. It is a waste of public funds to reserve playfields for purposes other than school activities and compel the school to construct its own playfields. It is equally wasteful to allow public school property to lie idle and use public funds to construct identical facilities. It is true that it will require sound and skillful administration to knit together all agencies so that maximum use may be obtained from all facilities. However, it can be achieved by proper administration. The patterns of cooperation and coordination of those communities which have attained success should be studied and evaluated by communities which have been less successful. The community recreation program should be designed to serve the entire community throughout the year, and this can be accomplished when every agency directs its efforts to that end.

INDUSTRY AND RECREATION

In many communities industry provides for a substantial portion of the recreational program. Usually their facilities, finances, and personnel are utilized in activities for their employees and families. Occasionally others may participate as guests in specified activities and at specified times. The program ranges from sponsored teams in an industrial league at the YMCA to a full-year program in all activities. The extent and nature of the program depends upon the needs and interests of the employees and the practices of the industry. The Timken Roller Bearing Company of Canton, Ohio, exemplifies an industry which employs a director and staff to administer the recreational program for its employees. Extensive facilities and many types of equipment are furnished for the enjoyment of those who participate. All members of the family are taken into consideration, and provision is made for their needs and interests. Bus service is provided for the youth, and instruction is given in a variety of activities. Some industries not only provide for their own employees but also contribute to the community program either financially or through the use of facilities. Industrial management may participate with representative labor unions or may provide a program independently. The extent of participation would depend upon the relationship between the representatives of management and labor. In some communities, where one industry provides employment for most of the populace, the public recreational program is provided by that industry. There are some excellent examples which demonstrate the cooperation between industry and the community, resulting in a generously supported program in which all may participate. There are other examples where little thought has been given to the recreational needs of the employees of the community. The Hobart Company in Troy, Ohio, and the Hershey Company in Hershey, Pennsylvania, also are examples of industries which have recognized the benefits to be gained from a recreational program for their employees and their communities.

RELIGIOUS ORGANIZATIONS AND RECREATION

Organizations whose purpose is to provide recreational opportunities in a religious atmosphere are the YMCA and YWCA. Recreation is only one phase of their multipurpose program, but in many instances it is one of the most important. The gymnasium has long been associated with YMCA and YWCA organizations. It is within this program that a substantial portion of a community's recreational program often takes place. Other agencies within a community frequently look toward these organizations for leadership and facilities. Churches, clubs, industries, and independent groups participate in basketball, volleyball, bowling, swimming, wrestling, physical conditioning, and many other programs provided in the YMCA and YWCA buildings. Either or both associations may own and operate camps for members and sponsored individuals or groups. Both associations give leadership in the formation of day camps, hiking parties, field trips, and a great variety of outdoor activities. They cooperate with other agencies in the mutual use of community facilities. Their programs encompass the needs of all ages, races, and creeds. They are community-supported and community-controlled through committees and boards of laymen who contribute their service and time without remuneration. The professional staff work through and for the community boards, who are elected from interested lay personnel. The Jewish Community Centers and Catholic Youth Organizations also operate in a manner similar to the aforementioned associations. Many alter their programs and purposes as determined by local conditions and needs. Their financial support may come wholly or in part from the community at large—for instance, through the Community Chest—or it may come solely from members of their particular faith. In some communities there may be other organizations which provide for recreational needs in surroundings dedicated toward a religious concept.

THE RECREATION STAFF

In order for a community to secure the greatest recreational good from its investment in facilities, materials, and personnel, it is essential that a qualified staff be secured to aid and direct its evaluation, organization, and administration. Evaluation may indicate a need for changes in the present structure, or it may support its continuation. The National Recreational Association and the American Association for Health, Physical Education, and Recreation have a wealth of material available for use in evaluation, organization, and administration of all types of community recreation. Suggestions which will be of value to the administrator and his staff will include:

1. That all policies concerning working relationships with other community agencies be available in written form.
2. That an official, qualified citizen's committee or board actively participate in policy-making or in advisory capacity, whichever function is intended.
3. That arrangements be made through all available media for adequate publicity on organizations, administration, program, activities, needs, objectives, policies, and services.
4. That an accurate and complete method be provided for recording and reporting this information.
5. That an accurate and complete record be established and maintained for the receipt and use of funds, facilities, and supplies.
6. That an accurate and complete personnel policy be established and maintained and that an evaluative record of performance be included.
7. That a carefully prepared plan be established for the recognition of those who contribute their time and talents toward making the program possible.
8. That all participants be made fully aware of rules and regulations, procedures, and penalties in the phases of the program which are competitive and for which recognition is given.
9. That policies and procedures be established and publicized concerning legal responsibilities, particularly where accidents are involved.
10. That rules and regulations concerning the use of equipment and facilities be established and publicized.
11. That complete and fair working rules and regulations be on record and known to all staff personnel for both internal and public relations.

12. That adequate authority be granted to all personnel to carry out assigned responsibilities.
13. That procedures be established and decisions be made judiciously and promptly for all protests or violations of recreational rules and regulations.
14. That an adequate method of financing be provided for the program which the community desires.

There are many other phases which these suggestions do not cover, but a successful program cannot be carried on without due consideration for the many relationships which are involved in a communitywide recreation program.

The success of any program depends upon the staff which directs it. Facilities mean very little unless the program is properly planned and directed. To insure this there must be sufficient and properly qualified personnel. Inasmuch as recreation personnel often appear in more than one capacity, there must be smooth working agreements among all of their employers. If they are school personnel and are scheduled for afterschool and summer employment, they must be compensated for their extra work. Some of this is made up in released time during regular school hours, but it is recommended that they be paid for their extra service. Their salaries may come from the board of education, from the recreation or park board, or from the community agency which sponsors the program. If the recreation personnel is under the control of a community agency other than the board of education, then they are paid by that agency whether they are fulltime employees or school personnel serving in dual roles.

RESPONSIBILITIES FOR CAMPING

The values inherent in camping have long been known and recognized by those who are in physical education in the schools. It generally was accepted that camping was an activity which was provided by the YMCA, YWCA, Boy Scouts, religious organizations, some voluntary civic groups or private organizations. Community groups often furnished financial support for individuals or groups so that they might enjoy the benefits of camping. This was largely a summer program, the gold mine in the sky for those youngsters who longed for the great out-of-doors. Boy and Girl Scout troops often secured or retained membership because of the fun anticipated in the camping trips. In some localities, camping became important enough for religious organizations to purchase or lease suitable sites. Where enthusiastic leadership was present, there usually was widespread recognition of the values of camping activities.

Schools have been rather slow to accept any responsibility for camps or camping. Often it was the school personnel who took scout troops on overnight or weekend camping trips or served on camp staffs during vacation periods. The more venturesome would chaperone groups from their religious organization or assist the YMCA in a camping venture. Some hardy families would go on rugged camping trips. The growth of large urban communities and the subsequent loss of the short trips to rural areas, rivers, and lakes have created an added interest in the benefits of camping.

There are excellent examples of school system participation in camping projects and even the owning and operating of camp areas solely for the use of school groups. Where this movement has been started, it usually spreads to other nearby communities, but it cannot be said that there is widespread acceptance of camping as a responsibility of the public schools. Perhaps the added financial burden is one of the main deterrents for the acceptance of camping as a school responsibility. There are many who would seriously object to adding the cost of the purchase and maintenance of camps and camping to the public tax duplicate. Others see no connection between camping and the long-accepted educational responsibilities of the public schools. In the minds of some, camping is fun and it is recreational, but it does not have a place in the program of public education. Others will concede the potential education values in camping, but will not accept it as a public responsibility. Boards of education often have been intrigued by the well-presented camping program coordinated with other phases of the school curriculum, but have not been willing to support the measures necessary to bring about the union. In some instances, this is not a major obstacle, since facilities are near at hand and the community is camp-minded. However, in many communities it is a tremendous struggle to keep the doors of the school building open for the traditional purposes of the school. In the latter, one could scarcely expect the acceptance of the added responsibilities for a camp or camping program. With the growth of the park-school and community-school concepts, and with the anticipated tremendous explosion in recreational needs, it will be well for all communities to plan in terms of future comprehensive needs.

To enter into a public school camping program is not a minor venture, particularly if it is to be comprehensive in scope. It is conceivable that a permissive program might be initiated by a board of education, in which it gave its permission for a teacher and a group of students to participate in weekend trips under school auspices. The trips might be for the purpose of extending laboratory experience in biology, forestry, geology, or in some similar subject area. Some of the benefits of camping would be realized and the venture could be called a part of a school camping program. It is also possible for a board of education to enter into an agreement with an organization such as the YMCA for the use of camp facilities by students and teachers. In some states, tax funds can be used to support some portions of the contractual costs, while in others the entire costs will have to be borne by sources other than taxes. These are examples of only nibbling at a school camping program.

For years, groups of students have planned camping trips with teaching staff members. One example might be a group of boys who wish to see some particular part of the country and prepare for the trip with one of their teachers. The plans could be extensive in nature, involving an entire summer vacation period and covering several thousand miles. They may consist of day camp trips by a teacher who takes a group from morning until evening and conducts camping activities. They may consist of the prospective candidates for football going to some camp site prior to the opening of school and engaging in camp activities. Generally this latter enterprise is closely governed by the rules of the athletic association of the state in which the school is located.

With the recent development of interest in cheerleading workshops, it was inevitable that the program would be extended to a week instead of only a Saturday session. What better place than a camp site to carry on the activities connected with cheerleading?

At present a number of schools conduct a preschool camp for their marching band members. It becomes a workshop in which the formations for the coming football season are worked out and practiced. The benefits derived from having the group together under camp conditions are quite gratifying to the director and the participating students. Schools may or may not sponsor the trip, but may give their approval for athletic or booster clubs to do it.

Camping may include all of the ruggedness inherent in the great out-of-doors, or it may be conducted under the protection of the most modern surroundings. In either case the phrase, "we were camping," carries with it an atmosphere of adventure, thrills, and something off the beaten path. School faculties frequently hold workshops at camp sites and find the results most gratifying. Although the program may be similar in format to that held in the school auditorium, the atmosphere of a suitable camp will contribute greatly to the enthusiasm for the affair. In order to accomplish the purposes of the workshop it is usually necessary to dispense with the outdoor type of existence and depend upon the more modern sleeping and dining quarters. Nevertheless, the beneficial effects of camping enhance the working of committees, speakers, forums, roundtables, and general meetings. Although these are only "camping cousins" of the more comprehensive school-camp programs, they do stimulate thinking about the far-reaching opportunties of camping. The extent of activities connected with camping seems almost endless. The future surely holds much in store for those areas which have only touched upon the school camping movement.

Some schools have taken full advantage of the potential in camps and camping. Boards of education have purchased camps or camp sites and have constructed the necessary facilities to carry on a comprehensive camp program integrated with the educational program of the school. They have extended the curriculum to include camping and those activities which can best be provided in a camp atmosphere. It would scarcely justify the expense for the board of education to purchase and outfit an extensive camp site if the only objective was to teach the accepted techniques of good camping. These can be taught under less ambitious, more economical conditions. However, to get the most effective results from this type of instruction, it is necessary to put the knowledge, skills, and attitudes into practice. There are some who will ask, if regular classroom subjects are to be taught, why go to a camp to teach them? This can be answered by the fact that the experience in a camping atmosphere and surroundings better achieves the objective of education through a sound and practical approach to learning. The situation offers and accommodates itself to direct learning in the solution of many community problems. The school-camp approach to education is not meant to be a new discipline, but a more effective extension and presentation of the present curriculum. Examples of how this can be done will be presented in the discussion of outdoor education.

If a board of education considers entering the school-camp phase of education, it needs to weigh certain fundamental policies and procedures. Equipment, facilities, supplies, and personnel must be provided in the regular instructional program. Their costs should be accepted as a part of the regular school program and must be included in the regular budget. All authorities and responsibilities should be designated in accordance with those prevailing in the regular school program. The camp facility must be administered like any other school facilities. It is often suggested or required that the student assume the cost of food and maintenance during his camp period. If there are particular hardships, this cost may be borne by contributions from other agencies within the community. The board of education should provide the instruction, the instructional materials, transportation, equipment, facilities, site, and special services. Some special services and substantial amount of community leadership is often available without extra cost to the board of education. This service and leadership is secured on the same basis as the vast amount of talent and time which is volunteered to community organizations such as the YMCA, the community welfare, the Red Cross, the Health and Tuberculosis Association and the Cancer Society.

RESPONSIBILITIES FOR OUTDOOR EDUCATION

Outdoor education is considered as education in and for the out-of-doors. It involves the use of the outdoors as a laboratory for teaching the knowledge, skills, attitudes, and appreciations essential for effective living. This implies not only efficient outdoor living but all phases of living which can be more effectively approached in this manner. Teaching about some aspects of the outdoors is already an integral part of classroom education. The life cycles of plants and animals, relationship of soil content to plant growth, the seasons and weather, conservation of soil and water supply, are all familiar examples of outdoor subjects now being taught in the classroom. In addition, the out-of-doors is a place for teaching. It is an environmental change contributing to the approach and method. It is essentially conceived as a better place to learn some of the subjects already being taught and an extension to other learnings which need to be included.

The case for outdoor education should be based upon these premises:

1. That all community resources should be placed in operation for their educational value.
2. That some of the general objectives of education can best be achieved in outdoor settings.
3. That certain competences for adequate living can be secured only through outdoor living.
4. That some phases of outdoor living and learning are essential to the future needs for living in this world of rapid and phenomenal change.
5. That much of the basic knowledge, appreciation, and attitudes concerning nature and the outdoors need to be better understood, and even are necessary for survival.
6. That outdoor education is an extension of experiences, such as field trips, which have become an accepted part of the curriculum of many schools.
7. That there are valuable contributions toward successful family living, which is fundamental to the preservation of democracy.
8. That increased motivation toward effective learning will come from the natural interest in the outdoors.
9. That the needs stemming from urban living and abundant leisure time can best be served through outdoor education.

These premises are based upon the needs of youth to feel self-sufficient in the outdoors, that the outdoors provides abundant opportunities for wholesome and vigorous living, that it provides the environment for relaxation and relief from tensions, that it introduces a great range of activities requiring many skills and stimulating many interests, that it contributes to personal and social development, that it offers adventure and exploration into the basic processes of nature, and that it challenges one to seek better understanding of the fundamental concept of human life and the relationship to God.

The following suggestions are offered as necessary for consideration before a comprehensive outdoor education program is launched:

1. A survey of available facilities, including extended school facilities, camps, forests, farming and gardening areas, lakes and streams, ranges, waste or abandoned lands, sanctuaries, ponds, and community property such as parks and buildings.
2. A survey of existing and functioning outdoor programs conducted by other community and state agencies.
3. A knowledge of the availability of qualified community leadership to aid in the support, development, and direction of a program adequate for school-community needs.
4. A knowledge of the curricular extension and improvement in the various subject areas of agriculture, horticulture, geology, biology, conservation, astronomy, forestry, animal husbandry, marketing, agronomy, and social sciences.
5. The effectiveness of learning from direct application of taught knowledge and skill.
6. The extent of community support for this additional approach to public education.
7. The extent of cooperation expected from other agencies already participating in some phase of outdoor education.
8. The extent of enthusiasm of the present school staff and administration for outdoor education.
9. The quality of instructional leadership among present staff members and the need for in-service teaching.
10. The amount and method of financing and the adequacy of evaluative criteria and techniques to determine the values obtained.

All these and perhaps more must be considered before any substantial steps can be taken to provide for a comprehensive outdoor program. No community needs to adopt a total program, even though it realizes the distinct advantages in doing so. A sound experimental approach may be preferred. Each community must make its own decision, based upon its own needs and interests.

YOUTH AGENCIES AND ORGANIZATIONS

Almost every community supports agencies and organizations for the benefit of its youth. These may range from organizations which offer only administrative counselling to those with extensive buildings and camp facilities. Some are founded and maintained by citizen groups whose major project is the recognition and assistance of youth in their community. Others are organized and carried on as local units of a national organization.

The objectives of community youth agencies are similar in some fundamental areas, but become peculiar in others. Moral and spiritual values have an important place in all agencies. Social and recreational activities appear to be a part of most youth organizations. If these activities are not included in the original objectives, they may be introduced as membership and participation inducement features. Other objectives may point toward specific goals peculiar to the founding and supporting organizations. School groups which are directed by community organizations usually have academic achievement as one of their objectives. Some groups are organized within the school with school approval and cooperation, while others are entirely independent of the knowledge or sanction of school authorities.

National organizations often adjust their regulations and support to accommodate local conditions and requirements; in some instances no adaptation is necessary. It is essential for the school to recognize these national organizations and to be acquainted with their aims, policies, and methods. The school ought not to, and perhaps cannot, insulate its students from the public and civic responsibilities which are often reflected in the programs of these organizations. It is most likely that all reputable youth-serving organizations are guided by outstanding citizens in the community, citizens who serve in school organizations and civic groups and work to accomplish the ideals of the supporting organization. However, school officials must guard against the intrusion of sectarian, partisan, or commercial propaganda and interests. They should be quick and definite in describing the functions of the public school and should in no way become an agency for any group which would compromise these functions. It is entirely possible that if school officials were not alert, a youth group professing worthy goals could gain the support of the school through insidious means. If an organization or individual is found to have some motives not compatible with the rules and regulations of the school, the board of education should take immediate action and bar them from the use of school facilities and personnel. Alertness and familiarity with youth-serving organizations can prevent subversive groups from gaining entrance into and using the schools as pawns for their purposes.

We are indebted to the American Youth Commission of the American Council on Education for an excellent study and presentation entitled, "Youth Serving Organizations." This manuscript was prepared under the auspices of the American Council on Education by Merrit M. Chambers and was published in April, 1941. In presenting the basic information, two questions are asked:

1. What are the general purposes and activities of the national youth-serving organizations which have local branches in my community?
2. Are there any national groups not represented in my locality whose aims and policies indicate that a local branch would be an asset to the youth of this community?

A comprehensive presentation of youth-serving groups is then made, which offers important information concerning each. Among the more common groups are the following:

1. The American Junior Red Cross, which has for its stated purpose service to others in health of mind and body so as to fit people for better service and worldwide friendship.
2. The Boys' Clubs of America, whose activities are mainly physical education and recreation.
3. The Boy Scouts of America, who promote through organization and cooperation with other agencies the ability of boys to do things for themselves and others, to train in scoutcraft and to teach patriotism, courage, and self-reliance, with emphasis upon character development, citizenship training and physical fitness.
4. Campfire Girls dedicated to the personal development of girls through group experiences in a program of leisure activities, cultivation of skills, democratic practice, and self-reliance.

5. The YMCA, which promotes worldwide fellowship united in common loyalty to Jesus Christ. This is done through social education, leadership, citizenship, and community welfare. Social and recreational life are emphasized in order to gain the ideals of Christianity and promote a better society.
6. The YWCA, founded to advance the physical, social, intellectual, moral and spiritual interests of young women upon the foundation of the Christian beliefs.. The aims include praparation for a full life and development of character through social, cultural, and recreational activities.
7. The 4-H Clubs, which promote desirable standards for farming, homemaking, community life, and citizenship through demonstrations, exhibits, judging, farming experience, and social and recreational activities.
8. Future Farmers, which strengthen confidence in farming, create more interest in varied forms of farming, improve rural life with goals of thrift, scholarship, and organized recreation.
9. Christian religious groups which build Christian character, develop the individual, provide service, promote the welfare of the church and a Christian society among men. The program consists of religious, social, and recreational activities.
10. Aleph Zadik Aleph of B'Nai B'Rith, which emphasizes patriotism, love of justice, tenets of Judaism, a healthy body, an active mind, a wholesome spirit, and gentlemanly conduct, and uses such activities as debate, social affairs, oratorical and athletic tournaments to accomplish these goals.
11. Catholic Boys Brigade of the United States, which brings Catholic boys under the influence of Catholic training and instruction through association and activities for greater service to God, country, and fellowmen. Activities include drills, physical exercise, first aid, recreation, civic duties and athletics.

This brief list includes only a few of the vast number of youth-serving organizations. The few remarks made about each one cannot begin to describe or give full credit for the extent and quality of work which they perform. The full nature and quality of their programs may be determined by directly contacting their offices.

What has this to do with schools and administration in physical education? As has been previously stated, school personnel should be familiar with the goals and policies of youth-serving groups in their communities. They serve the same youth during the afterschool hours and influence them greatly. Their contributions often dovetail with the school program. They often wish to use school facilities and frequently depend upon school personnel for leadership. Qualified physical education teachers are particularly in demand. Most of the groups include recreation, physical and social activities, and cultural goals in their programs. It behooves every physical education teacher to contribute to the community through youth-serving groups.

RESPONSIBILITIES TO OTHER AREAS

When physical education teachers start a new job or begin a new year in a school, there are many people and departments with whom they must work. For the best results and the greatest satisfaction, it is essential that this work be carried on in a harmonious manner. The physical education teacher must realize that his department offers only one phase of the total educational program. He must be aware that other teachers have a strong interest in the promotion of their work. If each teacher respects the program and work of others, all worthy educational activities will prosper. The welfare of the students must always be uppermost in the plans and actions of the teacher.

The physical education teacher must know to whom he should report. Most frequently these people are the principal, the director, and supervisor. If there is any uncertainty, it is essential to work with the principal. The teacher must understand the rules and regulations, his prerogatives, the school's philosophy, and the normal administrative procedures. This body of material is written in most schools and is a part of the material issued before the opening day. It is not only desirable but necessary that the teacher become familiar with this information. It is well to ask questions if he is a beginner, and to be helpful to beginners if he is experienced.

Every physical education teacher must work closely with every classroom teacher. It is essential to remember that teachers want their classes to begin on time and that their students must be in the room and ready for work. They should never be detained in the gymnasium, thereby causing tardiness in the next class. It is also important to remember that the students should be suitably groomed when they leave the locker room. To have them uncomfortable or disheveled in the halls or in the following class, because of operations in the physical education department, does not build friends among other staff members. Physical education teachers can offer much to the general deportment of the school by keeping their students well disciplined and dismissing them promptly.

There are numerous opportunities for the physical education teacher to work with the various other departments in the building or buildings. The vocal and instrumental departments often cooperate and coordinate their work with the physical education department. This cooperation may consist of the interdepartmental use of equipment or the coordination of activities for a major public presentation. Such cooperation can become a major attraction of the school year.

Frequently oportunities arise for the departments of physical education, art, and drama to coordinate their work. Although the inclusion of dance routines may be found more often in musical department productions, it is not uncommon for the dramatic department to need help from the physical education staff. There are times when special events by the physical education department may be presented between the acts of a play. The art department correlates its work with the drama and music departments and often makes important contributions to the physical education department. Any school system which has a core program affords many opportunities for integrated work. For the best results, it is necessary to have coordinated planning and operation. Once this coordination is achieved, gratifying results are obtained for students and teachers alike. The interpretation of physical education activities can aid substantially in a better understanding of history. A presentation of the physical activities of Bismarck's Germany can be shown as a reflection of the German culture of that period. Denmark's culture is interpreted through its physical education. The ideals of democracy can be demonstrated and explained through physical education activities.

It is quite possible for the alert and cooperative physical education teacher to correlate activities with almost all departments in his school. In most cases it requires more work and certainly more planning to correlate and integrate the activities of more than one department. However, educational dividends are great and certainly within the responsibilities of those who wish to do an outstanding job in education.

Chapter 16

PROFESSIONAL ORGANIZATIONS IN PHYSICAL EDUCATION, ATHLETICS, AND RECREATION

PROFESSIONAL groups are essential to the health and growth of a professional field. It is not essential that the groups be organized, but the continued activity of a group usually results in its formalization into a kind of organization. Professional organizations have been formed to meet one or more specific purposes. As the organization lives year after year, its original purpose may be forgotten or may have been served. The organization persists, however, and usually finds new goals toward which it can work.

There are several important professional organizations in the field of physical education. The administrator and the teacher should know about them and should be active in those which they can serve and which render a service to them in turn.

The purpose of this chapter is to give information which will enable the reader to understand the nature of the professional organizations listed. Those included in the chapter devote their interests principally to the activities of schools and colleges, thus serving the professional personnel in education. Insofar as it is possible, the description of each organization will follow a standard pattern. Because an organization may have interests and activities which touch upon several fields, the listing of organizations will be alphabetical rather than by fields.

1. Name. American Association for Health, Physical Education and Recreation, founded in 1885 as the Association for the Advancement of Physical Education. The Association became a department of the National Education Association in 1937, and adopted its present name in 1938.

2. Address. Executive offices are located at 1201 Sixteenth Street, N.W., Washington 6, D. C.

3. Publications. The Association issues the *Journal of Health, Physical Education, Recreation,* published monthly September through May, and *The Research Quarterly,* published in March, May, October and December of each year. The Association also publishes books, monographs, brochures, conference reports, and yearbooks. A list of available publications can be obtained by making a request to the Washington office.

4. Membership. Membership is open to persons working in any of the fields represented in the Association. Membership is classified as Fellow, Professional, and Student. Persons who are Fellows, or who pay the higher rate ($15) for Professional membership receive the *Journal,* the *Research Quarterly,* and the *National Education Association Research Bulletin.* Professional members who pay an annual dues of $10 and Student members who pay dues of $6 receive the *Journal* and the *Research Quarterly.* An undergraduate membership of $3.50 entitles the student to the *Journal.*

There were 23,751 members enrolled in 1960. The Association has grown from a membership of 10,585 in 1945 to its 1960 figure and will continue this growth as more persons enter the professions of health, physical education, and recreation.

5. Meetings. The Association holds a national convention annually. The convention site, which changes each year, is selected in a geographic area represented by one of the district associations. The annual convention is the official meeting of the Association.

6. Services to the profession. The Association renders a number of services to the profession. A statement by Esslinger indicates the extent of services.

The Association is currently involved in a program of action which includes annual conventions, national conferences and workshops, consultant services, representation in other national and international groups, publications, informational and public relations programs, and specific services to state associations and individual members. It is concerned with raising professional standards, improving programs of instruction, promoting more nationwide activity in our specialized areas of education, creating and sustaining professional interest, informing the public of the contributions of our areas, and building better understanding of the significant role played in our society by health, physical education, athletics, outdoor education, recreation, and safety education.[1]

As noted above, the Association has published a sizable list of items, including books, reports of conferences, and brochures. These are available to members at nominal costs. Those which can be used for community public relations can be purchased in bulk at low cost. The Association also cooperates with other organizations in the preparation and publication of yearbooks, conference proceedings, and monographs.

Through the services of its consultants on the headquarters staff the Association aids local organizations, institutions, and groups of professional people in meeting their particular problems in health, physical education, and recreation. Local matters may be the status of the physical education requirement, the qualifications of teachers, the need to plan new facilities, and gaining support for securing funds for new facilities.

The Association sponsors conferences and workshops, often in cooperation with other organizations. Between 1951 and 1959 the Association sponsored twenty-four conferences and one workshop. Examples of conferences are the following: National Conference of Physical Education in Elementary Schools (1951), National Conference of Physical Education for College Men and Women (1954), National Conference on Health Education for All Prospective Teachers (1956), National Conference on Social Changes and Implications for Physical Education and Sports Programs for Women (1958), and National Conference on the Science Core in the Physical Education Professional Program (1959).

[1] Arthur A. Esslinger and Carl A. Troester, Jr., "Our Association Today," *Journal of Health, Physical Education and Recreation,* April, 1960, p. 24.

Nineteen professional organizations are affiliated with the Association.

The AAHPER is the only organization serving the entire profession in schools, colleges, and community work. It is by far the largest of the organizations, and is most actively concerned with the growth and status of all the named fields. As a department of the National Education Association, it is a member of the family of organizations which are constantly concerned with professional matters in education and with the improvement of the educational services to children, youth, and adults. It is the organization to which all persons working in any of the fields should belong.

The considerable growth in size of the national organization has been accompanied by a lessening of the part which any individual member may feel that he plays in the activities of the association. The creation of sections whose programs are built around only one phase of the Association's interests has retained relatively smaller group meetings to offset the bigness of the general meetings. The section device is an acknowledgment of specialization and also a means of dividing interests in the total program of physical education.

The new teacher in the field, as well as the one who finds that the national meetings offer a frustrating experience in trying to select a possible program out of the numerous offerings, will find in the state and district associations opportunities to become acquainted with others who live in the same region, to take part in Association activities and be recognized for their contributions, and to work actively in the organization throughout the year. Participation in the meetings and affairs of the state associations is an obligation of every teacher and administrator of physical education. In 1960 there were fifty-two state units, including Puerto Rico and the District of Columbia. Attendance at district conventions broadens one's acquaintance and can lead to active participation at this level, also.

Although a national association exerts tremendous influence upon the thinking in the field, the implementation of recommendations and plans is done at the local level, hence the strength of the profession nationally is based upon its local strength. It is important, therefore, that every member of the profession be an active member of his state organization, as well as an enrolled member of the AAHPER.

Reference has been made to district associations, of which there are six: Central, Eastern, Midwestern, Northwestern, Southern, and Southwestern. Each district encompasses a number of states and conducts a regional meeting each year. The district in which the national Association holds its annual meeting does not have a separate meeting that year but joins with the national organization.

Although district and national meetings are large and tend to engulf the individual, the larger meetings attract people from wider areas and extend the communication of ideas and experiences. The larger meetings also are able to secure nationally and internationally prominent people to appear on their programs. Finally, actions taken in the form of resolutions carry more weight because they represent more people and a wider geographic area, and they tend to bind together a larger segment of the profession. The district and national conventions do serve important purposes.

1. Name. American Academy of Physical Education. The Academy was founded in 1904–1905 to bring together persons doing original research in the field of physical education, and to promote interest in scientific investigation. The organization was active until World War I and was revived about 1924. The current form of organization was adopted in 1930.

2. Address. Probably the address of the current president, who is elected annually, is the address of the Academy for the year. Communications addressed to the Washington office of the American Association for Health, Physical Education and Recreation will reach the officers of the Academy.

3. Publications. These include papers and reports presented at annual meetings.

4. Membership. "Membership consists of (a) active fellows (not to exceed 100 at any time), (b) associate fellows; (c) corresponding fellows; (d) fellows in memoriam, (e) honorary fellows in memoriam, and (f) fellows retired."[2] Membership is by election of a two-thirds majority of all votes cast.

[2] Edward F. Voltmer and Arthur A. Esslinger, *The Organization and Administration of Physical Education,* 3d ed., Appleton-Century-Crofts, Inc., 1958, p. 492.

5. Meetings. The Academy meets annually, usually at the time of the annual meeting of the American Association for Health, Physical Education and Recreation.

6. Services to the profession. The Academy serves the profession through stimulating needed research, through disseminating professional information within the country and in foreign lands, through supporting legislation dealing with physical education, by encouraging promising individuals to enter the profession, and by recognizing scholarly achievements with appropriate awards and citations. The Academy elects to membership as corresponding fellows the most outstanding physical educators of foreign lands. Through these fellows there is an interchange of research materials and ideas which benefit all who are involved.

1. Name. The American College of Sports Medicine was organized in September, 1954, and incorporated in 1955. In this title the term *sports* is defined broadly to encompass the whole field of physical education, including competitive athletics, exercise therapy, and all types of exercise activities practiced by peoples of the world.

2. Address. The address of the current president of the organization is its official address. Because the organization is affiliated with the AAHPER, the name and address of the president can be obtained from the office of the Executive Secretary of the AAHPER.

3. Publications. The proceedings of the meetings are published. As of April 1961 the *Journal of Sports Medicine and Physical Fitness,* the official journal of the Fédération Internationale de Médecine Sportive, is also the official journal of the American College of Sports Medicine.

4. Membership. Members are drawn from all fields engaged in work related to the effects of exercise upon the person. Three major groups are represented: medical practitioners from the various specialties, scientists with specialized training in one of the disciplines, and what may be termed applied scientists, including the physical educators, therapists, and general educators.

5. Meetings. The College meets annually. The organization is affiliated with the AAHPER and usually meets at the time of the latter's annual convention.

6. Services to the profession. The purposes of the College are

(1) to promote and advance scientific studies dealing with the effect of sports and other motor activities on the health of human beings at various stages of life, (2) to cooperate with other organizations concerned with various aspects of human fitness, (3) to sponsor meetings of physicians, physical educators, and other scientists whose work is relevant to sports medicine, (4) to make available postgraduate education in fields related to the objectives of the College, (5) to initiate, encourage, and correlate research, and (6) to publish a journal dealing with scientific aspects of activity and their relations to human fitness.[3] To bring together trained persons from many fields who study the effects of exercise and of sports upon individuals is a tremendous service. In the early years of the American Association for the Advancement of Physical Education and of the Society of College Gymnasium Directors, the concern of the members at the annual meetings was the effects of exercise upon individuals. Investigations which had been conducted by members of the groups were reported and discussed. The rapid growth of physical education in schools and colleges during the twentieth century utilized the time and energies of the professional physical educator to the point where he did very little research in this area. Other fields of science have developed with great rapidity, and new divisions have developed within them. Research in the science fields is complex and profuse. To have an organization which can again bring together the research interests of the various disciplines including physical education is of benefit to all.

1. Name. College Physical Education Association, founded in 1897 as the Society of College Gymnasium Directors. In 1933 the present name was adopted.

2. Address. The address of the Association is the address of the current Secretary-Treasurer, and is printed in the annual proceedings. The Secretary-Treasurer as of 1962 is M. M. MacKenzie; his address is Teachers College, Columbia University, New York 27, New York.

3. Publications. The Association annually publishes the *Proceedings,* which carry a full report of the papers and speeches given

[3] "American College of Sports Medicine," *Journal of Health, Physical Education, Recreation,* February, 1960, p. 33.

at the annual meeting, the minutes of the business meeting, the constitution and bylaws of the organization, and the roll of members.

4. Membership. There are two types of membership in the Association, active and honorary life. "Active members are men actively engaged in teaching or administering one or more of components of college physical education, men with teaching experience pursuing graduate study, or men engaged or interested in allied fields."[4] Honorary Life membership may be conferred upon active members or former active members by a two-thirds affirmative vote of the members in attendance at a regular business meeting. The enrolled membership of the Association is above seven hundred. Between 1945 and 1960 the membership increased three-fold.

5. Meetings. The Association holds an annual meeting, usually of two to three days' duration in the last week of December. The meeting sites are selected in various geographical areas. In 1958 the members voted to make the Western College Men's Physical Education Society a division of the Association. Whereas in the earlier years of the Association the membership was almost entirely from the New England, Middle Atlantic and Midwestern states, now the members represent colleges and universities in forty-nine of the fifty states, and in Canada, Puerto Rico, New Zealand, and England.

The business of the organization is conducted at a business meeting which is held at the time of the annual meeting. During the period between meetings the Executive Council acts for the Association.

6. Services to the profession:

a. Publications: In addition to the annual *Proceedings,* which are sent to all members and which can be purchased by anyone, the Association publishes important committee reports. Reports on gymnasium planning and construction, facilities for health, physical education and athletics, the physical education curriculum, terminology, and fitness have been published by the Association. Informational brochures are prepared and printed for distribution when a special need arises. The brochure dealing with the subject of credit for military service is an example.

b. Cooperative relationships. The Association, through its membership on joint committees, and through its representatives to other organizations,

[4] Article I, Section 2 of the By-Laws, *Proceedings,* College Physical Education Association, 1958, p. 238.

works closely with several professional associations. The *Proceedings* for 1958 lists seven areas in which the Association has committee or representative relationships with one or more professional organizations.

c. Through its officers and committees the Association offers assistance to members who meet especially difficult situations in their institutions.

d. The Association encourages research through its own Research Section and through the cooperation of the membership on approved projects.

The College Physical Education Association is the only professional organization in the field whose principal concern is the total program of college physical education for men.

1. Name. National Association for Physical Education of College Women, formed in 1924 as an outgrowth of the Association of Directors of Physical Education for Women. The organization consists of five district associations: Central, Eastern, Midwestern, Southern, and Western. The Eastern Association was the original one.

2. Address. Because the organization functions principally through its district associations, the addresses will be those of the officers elected biennially. Since it is an affiliated organization of the AAHPER, communications to the national organization can be addressed to the executive office of the AAHPER in Washington, D.C.

3. Publications. Reports of conferences, meetings and workshops are prepared by the organizations and distributed to their members.

4. Membership. Membership is open to all teachers of physical education for college women. In the early years of the organization membership was open only to heads of departments of four-year colleges and universities. In 1946 staff members were invited to become non-voting associate members, and in 1948 they were granted full membership.[5] Membership may be held in the district organization and in the national association. In 1960 the Eastern Association for Physical Education of College Women had a membership of 274. Of this number 165 were also members of the National Association for Physical Education of College Women.[6]

[5] Taken from Elizabeth Beall, "President's Message," *Business Report,* Eastern Association for Physical Education of College Women, February, 1960, p. 3.

[6] Figures on membership are taken from the *Business Report,* Eastern Association for Physical Education of College Women, February, 1960, pp. 8–17.

5. Meetings. Regular meetings are held biennially. In between these meetings regional meetings and workshops are conducted by the Association.

6. Services to the profession. The Association serves its members and the profession at large through the papers presented and deliberations carried on at its biennial meetings, through official actions taken by the Association and its officers, through the work of its committees, and through the workshop which it sponsors.

In 1949 the Association sponsored the First International Congress on Physical Education for Girls and Women at Copenhagen, Denmark. The success of the first congress resulted in the scheduling of a Second Conference in Paris in 1953.

1. Name. National Education Association of the United States. The National Teachers' Association, founded in 1857 "to elevate the character and advance the interests of the profession of teaching and to promote the cause of popular education in the United States," was the forerunner of the NEA. In 1870 two other organizations which had grown up separately united with the National Teachers' Association to form the National Educational Association. These groups, the National Association of School Superintendents and the American Normal School Association, became the first department of the NEA. The NEA was incorporated under the laws of the District of Columbia in 1886. The present name was adopted in 1907.

Today the NEA represents the education profession of the United States in all its aspects. In order to carry on the work of the many different groups, organizations known as departments have either developed with the NEA or have become affiliated with it as one of its departments. The American Association for Health, Physical Education, and Recreation is a large organization in its own right but also is a department of the NEA. There are currently (1960) 31 other departments.

2. Address. The NEA has its own building at 1201 Sixteenth Street, N.W., Washington 6, D.C. An Executive Secretary manages the operation of the Association's central office. Policies guiding the activities of the entire organization are established by the Representative Assembly.

3. Publications. The NEA publishes a large number of books, pamphlets, periodicals, and films on every conceivable subject in education. A publication list for any recent year will contain over one thousand titles. The list is free and may be obtained from the NEA office in Washington, D.C.

4. Membership. There are five classifications of members: Active, Life, Associate, Retired, and Student. Active membership is open to any person actively engaged in the teaching profession or other educational work, and associate membership is open to any person interested in advancing the cause of education but who is not actively engaged in educational work. The annual dues are the same for both classes, but the associate member may not hold an office or vote for delegates to the Representative Assembly.

Membership in the NEA reached a total of 713,994 in May, 1960. The organization is aiming at a goal of one million members.

5. Meetings. The Association holds an annual convention in conjunction with the meeting of the Representative Assembly. Departments of the Association may hold their own annual meetings at other times and in other locations. The AAHPER conducts its annual meeting in the spring of the year, whereas the NEA usually meets in the early summer. In a sense the NEA is a federation. Prior to September, 1960, a person could be a member of one of the departmental organizations without being a member of NEA. Beginning with the NEA membership year of 1960–61, departments requesting affiliation must include the requirement of NEA membership in their respective constitutions.[7]

6. Services to the profession. The NEA provides many services, only a sample of which can be listed here.

a. Publication and distribution of educational materials, including books, pamphlets, periodicals, reports, and films.

b. Provision of consultants in many fields, e.g., in elementary education, audio-visual education, and curriculum revision.

c. Sponsorship of conferences which deal with specific problems in education. Reports of these conferences are made available to the education profession.

[7] *NEA Handbook, 1960–61,* National Education Association of the United States, 1960, p. 41.

d. Information and assistance about the work of teachers' associations is supplied to members.

e. Preparation of legislation affecting teachers, and sponsoring of such legislation.

f. When called upon, the NEA will investigate situations in which teachers' rights are jeopardized, or in which working conditions are intolerable.

g. Conduct of a continuing public relations program in the interests of education.

A professional education association may become affiliated with the NEA upon approval of the Executive Committee. There are two classes of affiliates: State and Local. The number of these affiliated associations is large. They exist in each state, in Puerto Rico, and in the District of Columbia, and provide opportunities for teachers to become participants at local levels in the activities of a professional education association. The importance of local participation is as significant in these affiliated associations as in state units of the AAHPER.

1. Name. The Society of State Directors of Health, Physical Education, and Recreation was organized in 1926.

2. Address. As an affiliated organization, the Society will receive communications addressed to the office of the AAHPER. A list of state directors is published in the *Journal* together with a report of the annual convention of the AAHPER, but the officers of the Society of State Directors are not indicated.

3. Publications. Reports of the committees are published and given selective distribution. Reports of broad interest are printed in the *Journal of Health, Physical Education, Recreation.*

4. Membership. State directors are eligible for active membership, and their professional assistants and past state directors for associate membership. The active membership is limited to the number of state directors holding office. The number of states which have the position of director or its equivalent in 1960 was 32, plus the District of Columbia.[8]

5. Meetings. The Society holds its annual meeting in conjunc-

[8] "State Directors of Health, Physical Education, Recreation." *Journal of Health, Physical Education, Recreation,* December, 1960, p. 44.

tion with the annual meeting of the AAHPER. The meetings are open to anyone who wishes to attend.

6. Services to the profession. As the title indicates, the members of the organization occupy positions in their states through which they can influence physical education on a statewide basis and can look after the concerns of physical education in the activities of the state education department and the state government. The Society is the means by which its members, who are in positions of leadership in their respective states, can share their experiences and can aid each other in their work of promoting and improving physical education programs.

Although the membership of the Society is limited, its nature is almost that of a central nerve organ to which stimuli (information) are being sent from the entire field. It has the broadest of interests and a great potential for stimulating the advancement of the entire field of physical education.

A number of helpful studies have been made by the Society. Among them are "The National Physical Achievement Standards for Boys," "The National Physical Achievement Standards for Girls," "Credit for Physical Education," "Physical Education and Athletics," and the "National Study of Professional Education in Health and Physical Education."

The Society also prepares a statement of policy on matters in the field, e.g., statements concerning football for elementary and junior high school boys, junior Olympics, and interscholastic boxing.

1. Name. Division for Girls and Women's Sports (AAHPER), although not a separate organization, has functioned in the field of girls' and women's athletics with the force of an association. Prior to June 1, 1957, this organization was known as the National Section for Girls and Women's Sports. The organization grew out of a Committee on Women's Athletics which met in 1917, and later became the Women's Athletic Section of the American Physical Education Association. As a division of the AAHPER, the organization continues its activities in the field of athletics for girls and women.

At the meeting of the AAHPER held in Kansas City, Missouri, in March, 1958, the Division was given permanent status.

2. Address. The address of the executive office is the address of

the AAHPER. The name of the vice-president is listed in the *Journal of Health, Physical Education, Recreation* and she may be considered as the executive officer of the division during her term of office.

3. Publications. Under the previous organization the section edited the guides and official rules for women's sports. As a division of the AAHPER it maintains a standing committee on Sports Guides and Official Rules to advise on the content of these publications. State committees of the division publish materials to serve the needs of their local groups.

4. Membership. All active women members of the AAHPER are eligible for membership in the division. The enrolled members are those who attend meetings of the division and who sign the division roster. It is estimated that the membership is about 10,000 for all districts and the national organization.

5. Meetings. The division meets as part of the annual convention of the AAHPER. The division includes five sections, each of which has its own chairman and prepares its own program for the annual meeting. These sections are: Individual and Dual Sports, Officiating, Philosophy and Standards, Sports Leadership, and Team Sports.

6. Services to the profession. All matters pertaining to sports for women are the concern of this division. During its history the National Section for Girls and Women's Sports has exerted profound influence upon sports and athletics for girls and women through the establishing of policies governing their conduct and practice, and through the development and publication of official rules for women's sports. The Division continues the program of the former NSGWS and continues to give direction to these programs on a nationwide basis. Among the publications which have been of value to the physical education profession are *Standards in Athletics for Girls and Women, Desirable Practices in Athletics,* and *Special Events in the Physical Education Program.*

Writing on the subject of the future of the Division, Thelma Bishop states:

> The work now being done . . . will continue, since that service is eminently suited to present and future needs, but we will be doing it better and more thoroughly. We will also add other services. One of the

first needs discussed here was the need for American women to change habits and attitudes for better body maintenance. In 1985, the Division for Girls' and Women's Sports will have a well-established pattern for continuous and effective interpretation of this need to girls and women; for stimulating participation of all girls and women in sports; and for upgrading the experiences possible through sport participation. The Division will give continued and strong leadership in testing, developing, modifying and inventing new sports needed to fit space, age, and time limitations. Present services are geared primarily for girls in school, officials, physical educators, and recreation personnel. In the future, the Division will give similar services in the area of sports to lay women of all ages. The Division will give added help and service on the international level.[9]

Another important service which the Division provides is the rating of officials for women's sports. The Women's National Officials Rating Committee is a committee of the Section of Officiating. Standards which officials are expected to meet are promulgated by the committee, and official raters who may conduct rating sessions are designated by the committee.

1. Name. Phi Delta Pi, National Professional Physical Education Fraternity for Women, was organized at the American Gymnastic Union in Indianapolis in 1916.

2. Address. The address of the current president is the official address. It may be obtained by writing to the office of the AAHPER in Washington, D.C.

3. Publication. *The Progressive Physical Educator,* published twice yearly, is the official publication of Phi Delta Pi.

4. Membership. Active membership is possible only at institutions which have chapters of the fraternity. Where a chapter exists, only students of physical education are admitted. An institution having a major department in physical education (for women) may seek the organization of a chapter on its campus. "A college or university wishing to establish a chapter may petition the National Council. A temporary club must be organized and if this club meets the standards of the Fraternity, it will be installed as a chapter."[10]

[9] Thelma Bishop, "Division of Girls and Women's Sports," *Journal of Health, Physical Education, Recreation,* April, 1960, p. 95.

[10] Charlotte W. Holmes, "Phi Delta Pi—Who? What? Why?" *Journal of Health and Physical Education,* February, 1940, p. 79.

There are alumnae chapters in various cities throughout the country to which a former active member may belong. Persons who are working in the profession and "who have become acquainted with the Fraternity and its work, have applied for affiliation with it, and have met the requirements for membership" are accepted as special members with all the privileges of alumnae members. The total membership in 1940 was over two thousand.

5. Meetings. The Fraternity holds its meetings at the time of the national convention of the AAHPER.

6. Services to the profession. The fraternity serves the profession through its official publication, through the publication and distribution of special reports, through requiring high scholastic and professional standards as qualifications for membership, and through its study of important problems. A Vocational Placement Bureau is maintained to serve its members.

BIBLIOGRAPHY

Ainsworth, Dorothy S., "The National Association of Physical Education for College Women," *Journal of Health and Physical Education,* November, 1946, p. 525.

"AAHPER, Yesterday, Today, Tomorrow," *Journal of the American Association for Health, Physical Education, and Recreation,* April, 1954, p. 31.

"AAHPER's Section on Girls and Women's Sports," *Journal of the American Association for Health, Physical Education, and Recreation,* April, 1953, p. 32.

A description of the purposes, organization, and platform of the NSWA.

Ayars, George W., "The Society of State Directors of Health and Physical Education," *Journal of Health and Physical Education,* February, 1946, p. 68.

Bishop, Thelma, "Division of Girls and Women's Sports," *Journal of Health, Physical Education, Recreation,* April, 1960, p. 94.

An attempt to predict the development of the division during the next twenty-five years. Emphasis is given to work which is going on as it bears upon the work which is to be done.

Brace, David K., "The Academy of Physical Education–An Explanation,"

Journal of the American Association for Health, Physical Education, and Recreation, September, 1953, p. 31.

"Division for Girls and Women's Sports," *Journal of Health, Physical Recreation,* October, 1958, Part II, pp. 80–81.

In the summary of division meetings and activities, the work of the DGWS is reported in detail for the year 1957–1958.

Holmes, Charlotte W., "Phi Delta Pi—Who? What? Why?" *Journal of Health and Physical Education,* February, 1940, p. 79.

Locke, Mabel, "The Section Becomes a Division," *Journal of Health, Physical Education, Recreation,* April, 1958, p. 60.

An explanation of the organizational changes which occur when the former National Section for Girls and Women's Sports become a Division for Girls and Women's Sports.

McCloy, C. H., "What is Sports Medicine?" *Journal of Health, Physical Education, Recreation,* January, 1958, p. 45.

Primarily the article lists the problems which represent the areas of interest in the field of sports medicine.

Nash, J. B., "The American Academy of Physical Education," *Journal of Health and Physical Education,* January, 1946, p. 8.

Brief history of the organization and growth of the Academy. A list of awards made prior to 1946 is given.

Osborn, Vivian, "National Women's Official Rating," *Journal of Health and Physical Education,* April, 1938, p. 216.

Sets forth the method of organizing a rating board, the services which the National Committee can render, and the relationships between the National Boards and the National Officials' Rating Committee.

Soladay, Doris, "Functions and Purposes of NSGWS," *Journal of Health, Physical Education, Recreation,* October, 1956, p. 51.

A brief historical summary of the section is given. Standards in girls' and women's sports which the organization promulgates are reviewed.

APPENDIX

Physical Education
ACTIVITY CARD
The Rice Institute

Fr.

No.______________ Date________________________ So.

Classification________________________________

Present this card to obtain permission to use the Physical Education facilities and to check out authorized uniforms and equipment. Jr.

Prof. of Physical Education Sr.

FIGURE 1. Identification Card–Front Side

Conditions

I agree to:

(a) abide by the regulations set up for the use of the Physical Education equipment and facilities (Secure "Bulletin of Information" from the Physical Education Office)

(b) not hold The Rice Institute or the employees of the Physical Education Dept. liable for accidents, damages or losses incurred in the use of the Physical Education equipment and facilities.

____
Signed

FIGURE 2. Identification Card–Reverse Side

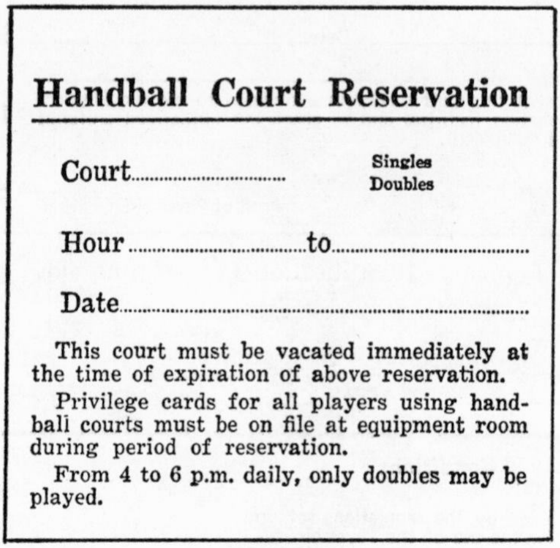

Handball Court Reservation

Court.................................. Singles Doubles

Hour.................................. to..

Date..

This court must be vacated immediately at the time of expiration of above reservation.

Privilege cards for all players using handball courts must be on file at equipment room during period of reservation.

From 4 to 6 p.m. daily, only doubles may be played.

FIGURE 3. Court Reservation Card

Health, Physical Education and Recreation

QUEENS COLLEGE

Permanent Record Card

M.............. F..............

Last Name .... First.............................. Middle.............................. Restr..............

....

MEDICAL RECORD

Date .... Height.............. Weight..............

Diagnosis ....

Classification ....

Remarks:

Physical Education V		
Date	Grade	Instructor
Date	Grade	Instructor

COURSE RECORD

Physical Education I		Physical Education II		Physical Education III		Physical Education IV					
Term	Grade	Term	Grade	Term	Grade	Term	Grade	Term	Grade	Term	Grade
Activities		Activities		Activities		Activities		Activities		Activities	
Instructor		Instructor		Instructor		Instructor		Instructor		Instructor	
Comment		Comment		Comment		Comment		Comment		Comment	

FIGURE 4. Student Permanent Record Card—Front Side

Last Name .... First .... Middle ....

Home Address .... Home Telephone ....

Date Entered College .... Date of Birth ....

High School Varsity Team Experience (Name of Sport and Seasons Played)

INTERCOLLEGIATE RECORD	INTRAMURAL RECORD

HR51-2M-55 142

FIGURE 5. Student Permanent Record Card–Reverse Side

UNIVERSITY
Department of Health and Physical Education

Date..., 19...........

My dear Mr...

A check of your basket shows that a..
is missing. Unless you can produce this article, you will be charged
$......................for it.

This charge is payable at the Office of the Bursar,
All college credits will be held until
it is paid.

It is imperative that you give this matter your immediate attention.

Chairman

FIGURE 6. Notice of Articles Missing from Basket

UNIVERSITY
Department of Health and Physical Education

351

Date...19...........

Mr. ________________________________

The following amount is due for articles not returned to equipment room. Please pay this at the Office of the Bursar,

Signed ....

NOTE: All credits in the college are withheld until this bill is paid.

Articles	Amount
TOTAL	$

FIGURE 7. Bill Form for Articles Taken or Lost from Basket

THE RICE INSTITUTE
DEPARTMENT OF PHYSICAL EDUCATION

CLASSIFICATION ________ REMARKS: ________

MAJOR SUBJECT ________

ACTIVITY	ATTENDANCE RECORD														ACTIVITY	KNOW-LEDGE	ASSIGN-MENT	FINAL GRADE

NAME ________ HOUR ________

FIGURE 8. Instructor's Class Record Card

THE RICE INSTITUTE
DEPARTMENT OF PHYSICAL EDUCATION

________ with regular class on ________
(name in full) (days)

at ________ made up an absence on ________.
(hour) (date)

Reported out at ________ Reported in at ________
(hour) (hour)

Activity engaged in ________

Instructor supervising make-up ________
(signature of instructor)

Note: Three absences are permitted each semester. Excused absences in excess of three may be made up at times other than class hours at the rate of one a day. In making up an absence 40 minutes exclusive of shower and dressing must be devoted to activity. This slip should be filled in and filed in the Physical Education Office.

FIGURE 9. Report on Make-Up of Absence

INDEX